WORLD
POWER

WORLD POWER

SOVIET FOREIGN POLICY UNDER BREZHNEV AND ANDROPOV

Jonathan Steele

Michael Joseph
London

First published in Great Britain by Michael Joseph Ltd
44 Bedford Square, London WC1
1983
© Jonathan Steele 1983

ISBN 0 7181 2297 6

Typeset by Rowland Phototypesetting
Bury St Edmunds, Suffolk
Printed in Great Britain by
Hollen Street Press, Slough, and
bound by The Dorstel Press, Harlow

ACKNOWLEDGEMENT

Many people, directly and indirectly, have contributed to this book. I would particularly like to thank the *Guardian*, which dispatched me so often to the Soviet Union and let me report its activities in such critical areas as Afghanistan, Cuba, Czechoslovakia, and Poland. My special gratitude goes to its present editor, Peter Preston, for giving me most of these assignments, as well as leave of absence to write the major part of this book. Among those who read and commented on draft chapters, I want to thank Ian Black, Victoria Brittain, John Gittings, Jonathan Mirsky, Peter Osnos, and John Rettie. Geraldine Petley typed the final version at amazing speed. Geoffrey Stern was an eagle-eyed critic of the entire draft. Ruth Steele gave constant encouragement and unflagging support.

CONTENTS

INTRODUCTION

At a recent exhibition in Paris of early Soviet art I came across a poster of a Russian factory worker astride a horse. The folds of the giant red banner he was carrying rippled majestically in line with the flow of the horse's mane. Dated 1918 and signed by Leon Trotsky, the motto of this dashing picture was stark: "To horse, proletariat! The workers' revolution needs a powerful Red cavalry."

Bizarre requirement, one might think. But it was rationalized at the time by the necessity of self-defense and the desire to spread the message of Soviet power. Sixty-five years later the same twin motives have given the workers' revolution the equally strange "requirement" of hundreds of independently targetable nuclear warheads and Soviet military command posts in places as distant as Addis Ababa, Budapest, and Kabul.

The paradoxes of Soviet security policy are almost as old as the revolution itself. Yet in no period of Soviet history have they been as acute as in the Brezhnev era, a time of "détente" that was matched by an unparalleled growth in Soviet military might.

Under Leonid Brezhnev the Soviet Union became a world power. It acquired an arsenal of long-range missiles that can reach any part of the globe within minutes. Its navy patrols the world's oceans. Its political interests rival those of its only serious competitor, the United States. All this is a vast change from 1964 when Nikita Khrushchev was removed from power in the Kremlin. At that time, though embracing more than half the landmass of Europe and Asia combined, the Soviet Union was still a continental rather than a global power, in no way comparable with the United States in military might.

But what is its power for, and why has it grown? Some claim that the Soviet Union is aiming to dominate the entire globe. At his first press conference as president, Ronald Reagan confidently declared, "I know of no leader of the Soviet Union, since the revolution and including the present leadership, that has not more than once repeated . . . their determination that their goal must be the promotion of world revolution and a one-world socialist or communist state."[1] Reagan was perhaps referring to the final words of the now superseded Soviet constitution of 1924, which indeed say that "the USSR . . . will mark a decisive new step toward the union of the workers of all countries in one World Socialist Soviet Republic."[2]

On the other side are fellow-travelers and apologists for the Soviet Union who argue that its every action is guided by an unswerving desire for peace. They, too, have numerous Soviet texts on which to base their case.

In spite of the increasing alarmism in most Western governments about Soviet intentions, there has been an astonishing decline in Russian studies and in the availability of professional expertise from Russian-speaking observers of the Soviet scene, whether they be diplomats, journalists, or academics. In the United States the number of graduate students in Russian studies has dropped to its lowest point since the Second World War, leading to an estimate that in 1982 the Soviet Union had three times as many specialists on American foreign policy as the United States had on Soviet foreign policy.[3] The situation in Britain was little better. The most recent official report found a picture of stagnation in the number of undergraduates and graduates studying Russian throughout the 1970s.[4]

Partly because they feel unsure of Soviet intentions, and sometimes because of a deliberate desire to misrepresent the facts, many Western decisionmakers insist that the only basis for Western policy toward the Soviet Union should be the nature of Soviet capabilities. What matters is not what Moscow is likely to do, but what it can do. This inevitably leads to a "worst case" analysis of Kremlin options in any crisis—an approach that encourages pessimism, if not paranoia. It tends to weight the discussion in favor of military quantification rather than political judgment. Emphasis on Soviet military capabilities is a reasonable starting point for those who design weapons, but it should not be the primary or sole guide for those who design Western policies.

The central argument of this book is that there is a sufficient body of evidence, based on Soviet practice, to throw light on the Kremlin's thinking and intentions. Careful analysis of the Kremlin's record—where the Soviet Union has intervened and where it has not, what its leaders have said and what they have done, when they have moved quickly and when they have been slow to react—can offer a guide to their motives and the likely patterns of future action.

Public statements that pour out of the Kremlin and its agencies in tidal quantities also have their value. While they, like those of other countries' spokesmen, are often designed to conceal more than they reveal, they cannot be totally ignored. Nor can discussions with Soviet Union officials, academics, and journalists be ruled out as clues to Soviet thinking. Soviet leaders' private and sometimes unguarded conversational comments to Western visitors during the period of détente also provide a useful source of information.

The combined weight of this evidence, as well as the recent historical record, suggest that Soviet policy is less adventurous, energetic, and threatening than conventional Western wisdom proclaims. Phrases like "expansionism," "the Soviet threat," "nuclear blackmail," and "appeasement" are bandied about in the West with little effort to examine what they mean or whether they apply to reality.

Of course one should not forget the lasting features of the Soviet system—the centralized bureaucracy, Russian domination of the numerous national minorities, the Communist party's monopoly of power, the controlled press, intolerance of dissent—but within these confines there have been significant changes in

Soviet society since the war. The same is true of Soviet foreign policy. The image of a remorselessly expanding Soviet Union, which was formed in the 1940s when Stalin imposed Soviet control over the Baltic states and Eastern Europe, is no longer valid in the 1980s.

Within the continuing context of a missionary ideology and a publicly pro-claimed faith in the eventual triumph of socialism over capitalism, the Kremlin's perceptions of the world have undergone important changes. Soviet foreign policy, far more than Soviet domestic policy, is circumscribed by an external environment that no planner can control. Soviet policymakers have to operate in an international context which is overwhelmingly hostile to, and suspicious of, their intentions. The constraints this imposes on the Kremlin have gradually created a pattern of Soviet activity that differs from what policymakers in an ideal world would pursue, but is the reality to which they and their successors have become accustomed. Hopes are frustrated. Plans are abandoned. Eager-ness becomes caution.

The second main argument of this book is that the Soviet Union is a society with a tired regime and a host of foreign and domestic problems.

- The growth of its strategic nuclear power has been a response and reaction to initiatives of the United States.

- In Europe, it is a conservative, status quo power, more concerned to hold on to its postwar conquests in Eastern Europe than to advance further westward.

- It gains more from trading with the capitalist West than from subsidizing the economically inefficient East.

- In Asia its primary objective is not external but internal: how to develop the vast resources of Siberia.

- In the Third World it seeks, like other industrial nations, to enlarge its power and influence by diplomatic, economic, and political means.

- It sees the strengthening of the Soviet Union at home as the main guarantee of an eventual spread of socialism abroad, and not vice versa.

- Only in the most exceptional cases, such as Afghanistan, has it been prepared to defend a revolution abroad, and even then it has acted primarily out of fear for Soviet security.

- In general, its aid for what it calls the anti-imperialist cause has been cautious, grudging, and calculated to avoid risk.

This leads to the book's third argument. Yuri Andropov is having to adjust to the fundamental paradox of the Brezhnev era. While Soviet military power increased in the 1960s and 1970s, its political influence declined. In almost every region of the world, whether it be the United States and the Western hemisphere, the Middle East, Asia, Eastern or Western Europe, the Kremlin faces major problems.

- Détente with the United States, which the Russians in the early 1970s expected to become a permanent feature of East–West relations, has collapsed and almost died.

- The Soviet Union is still in dispute with China, its largest and most powerful neighbor.

- In the Middle East the Soviet presence, once strong in the 1960s, is now virtually eliminated from the central axis, the Arab–Israeli conflict.

The Soviet Union should be judged not only by the size of its arsenal or the rhetoric of its leaders but by results. In the 1970s they have not been impressive.

My fourth argument is that Soviet foreign policy can only be properly understood if it is looked at through Soviet eyes. The world that the Kremlin's leaders plan for and react to is the world that they see. Things may seem clear and unambiguous to policymakers in Washington and London, but they are seen differently in Moscow, and when it comes to the making of Soviet foreign policy, it is Moscow's perception that counts. The West cannot understand the Soviet Union if it does not try to imagine how the Soviet Union sees the West.

Last, a word about what this book is not. East–West relations are frequently discussed as though they were a cycle of action and reaction in which each superpower fails to perceive the other's motives. While this is a reasonable and, in general, accurate way of looking at the conflict between the United States and the Soviet Union, this book does not aim to reproduce it. It deliberately focuses on the Soviet view of the world and makes no attempt to analyze American policy in equal depth. I have chosen this approach for two reasons. First, Soviet foreign policy is only partly explicable by virtue of its relations with the United States. We risk taking an excessively Western-centered attitude to international affairs if we assume that Soviet policy is entirely related to what the United States has done or may do. Second, whereas the number of studies of American foreign policy is legion, studies of Soviet policy are far fewer. Many of those that do exist take a prescriptive stance. What should the West do about the Soviet Union? How can the West best deal with Moscow? And so on. I abstain from that approach here. The time has come to look at Soviet foreign policy dispassionately and afresh. Discard the received assumptions of the Cold War. Forget the myths of Soviet apologists. Practical responses should proceed from a realistic assessment of what Soviet policy is.

PART ONE

The Center

1

THE ANDROPOV
INHERITANCE

*We know well that the imperialists will never meet our
pleas for peace. It can only be defended by relying on
the invincible might of the Soviet armed forces.*

Yuri Andropov
November 12, 1982[1]

The coffin was open in the Russian tradition. Inside, on a bed of blood-red
drapery lay the body of Leonid Ilyich Brezhnev, ruler of the Soviet Union for
eighteen years, his bushy eyebrows, puffy cheeks, and protruding upper lip now
turned upward toward the Kremlin wall. Carrying the coffin on their shoulders,
the honor guard of Soviet army officers paused before the Lenin mausoleum and
the funeral orations began.

"Comrades, our party, our people and all progressive mankind have suffered
a heavy loss," Yuri Andropov, Brezhnev's successor, declared.[2] It was a
predictable start, but as Andropov's short speech continued, observers noticed
some remarkable features. Less than half was devoted to praise of the dead
leader. Though extolled as a "tireless fighter for peace," no mention was made
of any successes or achievements associated with Brezhnev. Indeed, Andropov
devoted the major part of his oration to sketching out the tasks that faced the
party in what he called "the complicated international situation." First came the
need to raise the Soviet people's standard of living, then the strengthening of the
community of socialist states, extending cooperation to developing countries,

and upholding the cause of détente. Finally, in words that echoed Brezhnev's last public remarks on the anniversary of the October Revolution, Andropov pledged that the party and state would uphold "the vital interests of our homeland and maintain great vigilance and readiness to give a crushing rebuff to any attempt at aggression."[3]

Andropov was not Brezhnev's first choice as his successor, a fact that no doubt explained the unusually businesslike and unemotional tone of his funeral oration. But the flatness of the Andropov speech was also an appropriate and accurate reflection of the legacy Brezhnev had left behind. Eighteen years after Brezhnev became general secretary of the party, and sixty-five years after the revolution, the Soviet leadership still felt itself on the defensive. Although Brezhnev had scored some successes in foreign policy, they were overshadowed by a conspicuous sense of failure in his primary objective of securing better relations with both China and the West.

It was no accident that the only other Politburo member to speak at the funeral was the minister of defense, Marshal Dmitri Ustinov. His support had ensured Andropov of victory in the political jockeying over who should inherit Brezhnev's job. His constituency, the 3.7 million-strong Soviet armed forces, was the linchpin of the country's foreign policy. Between them, Yuri Andropov, for fifteen years the head of the KGB, in charge of the Soviet Union's internal security police and its border guards, and Dmitri Ustinov symbolized the forces of inward-looking vigilance and outward-looking strength.

Brezhnev left a country that was incomparably stronger in military terms than when he took over in October 1964. He presided over a massive buildup in Soviet nuclear strength that gave the country parity with the United States at the end of the 1960s. His other major achievement—the establishment of détente with the West—was linked to this, and indeed depended on it. In Western Europe Brezhnev managed to negotiate a settlement of most of the outstanding political issues left after the Second World War. The peace treaty with West Germany in 1970, the Quadripartite Agreement on Berlin in 1971, and the Helsinki Final Act of 1975 recognized the territorial status quo and laid the basis for a new relationship between the Soviet Union and Western Europe. Brezhnev also helped to evolve a more stable modus vivendi with the United States in the early 1970s. Four meetings with American presidents in two and a half years symbolized a degree of cooperation and dialogue that had never occurred before. Yet détente did not last. On Brezhnev's death Andropov inherited a situation of increased tension and risk. A new Cold War was underway, characterized by American efforts to put economic and political pressure on the Soviet Union to change its foreign and defense policy and liberalize its internal system. The three major states of Western Europe, though more willing than Washington to maintain normal relations with Moscow, were led, on Brezhnev's death, by governments that were more anti-Soviet than those of the early and mid-1970s. Prime Minister Margaret Thatcher, Chancellor Helmut Kohl and

President François Mitterrand were all less committed to détente than their predecessors.

In Eastern Europe and the Far East Andropov took over two daunting sets of problems with which he had been associated during the earlier part of his career. As head of the Central Committee's department for liaison with the Communist parties of socialist countries, Andropov had been a principal advisor in both areas from 1957 to 1967. For three years before that, including the time of the uprising in Hungary in 1956, he had been Soviet ambassador in Budapest. In 1963 and 1965 he led Soviet delegations to Peking shortly before relations between the two Communist parties broke down completely. He was with the then prime minister, Alexei Kosygin, on an important trip to Hanoi in February 1965 just as the United States escalated its military involvement in Indochina. As a member of the Politburo from 1967 onward, he must have been closely consulted by his colleagues in the leadership as they tried to contain the growth of an independent China and maintain stability in Eastern Europe. Both efforts failed. The buildup of Soviet forces on the Chinese border in the second half of the 1960s gave a military dimension to what had previously been a political and ideological conflict. It also prompted a new relationship between China and the United States. Soviet attempts to resume a dialogue with China had begun to show tentative results at the end of the Brezhnev era, but Andropov must have known that the chances of an early resolution of the dispute without substantial Soviet concessions were not high.

In Eastern Europe the crisis over the Solidarity trade union movement in Poland was not yet over in spite of the imposition of martial law. The Polish party had to be rebuilt after a spate of defections and would then have to restore its authority over a disgruntled and disappointed population. The crisis had shown the difficulty of finding a political consensus that could prevent periodic outbursts of national rebellion and consumer unrest. In Czechoslovakia in 1968 Brezhnev had sent in Soviet tanks to reverse a trend toward pluralistic reform. In 1981 the techniques of repression were more subtle, but the underlying problems remained the same. Indeed, they were sharpened by mounting economic difficulties. Falling growth rates, higher prices for imported energy, and the inadequacies of a centrally planned economy were limiting the prospects of buying popular loyalty through a steady increase in living standards.

In the Third World, Andropov inherited an undeclared but apparently hopeless war against rebels in Afghanistan. The Soviet invasion three years earlier had lost Moscow the support of the Islamic world and most members of the nonaligned movement. It spoiled relations with Iran, one of the Soviet Union's most important neighbors, and with Pakistan. Elsewhere in the Middle East, Soviet influence was minimal. In Africa the Soviet Union was giving heavy backing to Angola and Ethiopia but had made little headway with other states on the continent. In Latin America its only client, Cuba, was still largely isolated more than twenty years after Castro's revolution.

Faced with this legacy of problems in spite of the enormous increase in Soviet military might during the Brezhnev era, how will Andropov and his colleagues act in the 1980s? Those who seek a quick way of predicting Soviet actions in a host of complicated international crises are bound to be disappointed, since the Soviet leadership itself cannot yet know what it will do. The history of Soviet policy is as full of hasty improvisation, changes of mind, and impotent delay as that of any other nation. What can be said is that Andropov will be governed in his decisions by personality, experience, and the prevailing attitudes of his generation.

In contrast to Brezhnev, Andropov is something of an intellectual. Both men came from working-class families. Brezhnev's father was a steelworker, Andropov's a railwayman. Both graduated from technical institutes—Brezhnev in agronomy and land reclamation, Andropov in water transport problems. (He worked for a time in 1932 as a Volga boatman.) Yet Andropov appears to have a more inquiring mind. He took the trouble to try to learn foreign languages, including English, and while he was ambassador in Budapest, the notoriously difficult Hungarian tongue. Whereas Brezhnev was an extrovert, whose main hobbies were outdoor pursuits, Andropov's tall and stooping appearance conveys a more professorial image. His children are members of the Moscow intelligentsia; his son was a researcher at Moscow's Institute for the Study of the United States and Canada before joining the diplomatic service, his daughter is a journalist married to an actor.

In spite of the difference in temperament and a seven-year gap in age, Brezhnev and Andropov belonged to the same political generation. They were at school at the time of the revolution and grew up in a period when the Soviet Union and its Bolshevik leaders were trying to extend their power, in the face of domestic resistance and foreign intervention, against an "enemy within" and an "enemy without." Schooled in a climate of personal, political, and national insecurity, their natural approach to problems was one of caution.

In career terms their political generation benefited from Stalin's purges. The virtual elimination of the elite that had ruled in the 1930s allowed men like Brezhnev and Andropov rapid promotion. In 1939 at the age of thirty-three Brezhnev was party secretary in charge of a major industrial province in the Ukraine. In 1940 at the age of twenty-six Andropov was first secretary of the entire Communist Youth Organization in the Karelo-Finnish Republic. Their unexpected advance on the backs of the victims of arbitrary purges must have left a deep fear of failure. In personal terms their generation underwent an even more crucial experience. No Western politician who has negotiated in the Kremlin or dealt with Soviet officials has failed to be struck by their frequent references to the Second World War. No issue unites the Soviet leadership more firmly with ordinary people than the shared trauma of the Nazi invasion. The constant invocations of the horrors of an occupation that left twenty million Soviet dead, the ubiquitous war memorials with their always newly placed flowers, and the unsolicited assurances from Russians to any foreign visitor to "please understand that all we want is peace" are reflected in the emotions of the men at the top.

Willy Brandt recalls how tears came to Brezhnev's eyes at a state banquet when Brandt read him a letter from a German soldier, written shortly before his death on a Russian battlefield: "I know that our armies will leave this land in a trail of misery. Nothing will remain but suffering, destruction, and perhaps hatred, yet I wish for nothing better than to meet these people one day in peace and as a friend."[4] Richard Nixon found himself touching the same chord at a dinner in San Clemente. "I only hope that Russians and Americans in future generations may meet as we are meeting, in our homes as friends because of our personal affection for each other, and not just as officials meeting because of the necessity of settling differences that may exist between our two countries," he told Brezhnev. "As my toast was translated, Brezhnev's eyes filled with tears. He impulsively got out of his chair and walked towards me. I rose and walked towards him. He threw his arms around me with a real bear hug and then proposed an eloquent toast to Pat and our children and all the children in the world."[5]

It would be easy to dismiss these gestures as the cloying sentimentality of an old man, loosened by a good meal. But they have been repeated too often by other Soviet leaders to be overlooked. Even the most skeptical Western adversaries of the Soviet Union have, at least in brief moments, come to accept their validity. After a long evening alone with Brezhnev and his interpreter at a hunting lodge north of Moscow, Henry Kissinger concluded that "there was also in Brezhnev a clearly evident strain of the elemental Russian, of a people that has prevailed through endurance, that longs for a surcease from its travails and has never been permitted by destiny or the ambitions of its rulers to fulfill its dream."[6] In 1977 William Colby, then director of the CIA, told Congress, "You will find a concern, even a paranoia, over their own security. You will find the determination that they will never again be invaded and put through the kinds of turmoil that they have been under in many different invasions."[7]

The Nazi invasion was a trauma that scarred most of Brezhnev's generation of Soviet leaders. Brezhnev himself served as a political commissar throughout the war, attached to various units in the Ukraine. His longest service was with the Eighteenth Army, which was involved in several bitter battles, stopping the Nazi drive into the Caucasus, assaulting the Germans at Novorossiysk and then forcing them slowly westward into Czechoslovakia. In 1943 Brezhnev narrowly escaped death when a landing craft in which he was traveling hit a mine.

Yuri Andropov was on the Finnish front during the war, setting up partisan units to operate behind enemy lines. Mikhail Suslov, the veteran ideologist who died in 1982, was a commissar on the North Caucasian front throughout the war, serving for a time as chief of staff of partisan forces in the Stavropol region. Dmitri Ustinov was chief commissar in charge of armaments after 1941, and played an important part in rescuing the arms industry from the Nazi invaders by moving it back beyond the Urals.

The end of the war and the subsequent growth in Soviet terrain, influence, and power did not remove the sense of being encircled. The Western strategy of containment, the postwar American policy of creating "forward bases" in many of the countries on the Soviet Union's periphery, and the development of intercontinental rocketry left Moscow vulnerable to a new threat. In spite of the reincorporation of the Baltic states under Russian control, and the creation of a buffer zone in Eastern Europe, the Soviet Union could still be hit by strategic bombers or missile attack.

The brief hopes of a friendly China on its eastern borders after Mao's victory over the Nationalists in 1949 were soon abandoned. As China developed a nuclear potential in the second half of the 1960s and formed a tentative strategic alignment with the United States a decade later, Moscow found itself with a new cause for alarm. "We have four potential opponents to take into account," says Georgi Arbatov, the director of Moscow's Institute for the Study of the United States and Canada. "The United States with its strategic and conventional weapons, the NATO allies in Europe, Japan, and China."[8]

Beside the four areas that Arbatov listed, the view from the Kremlin encompasses neighbors who are in no way models of stability or friendliness. On the Soviet Union's southern border is the Middle East, an area of considerably greater geographical significance to the Soviet Union than to the West, as the Kremlin frequently points out. Yet long before the Soviet Union became active there, this was a region where British, French, and American interests were pervasive. Today, in spite of a climate of strong Arab nationalism, Western influence remains deep. The Eastern European states, although nominally allied to the Soviet Union, are friends on whom Moscow cannot be sure of relying at a time of crisis. A powerful sense of nationalism lurks beneath the veneer of publicly proclaimed Communist fraternity, making Moscow feel perpetually insecure.

Surrounded by uncertain friends and hostile neighbors, it is hardly surprising that Soviet leaders look enviously at the United States, with its ocean frontiers on the east and west, and peaceful borders to the south and north. "I recently suggested to a group of American senators that the United States change geographical places with us," remarks Vadim Zagladin, the deputy head of the Central Committee's international department. "They were quick to turn the idea down."[9]

Andropov took over a Kremlin that seemed collectively to have slowed down in the last few months of Brezhnev's life. Brezhnev had been dogged by ill health since 1974. He would disappear from public view for several days or weeks without any official explanation either while he was away or when he returned. This led to inevitable speculation about the implications for foreign policy, and visiting politicians who met him always spent some time watching for clues to his physical condition. They found his health varied unpredictably. Sometimes he would read entirely from a prepared text. His speech was slurred. He moved stiffly.

When he gave his long report to the Twenty-Sixth Party Congress in February 1981, the Soviet television cameras unexpectedly broke off their live coverage after seven minutes. Observers in the hall saw the Soviet leader perspiring heavily and frequently wiping his face. In the absence of any official Soviet information, outsiders could only guess at his condition. Unconfirmed reports said he received injections for a nerve affliction in his jaw, required blood transfusions for a mild form of leukemia, and wore a pacemaker for a bad heart condition—the weakness that eventually caused his death. The only bulletin ever published on Brezhnev's condition was the one that announced his death.

Yet Brezhnev's fluctuating health did not seem to affect Soviet foreign policy before 1982. Moscow took some vigorous actions during that time, including its operations in Angola, Ethiopia, and Afghanistan. Brezhnev visited India and West Germany in 1980 and 1981. But the following year the Kremlin seemed to stagnate. The two men who had deputized for Brezhnev at Politburo meetings for the last few years, Andrei Kirilenko and Mikhail Suslov, were both out of action. Kirilenko was absent from most public functions, apparently suffering a political eclipse. (He was removed from the Politburo a few days after Brezhnev's death.) Suslov died in January 1982. His death seemed to hit Brezhnev hard. He looked frail and overwrought as he stood over Suslov's grave by the Kremlin wall and pronounced a strange atheistic benediction: "Sleep peacefully, dear friend."[10]

Brezhnev had increasingly concentrated power in his own hands in the last few years. In the early period after Khrushchev's overthrow in 1964, the Kremlin leadership was a genuine collective in contrast to Stalin's rule and the latter part of Khrushchev's. But a jockeying for preeminence soon began, and Brezhnev emerged as the senior man in 1970. Although victorious, Brezhnev showed a skillful willingness to compromise and balance off the pressures from the various interest groups within the Soviet bureaucracy. This was symbolized by the promotion into the Politburo in April 1973 of the foreign minister, Andrei Gromyko, the defense minister, Marshal Andrei Grechko, and Yuri Andropov, then head of the KGB.

Brezhnev's style was cautious and gradualist. He was less interested in initiating change than in arbitrating between diverse corporate views, whether they came from the army, the KGB, the supporters of heavy industry, or the agricultural lobby. He was a good committee chairman, presiding over a series of policies that were bound to be conservative since they were the product of a consensus between conflicting priorities. It is hard to believe that Brezhnev had a long-term plan.

Though a moderate in style and approach, Brezhnev was determined to remain in charge. In 1975 and 1976 he ousted Alexander Shelepin and Dmitri Polyansky, two of the longest serving members of the Politburo. In 1977 he removed Nikolai Podgorny as chairman of the presidium of the Supreme Soviet (i.e., the Soviet president) and took the job himself. Thereafter, he was showered with lavish publicity and praise, though still not on the scale of Stalin and Khrushchev. He surrounded himself with loyal colleagues by coopting former associates from his days as a party official in Moldavia and the Ukraine. Yet even while he secured himself against any challenge and developed a small-scale personality cult, his administration remained a collective operation. It was this that enabled it to function even during his periods of illness, at least until 1982.

Brezhnev's authority over Soviet foreign policy rested on his role as head of the three main decision-making bodies. As general secretary of the Central Committee since 1964 he chaired the Politburo, the supreme policy-making committee in the Soviet Union. During the 1970s it had an average membership of fifteen men. As chairman of the presidium of the Supreme Soviet since 1977, Brezhnev was the official head of state. He was also commander-in-chief of the Soviet armed forces and chairman of the Defense Council. This body, rarely mentioned in the Soviet press, appears to include the defense minister, the prime minister, the foreign minister, the head of the KGB, and some other full members of the Politburo. The chief of the General Staff and other military advisors may attend on occasion. Its membership suggests that the Defense Council considers all major security and foreign policy issues and makes recommendations to the full Politburo, making it in effect the highest Soviet body dealing specifically with politico-military matters.

Foreign policy planning is handled by two departments of the Central Committee—the International Department (which deals with general foreign issues, national liberation movements, and nonruling Communist parties) and the Department for Liaison with the Communist and Workers' Parties of the Socialist Countries, i.e., Eastern Europe, those Third World countries with Socialist systems, and—in the days when the Soviet party still had relations with them—the Chinese Communists. This is the department that Andropov headed from 1957 to 1967. The Foreign Ministry reports to these two committees rather than vice versa.

Brezhnev made several changes in the management of Soviet foreign policy, marking its growing complexity and importance. He enlarged the personal staff who served him as general secretary, putting one trusted aide, Andrei Alexandrov-Agentov, in charge of a team dealing with relations with the United States, and another, Anatoly Blatov, in charge of relations with Eastern and Western Europe. In 1978 he set up a new Central Committee department of international information. Headed by Leonid Zamyatin, the former director-general of the official news agency, Tass, it became in effect the Kremlin's press office, holding news conferences and granting interviews to Western journalists in a way that Brezhnev himself had never done and Gromyko only rarely had.

One important trend under Brezhnev was the extra weight the armed forces gained in policymaking. Whereas the Politburo has several sources of advice on foreign policy—the Foreign Ministry, the Central Committee, the KGB, and the various academic institutes—it relies for military advice entirely on the armed forces. Their monopoly of competence clearly gives them a powerful voice in decision making. They carry weight over and above their numerical representation in the key committees by virtue of several factors—Soviet reliance on military might as a major foundation for foreign policy, the Kremlin's continuing commitment to defend Eastern Europe, the new confrontation with China, and the determination to maintain strategic parity with the United States. When it comes to decisions on allocating resources within the Soviet budget, the armed forces form an influential alliance with the heavy industry lobby.

Brezhnev's close support for the armed forces became increasingly evident after 1976 as a result of a process that one writer has called "the militarization of Brezhnev."[11] His wartime career was given massive publicity in the Soviet media. He appointed a close associate, Dmitri Ustinov, as defense minister on Grechko's death in 1976. He had himself made a marshal of the Soviet Union. Long before that, Brezhnev had given the armed forces important assignments on the Sino-Soviet border and in Czechoslovakia. He was also, from the very beginning of his tenure as general secretary, a keen exponent of military and patriotic themes in his speeches. Whereas Khrushchev had tried to mobilize the Soviet people by a brand of populism and utopian exhortation (overtaking the United States economically within twenty years, abolishing rents, and so on), Brezhnev preferred a nationalistic appeal. This was partly reflected in several large-scale development projects for which volunteers were summoned from all over the Soviet Union, such as the second Trans-Siberian railway and the Baikal-Amur main line, which were designed as pioneering ventures to open up new regions of the Soviet motherland; and partly by boosting the image of the armed forces as a symbol of national pride, power, and prestige.

The long series of arms control talks with the United States which began in 1969 also helped to increase the armed forces' role in foreign policy by institutionalizing their position as a voice in the process of détente. General Nikolai Ogarkov, then first deputy chief of the General Staff, was the second-ranking member of the Soviet SALT delegation in the 1970s. Several other officers served in Soviet delegations subsequently.

A second significant trend under Brezhnev was the increasing use of professional experts as foreign policy advisors. The establishment of academic institutes to advise the Central Committee began under Stalin and was expanded under Khrushchev, whose colleague, Anastas Mikoyan, announced in 1956 that the Soviet Union "seriously lags in the study of the contemporary stage of capitalism. We are not engaged in a deep study of the facts and figures, but often limit ourselves to seizing upon individual facts . . . for propaganda purposes."[12] Shortly afterward, the Academy of Sciences created an Institute of the World Economy and International Relations (IMEMO). In just under twenty years, between 1956 and 1974, the height of détente, the number of specialists rose sevenfold. In 1974 IMEMO had 572 research associates, while another 725 worked in four institutes that had branched out from it—the Institute for the Study of the United States and Canada, the Institute of Africa, the Institute of Latin America, and the Institute of the International Workers' Movement.[13] Other policy-linked bodies were the Institute of Oriental Studies and the Institute of the Far East. The directors of some of these institutes, such as Nikolai Inozemtsev, head of IMEMO, and Georgi Arbatov, head of the Institute for the Study of the United States and Canada, became members of the Central Committee, a clear sign of their importance. Since the 1960s, Andropov has shown a particular interest in encouraging these institutes.

Each institute is staffed by professional research workers, journalists and diplomats on secondment from their normal professions. In contrast to prewar and early postwar days, when the Soviet Union had diplomatic links with only a few states, it now has a growing pool of specialists with direct experience of life abroad. They move regularly between the three fields of research, diplomacy, and journalism. One Western analyst has pointed out that these men "tend to be modernizers, and even Westernizers in Soviet politics, and strong supporters of détente. They have a sense that xenophobia and Cold War relations with the West are associated with reaction at home and with a fundamentalist, ultra-nationalist mentality that bodes no good for them personally or the values to which they adhere."[14] While the older generation of advisors came to international studies through dedication to the international Communist movement, the younger generation often choose their careers because of a fascination with the West and a desire to travel. They may be driven more by intellectual curiosity than any zeal to promote change in the West. Their basic viewpoint is still Marxist, but they tend to be less interested in general ideological explanations for world developments than in detailed local information on social, economic, and political factors.

Take, for example, a man like Alexander Bovin. Born in 1930, he became a leader of a group of consultants in the International Department of the Central Committee in the late 1960s under Andropov. He travels frequently to the West in his current capacity as political observer for the newspaper *Izvestia*. Commenting on a range of international issues, he has become one of the most outspoken Soviet journalists (see chapter 7 for his key article on Afghanistan), and with his long hair and preference for open-neck shirts, even when appearing on television, he fails to conform to the normal Western stereotype of a gray-suited "regime hack." Vadim Zagladin, born in 1927, has been first deputy head of the Central Committee's International Department since 1975. A graduate of Moscow's Institute of International Relations, which trains many Soviet diplomats, he taught history there for five years before joining Moscow's best foreign affairs weekly magazine, *New Times*. Fluent in English, French, and German, and a sharp-witted analyst of Western politics, he often doubles at press conferences with the Kremlin spokesman, Leonid Zamyatin. Both Zagladin and Bovin have served as Brezhnev's speech writers. Men like these (both belong to the roughly three hundred-member Central Committee or its auditing commission) wield considerable influence as advisors. They will probably gain more under Andropov who worked as one of them for a time himself.

Andropov's own career has been closely connected with foreign affairs for the last thirty years. His leadership of the KGB from 1967 to 1982, during which he supervised the clampdown on would-be émigrés, nonconformist intellectuals, and dissidents, earned him a miserable reputation in the West, but probably the gratitude of his colleagues. One of the by-products of détente was bound to be an upsurge in demands for political liberalization at home. Andropov successfully controlled it without resorting to the all-out terror of Stalin or allowing it to infiltrate the ranks of the party.

In spite of years of supervising aspects of foreign affairs, Andropov has no personal experience of the West. He has never traveled outside the socialist world (unless one counts Yugoslavia which he has visited three times). His KGB job kept him away from direct participation in any of the East–West negotiations or summit meetings during the period of détente and the *Ostpolitik*. But as a member of the Politburo and the Defense Council he was privy to the key policy debates and discussions. As head of the KGB he had his own channels of information on Soviet performance around the world.

Hungarians who dealt with Andropov during his time as Soviet Ambassador in Budapest, as well as Western diplomats and politicians who have met him since he became party leader, agree in general that he is a quiet, controlled man, alert in his questions, and modest in manner. Unlike Brezhnev, he hides his emotions —some would say to the point of being cold. He is well-briefed and in command of the issues. When he met the West German President the day after Brezhnev was buried, he was so confident that the Foreign Minister Andrei Gromyko had nothing to say during a ninety-minute meeting.

Andropov is likely to strengthen the two trends that began under Brezhnev— a greater role for the specialist advisors (the *pomoshchniki*), and a closer integration of the army into foreign policy planning. He is believed to have won the competition to succeed Brezhnev by gaining the support of Dmitri Ustinov and the military establishment. At the first Central Committee meeting after Brezhnev's funeral, Andropov promised "to provide the army and navy with everything necessary."[15] Most of the Soviet Union's foreign policy problems have an important military dimension—détente with China, a potential settlement in Afghanistan, maintaining stability in Eastern Europe, and the series of arms control talks with the United States. The army's voice is bound to carry weight in policy discussions. But whereas Brezhnev's link with the top brass was partly a survival of cronyism from the Second World War, under Andropov the link between the army and the party leadership is based on the new and increased role of the military in serving Kremlin goals.

Twenty-five years ago Andropov was one of those who helped to promote the concept of expert consultants in the Central Committee as a more streamlined alternative to the Foreign Ministry. Now that he occupies the top party job he is expected to continue the process. His first months in office showed a greater flair for public relations in foreign policy than Brezhnev had. A flurry of new or newly-packaged arms control proposals put Western governments on the defensive. His overtures to China showed a flexibility and willingness to explore possible concessions in the hope of advancing the negotiations. He demonstrated more urgency in the search for an agreement with Pakistan which might lead to a withdrawal of Soviet combat troops from Afghanistan. The Andropov administration seems set to be more professional and efficient in foreign policy than the one that Brezhnev led.

2

THE SOVIET VIEW
OF NATIONAL
SECURITY

We shall do our utmost to ensure that the proponents of military adventurism never catch the land of the Soviets unawares, and that the potential aggressor knows that a crushing retaliatory blow will inevitably await him.

Leonid Brezhnev
November 7, 1982[1]

It is important to stress how deeply Soviet foreign policy is primarily a policy of national security. Indeed, it can plausibly be argued that until the mid-1950s the Soviet Union had no comprehensive foreign policy. Its policy was mainly geared to territorial concerns and the making of deals with actual or potential invaders. By comparison with the West, its diplomatic missions abroad were sparse and small. Self-sufficient in raw materials, it derived only a tiny fraction of its national income from foreign trade.

Brezhnev and Andropov were brought up in a climate in which the world beyond the Soviet borders was seen more as a threat than a promise. The Soviet Union could survive on its own, if only the outside world would let it be.

The Bolsheviks' initial feeling of vulnerability fitted easily into the centuries-old Russian experience of foreign intervention. Napoleon's well-known march on Moscow was preceded by incursions from Poles, Swedes, and Germans. The

15

Mongol invasion of 1237 destroyed the old Russia based in Kiev and suppressed its culture for two hundred and fifty years. In spite of its other successes, the October Revolution conspicuously failed to guarantee Russia against further invasion. Indeed, it heightened the threat from abroad. The missionary hopes of Soviet revolutionaries for a new society were matched by the missionary hostility of the revolution's enemies. Churchill talked of strangling the revolution in its cradle. Hitler saw his attack on the Soviet Union as a crusade against Bolshevism.

Every Soviet schoolchild is reminded that the Soviet Union has been invaded twice since the revolution. The first occasion was in 1918. "The exploiting classes overthrown by the revolution mounted a civil war against the power of the workers and peasants. . . . Led by the leading circles of England, the USA and France, the imperialists organized military campaigns against our country. From all sides, north, south, east and west, the attacking hordes of interventionists and White Guards poured on to our territory," as *Pravda* put it on the fortieth anniversary.[2]

Whatever exaggeration or distortion there may be in this analysis, it is part of Soviet historiography and the received perception of Soviet leaders. Although the young Soviet republic managed to defeat the interventionists, the experience fostered a powerful feeling of encirclement, which still continues. Having failed to conquer it militarily, the capitalist states tried to weaken the Soviet Union by diplomatic isolation and economic boycott. The result in Moscow was a deeply ingrained feeling of living in a state of siege. The Soviet leadership was aware of two strands of Western thought vis-à-vis the new Soviet state. One sought confrontation. The other was prepared to tolerate accommodation. Lenin envisaged a period of peaceful, though temporary, coexistence between the Soviet Union and the capitalist states, during which Soviet policy should aim at encouraging the West's proponents of accommodation. The Soviet Union should seek trade, aid, and recognition from them, and play the traditional game of international diplomacy in order to build up Soviet strength before imperialism's inevitable attack. Lenin was convinced that no lasting accommodation was possible because the West would never come to accept the permanent existence of the Soviet state. Behind the accommodationists' smiles lurked intentions just as hostile as those harbored by the advocates of outright confrontation with the Soviet Union by force of arms.

While the strongest impression left by the first invasion of the Soviet Union shortly after the revolution was to enhance the Bolsheviks' feeling of encirclement, the issue raised by the Nazi invasion was the need for preparedness. Like many of Stalin's mistakes, his actions in the months preceding Hitler's attack are no longer discussed in the Soviet press. But every member of the present generation of Soviet leaders is aware of Stalin's grotesque failure to prepare adequate defenses against the Nazi threat. In his denunciation of Stalin at the Twentieth Party Congress in February 1956, Khrushchev pointed out that "the annihilation of many military commanders" in the party purges had enormous consequences. Stalin also failed to heed the warnings from foreign governments and Soviet agents abroad that Hitler was preparing an attack. The army was not properly mobilized or supplied. Mass production of armaments was barely underway. "Did we have the time and the capabilities for such preparations? Yes, we did," Khrushchev argued.[3]

It is hardly surprising that he and his successors determined that they would not be caught out a second time. If it sometimes seems that the Soviet Union is rearming to an unnecessarily high degree and overinsuring against any conceivable outside attack, this is partly an overreaction to the mistakes of the last war. The Kremlin is not going to be surprised again. It has also abandoned the old Russian policy, adopted by necessity more often than choice, of territorial defense in depth. No longer will an enemy be allowed to penetrate inside Russia as Napoleon and Hitler were. The horrors of the Nazi occupation confirmed the Soviet leadership in the view that the only way to deter any future invasion is to maintain a formidable fighting machine geared to forward defense and poised, if necessary, to launch a preemptive attack on enemy territory in a developing crisis. In Eastern Europe Stalin created a buffer zone of Soviet-dominated allies, designed to absorb the first shock of any enemy ground attack. On the border with China, when tensions mounted in the mid-1960s, Brezhnev and his colleagues built up a massive military curtain of strength consisting of roughly half a million men and partly using Mongolia as another buffer zone. "We have 22.4 million square kilometers of territory and we want to defend every single one of those kilometers," says Vadim Zagladin.[4]

Immensely powerful on land, the Soviet leadership still found itself, for more than a decade and a half after the Second World War, vulnerable to air attack and lacking any credible deterrent to counter the threat of the new technology, the atomic bomb. It was not until the mid-1950s that Moscow developed a long-range bomber that could cross the Atlantic. The first intercontinental rockets, launched in 1957, were unreliable for several more years. Although Moscow had tested an atomic bomb in 1949, it had no means of delivering it for ten years. During that long period of nuclear monopoly, the United States had been building up military bases on the Soviet periphery. Soviet sensitivity about violations of its air space was a powerful factor in the crisis over the American U-2 spy plane that the Russians shot down in 1962. Roy and Zhores Medvedev have described how embarrassed the Soviet leadership felt by its helplessness to prevent American overflights.[5] For years the Kremlin had been able to detect, but not obstruct, the flights, which were designed, it assumed, not only for espionage but as a device for political intimidation, often coinciding with Soviet national celebrations. The Soviet leaders did not publicly protest, for fear of advertising their own powerlessness. When they finally managed to shoot down a U-2 after ten years of American impunity, Khrushchev exulted. "We were sick and tired of being subjected to these indignities. They were making these flights to show up our impotence. Well, we weren't impotent any longer."[6]

The gradual development of a Soviet nuclear potential prompted a profound change in Soviet foreign policy. At the Twentieth Party Congress, Khrushchev modified Lenin's view that war between capitalism and communism was inevitable. Although he expected capitalist states to launch most wars, Lenin had also envisaged in certain circumstances the possibility of an "offensive revolutionary war" by a socialist state against bourgeois countries. The atomic bomb made that kind of war irrational. Equally, by the late-1950s, an attack on Russia could not be profitable for an aggressor. The new reality was a major factor in the split between Khrushchev and Mao, who argued that the Soviet Union should no longer be afraid of confronting the United States now that Moscow had acquired the power to threaten it with nuclear weapons. By contrast Khrushchev believed that war between capitalism and socialism was no longer inevitable, and that the socialist world should concentrate on defeating capitalism by peaceful competition.

The paradox of nuclear weapons was that while they removed any rational calculation in favor of war they heightened the destructive potential available to an enemy who might behave irrationally or make a miscalculation. In the hands of responsible statesmen the atomic bomb might be a reassuring mutual deterrent. In the hands of madmen or gamblers it was the stuff of nightmares. As far as the Kremlin was concerned, Mao was a madman who would sacrifice the world because he thought that more Chinese would survive than other people. "I remember how Mao said: 'Let 400 million Chinese die; 300 million will be left.' Such is the psychology of this man," Brezhnev warned Nixon in one of their talks.[7]

In the Kremlin's view the danger posed by the Americans was only slightly less. The Americans were well ahead in the arms race, and the Russians were continually afraid—and remain so—that Washington might launch an all-out preemptive strike or touch off what would be intended as a "limited" nuclear war with missiles launched from Western Europe alone. In either case it would be a tragic miscalculation, since Moscow would be able and willing to retaliate on the continental United States.

Robert McNamara, President Kennedy's defense secretary, has pointed out that in 1962 the U.S. Air Force wanted to develop forces that would give Washington a first-strike capability. The Russians believed this was Washington's intention and responded by expanding their own strategic nuclear program. If McNamara had been a Kremlin decision maker he would have done the same thing, he has said, although "I see no evidence that they would accept the risks associated with a first strike against the United States."[8] He went on to say, "The Russians are people that I would not trust to act in other than their own narrow national interest, so I am not naive. But they are not mad. They have suffered casualties and their government feels responsible to their people to avoid those situations in the future. They are more sensitive to the impact of casualties on their people than we appear to be in our statements."[9]

Paul Warnke, Jimmy Carter's chief arms control negotiator, has offered another reason for Soviet concern. "In my negotiations, I had the feeling that the Soviets were more serious than we were—not because of any philanthropic impulses, nor because they're nice guys, but because they recognize their political system is infinitely more fragile than ours. If Moscow disappeared, there'd be dancing in the streets in the Ukraine, in Latvia, Estonia, and Lithuania."[10]

These then are the three factors behind the Kremlin's security fears: a sense of geographical encirclement; the knowledge that their ideological enemies have invaded them twice and have the power to do so again; and awareness that the next war is likely to be the last. If the chances of a third invasion seem less these days, the Kremlin does not ascribe this to any permanent shift in its opponents' attitudes, and certainly not to goodwill. It sees it as almost entirely the result of increased Soviet military might and a consequent shift in the balance of world power. In contrast to 1919 when the Soviet Union was weak and to 1941 when it was unprepared, it is strong and vigilant today.

What are Moscow's priorities in relation to the West? The primary one is to gain Western respect. This may seem an odd desire for a missionary system that claims to represent "the most advanced ideas of our age," in the words of Brezhnev's speech on the fiftieth anniversary of the October Revolution.[11] But Russians have long had a fragile relationship to the rest of European culture, a sense of belonging to the West but not being recognized as such. Since the revolution this desire for recognition has been compounded by the manifest contempt and hostility accorded in the West to Soviet socialism. "Our new post-revolutionary society was considered illegitimate, and condemned to be treated as a bastard of history," says Arbatov.[12] "I get angry when I hear how condescendingly many Americans talk of the Russians. Our people have a right to some respect for what they have achieved in spite of enormous difficulties."[13]

Richard Nixon, himself a man with a pronounced inferiority complex, remarked how Russian leaders "crave to be respected as equals."[14] Henry Kissinger contrasted his first meeting with Brezhnev with similar encounters with Mao. "Equality seemed to mean a great deal to Brezhnev. It would be inconceivable that Chinese leaders would ask for it, if only because in the Middle Kingdom tradition it was a great concession granted to the foreigner. To Brezhnev it was central. . . . He expressed his pleasure when in my brief opening statement I stated the obvious: that we were approaching the summit in a spirit of equality and reciprocity. What a more secure leader might have regarded as cliché or condescension, Brezhnev treated as a welcome sign of our seriousness."[15] Willy Brandt found Brezhnev anxious that Russians and Germans should "respect" each other.[16]

Soviet leaders are sensitive to the insulting language of the Cold War, which is often permeated with punitive overtones reminiscent of the scolding attitude of a parent to a child, a judge to an accused, or an animal trainer to a savage beast.

Western decision makers talk not of Soviet actions but of Soviet "behaviour" or "conduct." They judge whether it is "responsible" or not. A favored cliché is "the carrot and the stick," as though the Soviet Union is a donkey that can be manipulated by simple means. Under the Reagan administration this kind of language gained currency again, as the new president in his first press conference accused the Soviet leadership of reserving the right "to commit any crime, to lie, to cheat."[17] To the Russians these words were demeaning and an insult. They symbolized a reversion to the old strain in American attitudes toward the Russians, which has long angered Moscow, the notion that the Soviet Union is beyond the pale of civilization and can only be allowed into the international community if it changes its ways.

The Russians long for the West to adopt the alternative "realistic" view of the Soviet Union as a state with a legitimate interest in its own security. They also hope that the West will recognize that the Soviet Union is entitled to want to spread its influence by diplomatic, economic, and political means like any other major power. In spite of his many criticisms of Kissinger, Arbatov looked back to him fondly when contrasted with Zbigniew Brzezinski. "In Kissinger's view the Soviet Union is merely another actor on the world stage, which can be anything according to circumstances, from irreconcilable enemy to traditional rival right up to partner. For Brzezinski the USSR is above all an illegitimate type of society with which normal relations are impossible as long as fundamental internal changes have not occurred."[18]

The Russians want respect not only because they want to come in out of the cold psychologically and see an end to the recurring insults and contempt of the West. They also seek respect as a political goal. It would mean, they hope, the West's abandonment of economic, political, and nuclear pressure on the Soviet Union—what Brezhnev and other Soviet leaders have called the policy of "diktat" and dealing with the Soviet Union "from positions of strength." In its stead, they say, the two systems should compete and cooperate on peaceful terms.

In all the Reagan administration's talk about preventing Western Europe from becoming too dependent on the Soviet Union for natural gas, the actual history of economic relations between Moscow and the West has usually been forgotten. The number of occasions on which the Soviet Union has attempted to exert economic leverage over the West is very small. Even at moments of severe economic crisis for Western Europe, such as the Arab oil embargo in 1973, Moscow made no effort to add to the West's difficulties. The West, by contrast, has frequently been an unreliable partner. Before the Second World War the United States had been the largest Western exporter to the Soviet Union, but in spite of the wartime alliance and the Soviet Union's enormous war damage, it stopped Lend-Lease aid as soon as the war was over. In 1949 it launched what amounted to economic warfare against Moscow as part of its containment policy. The Export Control Act of 1949, which was tightened up in 1962, listed hundreds of items of "military or economic significance" that could not be sold to the Soviet Union or its Eastern European allies without a special license. In 1951 Congress withdrew most-favored-nation trading status, which had been granted in 1935. Under Nixon, trade with the Soviet Union leaped ahead again and most-favored-nation status was due to be restored. But critics of trade reciprocity regained their strength, and the Reagan administration resorted to economic warfare once again.

Reagan and his officials talked of the Soviet Union's declining rate of growth, its agricultural problems, and the burden of the arms race on its domestic economy as evidence that it would be vulnerable to outside pressure. In diplomatically understated terms, Reagan said in London in 1982, "We ask only for a process, a direction, a basic code of decency—not for an instant transformation."[19] The Kremlin saw this as unjustified interference, and another example of American failure to grant Moscow respect.

The switch in American policy under Carter and Reagan toward a more hostile stance against the Soviet Union was a particular disappointment for Brezhnev. He and his colleagues had hoped that Moscow's achievement of strategic nuclear parity, or what was also called the "rough equivalence" of each side's nuclear arsenals, would finally unlock the door to Western respect. Even if the West was unwilling to recognize the legitimacy of the Soviet system and the Kremlin's justified security fears it would have to acknowledge the facts of Soviet power. Their feelings were well embodied in the remark by Vasily Kuznetsov, a deputy foreign minister, as he negotiated the details of the withdrawal of Soviet nuclear weapons from Cuba after the missile crisis of 1962: "You Americans will never be able to do this to us again."[20] Put in more conventional diplomatic language, parity was seen by Moscow as the essential condition for Soviet–American relations to rest in future on détente or "the relaxation of tensions," as the Russians call it. When the two countries signed a document on the Basic Principles of Mutual Relations, during Nixon's visit to Moscow in 1972, it cited as essential conditions, "observance of the principle of equality and equal security, respect for each other's interests and the peaceful settlement of differences."

Détente, based on parity, offered Moscow numerous advantages. It reduced the risk of war. It opened the way to a stabilization of the arms race. It increased the chance for East–West trade to develop and the restrictions on the transfer of Western technology and capital to the Soviet Union to be lifted. As the cornerstone of a new Western approach to foreign policy, it would lead—so Moscow hoped—to recognition of the status quo in Europe. Instead of the old policy of trying to "roll back" communism, the West would formally accept the Soviet sphere of influence in Eastern Europe. This would be shown by Western recognition of the German Democratic Republic and Poland's postwar western frontiers.

Beyond Europe, parity would provide the Soviet Union with an assured role in international crisis management. The Russians do not admit to being a superpower, which they see as a Western term that denies the class essence of the Soviet Union and the United States. There can be no "convergence" between capitalism and socialism, and Soviet society is totally different from that of the United States. But, they argue, as *The History of Soviet Foreign Policy* puts it, that they have become "one of the greatest world powers, without whose participation not a single international problem can be solved."[21] This should mean that their views be consulted, and their interests represented, in any international settlement of regional tension, whether in the Middle East, the Persian Gulf, or Indochina. In the early days of détente they hoped for regular summit meetings with the American president and even now they call for continuing "dialogue."

The Kremlin wanted détente to be permanent, or as Brezhnev frequently put it, "irreversible." The Leninist concept of "temporary co-existence between socialism and capitalism" was stretched out to encompass the entire foreseeable future. Détente would not only consolidate a relaxation of international tension, it would also provide continuity and predictability in foreign policy—two values that Moscow has always sought from the United States. Brought up on a Marxist view of history as a series of protracted but inevitable social transformations, and accustomed to long or at least open-ended periods in power themselves, Soviet leaders find the Western election system irritating. They argue that it produces excessively frequent changes of leadership and policy, and leaves controversial policies vulnerable to demagogic attack. In 1971 Brezhnev complained that "the frequent zig-zags in US foreign policy, which are apparently connected with domestic political moves and short-term political considerations, have made it much more difficult to deal with the United States."[22] By the end of the 1970s when détente was dying, Arbatov spoke out bitterly against Washington's numerous policy reversals, culminating in the failure to ratify the second treaty limiting strategic nuclear arms (SALT II). "This is another indication of a clearly discernible political style—instability, high-handedness towards others, absolute lack of restraint, and readiness to subordinate important foreign policy issues to transient interests, including those of domestic maneuvering and rivalry. All this bears out the fears voiced in recent years by America's opponents and friends alike—that it is an unreliable partner in international relations."[23]

Soviet unhappiness with the unpredictability and vacillation of American policy was understandable. Under Brezhnev the Kremlin's main goal in Soviet–American relations, apart from the quest for respect, was stability. No Soviet leader made such sustained and consistent efforts to achieve a stable relationship with the United States as Brezhnev. Khrushchev had sought to promote peaceful coexistence with capitalism into the linchpin of Soviet foreign policy and looked for some accommodation with the West, but his own actions over Berlin and Cuba belied his words. His blustering impetuosity and eagerness to score a point against Washington were a far cry from Brezhnev's restrained moderation. Throughout the 1970s Brezhnev measured his actions abroad by the yardstick of Washington's likely response. What would the Americans do? Would this risk provoking them?

In the search for stability, Brezhnev and his colleagues obviously could not totally abandon their commitment to the socialist cause. But even in their public presentation of Soviet policy, they adopted a cautious tone. At the Twenty-third Congress of the Communist Party of the Soviet Union (CPSU) in 1966 they defined the goals of Soviet foreign policy as follows:

"1. Ensuring, together with other socialist countries, favorable international conditions for the construction of socialism and communism;

2. Consolidating the unity and cohesion of the socialist countries, their friendship and brotherhood;

3. Supporting the national liberation movement and engaging in all-round cooperation with the young developing states;

4. Consistently standing up for the principle of peaceful coexistence between states with differing social systems;

5. Giving a resolute rebuff to the aggressive forces of imperialism;

6. Safeguarding mankind from another world war."[24]

By 1977, when the party promulgated a new constitution for the USSR, the state interests of the Soviet Union had moved more explicitly to the top of the list of priorities. The constitution now states: "The foreign policy of the USSR is aimed at

1. Ensuring international conditions for building communism in the USSR;

2. Safeguarding the state interests of the Soviet Union;

3. Consolidating the positions of world socialism;

4. Supporting the struggle of peoples for national liberation and social progress;

5. Preventing wars of aggression;

6. Achieving universal and complete disarmament;

7. Consistently implementing the principle of the peaceful co-existence of states with different social systems."[25]

In the new constitution the first two goals of the USSR's foreign policy are thus clearly stated as the promotion of direct Soviet national interests. The third one amounts to the defense of existing socialist states, i.e., the USSR's Eastern

European allies and the other socialist states with whom the Soviet Union has treaties of friendship and cooperation, although the phrase "consolidating the positions of world socialism" is vague enough to leave it to Moscow to decide when and how to act. After that, in clause four, comes the national liberation movement. Here again there is an interesting change since 1966, another apparent swing away from internationalism. The promise of "all-round cooperation with the young developing states" has been dropped, reflecting the Soviet Union's disappointment with the way events have turned out in many parts of the Third World. Clause four suggests that the Soviet Union will be more selective in its aid in the future.

The primacy given to the defense of state interests in the 1977 constitution would not be remarkable in any other country. It is the cardinal principle of every state's foreign policy. For the Soviet Union, however, it is interesting in the light of the long debate within the communist movement over the role of internationalism, particularly in the early years after the revolution. The fact that the current Soviet establishment unashamedly promotes its own state and party interests reflects conditioning caused by decades of feeling encircled and under threat from the capitalist world. Two invasions since the revolution, as well as the recurring efforts at boycott and containment, have convinced Soviet party members that the survival of the USSR is the essential condition for the development of socialism in other parts of the world. Soviet party theorists are sensitive to the charge that they may be neglecting the cause of internationalism. In 1981 Zagladin wrote in *Pravda* that the might of the socialist community, headed by the Soviet Union, was vital for the struggle for peace and socialism everywhere.[26] Yuri Krasin, the pro-rector of the Academy of Social Sciences of the Central Committee of the CPSU, argues that the working class's "most important historical task" is to prevent a thermonuclear catastrophe. "Marxist–Leninists are opposed to the dissolution of the communist movement in some sort of boundless and amorphous internationalism," he goes on. "It is perfectly clear that no countries, the socialist included, can afford to pursue a foreign policy which utterly ignores national state interests. . . . The Soviet Union's defense of its state interests, of the interests of a nation building a new society, does not run counter to proletarian internationalism; on the contrary as history shows, it is a factor making for a change in the world balance that accords with the interests of all progressives."[27]

Moscow claims that its achievement of parity with the United States "paralyzes the aggressive actions of imperialism" and "hinders the export of counter-revolution and actions taken to counter the national liberation movement."[28] This means that peaceful competition between the two rival social systems of socialism and capitalism can go ahead unfettered by the threat of nuclear and conventional war. Peaceful coexistence does not put an end to the ideological struggle. On the contrary it creates the conditions in which the superiority of socialist ideas is bound to emerge. That, at least, is the theory. But behind this thesis of official optimism there lurks as always an antithesis of pessimism. As capitalism's leaders realize that they are doomed, they will resort to "the most refined methods of ideological subversion,"[29] forcing the Soviet Union to be ever more vigilant. "Even such forms of international intercourse as trade, cultural and scientific-technical ties and so on, which are generally accepted and have enjoyed a good reputation for centuries, when passed through the intellectual meatgrinder of these people are immediately turned into their opposites, into sinister weapons of subversive activity."[30] So yet again the Soviet Union has to be on its guard, anxious, alert, and on the defensive.

Worse still, the capitalists may revert to violence and war. The former minister of defense, Marshal Grechko, put it clearly enough in 1974 at the very height of détente: "The weakening of the positions of imperialism and the capitalist system's feeling of doom intensify the aggressiveness and adventurism of reactionary-monopolistic circles. Here and there they provoke military conflicts, which are directed against the Soviet Union, the entire socialist community and the forces of national liberation.

"The militarists vainly attempt to overcome the insoluble internal social, economic, and ideological contradictions of the capitalist system to weaken the world socialist system and to deal with the international worker and liberation movement by the path of political subversion, blackmail, and aggressive wars."[31] This, then, is the paradox of parity and peaceful coexistence. As the capitalists realize that they are losing the ideological struggle, they go back to military methods, and thus force the Soviet Union and its allies to increase their own military strength.

What seemed in the early 1970s to be largely a gloomy Soviet prediction had become a reality under the Reagan administration a decade later. In Washington, officials were talking of restoring American military superiority and using economic leverage to force the Soviet Union to change its system under threat of war. "The Soviet Union would have to choose between peacefully changing their Communist system in the direction followed by the West, or going to war. There is no other alternative and it could go either way," according to Richard Pipes, former advisor on Soviet affairs on Reagan's National Security Council.[32] Détente was barely mentioned, let alone pursued. The Pentagon was proposing the biggest peacetime increase in American military spending ever.

It was perhaps no surprise that at the end of the Brezhnev era Georgi Arbatov summed up Moscow's mood in a sentence that conveyed a deep Russian yearning for respect, understanding, and peace—a yearning that, he seemed to fear, might never be fulfilled: "I often think that Americans have had unheard-of luck throughout their history, perhaps too much luck so that they cannot understand or have deep sympathy for people whose own history has been much less fortunate."[33]

3

THE GROWTH
OF SOVIET POWER

*There is a pervasive fallacy that America could have
the power to order the world just the way we want it to
be. It assumes, for example, that we could dominate
the Soviet Union—that we could prevent it from being
a superpower—if we chose to do so. This obsolete idea
has more to do with nostalgia than present-day reality.*

Cyrus Vance
former U.S. Secretary of State[1]

The director of the U.S. Central Intelligence Agency, William Casey, has a map
of the world in his office. Dozens of countries are colored red—not, as it might
have been in the days of the British Empire, in order to mark the loyal colonies
of the Crown. Casey's red crayon picks out countries "under a significant degree
of Soviet influence," altogether some fifty nations. This was double the number
of ten years before, he told a meeting of the American Legion in 1982.[2] The CIA
director refused to name the unfortunate countries or explain the basis of the
classification. But after his speech an agency spokesperson revealed to reporters
that the red crayon could mark a country not actually under Soviet control but
facing an insurgency backed by Moscow. Thus a right-wing country like El
Salvador might be colored red.

Adversaries of the Soviet Union have always found it easy to produce rough
evidence of an increase in Soviet power. The number of nations under Soviet

influence has clearly increased since 1945. The size of the Soviet arsenal, conventional and nuclear, has grown dramatically. The Soviet Navy is no longer a coastal force, but has acquired a global reach. Soviet diplomats and military advisors work in scores of countries on every continent. Compared to 1945, Soviet power at the end of the Brezhnev era has obviously grown. But has it really grown compared to 1972 or 1962? Will the Soviet Union inexorably advance if the West leaves open "a target of opportunity"? Is there, as Kissinger now puts it, "an unprecedented Soviet geo-political offensive all over the globe"?[3] What are the purposes of Soviet power? Is it axiomatic that every Soviet foreign policy move is hostile in intent, and that Moscow always favors conflict and rejects international settlements? Does the rest of the world, in short, face a "Soviet threat"?

The almost forty years since the Second World War have provided enough of a panorama of Soviet activity for some patterns to emerge. Inevitably they are nuanced and complicated. Yet how often is a simple picture of Soviet expansionism held up in the West, as though there were no doubts about it? Soviet advances are remembered. The withdrawal of Soviet troops, even under Stalin, from Iran, China, Czechoslovakia, and Denmark are conveniently forgotten. Khrushchev's move into Hungary in 1956 is an indelible memory in the European mind. His removal of troops from Rumania in 1958 is overlooked. Brezhnev's intervention in Afghanistan in favor of an allied regime is the stuff of frequent comment. His unwillingness to send troops to Vietnam to defend an ally against massive attack is rarely remembered. Soviet power has been used at times rashly, at times with caution. In the Middle East, Moscow has persistently urged its Arab friends to accept the existence of Israel, even at the cost of weakening Soviet links with the Arab radicals. In Latin America, the Soviet Union defended Castro but deserted Allende. In Africa it supplied arms to the Movimento Popular de Libertação de Angola (MPLA), which took power in Angola, but only limited amounts to one group in Zimbabwe and none to Robert Mugabe's victorious ZANU. In the Horn of Africa it supported the right of the Eritreans to independence in the 1950s, then ignored them for twenty years; and finally, after a Marxist regime came to power in Ethiopia in 1975, turned one hundred and eighty degrees to oppose it by force.

These contradictions and inconsistencies in the Soviet Union's use of power cast grave doubt on the notion that the Kremlin has any master plan in foreign policy. They have all the hallmarks of short-term decision making that characterize other countries' activity abroad. A last-minute compromise here, a panic reaction there, in this country the hope that uncritical backing of an unpopular ruler will bring dividends, in that country the fear that failure to act will be worse than intervention—these are the common currency of great-power diplomacy which Moscow also employs. The stakes differ widely on each continent. The Soviet Union has always been more concerned about countries on its immediate periphery than those in the remoter parts of the Third World. Southern Africa and Latin America are lower on the list of Soviet priorities than Asia and the Middle East. The core of Soviet policy since the Second World War has been its relationship with the United States, although competition has taken place largely in Europe. Overarching Europe, the Soviet Union engaged in a frantic arms race in the hope of blunting American nuclear superiority.

It would be wrong to suggest that the zigzags in Soviet foreign policy mean that Moscow has no long-term goals. The Kremlin still hopes for the eventual triumph of socialism throughout the world. But it sets no time limit and does not believe in the "export" of revolution. Each country will make the transition to socialism, depending on its own internal social and economic processes. Moscow expects that what it calls the international "correlation of forces" will gradually and inevitably produce a transfer of power all over the world to the benefit of the socialist camp.

The "correlation of forces" is a vague and elastic term that can be used to argue that an historically inevitable shift toward socialism is underway. Under Khrushchev and Brezhnev, the "correlation of forces" included not only the growth of Soviet power and the relative decline of the West, but the anticolonial drive of the Third World and internal developments in the capitalist countries, such as the peace movement and rising trade union militance. Soviet strength was seen as the sine qua non for the switch in the correlation of forces toward socialism. On this point the Soviet Union's national ambitions for increased status in the world coincided with the revolutionary imperative of Leninist theory. Moscow wants power in order to defend the Soviet Union against the military threat posed by the United States and its allies. It wants power as a source of international prestige, and in order to strengthen the "socialist community" and encourage anticapitalist tendencies in the rest of the world.

It is important to distinguish between the realms of state relations and class struggle. While denying that there is a Soviet military threat, the Kremlin makes no attempt to hide its view that socialism is a "threat" to capitalism and imperialism. But it argues that this is a struggle waged by ideas that cross national boundaries and are international in character, putting down roots in accordance with local circumstances, class inequalities, and the degree of capitalist oppression in different countries. This is similar to Western arguments that the desire for "human rights" such as liberty, democracy, and justice overrides national boundaries and is universal.

It does not follow, therefore, that the Soviet wish for power is "expansionism" in the sense of a drive to impose its will on foreign nations or subordinate their interests to its own. Nor can the Kremlin's desire for an increase in Soviet power automatically be equated with a "geopolitical offensive," as often alleged in the West. The value of power is more diffuse and longterm, a mark of status, and an ingredient in what the Kremlin sees as the inevitable historical transition from capitalism to socialism.

THE SOVIET NAVY AND OTHER INTERVENTION FORCES

However vague Moscow's long-term political goals may be, one trend has been constant. Soviet military power has grown and grown. The Soviet Union's nuclear arsenal expanded rapidly in the 1960s and continued to grow in the 1970s throughout the era of détente. In Central Europe Soviet conventional forces have regularly been modernized. At sea the Soviet Union has switched the operations of its navy over the last twenty years from coastal defense to forward deployment. Its battleships maneuver in every ocean of the world. Their numbers have dramatically increased. In addition, Moscow has built a large merchant marine and an ocean-going fishing fleet, which, under the centralized Soviet system, can easily be put at the service of the navy. At the same time the Soviet Union has acquired the ability to lift Soviet troops and heavy equipment by air to war theaters far from its shores.

Apart from the growth of the Soviet nuclear arsenal, the expansion of Soviet sea and airlift power became the main new factor for alarm and suspicion in some quarters in the West during the Brezhnev period. It also seemed that Moscow was increasingly willing to use its newfound power.

No two events in the 1970s were more decisive in reinforcing an aggressive image of Soviet policy than Moscow's massive airlift of arms and equipment for Cuban troops in Angola in 1975 and its invasion of Afghanistan at the end of 1979. The two operations seemed to reflect a new boldness in what became known in the jargon as the "projection of Soviet power." In Angola the world saw the first sudden shipment of large quantities of Soviet weaponry by air to a distant battlefield. In Afghanistan Soviet troops crossed an international frontier into a country that was not part of the Soviet sphere of influence for the first time since the Second World War. In addition, in November 1977, the Russians mounted an almost round-the-clock airlift of tanks and heavy weaponry to Ethiopia to help repulse the Somali occupation of the Ogaden. Adversaries of the Soviet Union treated the events as proof that Moscow was more eager than ever to exploit "targets of opportunity" wherever they might arise. What was new was Moscow's willingness and ability to do so a long way beyond Europe. The implications for the Third World were said to be dire.

The difficulty with this interpretation of Soviet policy was its blurring of several separate ideas. Those who used the phrase, "power projection", often gave it, consciously or unconsciously, a sinister meaning, as though it were synonymous with aggression. This allowed them to evade the issue of the legitimacy of Soviet actions. Were Soviet actions in Afghanistan really the same as those in Angola and Ethiopia? It also confused what was new and what was not. When the Russians sent a batch of rifles to liberation movements or friendly governments in Africa in the 1960s, this was also "power projection." The difference in Angola and Ethiopia in the 1970s was one of degree. At the same time, the new phrase was often employed to give the impression that the Soviet Union had overtaken the West in its ability to intervene militarily in the Third World. The streak of alarmism that assumes Moscow is always stealing a march on the West and forging ahead in some branch of military technology had appeared again in a new context. Among some Western observers there was even a suggestion that Moscow was responsible for the turbulence of the Third World, and that its new "power projection" was fomenting revolution in different parts of the globe.

Moscow's interventions in Angola, Afghanistan, and Ethiopia undoubtedly destroyed the easy Western assumption that its own forces could operate in the Third World virtually without challenge from Moscow. Throughout the 1950s and 1960s American, British, or French forces intervened in a host of foreign countries (Lebanon, the Dominican Republic, Egypt, Malaysia, and many others) without having to worry about a potential clash with the Soviet Union. As a nation with great-power ambitions, the USSR was likely to wish to break the West's monopoly eventually.

Until the Angolan civil war, Moscow had not been able to make the decisive difference in any Third World conflict. In earlier anticolonial conflicts, its help had been low-key and in some cases exclusively clandestine. In Vietnam it was massive, but still subsidiary to the efforts of the local protagonists. Angola was the first place where Moscow was able to turn the tide openly and convincingly, yet even here it acted at the prompting of and with help from an ally, Cuba. Some Western analysts argued that Moscow used Cuban troops in Angola as proxies or surrogates for its own, so that the Kremlin could avoid any international blame. The assumption is that Moscow masterminded the operation. But the evidence suggests that Castro, not Brezhnev, took the initiative. (Similarly, there is no evidence that Moscow encouraged the Vietnamese to invade Kampuchea in 1978—the other case most often cited for the "Soviet proxy" theory.)

Nevertheless, success in Angola was a major factor behind the Kremlin's move into Ethiopia two years later and probably encouraged it to take the risk of invading Afghanistan in 1979. Militarily and politically, however, the invasion of Afghanistan was different from the Soviet Union's operations in Angola and Ethiopia. The move into Afghanistan was a combined land and air offensive at very short range from the Soviet frontier. It was aggression, since it was intended to remove the government of an independent state. The reasons for Moscow's intervention will be discussed later. Here, the argument is that the invasion of Afghanistan was not typical of Soviet actions in the Third World in the 1970s. The overall record of Soviet policy is mixed, a combination of caution as well as radicalism, of stagnation as well as advance, and of opportunities ignored as often as seized. If "expansionism" means the use or threat of force to achieve political advantage beyond a nation's own frontiers, the case can be argued that there was a decline in Soviet expansionism from Stalin via Khrushchev to Brezhnev.

This is borne out by a study by Stephen Kaplan of the Brookings Institution in Washington, who found that between January 1946 and December 1975 the USSR had used military force as a political instrument 156 times.[4] Three-fifths of the incidents in which Moscow used combined operations in a substantial display of politico-military power occurred before Stalin's death.[5] In a separate study with Barry Blechman, Kaplan found that the United States had used military force as a political instrument 215 times over the same period, i.e., about 40 percent more frequently than the Soviet Union.[6]

The greatest increase of people and territory under Soviet control took place during Stalin's rule. The Nazi–Soviet nonaggression treaty of August 1939 was followed by the seizure of the three Baltic states, Eastern Poland, and, a few months later, after Finnish resistance was painfully overcome, large tracts of Finland. (Most of these territories had formed part of the Tsarist Empire.) At the end of the war the Soviet Union annexed smaller parts of Rumania, and Czechoslovakia and half of what formerly had been German East Prussia. Soviet troops occupied Poland, Hungary, Rumania, Bulgaria, eastern Germany and North Korea. But the story of Stalin's military operations in the postwar period also contains cases of withdrawals. Soviet troops left Yugoslavia after only a brief stay, as Stalin felt secure that the local Communists would consolidate their power. In parallel with an American withdrawal from Czechoslovakia in December 1945, Stalin pulled out his own troops. In the spring of 1946, Soviet troops evacuated the strategically important Danish island of Bornholm and the northern provinces of Iran. Stalin felt his chance of a good long-term relationship with both countries would be better served by a military retreat. The foreign policies of neighboring states were more important to him than their internal political system. On his immediate borders he wanted buffer states which would be, in the words of the Yalta agreements, "friendly" to the Soviet Union. He offered to withdraw Soviet troops from East Germany in favor of reunification, provided the new German state was neutralized. In Asia, after giving some support to the Chinese Communists, Stalin withdrew his troops from Manchuria in April 1946, long before a Communist victory in the civil war was assured.

In the two great Cold War crises of Korea and Berlin, Stalin's behavior, although provocative, showed significant elements of military caution. He did not attempt to interfere with the Western airlift into blockaded Berlin. Soviet ground and sea forces played no part against the United Nations forces as they routed the North Koreans, while the limited number of Soviet pilots reported in North Korea confined their flights to air space controlled by the North Koreans. When Yugoslavia defied Moscow in 1948, Soviet troops were not sent in.

It was Khrushchev who took the biggest risks against the West and showed the first signs of interest in the Third World. Stalin had seen the world in terms of "two camps," one socialist, the other capitalist, with no room for any intermediate zone. Khrushchev saw the political potential of the developing countries. But during his period of rule policy vacillated, partly reflecting strains within the Politburo during the uneasy transition from Stalin's long rule. In the early years after Stalin's death, the Kremlin looked for conciliation all round. Soviet troops left Austria in 1955, once its neutrality was guaranteed by treaty, and pulled out of the Finnish naval base of Porkkala. Khrushchev apologized to Tito for previous Soviet pressure on Yugoslavia.

The turning point came with the upheavals in Hungary and Poland in 1956, which demonstrated that Stalin's buffer states were by no means stable. Moscow's anxiety about West Germany increased, not only because of its rearmament but also because of new concern about the relationship between a strong West Germany and a weak Eastern Europe. In trying to force Western concessions over Berlin, Khrushchev twice provoked crises, once in 1958 and again, more seriously, in 1961. In 1962 he dispatched nuclear missiles to Cuba in the most dramatic escalation of East–West tension since the Cold War had begun.

Khrushchev moved away from what can be described as Stalin's continental isolationism. The upsurge in decolonization of the Third World excited Khrushchev's imagination, and he eagerly embraced the new anti-Western figures who appeared on the world stage, Sukarno, Nasser, Nkrumah, and Ben Bella. Soviet military aid was offered to regimes whose foreign policies or strategic positions made them potential allies against the West, while the Kremlin turned a blind eye to their frequent repression of local Communist parties and the organized Left. But it is important to remember that the first direct Soviet involvement in Third World arms deliveries in 1955—the deal with Nasser—took place on Egypt's initiative, not Moscow's, and after the West had created the Baghdad Pact. The dispatch of Soviet pilots to the Congo during the crisis of 1960 was also at local request, and proved to be short-lived.

With Khrushchev's overthrow, Soviet "power projection" moved into a third phase. Kremlin policy under Brezhnev was mostly marked by caution in the application of force. There were no attempts to challenge the West politically on the central terrain of the East–West divide in Europe or Berlin. While Soviet power, both conventional and nuclear, was continually built up, its deployment was primarily related to the perceived threat from U.S. strategic forces.

As Soviet power developed, so the agenda of Soviet foreign policy changed. Moscow was seen to be growing stronger militarily and the call on its resources from countries in the Third World became more insistent. It was increasingly expected to help liberation movements and "progressive" regimes. Its wish for international recognition as a world power also encouraged it to play a more vigorous role.

One of the major instruments of its new power was the Soviet Navy. Yet in assessing Soviet intentions, one must first consider where the navy has come from, and the point it has now reached. In a sense it is surprising that it took the

Soviet Union as long as it did to build up its sea power. For the last ninety years of its existence, the Tsarist Empire had been confronted by mainly maritime powers along its four separate coasts, the Baltic, White Sea, Black Sea, and Pacific. Russia found herself more often attacked than attacking. It was not until the 1930s that Stalin invested seriously in improving the country's naval resources by extending its shipyards and building new ones, safe from coastal attack, on the Volga, in the north, and on the Pacific. He launched a ship-building program centered on submarines, torpedo boats, and shore-based aircraft. In the immediate aftermath of the war, Stalin still saw the potential naval threat to the Soviet Union in traditional terms as a seaborne invasion with amphibious landings of enemy troops. Stalin continued his prewar naval construction program but also invested heavily in civilian ships, deciding that it would be cheaper and more efficient to increase the supply of protein to the Soviet people by building a fleet of deep-sea trawlers and factory ships rather than sinking more resources into collective farming.

Khrushchev expanded the Soviet Union's merchant marine a few years later as part of his drive to increase foreign trade. With his more outward-looking foreign policy, Khrushchev saw that hard currency could be earned by selling space on Soviet ships and limiting the transport of Soviet freight on foreign ones. Seven of the country's thirteen largest shipyards were converted from naval to civilian use. This switch coincided with a downgrading of the fear of seaborne invasion. The Kremlin's military planners now saw the main naval threat from the West as likely to come from nuclear strikes from American aircraft, operating from carriers. This prompted a profound change in strategy. Cutting back their naval ship-building by 60 percent, they halted the building of cruisers and medium-sized submarines. The new Soviet plan was to counter American carrier groups with missile attacks from shore-based aircraft and destroyers.

Another technological leap by the United States forced a third change in Soviet strategic thinking. American development of the world's first nuclear-powered submarine, able to go deeper and undetected for longer distances than conventional submarines, alarmed the Kremlin. Increases in the range of carrier-borne aircraft also meant that coastal defense was not enough. The Kremlin's response was twofold. First, in 1958, it decided to make the building of its own nuclear submarines a main priority. Then when Kennedy accelerated the production of nuclear-armed Polaris submarines, the Kremlin took a crucial decision. In October 1961 the Soviet defense minister, Marshal Rodion Malinovsky, revealed a shift in naval strategy from coastal defense to forward deployment. The decision was to have major implications for what the West was to call "the global projection of Soviet power." But as Michael MccGwire, one of the West's leading students of Soviet naval issues, has observed, "Most specialists in the field now accept that the initial shift to forward deployment was a response to the threat to Russia from sea-based nuclear delivery systems . . . triggered by President Kennedy."[7] Under the new strategy, the Soviet Navy led by Admiral

Sergei Gorshkov moved outward into ocean patrolling with the aim of being continuously able to track American aircraft carriers or submarines and strike them on command. It also developed its own submarine-launched missiles.

Forward deployment began in the Mediterranean. The Soviet Navy first started regular patrolling there in the mid-1960s. But as American sea-launched missiles extended their potential range, Moscow increased its concern for the northwest corner of the Indian Ocean, the Arabian Sea. This area provides the best target coverage of Russia and China by a 2,500-mile missile. Soviet fears that it might be used as a launch area for Polaris and Poseidon were fueled by an agreement in 1963 for the U.S. Navy to build a communications station at North West Cape in Australia and in 1966 by the British and American plan to turn the island of Diego Garcia, in the center of the Indian Ocean, into a military stronghold. The Soviet Navy began its own patrols and started to look for shore facilities in Somalia and South Yemen (Aden). To deal with U.S. submarine bases in North America and the transit routes across the Atlantic, it also tried to develop facilities in Cuba and Guinea.

By the early 1970s, the Kremlin found itself, for a number of different historical reasons, with a pattern of maritime responsibilities a long way from its shores. It had a large civilian fleet to protect. It had embarked on a substantial hydrographic research program in order to develop its sonar and other sub-marine-tracking technologies. It had a fleet of nuclear submarines and a large surface fleet of ocean-going cruisers, destroyers, and frigates. The development prompted a major debate within the Soviet leadership over the role of naval power in war and peace. A long series of writings by Admiral Gorshkov in 1972, which advocated a more assertive use of naval power as a necessary adjunct of great-power status, were punctuated by delays in publication. This, as well as the differing tone of review articles, suggested considerable disagreement. By the mid-1970s the trend of official naval pronouncements, plus the decision to build longer range amphibious ships and a light aircraft carrier, convinced Western experts that the Soviet leadership had come to accept the relevance of naval power, including general-purpose surface forces, in time of war.

In peacetime the Kremlin has used the navy in the classic role of showing the flag on courtesy calls at foreign ports as a way of trying to gain prestige and influence. In the absence of a reliable overland route through China, it sent most of its arms shipments to Vietnam during the war by sea. It has also deployed warships at times of crisis as a reminder to potential aggressors, as in the 1967 and 1973 wars in the Middle East, in the Bay of Bengal in 1971 during the Indo–Pakistan war, in the South China Sea after the American mining of the Vietnamese harbor of Haiphong, and off Angola in 1975. But MccGwire points out, "none of these examples provide evidence of Soviet readiness actually to engage Western naval forces in order to prevent them from intervening against a Soviet client state."[8]

Clearly, the Soviet Navy has gradually been taking on a larger logistical role in

Third World crises. In 1973 Soviet landing ships took Moroccan troops to Syria and also ferried military supplies there from the Black Sea. Warships armed with surface-to-air missiles stood off the coast in a position to protect aircraft landing at the resupply airfields in Egypt and Syria. In 1978, during the crisis over the Ogaden, Soviet warships took weapons from South Yemen which were then put on landing ships for delivery to Ethiopia. This use of the Soviet Navy in a secondary role in foreign conflicts is new. But it falls a long way short of suggesting that the Soviet Union is ready to intervene in direct naval hostilities against a Third World state or confront the Western navies.

Comparisons of the Soviet Navy with Western naval strength show a clear Soviet inferiority. In 1981 Admiral Thomas Hayward, chief of U.S. Naval Operations, said: "I would not trade the U.S. Navy for the Soviet Navy under any circumstances. Our forces today are modern and sophisticated, embodying some of the most advanced technology American industry can produce. Our capabilities are improving across the full spectrum of naval warfare with the addition of new ships, submarines, and aircraft to the fleet."[9] In 1981 the U.S. and other NATO navies had twice the naval tonnage of the Soviet and other Warsaw Pact navies. NATO had 403 major surface fighting ships compared with the Warsaw Pact's 281. Since the early 1960s NATO has deployed more than twice as many fighting ships as the Soviet Navy and will continue to outproduce it in the foreseeable future.

When it comes to the issue of naval forces for local intervention around the world, "the U.S. Navy's amphibious lift capacity and ability to project power ashore are clearly unmatched in the world today," as Reagan's navy secretary, John Lehman, conceded.[10] With the construction of three ships that can carry helicopters and vertical take-off planes, the Soviet capacity to apply force beyond its borders has improved in recent years, but it is still well behind that of the United States. Contrasted with the 190,000 U.S. Marines, the Soviet Union has only 12,000 naval infantry, a smaller marine force than those of Brazil, South Korea, or Taiwan.

The 55,000 Soviet airborne troops are merely half the number of soldiers assigned by the United States to its own Rapid Deployment Force. The United States has a huge advantage in amphibious vessels. The largest Soviet amphibious ship, the *Ivan Rogov*, at 13,000 tons is barely a third of the size of the five 39,000-ton American Tarawa-class helicopter assault ships. Compared with the thirteen American aircraft carriers, able to launch 800 jet fighters, the Russians do not possess a single carrier for advanced jet aircraft. The one advantage that the Russians have over the United States is in short-haul transport aircraft. These can carry more equipment than U.S. transport planes. But this is more than offset by the longer range and in-flight refueling capacity of American aircraft. Indeed, at the end of 1981 a NATO study conceded that "military scholars report that there are no current indications that the Soviets are developing a rapid deployment force similar to that of the United States since

they do not perceive the present need for such a development. The current
structure of Soviet armed forces is based upon doctrinal requirements to face
NATO forces in Europe and China in the Far East."[11]

Faced with this imbalance it is perhaps not surprising that in 1977 the Soviet
Union was prepared to enter into discussions with the United States on limiting
naval deployments in the Indian Ocean. Throughout the 1970s, India, Sri
Lanka, and the other states in the region pressed hard for "a zone of peace."
Every year since 1971 the United Nations General Assembly had called on the
great powers to agree to such a zone. Although the USSR had some reservations,
Brezhnev had declared himself in favor of negotiated limits as early as June
1971: "We have never thought and do not think now that it is an ideal situation
when the navies of the great powers are sailing for a long time at the other end of
the world, away from their native coasts. We are ready to solve this problem but
to make an equal bargain."[12]

Kissinger was against the project, but under Carter talks with the Soviet
Union began in June 1977. The Americans proposed that each side pledge not to
increase its naval strength in the Indian Ocean, or acquire new bases or expand
existing facilities. This meant that the Soviets would maintain their constant
deployment of eighteen to twenty ships, one-third to a half of them combatants.
The United States would keep its three-ship force stationed at Bahrein (a
command ship and two destroyers) and send three carrier task forces a year for
visits of a month or two at a time. After four sessions of talks, during a period
when the Carter administration was beginning to take a more assertive anti-
Soviet line, they were broken off. Arms control proponents in Washington felt
the weight of advantage was on the American side since the U.S. had superiority
whenever one of its task forces entered the Indian Ocean. Hawks feared that the
Soviet Union's proximity to the area gave it the capacity to dominate the area
without needing ships. It could mass troops on the borders with Iran and Turkey,
and send medium-range bombers into the region from Soviet territory, as well as
two airborne divisions. Division within the administration plus the collapse of
the Shah led Washington to plan for a real American buildup in the region. The
Indian Ocean talks collapsed. With them went the best chance of an agreed
ceiling on U.S. and Soviet naval deployments that has yet occurred.

THE NUCLEAR ARMS RACE

Over the last thirty years the USSR has built up and continues to develop a
formidable nuclear arsenal. Although the United States was the first country to
embark on the nuclear escalator, it is not true to say, as Soviet spokesmen do,
that the Americans took the first step in every subsequent weapons development. Within the last two decades, in particular, Moscow has pioneered a number of weapons that have given Washington grounds to fear that Moscow might

gain the ability to launch a successful first strike. These American fears were not in themselves unreasonable. After all, each superpower's doubts about the other side's capabilities, let alone their intentions, stem from the fact that they have chosen a different mixture of weapons for their arsenals. If the U.S. and Soviet stockpiles consisted of the same types of weapons, it would be easy to calculate which side had more. But since each country's arsenal is different—the U.S. putting more emphasis on submarine-launched missiles, the USSR on heavy land-based rockets, the U.S. pushing ahead in the development of low-flying, radar-avoiding cruise missiles, the USSR pioneering antisatellite technology— the debate about their rival strengths defies easy resolution. Nor is it clear what the primary purpose of each side's weapons is. When the Soviet Union started to develop a high-energy laser-beam weapons program in the mid-1960s with the power to incapacitate American satellites, was this a defensive move to blunt the American potential for attack, or meant to give Moscow the chance to knock out American warning systems in advance of a Soviet attack? The distinction between "defensive" and "offensive" weapons has always been difficult, and nowhere more so than in the field of nuclear strategy which has relied heavily on the concept of "mutual assured destruction." Each side is deterred by the knowledge that the other will always have enough power to retaliate. Attack means suicide. If either side breaks out of this pattern and reaches a position of superiority where attack no longer means suicide, then the danger that it might launch a nuclear war will grow. The current Western debate about whether Moscow has acquired superiority, or could acquire it if Western arms programs are not stepped up, has generated more heat than light. In a sense it is academic. What matters is not superiority as such, but the perception of superiority. If one superpower believes it has superiority, and this belief is shared by the other, then a decisive imbalance has been reached. One side will have "won" the arms race.

This is far from being the case with Moscow, for there is no evidence that the Kremlin thinks it has "won." On the contrary, it still feels, as it has always done, that it is behind the Americans. In 1981 it greeted the Reagan administration's plans for a massive increase in arms spending with anxiety, knowing that the need to match them would impose fresh strains on the Soviet economy.

The relevant questions to be asked about the growth of Soviet nuclear power are not technical but political. They should focus on intentions rather than capabilities. Did the Russians start the nuclear arms race? Did they take any decisive steps in it? If so, why? Are they trying to gain nuclear superiority, or do they prefer parity? Suppose they gained nuclear superiority, what would they be likely to do with it? Do they believe in the concept of "nuclear blackmail"—the notion that possession of nuclear weapons gives a country power to impose its will on nonnuclear nations, or that a clear lead by one of the superpowers in the arms race would give it similar power over the other?

No dispassionate analyst of history can doubt that for four years, until the first Soviet atom bomb test in 1949, the United States had a nuclear monopoly.

American officials made no secret of the fact. They boasted of it openly as proof of their country's global power in the aftermath of the Second World War, and they set about creating a ring of bases in many of the states close to the Soviet Union, from Britain and France to Greece, Turkey, and Japan, as well as in Alaska and the continental United States. Even after Stalin acquired the bomb, the United States was immune to threat for another five years. Not until 1954 did Moscow flight-test aircraft with a sufficient range to reach the heartland of the United States. Soviet strategists were concentrating on other delivery systems. In 1957 Soviet rocketry achieved its first breakthrough. A Sputnik satellite was launched into space and an intercontinental missile tested.

The impact of the sudden demonstration of Soviet advances in long-range rocketry was dramatic and immediate in the United States. It captured people's imagination as a breakthrough in the romantic field of space travel and provided a powerful boost to the image of the Soviet Union as an advanced industrial power. It was also the first step in the developing asymmetry of the arms race, foreshadowing the future problem of measuring each side's arsenals. For Moscow, there was strategic sense in producing rockets rather than bombers. Unlike the United States, the Soviet Union had no allies near its main opponents' territory and therefore no chance of friendly bases. Rockets gave it the swiftest and most efficient method of ending the American monopoly in nuclear delivery systems. In January 1960 the Kremlin concluded a long review of Soviet defense policy with the announcement that the newly formed Strategic Rocket Forces were to be the linchpin of the country's defense.

These Soviet moves soon had a political effect in the United States, where hawkish politicians have often accused their opponents of being "soft on Communism." In the 1960 election campaign Kennedy charged the Republican administration with allowing a "missile gap" to develop in the Soviet Union's favor. After his inauguration in January 1961, Kennedy launched a rapid acceleration of the Polaris nuclear-armed submarine program and a doubling of the production rate of land-based missiles. The new administration also started public discussion of the feasibility of "limited nuclear war" and the advantages of a "counterforce strategy" in which the United States would put more emphasis on being able to destroy Soviet missiles in their launching pads than on hitting Soviet cities.

During Eisenhower's presidency the National Security Council had already analyzed the implications of alternative nuclear war-fighting strategies, but it was the Kennedy administration that in January 1962 changed the U.S. targeting system so as to stress "counterforce." Defense Secretary Robert McNamara announced the shift in June 1962. McNamara has since denied that Kennedy intended it as a step toward a first-strike capability, but he conceded that the U.S. Air Force wanted it to be one. Critics of the new strategy focused on the threat it implied to the Soviet Union's rocket systems, and the fear that the Russians would be bound to have of a sudden American preemptive strike.

Kremlin anxiety was probably a major reason for Khrushchev's decision in the summer and autumn of 1962 to dispatch medium-range ballistic missiles and IL-28 bombers to Cuba capable of carrying nuclear weapons. Two years earlier Khrushchev had talked vaguely of using rockets to defend Cuba, but by the time the decision was taken in 1962 it looked more like a hasty effort to counter the new Kennedy intercontinental missile program than a device to help Castro. Some observers have seen it partially directed against Berlin with the aim of forcing the West to agree to an acceptable settlement in Europe.[13] Kennedy's insistence on an immediate retreat by the Soviet Union, rather than any suggestion of a global deal with Moscow, had profound repercussions in the Kremlin. It prompted Khrushchev's successors to undertake a massive long-term nuclear buildup so as to avoid any future humiliations. Within the United States it served to justify the prevailing American tendencies toward dealing with Moscow from a position of strength.

By the end of the decade, however, the missile buildup backed by Brezhnev and his colleagues had reached the point where the United States had to acknowledge that an American first strike would be excessively costly in American lives. As Kissinger put it in his memoirs: "For most of the postwar period the Soviet Union had been virtually defenseless against an American first strike. Nor could it improve its position significantly by attacking since our counterblow would have posed unacceptable risks."[14] The post-Cuba Soviet missile buildup changed the picture. By the time the Nixon administration entered office in January 1969, "the estimate of casualties in case of a Soviet second strike stood at over fifty million dead from immediate deaths (not to mention later deaths from radiation)." Kissinger concedes: "To pretend that such a prospect would not affect American readiness to resort to nuclear weapons would have been an evasion of responsibility."[15]

Kissinger's evaluation laid the basis for the concept of strategic parity which was to underpin and lead to the two U.S.–Soviet treaties limiting strategic arms (SALT). Parity meant that each side was recognized to have an assured chance of responding to a first strike by the enemy with a devastating counterattack of its own. But parity did not mean equality, in the sense that each side was recognized to have an *equal* chance of responding to a first strike. This was the fatal flaw in the SALT process. As one side continued to develop new weapons and modernize old ones, the other side feared that this might lead to a first-strike capability. In the United States, meanwhile, which had enjoyed nuclear superiority for two decades, it was hard for politicians to accept the ambiguous concept of "parity" and abandon the notion of staying ahead of the Soviet Union.

Parity and equality became hopelessly confused in the public debate. Like Kennedy eight years earlier, Nixon had used the presidential campaign of 1968 to accuse his opponent, Hubert Humphrey, the then vice-president, of creating "a security gap" for the United States. Nixon called for a return to unequivocal nuclear superiority over the Russians. After his victory, Nixon blurred the issue, adopting the term "sufficiency" which "I think is a better term, actually, than either 'superiority' or 'parity.'"[16] This semantic juggling was mainly designed to conceal the tussle within the administration over the terms of a continuing American buildup.

Nixon's charge of a "security gap" was as spurious as Kennedy's alleged "missile gap" in 1960. The Russians had indeed increased their nuclear arsenal since the Cuban crisis at a phenomenal rate. The number of Soviet intercontinental ballistic missiles rose from 190 to nearly 860 between 1964 and 1968, while the number of submarine-launched missiles quadrupled from 29 to over 120. But the Americans were still ahead in 1968.

Even so, the United States went on with a further jump on the nuclear escalator, with the predictable result that the Russians followed suit a few years later. In 1968 the Johnson administration flight-tested the first missiles with multiple independently targeted warheads (MIRVs). This technological development could double or triple the offensive power of the United States by putting several warheads on each missile. Had the incoming Nixon administration stopped the MIRV program, it might have achieved a genuine halt to the arms race. Instead, it pushed on with MIRVs. Although the United States and the Soviet Union subsequently reached three agreements on nuclear weapons (SALT I in 1972, the Vladivostok accords in 1974, and SALT II in 1979), each one was undermined by its failure to deal with new generations of weapons that were still on the drawing boards or in the testing stage.

SALT I ignored MIRVs. While it conceded that the Russians could retain their newly acquired lead over the United States in missile launchers, it assumed the American monopoly of MIRVs gave the United States a substantial lead in nuclear warheads. In 1973 the Soviet Union tested its first MIRVs. This worried Washington, which suddenly saw the Soviet monopoly of very heavy missiles being turned by MIRVs into a potential first-strike arsenal. (The Americans had deliberately chosen to specialize in lighter and more accurate missiles and had no heavy ones in their inventory.) In response they began to develop a powerful new missile, the MX.

The Vladivostok accords for the first time laid down the principle that each side must have an equal number of launchers (missiles, bombers, and submarines) with a subceiling of deployed launchers with MIRVs. But they said nothing about stopping MIRV testing nor the low-flying cruise missile, which the Americans were just beginning to develop and which, with its ability to evade enemy radar, was the next generation of weapon that could give its owners a first-strike potential. Five years later SALT II put some limits on the cruise, though not an absolute ban, but said nothing about the new American MX missile, which was heavier and more powerful than its predecessors. Every superpower agreement thus locked the stable door after the most lethal horse had already bolted, and each time the horse was American.

The Soviet Union bears some responsibility for the nuclear arms race. Its early emphasis on rocketry, its decision to MIRV its heaviest missiles, its research into laser weapons raised the prospect of a first-strike potential. In the early 1960s Khrushchev foolishly boasted of having an antiballistic missile system which could knock out incoming American missiles as accurately as "hitting a fly in outer space."[17] The boast was spurious and was probably designed to conceal Soviet weakness in strategic weapons, but it played into the hands of Pentagon hard-liners who used it to justify their own plans for new weapons. Under Brezhnev the Kremlin did not indulge in trumpeting the specific qualities of its weapons, whether true or false. On the contrary, it made the opposite political mistake of maintaining excessive secrecy about the size of its nuclear arsenal and of inhibiting all public debate about its arms budget.

As a result, Western analysts have long been divided over the amount the Soviet Union spends on arms each year. Some have sought to calculate it by taking the published Soviet figure and adding on estimated research and development expenditures. Others, including the CIA, take the "building-block approach" of estimating the cost of all the components of the assumed Soviet defense effort. However it is calculated, the Soviet defense budget almost certainly consumes a higher proportion of the gross national product than United States defense spending does. Given the smaller size of the Soviet GNP, this is not surprising. After taking into account the difficulty of comparing the ruble costs of estimated Soviet defense with the dollar costs of American defense, it may be that Moscow spends even more than Washington in absolute terms.

Yet the fact remains that whatever the Soviet ruble buys in nuclear arms, it has not put Moscow ahead in offensive power. The 1982 yearbook of the Stockholm Institute for Peace Research (SIPRI) calculated that the U.S. had 9,540 warheads in mid-1982 compared with 8,802 Soviet ones. The annual survey of the military balance for 1982/83 prepared by the International Institute for Strategic Studies calculated the number of Soviet warheads as roughly 7,300 and U.S. warheads as 9,268. Nor is it possible to argue, even under a "worst-case scenario," that the USSR has a serious possibility of launching a successful first strike. To knock out America's land-based missiles, Soviet weapons would have to be fired in perfect sequence and without electronic or computer malfunction. The warheads would have to be released accurately at the correct altitude and velocity, taking into account the highly complex effects of gravitational drag as they reentered the earth's atmosphere. They would have to deal with possible deviations caused by the polar magnetic field which have never been closely tested. Finally, they would have to overcome the grimly named problem of fractricide—the as yet unknown repercussions of an exploding warhead on the trajectory of other incoming warheads. Even if, against all expectations, the Russians hit every U.S. land-based missile before Washington launched them in retaliation, the Americans would still have the other two parts of its so-called triad—its submarine-launched missiles and its strategic bomber force—which together provide 75 percent of its arsenal. On a purely quantitative basis it is the Russians who are theoretically more vulnerable to a first strike since three-quarters of their arsenal is on land. As for their missile-carrying submarines, only 15 percent are on active station in the open ocean, compared with 55 percent of the U.S. submarine fleet. The Soviet strategic bomber force is relatively small and obsolescent by American standards.

In practice, whatever the difference in the two sides' respective deployments, neither is far enough ahead of the other to be able to bank seriously on a successful attack. Brezhnev accepted this parity. At no time under his leadership did the Soviet Union suggest that it wanted to overtake the United States. In his speech at the Twenty-Sixth Party Congress in February 1981, Brezhnev declared, "We have not sought, and do not now seek, military superiority over the other side. That is not our policy."[18] By contrast every American administration since nuclear weapons were invented has tried to maintain the U.S. lead. The Reagan administration adopted a defense policy based on the premise that the United States should be able to win a nuclear war.[19]

In recent years considerable public attention has been focused on intermediate-range nuclear missiles in Europe. These weapons, which were first deployed by the United States to threaten Soviet territory from forward bases and aircraft carriers on the Soviet periphery, had been largely ignored in Western discussions of arms control for almost two decades. Of course they concerned the Soviet Union and added to the Kremlin's sense of being encircled. It had no comparable way of moving nuclear weapons close to the American heartland with the exception of using Cuba, and its brief effort to deploy them there ended in humiliation in 1962. Coupled with the separate French and British missiles, the American "forward-based" systems posed a significant threat to the Soviet Union. To counter them, Moscow deployed land-based missiles in the western parts of its territory that could strike targets in America. The Americans chose not to match Soviet superiority in land-based missiles in Europe, and indeed, during the 1960s, McNamara withdrew U.S. Thor and Jupiter missiles in favor of less vulnerable submarine-launched Polaris missiles.

In spite of the asymmetry in intermediate-range weapons, in which the Americans enjoyed strategic options denied to Moscow, the issue was an item of low priority in East–West discussions. The Russians made occasional undramatic attempts to raise it, but to the surprise and delight of the Ford administration, Brezhnev dropped his reference to American forward-based systems when the two leaders met at Vladivostok in 1974. The issue only came alive in 1977 after the Soviet Union had begun to replace its aging SS–4 and SS–5 missiles with the new SS–20. The SS–20 has three warheads and is more accurate than its predecessors.

Since the early 1970s the United States had been developing a new medium-range, land-based missile, the Pershing II, with a view to its possible deployment in Europe. The SS–20 provided a justification. NATO responded to the SS–20 deployments with a decision in December 1979 to deploy 108 advanced Pershing II missiles in West Germany plus 464 cruise missiles there and in other countries of the alliance, starting in 1983. The decision caused strong protest in Moscow and considerable criticism in Western Europe. No one could doubt that the SS–20 was a powerful and menacing weapon, but "a good case can be made for regarding the SS–20 as modernization," as Raymond Garthoff, a former U.S. ambassador to Bulgaria, has written.[20] It "does not give the Soviet Union any nuclear capability against Europe alone that it did not have in overflowing measure before," wrote McGeorge Bundy, who was national security advisor in the Kennedy and Johnson administrations.[21] Every long-range Soviet strategic missile that can hit the United States can also hit Europe. To the Russians, however, NATO's counterweapon, the Pershing II, added a whole new dimension. Bundy again: "The Pershing II missiles can reach the Soviet Union from West Germany in five minutes, thus producing a new possibility of a super-sudden first strike—even on Moscow itself. This is too fast. We would not like it if a Soviet forward deployment of submarines should create a similar standing threat to Washington."[22]

Soviet spokesmen used this argument strongly against the Pershing II, as well as the ground-launched cruise missile, which, although slow, is seen by them as a strategic threat. Either weapon could conceivably knock out Soviet radar and command-and-control centers in western Russia, leaving the entire Soviet retaliatory arsenal impotent. They also claimed that the new weapons would give the United States the temptation of trying to launch a "limited" nuclear war on the Soviet Union with missiles fired from Europe, in the hope that Moscow would retaliate on Europe alone. The Russians have continually insisted that they do not believe in the concept of "limited" nuclear war themselves. The defense minister, Marshal Ustinov, wrote in July 1981: "Could anyone in his right mind speak seriously of any limited nuclear war? It should be quite clear that the aggressor's actions will instantly and inevitably trigger a devastating counterstrike by the other side. None but completely irresponsible people could maintain that a nuclear war may be made to follow rules adopted beforehand with nuclear missiles exploding in 'gentlemanly manner' over strictly designated targets and sparing the population."[23]

Soviet insistence that, in the words of Marshal Ustinov, "there is no guarantee that such a war will not grow into a universal nuclear conflagration" was consistent with long-term Soviet security goals.[24] Moscow cannot allow the United States to believe it has a chance of an easy preemptive strike against the Soviet Union. Nor can it permit the United States and NATO to think it could intervene in the case of trouble within Moscow's Eastern European domain. To warn that any Western attempt to play with fire in Europe would lead to a worldwide holocaust makes political sense for the Kremlin.

Moscow's rejection of the concept of "limited" nuclear war was in line with

Soviet party thinking throughout the Brezhnev era. Under Khrushchev, in the early years of the nuclear age, Soviet military thought on the feasibility of victory in a nuclear war was in a state of flux. Some senior army officers, concentrating on the study of possible scenarios for war and the methods of waging it, concluded that nuclear weapons increased the advantages to be gained from surprise attack. Marshal Pavel Rotmistrov wrote in 1955 that "the duty of the Soviet armed forces is not to permit an enemy surprise attack on our country, and, in the event of an attempt to accomplish one, not only to repel the attack successfully but also to deal the enemy counterblows or even pre-emptive surprise blows, of terrible destructive force."[25]

As a politician rather than a professional military strategist, Khrushchev took a more detached line. He believed that the capitalists could be prevented from unleashing a war through the threat of massive retaliation. It was unnecessary for the Soviet Union to consider how to fight and win a nuclear war. He was bitterly criticized by Mao for taking what the Chinese called a defeatist position.

Meanwhile, debate continued among Soviet military planners. A former chief of the General Staff, Marshal Vasily Sokolovsky, argued in 1962 in a book called *Military Strategy* that because the capitalists might unleash a nuclear war, the Soviet Union had to prepare and provide for war because "victory in a future war will not come by itself."[26] This difference of emphasis between the political doctrine that nuclear war is futile and the military view that victory must be prepared for remained valid in the Brezhnev era. Soviet policy was as contradictory as Western policy in trying to justify the value of what were admitted to be suicidal weapons.

David Holloway, one of the foremost Western experts on Soviet nuclear thinking, has pointed out that "it has been difficult for the party to accept that nuclear war could permanently reverse the course of history and lead to the defeat of socialism. The military stress on preparing to fight and win a nuclear war has been reinforced by the ideological belief that, if nuclear war did take place, it would be the decisive contest between socialism and capitalism and that socialism would emerge victorious."[27] In an article in the *Soviet Military Encyclopedia* in 1979, Chief of the General Staff Marshal Nikolai Ogarkov wrote that "Soviet military strategy proceeds from the fact that if nuclear war is forced on the Soviet Union, then the Soviet people and its armed forces need to be ready for most severe and prolonged trials. The Soviet Union and the fraternal socialist states in that case will, by comparison with the imperialist states, possess definite advantages, conditioned by the just goals of the war, and the progressive character of their social and state order. This creates for them objective possibilities for attaining victory. However, for the realization of these possibilities timely and all-round preparation of the country and the armed forces is necessary."[28] But Holloway argues that the chief aim of Soviet military preparations has been to prevent a nuclear war, and that since the late 1960s strategic thinking has placed less emphasis on the idea of preemption. Brezhnev formally pledged in a message to the United Nations in 1982 that the Soviet Union would never use nuclear weapons first.

Christopher Jones, of the Harvard Russian Research Center, has pointed out that in the Soviet literature on the conduct of offensive nuclear actions by their ground forces, Soviet specialists "never discussed how to decouple a European nuclear war from a general one. In fact the Soviets have argued since the early 1960s that such decoupling is impossible."[29] Yet if the Soviet Union were ever to think of "winning" a war in Europe, it would have to manage a successful attack against NATO without provoking an all-out and general nuclear war.

Soviet actions have matched their words. They have based their intermediate-range missiles in a way that makes it more likely that a nuclear war in Europe would become a total U.S.–Soviet exchange. This is the reverse of the planned American deployments of Pershing II and cruise. All the Soviet SS–4s, SS–5s, and SS–20 s are based in the USSR, as well as at least half their FROG and SCUD tactical nuclear weapons, which have too short a range to reach NATO territory without being moved forward several hundred miles. The Soviet Union has provided its East European allies with some FROG and SCUD, but the nuclear warheads are retained by the USSR. Had Moscow been planning to try to limit a nuclear war to the Eastern European area of the Warsaw Pact and Western Europe, thus sparing Soviet soil, it would have based its nuclear forces differently. Most would have been placed in Eastern Europe itself.

Earlier in this chapter I argued that the key question in any discussion of Soviet nuclear policy concerned Moscow's intentions rather than its capabilities. Does the Kremlin believe in "nuclear blackmail"? Examination of the record suggests that it does not. In the study mentioned earlier of the way Moscow has used force to obtain political goals, Stephen Kaplan concluded that on many occasions, particularly under Khrushchev, Soviet leaders verbally raised the prospect of using nuclear weapons.[30] But in only one instance was data found confirming that Moscow had actually raised the alert status of nuclear forces. This incident was the Cuban missile crisis. Under Brezhnev there was no case. Kaplan concedes that it is impossible to be sure whether such alerts occurred, but he remarks that the Kremlin did not draw attention to them, as it might have been expected to do in the case of "blackmail," unlike American leaders who have several times publicly used the alerting and deployment of nuclear forces to make a political point in a crisis. He also points out that the normal levels of alert of Soviet strategic forces are lower than those of U.S. strategic forces. One case where Moscow may have thought of using nuclear pressure was the crisis over the Sino–Soviet border clashes in March 1969. Moscow raised the issue verbally in a veiled manner, but there is no proof that it ever went onto the alert. There is no case of Moscow using nuclear pressure on a nonnuclear state. The idea that the Soviet Union is some kind of nuclear bully, ready and eager to brandish its nuclear weapons and trample on Western nations, is a figment of Cold War propaganda. The historical record appears to confirm the repeatedly propounded Soviet view that Moscow's nuclear might is a reserve force, part and parcel of the "correlation of forces" that ensures the defense of socialism in a dangerous world. It is the weightiest component in the overall Soviet arsenal, but also the most dangerous and least usable part.

4

THE UNITED STATES: THE RISE AND FALL OF DÉTENTE

The Soviet view of the United States is inherently ambiguous. The United States is the object of envy and scorn; the enemy to fight, expose and pillory—and the model to emulate, catch up with, and overtake.

Alexander Dallin[1]

The treaty was signed, the documents exchanged, and then to the surprise of watching reporters Jimmy Carter walked forward and kissed Leonid Brezhnev on each of his puffy cheeks. It was a sudden unscripted impulse, the symbolic climax in Vienna's Hofburg in June 1979 of the long-drawn-out negotiations for a second U.S.–Soviet treaty limiting strategic arms (SALT II). In a sense it was also the culmination of a process of regular negotiations between Washington and Moscow which had already seen Brezhnev face to face with American presidents no less than five times in the space of little more than three years between May 1972 and July 1975. But the kiss in Vienna was tainted, as the four-year gap since the previous U.S.–Soviet summit might have suggested, and as the U.S. Senate's failure to ratify SALT II was soon to prove.

Looking back on that period in the early 1970s when Brezhnev greeted

Richard Nixon twice in Moscow, visited him in Washington once, and met Gerald Ford at Vladivostok and Helsinki, the observer finds it hard to believe that détente between the superpowers should have turned out to be so tender a plant. At that time the notion of a regular dialogue between the United States and the Soviet Union appeared natural and well-rooted. Summit meetings between the two leaders had become routine, and the process of negotiations seemed to have lasted long enough to have built up on both sides a powerful constituency in its favor.

Over that period the Western world was treated to a rare view inside the Kremlin, and found a Soviet leader who was unexpectedly emotional, ebullient, and fun-loving. The gray curtain that had fallen after Khrushchev's overthrow was lifted again, and Brezhnev was seen on stage, another character of apparent energy and enthusiasm but with more dignity and sophistication than Khrushchev. The West's discovery of Brezhnev did not produce the same excitement as the opening to China. Russia had never been so closed to the outside world. But Brezhnev and his colleagues suddenly seemed human. The Soviet leader invited journalists into his office and showed them his special locked cigarette case which would only open at preset times to prevent him from chain-smoking. Then he would put his hand in his pocket in triumph to show the second packet he could use when the case was locked.

Stories of his antics with foreign visitors leaked to the press. Kissinger revealed that Brezhnev's concentration was poor. He would hop up and down. His hands would fidget. Once he brought a toy cannon to a negotiating session, and spent more time trying to make it work than listening to the discussion. When the contraption finally went off with a roar, he strutted round the room like a victorious boxer. On his trip to the United States in 1973, Brezhnev cheerfully put on a cowboy belt with toy gun and holster as Nixon's plane flew him to California. As they crossed the Grand Canyon, Brezhnev said his favorite film star was John Wayne and imitated a fast draw. Introduced to several Hollywood actors at a cocktail party around Nixon's swimming pool at San Clemente, he showed a familiarity with old movies that, Nixon commented, "indicated either that he had been very well briefed or that he had been spending time in the private screening rooms in the Kremlin."[2]

Brezhnev was fascinated by powerful cars. From his various foreign hosts he had acquired a Rolls-Royce Silver Cloud, a Citroen-Maserati, a Mercedes, a Cadillac, and a Lincoln Continental. On one occasion he took Nixon for a ride at Camp David and hurtled down a series of hairpin bends at fifty miles an hour with tires squealing. "This is a very fine automobile. It holds the road very well," he told a shaken Nixon as they got out.[3]

Between his bursts of excitement and good humor Brezhnev seemed over-awed and surprised by the new warmth of American feeling toward the Soviet Union. At a state dinner in his honor at the White House in 1973, he greeted a broad cross-section of American politicians and businessmen in the receiving line. "Do they all support the new Soviet–American initiatives?" he asked Nixon incredulously several times. "Not only in this room but across the country," Nixon said in his toast, "regardless of whatever the organization may be, the overwhelming number of Americans support the objective of Soviet–American friendship."[4]

Brezhnev's doubts were soundly based. Within three years détente was to begin to decline, the blame for it largely on the American side. The United States found the psychological and political burden of giving up nuclear superiority and accepting parity too hard to bear. Americans misunderstood the radical changes in the Third World such as those in Angola, Ethiopia, Iran, and Nicaragua between 1975 and 1979, and the Soviet Union's minimal role in them. They also assumed, in line with old and mistaken Cold War thinking, that détente could be used to liberalize the internal Soviet system, and were unreasonably disappointed when it did not. The Russians, and Brezhnev in particular, were disappointed and tried to prevent the end of the thaw, even though, in the period up to 1974, as Kissinger was to remark, "the years of détente had been kinder to us than our adversaries."[5] The trouble was that the competitive instincts that remained dormant in the U.S.–Soviet relationship during détente eventually revived and became too strong. Détente had already come under attack from American critics, while Nixon was still in office. Gradually, during the latter half of Carter's term, those who argued that the United States should be more assertive vis-à-vis the Soviet Union and less eager to trade with it gained the upper hand in Washington, until with Reagan's election in 1980 their victory became complete.

Fragile though it turned out to be, détente will go down as one of Brezhnev's most impressive successes. Although the list of potential benefits was not seen clearly when the process started, détente produced the following outcomes for the Soviet Union:

1. Acceptance by the United States of Soviet strategic parity

2. The chance to limit the arms race, and thus reallocate investment to the civilian economy

3. An end to the East–West crisis in Europe and a shift of competition to the Third World

4. Easing of tensions on the Soviet Union's western flank, and the chance to concentrate on China

5. Recognition of Eastern Europe's postwar frontiers

6. The opportunity to increase imports of goods, technology, and capital from the West

Détente in the sense of a relaxation of tensions between East and West was not a new phenomenon in the Brezhnev era. Stalin's death in March 1953 and his successors' hopes for reducing the tensions of the Cold War led to East–West agreement on the neutrality of Austria, the exchange of ambassadors between Bonn and Moscow, and the Geneva conference of July 1955 when Khrushchev and Bulganin, the Soviet prime minister, met the British and French prime ministers and President Eisenhower. The conference produced little, and with the Anglo–French–Israeli intervention at Suez and the Soviet suppression of the Hungarian uprising the following year, East–West tension revived. In 1957 the Soviet Union's acquisition of intercontinental rocketry made the need for some U.S.–Soviet understanding seem more urgent. Once again it turned out to be hard to achieve. A tour of the United States by Khrushchev in 1959 led to false hopes of better relations which broke down with the U–2 spy plane incident in 1960. It was not until after the Cuban missile crisis of October 1962 that another brief period of détente began, marked by the establishment of a direct telex line between the Kremlin and the White House, the so-called hot line, and the Partial Test Ban Treaty in 1963.

This second thaw was disrupted by Kennedy's assassination and the subsequent pause in American foreign policy activity, and then by Johnson's escalation of military involvement in Vietnam. The Soviet Union was increasingly preoccupied with its deteriorating relations with China. Khrushchev's successors made a brief effort at the beginning of 1965 to compose their differences with China, at least over Vietnam, so that these would not obstruct their policy toward the United States, but the conflicting impulses in Washington, Hanoi, Peking, and Moscow could not be reconciled.

The two attempts at détente under Khrushchev failed also because neither side was consistent in its attitudes. Khrushchev vacillated from the bombastically antagonistic to the effusively friendly, while his provocative actions over Berlin and Cuba seemed to belie his overtures for better East–West relations. At home his eccentric and increasingly personal style of leadership did not command a solid consensus among his Kremlin colleagues. The United States explored the possibility of dialogue with Moscow, but was not ready to concede that détente between the two sides should be based on nuclear equality.

In the mid-1960s there was little chance of détente. The Americans were deeply involved in Vietnam and the Soviet Union was determined to build its nuclear arsenal to equal that of the United States. The only U.S.–Soviet summit in that period was a brief attempt to coordinate policy on the Middle East after the Six-Day War, rather than the authentic beginning of a new détente. Toward the end of Johnson's term tentative American overtures for strategic-arms-control talks in order to restrain the Soviet nuclear buildup were not taken up seriously in the Kremlin. Khrushchev's successors were still jockeying over the distribution of power. It was too early for them to agree on a ceiling to their nuclear arms program and a major new reorientation of foreign policy, although there was a consensus that Soviet diplomatic activity and public posturing must be more restrained than under Khrushchev. While the ousted leader was criticized in a *Pravda* editorial soon after his removal for "actions based on wishful thinking, boasting, and empty words" and for "voluntarism and subjectivism," the new Soviet leaders talked of "realism" and the complexity of the environment.[6] Whereas Khrushchev had often made precise predictions of when the Soviet Union would overtake the United States economically, they moved away from comparisons with the West. In the meantime, mindful of the lessons of the Cuban crisis and always conscious of the American submarine-launched missile program, they steadily built up the Soviet Union's military strength.

The crucial year was 1969. Several factors came together to prompt a change of strategy. A new administration in the United States appeared ready to accept the implications of Soviet nuclear might for Washington's previous military superiority. In Moscow, Brezhnev was receptive to the idea that the superpowers should engage in serious arms limitation. In Europe, the tentative negotiations for a treaty between West Germany and the Soviet Union renouncing the use of force speeded up in September with the election as chancellor of Willy Brandt, a man the Russians felt they could trust. Armed clashes between Soviet and Chinese troops in March prompted the Kremlin to think that an improvement of relations with the West could help it to deal more easily with Peking. Finally, there was the economic factor. Soviet leaders were becoming increasingly aware that growth rates would soon decline, as the country's labor surplus dried up and it ran out of easily exploitable reserves of raw materials. Continuing difficulties in agriculture were sharpened by a particularly severe winter in 1969 which caused serious shortages of meat. One solution was to abandon the Soviet Union's previous attempts at self-sufficiency and to look to the West for imports, not only of technology and capital, but also food.

By 1969 Brezhnev had moved a long way toward establishing himself as the preeminent leader in the Kremlin. As general secretary of the party, Brezhnev had differed with Alexei Kosygin, the chairman of the Council of Ministers, on several issues between 1966 and 1969. Evidence from their speeches during that period showed Brezhnev to be against economic decentralization, which Kosygin supported, and in favor of investment in agriculture. Kosygin preferred to put money into light industry and consumer goods. In March 1968 Brezhnev also indirectly criticized Kosygin's advocacy of importing foreign technology—a policy he was later to adopt himself.[7]

Brezhnev tried to take the final step toward preeminence at a Central Committee meeting in December 1969, when he strongly criticized Kosygin's economic reform and called for strengthening the party's role in enterprise management. His onslaught was not immediately successful, and over the next six months there were muffled signs of a power struggle, which no analyst of the confusing signals in the Soviet media had been able to illuminate satisfactorily.

The crisis ended in July with a compromise. Kosygin, who earlier had been rumored to be near resignation, was reconfirmed as prime minister, while the party congress, which Brezhnev wanted to hold early, was delayed until March 1971. But Brezhnev was the overall winner. From then on Kosygin's authority was second to that of Brezhnev, who soon took over some of Kosygin's own policies. To the outside world the signs of Brezhnev's preeminence became apparent when he held a four-hour private meeting with Willy Brandt in August 1970 shortly after the West German chancellor had joined Kosygin in signing the treaty renouncing the use of force. It was his first excursion into foreign affairs as party secretary. Brandt described Brezhnev and Kosygin as the number " '1-a' and '1-b' men in the Kremlin."[8]

He found Brezhnev at that time still somewhat uncertain, and heavily reliant on written notes. A year later when he was Brezhnev's guest for informal talks in the Crimea in September 1971, the general secretary's authority and self-confidence were clear. The official establishment of Brezhnev's leading role occurred at the Twenty-Fourth Party Congress in March 1971 when he launched a six-point "Peace Program." It called for a political settlement in Southeast Asia and the Middle East, the convening of a security conference in Europe, nuclear arms control, cuts in spending on conventional weapons, complete decolonization in the Third World, and the "deepening of relations of mutually advantageous cooperation in every sphere with states which seek to do so."[9]

In terms of détente, points two and six were the significant ones. Point two talked specifically of "proceeding from the final recognition of the territorial changes that took place in Europe as a result of the Second World War so as to bring about a radical turn towards détente and peace on this continent." Point six was developed in other sections of Brezhnev's speech, which produced a noticeable link between foreign trade and domestic Soviet development that had hardly been made at all at the previous congress five years earlier.

Brezhnev's strategy of moving toward arms control with the United States and reducing the Soviet Union's economic self-reliance was not reached without some hesitation and criticism at the top, as he hinted in the very next sentence after announcing the "peace program." He seemed to be trying to convince doubters who were wary of change when he said, "We declare that while consistently pursuing its policy of peace and friendship among nations, the Soviet Union will continue to conduct a resolute struggle against imperialism, and firmly rebuff the evil designs and subversions of aggressors. As in the past we shall give undeviating support to the people's struggle for democracy, national liberation, and socialism."[10]

The closed nature of debate within the Kremlin and the way in which Soviet participants adopt a mask of public obfuscation, punctuated by occasional code words, makes it impossible for outside observers to reconstruct all the arguments. Even the identity of supporters of different points of view is often unknown. Did the arguments between Brezhnev and Kosygin over domestic policy also stretch to foreign affairs? How much was the inner-party crisis of the first half of 1970 linked to détente?

Some Western analysts have talked of a split between "hawks and doves," "Left and Right," "orthodox and revisionists," or "traditionalists and realists." The Left is said to be "aggressive, militaristic, suspicious of the United States, hostile to détente," while the Right is "sober, moderate, concerned less about the danger of war with the United States than the benefits of mutual collaboration in specific areas."[11]

Other analysts identify six distinct "demand sectors" within the USSR's military-industrial complex. There is (a) the "ideological demand sector (the ideologues and conservatives of the party apparatus)," (b) the "security demand sector (police, armed forces and defense industries)," and (c) the "producer demand sector (heavy industry, construction and transport)." These three bureaucratic groups are said to form a coalition which competes for resources in the Soviet budget against three other groups: (d) the "consumer demand sector (light industry, consumer goods for industry, trade and housing)," (e) the "agricultural demand sector" and (f) "the public services and welfare sector."[12]

Marshall Shulman, who served as the secretary of state's advisor on Soviet affairs in the Carter administration, sees a dispute between champions of economic modernization who support peaceful coexistence, and "military interests and the orthodox party apparatus whose vested interest in an 'imperialist' enemy is combined with a fear of the effect of modernization on the system."[13] For them, détente holds the danger of a weakening of the ideological élan which is their stock in trade, an opening of the country to subversive influences, increased trouble with intellectuals and nationalist minorities, and an erosion of the image of the imperialist threat which legitimizes their power. They also fear that abandonment of self-sufficiency may lead to fatal dependence on the West, that détente will weaken Soviet political control at home and in Eastern Europe, and that foreign trade will not be very productive.

Although all these analyses throw useful light on potential differences of view within the Soviet elite, they come no nearer to naming definite protagonists of different standpoints in the Central Committee and the Politburo. Nor do they stress sufficiently that Brezhnev's policy was a synthesis of the respective arguments. While pressing for arms control agreements, he continued to increase defense spending. Although opening the country to trade, he clamped down on dissidents in a broadly successful effort to limit the internal political effects among individuals of the system's increased contact with the West. While increasing Soviet imports he took care to see that Soviet exports of oil and natural gas also went up, so that self-sufficiency was not replaced by Soviet dependence but by mutual interdependence between East and West.

The remarkable feature was the way Brezhnev and the majority of his colleagues stuck to the strategy of détente in the late 1970s in spite of its declining support in Washington. The only visible Soviet opposition came in the early days, when a Politburo member, Pyotr Shelest, lost his post as the party leader in the Ukraine a few days before Nixon's first visit to Moscow because he opposed it. After that the Politburo preserved a united front, symbolized by the promotion into its ranks in April 1973 of the minister of defense, Marshal Grechko, the then head of the KGB, Yuri Andropov, and the minister of foreign affairs, Andrei Gromyko.

The plenary meeting of the Central Committee at which the promotions were made was devoted to "strengthening foreign economic ties." Later that year Brezhnev visited West Germany and the United States and acted as host to the Japanese prime minister, Kakuei Tanaka, in Moscow. Linking political détente to "economic détente," his message to all of them was similar. The international division of labor should be broadened by "large-scale, and long-term economic ties."[14] He held out to Western businessmen and governments the prospect of massive investments in Siberia and the Soviet Far East, which would be paid back by the delivery of Soviet oil, coal, and natural gas.

For a time Brezhnev behaved like a commercial salesman. He regularly entertained Western tycoons with conversations in the Kremlin that warmly extolled the advantages of business with the Soviet Union. Observers began to refer jokingly to the "Soviet Union, Inc." with Brezhnev portrayed as a jovial chairman of the board. The Kremlin approved the purchase of a license to set up a Pepsi-Cola bottling plant near the Black Sea, and in exchange gave the company's chairman, Donald Kendall, a friend of Nixon's, the franchise to import Soviet vodka into the United States at special rates. "Vodka-cola" became a shorthand label for the new type of East–West barter arrangements.

The Politburo's commitment to increased economic ties with the West easily survived the first storms that blew up over détente in 1972. A coalition of U.S. congressmen led by Senator Henry Jackson and Representative Charles Vanik started to put pressure on Moscow to speed the pace of Jewish emigration, and in particular to abolish an exit tax that emigrants had to pay. The issue was sensitive in the Kremlin, which had traditionally blocked emigration and considered all would-be leavers to be ungrateful and disloyal to the Soviet system. Because most Jewish émigrés settled in Israel, the Kremlin was also coming under growing Arab criticism for strengthening the Zionist state. Yet in spite of these feelings, the Politburo gave in to American pressure and abolished the tax in March 1973. Success only whetted the appetites of the congressional campaigners, and throughout 1973 and 1974 they continued to demand written pledges from the Kremlin that Jewish emigration would increase. This was too much for Moscow. It was seen as an infringement of sovereignty and a blatant attempt to impose internal changes on the Soviet system. Although Jackson and his supporters subsequently forced new amendments to the U.S.–Soviet trade agreement, which the Politburo repudiated, Moscow continued to press the West for business and investment. Now the Kremlin put more stress on French, West German, and Japanese business, but the basic strategy of committing itself to economic détente remained. At the Twenty-Fifth Party Congress in 1976 Brezhnev openly praised the benefits of international business for the Soviet economy: "Like other states we strive to use the advantage that foreign economic ties offer with a view to mobilizing additional possibilities for the successful accomplishment of economic tasks, and for gains in time."[15] When the Carter administration imposed trade sanctions on the Soviet Union after the invasion of Afghanistan three years later, and Reagan extended them in a bid to prevent the sales of Soviet natural gas to Western Europe, Moscow tried hard to continue economic cooperation with its Western European partners.

On the political side, the Kremlin showed similar tenacity. It insisted on the ratification of the SALT II treaty even when the U.S. Senate showed reluctance to go along with it. When the Reagan administration came into office on a hard-line anti-Soviet platform, the Kremlin called for a dialogue. In spite of his good relations with France and West Germany, symbolized by summit meetings with their leaders in 1980, Brezhnev virtually ignored them in his speech to the Twenty-Sixth Party Congress in February 1981. Instead, he preferred to address the new American president, reasserting the primacy of U.S.–Soviet détente. "It is universally recognized that in many ways the international situation depends on the policy of both the USSR and the USA. . . . The USSR wants normal relations with the USA. There is simply no other sensible way from the point of view of the interests of our two nations and of humanity as a whole."[16]

The Politburo's constantly repeated adherence to détente over a period of ten years showed how valuable Moscow thought détente was. The single most important benefit was Washington's recognition that the Soviet Union had become its military equal. Vikenty Matveyev, one of the Soviet Union's most experienced political commentators, put it simply: "When we achieved parity, it was one of the greatest achievements of the whole postwar period. We cherish it dearly."[17] Georgi Arbatov saw American acceptance of détente as recognition of the futility of attempting to seek unilateral advantage over the Soviet Union. Washington had accepted the "principle of equal security" and a restructuring of international relations on the basis of peaceful coexistence.[18] When Nixon met Brezhnev in Moscow in May 1972, the Soviet leader referred warmly to Franklin Roosevelt as the first American president to extend diplomatic recognition to the Soviet Union.[19] To the Russians détente meant a renewal of that recognition. This was far more important than the economic benefits, which, as we have seen, only began to be stressed later. The first article of the document on the "Basic Principles of Relations between the USA and the USSR," which Nixon and Brezhnev signed in 1972, summed up the benefits as Moscow saw them: "The USA and the USSR will proceed from the common determination that in the nuclear age there is no alternative to conducting our mutual relations on the basis of peaceful co-existence. Differences in ideology and in the social systems of the USA and the USSR are not obstacles to the bilateral development of normal relations based on the principles of sovereignty, equality, non-interference in internal affairs, and mutual advantage."

Brezhnev told Nixon that he considered this statement even more important than the proposed SALT agreement.[20] The Americans found this hard to appreciate, as Kissinger's rather dismissive references reveal. "The Soviets are much addicted to declarations of principle. Probably they see in them an acknowledgement of equality and a device to create the impression that major progress is being made in bilateral relations. Perhaps there is something in Russian history that leads them to value ritual, solemn declarations, and visible symbols."[21] To Brezhnev and his colleagues, the "Basic Principles" promised an end to the tactics that the Soviet Union had endured from the West for fifty years—boycotts, pressure, isolation, and contempt.

Failure to understand détente's symbolic and psychological value for Moscow underlay much of the Western questioning of Soviet intentions. Was it a device to lull the West into a false sense of security? Did Moscow want quick gains in the name of détente which it would reject when the time was ripe? In one sense, of course, both sides saw détente as a form of long-term pressure on the other superpower, a way of changing traditional habits of confrontation into a new pattern of cooperation. At a press conference in Moscow at the end of Nixon's second visit to the Soviet Union in July 1974, Kissinger said that one of the purposes of summit meetings was "to see whether they can . . . construct a network of positive relationships that will prove an incentive for moderation and for a beneficial and humane conduct of foreign policy."[22] This sentiment was matched by repeated Soviet pleas that détente should be made irreversible. There was nothing sinister in that.

Where there is evidence of a wish to manipulate détente for short-term gains at the expense of the other superpower, it is largely on the American side. "To some extent my interest in détente was tactical, as a device to maximize Soviet dilemmas and reduce Soviet influence in the Middle East," wrote Kissinger in his memoirs. "In part it was domestic, to out-maneuver the 'peace' pressures so we could rally our public if a showdown proved unavoidable."[23] He also admitted that he hoped to use détente to split Moscow from Hanoi. During the October War in the Middle East, the White House considered whether to "induce Soviet caution by threatening the end of détente."[24]

The Russians were more committed to détente. In his analyses of Soviet actions during the October War in the Middle East, Kissinger wrote: "What seems to have occurred is that the Soviets sought to combine the advantage of every course of action: détente with us, enough support for their Arab friends to establish their indispensability if things went well, but not so much as to tempt a confrontation with the United States."[25] Other evidence suggests that the Americans were the more adventurous of the two superpowers in the early 1970s. They enlarged their military operations in Vietnam on the eve of Nixon's visit to Moscow in 1972. They supported the destabilization of the Allende government in Chile in 1973. They sought to oust the Russians from Egypt. They were more prepared for military confrontation with the Soviet Union. Kissinger described his efforts to forestall any possible Soviet intervention in the Jordan crisis of 1970 in stark terms. Recommending that the U.S. 82nd Airborne Division be put on full alert he wrote: "In my view what seems 'balanced' and 'safe' in a crisis is often the most risky. Gradual escalation tempts the opponent to match every move. . . . A leader must choose carefully and thoughtfully the issues over which to face confrontation. He should do so only for major objectives. Once he is committed, however, his obligation is to end the confrontation rapidly. For this he must convey implacability. He must be prepared to escalate rapidly and brutally to a point where the opponent can no longer afford to experiment."[26]

Brezhnev hoped that stability would avoid this "brutal" American readiness to take risks. For fifty years the debate within the Western establishments between advocates of accommodation and confrontation with the Soviet Union had swayed to and fro, although the "confrontationists" had the upper hand most of the time. The advent of nuclear weapons made the issues more urgent, and Brezhnev with his firm commitment to détente tried to resolve the debate on the American side once and for all in favor of the "accommodationists." At the beginning of the détente period, radicals in the Soviet camp as well as revolutionaries in the Third World, such as Castro and Qadaffi, accused Brezhnev of seeking stability at too high a cost. He was charged with sacrificing the chances of national liberation movements and failing to promote the struggle against imperialism because of excessive willingness to maintain relations with the United States.

Brezhnev's instinct was to stand firm. To him the alternative to stability was not the guaranteed advance of the socialist cause if only the Kremlin gave a little push. It was much more likely to be a switch toward a more assertive policy of American intervention abroad, as indeed happened after 1978 with the development of a Rapid Deployment Force, increased military assistance to Central America, and sanctions against the Soviet Union. As for revolution in the United States, Brezhnev had no expectation that this would happen soon. Again, it was more likely that the United States would swing to the right. Richard Barnet has pointed out that "if the Soviet elite has been quite content to wait a long time for a political conversion in the United States, the American elite has been less patient about changes in Russia."[27] Arbatov says he is convinced that the "historical superiority of socialism will lead to its inevitable long-term victory," but he modestly makes it clear that this is an article of Communist faith that is equally matched by devotees of the opposite view: "We Communists believe this. Otherwise we wouldn't be Communists. Just as, I presume, the champions of capitalism or the free market system are convinced of the superiority of their system and its eventual victory everywhere."[28] Coming closer to the more immediate issues, Arbatov echoes Brezhnev's particular caution: "The more farsighted men on our side are worried about the sharpening of some of America's problems—not because they find the present American system good, but . . . people can be led astray. They may listen to false prophets. This is exactly what happened in the 1920s in Italy and the 1930s in Germany."[29]

When détente eventually broke down (Ford instructed his staff not even to use the word during the 1976 presidential election campaign), the pressure against it came from forces in the United States. Three factors ultimately caused its death. One was the imbalance in its ideological costs, which were greater on the American side. In the Soviet Union the danger of "contamination" by Western ideas as a result of the slight opening of Soviet society which détente might entail was contained without serious internal upheaval by tightening the pressure on certain Soviet dissidents and pressing others into exile abroad. While the Soviet media had to modify their propaganda about the implacable hostility of the West, whose leaders were now seen as being "realistic," this was projected as a victory for the Soviet "peace policy."

Most Soviet citizens welcomed détente wholeheartedly. As for the notion that the Soviet Union had reached parity with the United States, this fitted the concept of historical progress that every Russian had learned and most wanted to believe.

Americans, by contrast, found it a threatening notion. Taught that their country was the world's most powerful nation and "the last, best hope" of mankind they found it hard to accept that their major ideological enemy had become their military equal and seemed immune to the liberalizing tendencies that détente was expected to bring. Coupled with defeat in Vietnam was American impotence in the face of the seizure of its diplomats as hostages in Iran. The mood of self-doubt was skillfully manipulated by right-wing American politicians in the second half of the 1970s. Instead of adjusting to a historical decline in the United States' relative power, they encouraged voters to think that "we have been pushed around by other countries for too long."

America's emotional reaction to its loss of global superiority was compounded by the second and third major factors that wounded détente—ambiguity over the area that it was meant to cover, and unrealistic expectations of its scope. Was détente meant to include the Third World? Nixon and Kissinger hoped that it would. From the outset of the administration they devised a strategy that was soon dubbed "linkage," by which agreement on strategic arms control was to be tied to Soviet "restraint" around the world. In a letter written to senior cabinet members in February 1969, Nixon said that "on the crucial issues of the day . . . I believe that the Soviet leaders should be brought to understand that they cannot reap the benefit of cooperation in one area while seeking to take advantage of tension or confrontation elsewhere."[30] This meant, Nixon went on, that the United States should keep open the option that there would be no arms control talks with the Soviet Union. Later, Kissinger talked of creating a balance of incentives and penalties, including trade agreements and grain sales, by which Moscow could be rewarded or punished for good or bad behavior. While he rejected Senator Jackson's efforts to control domestic Soviet policy by means of U.S. leverage, Kissinger hoped that Soviet foreign policy could be influenced. To support this argument Washington could point to the fact that Moscow had shown restraint in the past. Washington's bargaining position also seemed strong, since Moscow was eager to develop its trade with the United States and have its nuclear parity formally recognized. At times, too, the Americans thought they detected a Soviet desire for some kind of U.S.–Soviet condominium or system of joint consultations around the world.

Soviet ambivalence about parity played a role in confusing the issue. When Gromyko boasted at the Twenty-Fourth Party Congress in 1971, "Today there is no question of any significance which can be decided without the Soviet Union or in opposition to her,"[31] it may have sounded like a call for a formal share in world power. During the opening meeting of the second U.S.–Soviet summit, Nixon claims that Brezhnev told him: "We know that as far as power and influence are concerned, the only two nations in the world that really matter are the Soviet Union and the United States. Whatever we decide between us, other nations will have to follow our lead even though they may disagree."[32]

From the context it is clear that the Soviet leader was talking about policy toward China. Indeed the only areas on which there is any evidence of a Soviet wish for a condominium are China and the Middle East. In the one case they wanted to break up Washington's new triangular diplomacy by pressing the United States to work with them against China. In the other they sensed their influence was on the decline. To appeal for joint consultations with Washington on the Middle East was not so much a way of extending Soviet influence as preventing its further erosion.

Nuclear weapons were a special case. In June 1973 the Russians successfully pressed Washington to agree to a statement on the worldwide prevention of nuclear war. The agreement said that the United States and the Soviet Union would act "in such a manner as to exclude the outbreak of nuclear war between them and between either of the Parties and other countries." It also said that if relations between third parties appeared to involve the risk of nuclear war, the Soviet Union and the United States should immediately start urgent consultations. The treaty's message was that the two countries would act as policemen to prevent other nuclear nations from launching nuclear war.

This was a far cry from a global condominium. Indeed, it was the opposite, a device to make the world safe for the inevitable continuation of political upheavals by insulating them from nuclear war. A similar misunderstanding often affects Western views of détente. Brezhnev and his colleagues never saw East–West détente as a binding commitment to Third World restraint. They specifically denied it. In December 1972 Brezhnev declared that the class struggle between the two world systems would continue. "It cannot be otherwise, for the world outlook and the class aims of socialism and capitalism are opposite and irreconcilable. But we will strive to direct its historically inevitable struggle into a channel which poses no threat of wars, dangerous conflicts, and an uncontrolled arms race."[33]

Henry Trofimenko, the head of the department that studies American foreign policy in Moscow's Institute for the Study of the United States and Canada, put it bluntly: "American leaders pictured a deal along the lines of: 'We give you the status quo in strategic arms and you give us the status quo in the Third World.' . . . Inasmuch as the status quo in the Third World is mostly pro-American, as a consequence of U.S. economic domination, such an understanding wholly suited the United States. It is difficult to say what gave American leaders grounds to hope for such linkage, which is out of the question from our point of view."[34]

Shortly after Reagan took office, Brezhnev again dealt with the notion of a "code of conduct" in superpower relations. At a Kremlin dinner in April 1981 for the Libyan leader, Colonel Qadaffi, Brezhnev declared that the Reagan administration, "which is apt to see in all the events taking place in the world the 'hand of Moscow,' repeatedly launches appeals to the USSR and its allies to agree on the observance of some 'code of rules or conduct' in relations with the young states of Africa, Asia and Latin America. It is alleged that the world will be a calmer place in that eventuality." "If what is meant," he went on, "is certain 'rules' which would perpetuate imperialist brigandage, a policy of dictating to these states, the establishment of certain 'spheres of influence' etc., then of course we shall never agree to that." He called on Washington to apply the standards of the United Nations Charter, the Helsinki Final Accords and the agreements signed by the United States and the Soviet Union in the 1970s. The Soviet view was that these standards meant the following:

"Recognition of the right of each people to decide its domestic affairs without outside interference; renunciation of attempts to establish any forms of domination or hegemony over them or to include them in the 'sphere of influence' of any power.

"Strict respect for the territorial integrity of those countries; inviolability of their frontiers. No outside support for any separatist movements aimed at partitioning those countries.

"Unconditional recognition of the right of each African, Asian, and Latin American state to play an equal part in international life and to develop relations with any countries.

"Complete and unconditional recognition of the sovereignty of those states over their natural resources and also de facto recognition of their complete equality in international economic relations, support for their efforts aimed at eliminating the vestiges of colonialism and at eradicating racism and apartheid in accordance with the well-known decisions of the United Nations.

"Respect for the status of nonalignment chosen by the majority of African,

Asian, and Latin American states. Renunciation of attempts to draw them into the military-political blocks of big powers."[35]

Brezhnev's list of standards ignored the issue of support for national liberation movements, around which much of the original ambiguity of détente had revolved. The Kremlin was not about to elaborate the circumstances under which it might step up aid to these movements. Soviet attitudes on this were always pragmatic and flexible. Moscow wanted to be able to justify inaction, partly on the grounds that it did not believe in exporting revolution, but also because it preferred to see changes occur in the Third World without its help. The record suggests that when Moscow has taken action to support a movement it has taken a back seat rather than a leading role.

The Soviet Union's view of history as a dynamic process of constant struggle and of its own self-appointed role as the model of change is often underestimated in the West. Robert Legvold has rightly pointed out that "because our convictions about the Soviet Union have been so thoroughly shaped by the long interlude of Stalin's rule, and because his rule has always seemed so cynical, nationalistic, even anti-revolutionary, we have trouble taking seriously the residual force of earlier ideals."[36] Those portions of Brezhnev's speeches that talked about the triumph of communism or the opposition of two social systems, socialism and capitalism, were skipped over or pushed aside as so much verbiage. It was assumed they were ritual incantations without operational significance. Western observers found it hard to believe that Brezhnev had meant it when he boasted of the inspiration aroused by the Soviet Union: "It would be hard to overestimate the impact made on the masses in the rest of the world by the example of the successful development of the new society in a number of countries in various parts of the globe, a society without exploitation, without oppression and oppressors, a society administered for the people by the people. This example inspires hundreds of millions of the oppressed and fills them with hope for a happy future."[37] "Is the old man completely senile?" came the standard Western response.

Soviet leaders believe that the struggle between two social systems is the basic international reality of today's world. The enlargement of the world socialist system from being simply "socialism in one country" under Stalin to a "socialist commonwealth" of some dozen nations is considered a truly revolutionary development. The fact that in several Third World countries, from Cuba to Nicaragua or Algeria to Mozambique, progressive forces overthrew imperialism spontaneously and without Soviet help is seen as a vindication of the Soviet view of history. The lonely notion of encirclement by the capitalists, which was current under Lenin and Stalin and still remains as a powerful psychological factor for the Soviet leadership, now has a comforting ideological bedmate, the notion that in the world beyond the Soviet Union's borders the power of socialism is gaining ground. This trend first emerged under Khrushchev, but it was too new and his character was too impetuous for Soviet foreign policy to assimilate it under his leadership in a sophisticated way. Khrushchev's efforts to promote Soviet influence internationally were rash and simplistic. Under Brezhnev the Soviet Union's globalism was maturing into a subtle blend of restraint and intervention.

It was a long way from the "promotion of world revolution and a one-world socialist or communist state," which Reagan at his first White House press conference claimed as Soviet policy.[38] Western politicians found it hard to understand the contrast between Moscow's boast that the "correlation of forces" was moving in favor of socialism and its advocacy of correct state-to-state relations between the Soviet Union and capitalist countries. In Soviet thinking the "correlation of forces" is the basic substructure on which the international system of interstate relations rests. The latter is the product of deliberate policy processes and conforms to man-made rules, while the former depends on a stream of interacting variables that are beyond the control of decision makers. Brezhnev tried to explain this to Carter during their meeting in Vienna in June 1979: "Why pin on the Soviet Union the responsibility for the objective course of history and, moreover, use this as a pretext for worsening our relations?"[39]

While Brezhnev was praising the shift in the correlation of forces that had been produced by Soviet achievement of strategic parity, he was also embedding the Soviet Union more firmly in the existing international system. The new Soviet interest in the status quo was based on:

1. The desire for greater trade and commercial cooperation with the West, including hard currency

2. The desire for recognition by the international community as a great power

3. The need to prevent the United States from being provoked into abandoning parity, and trying to restore military superiority

4. Awareness of the slowness and unpredictability of any transition to socialism in the Third World, and the benefits of dealing with states regardless of their social systems

There was a fifth factor in the Brezhnev period that would have lowered any residual wish for the "promotion of world revolution" even further down Moscow's list of priorities. This was the split with China. Even when the Soviet Union was the world's only socialist state, its stormy relations with other parties in the Communist movement showed that there was no automatic harmony among Communists. The break with China reinforced the point that the triumph of socialism would not necessarily mean the triumph of internationalism. For Brezhnev the status quo was more comforting and less uncertain than the risks of an all-out "revolutionary" policy that would only produce more difficulties and upheavals than it was worth.

But Brezhnev and his colleagues were determined to take a greater role in shaping the international environment. This determination was no different from that of any other major power in history. American policy makers were never able to come to terms with this. Instinctively, they tried to stop it, either by force or lesser forms of pressure. Nor did they seem able to evaluate the exact nature of Soviet activism. When Kissinger wrote of the Soviet Union's "assault on the international order"[40] or asked if détente was only a tactic in an unending struggle "to overturn the world equilibrium," he betrayed an excessively static view of history. He underestimated the world's turbulence and overestimated the Soviet role within it. Who can seriously see the Kremlin as a controlling factor in the fall of the Shah, the tensions between Israel and the Palestinians, the conflicts between South Africa and its neighbors, the civil war in El Salvador, or the battle of the Falklands?

Kissinger hoped to control Soviet actions in the Third World by creating a web of restraint based on the threat of withholding arms control and trade agreements—what was called "Gulliverization." The idea was illusory, partly because the West would never be sufficiently united to agree on, let alone enforce for a long enough period, a consistent set of measures. It also assumed that Moscow would be prepared to overlook the United States' unilateral efforts to adjust the status quo in its own favor—China, Chile, and Egypt.

Kissinger's strategy was also doomed by its failure to appreciate Moscow's sense of international commitment and its wish to foster the extension of socialism if the circumstances were right. After a period of restraint over Vietnam, the Kremlin finally armed Hanoi for the last assault on the South when it decided that Kissinger had not delivered his side of the U.S.–Soviet trade bargain. In Angola the Kremlin moved when it saw that the guerrilla movement, which had majority international backing and which it had traditionally supported, faced the risk of defeat. The record shows that the Soviet Union has largely been cautious and slow to intervene in the Third World, but to expect it to refrain from ever acting at all, either by agreement or through fear of the consequences, is unrealistic.

Under the Carter administration the issues were differently posed. For the first years of Carter's term the mood of the administration's foreign policy was more relaxed and less interventionist than that of any of its recent predecessors. Carter talked of overcoming "the inordinate fear of communism" and his spokesmen played down the alleged role of the Soviet Union in local and regional crises in Central America and Africa. In October 1977 the administration even offered Moscow a joint role in the search for a settlement in the Middle East, in direct contrast to Kissinger's efforts to shut the Russians out. But Carter made more of the ideological struggle. Whereas Kissinger had played down the issue of human rights in favor of a more power-political approach to the Soviet Union, Carter reversed the stance. His international human rights campaign may have been primarily designed to restore the American public's self-

confidence and sense of moral superiority after the depression of Vietnam, but
the Russians saw it as directed against them. With its emphasis on the Soviet
Union's internal system and Carter's direct interventions, such as the letter he
wrote to the leading dissident, Andrei Sakharov, in January 1977, the new
administration was seen as more threatening than Nixon and Kissinger, who had
focused on Soviet activities abroad.

It was not long before Carter's ideological offensive spread to U.S. foreign
policy. His national security advisor, Zbigniew Brzezinski (whose Polish Catholic parentage and anti-Soviet academic background had already aroused Moscow's enmity years before), invited the Russians to join the North–South
dialogue on the side of the North. "We are challenging the Soviets to cooperate
with us or run the risk of becoming historically irrelevant to the great issues of
our time," he told an interviewer in May 1977.[41] Moscow found the language
insulting and the invitation a trap. "By appealing to the great-power economic
interests of the Soviet Union, it was intended to discredit it by this very same
great-powerism, to erase the distinction between the USSR as a state bearing no
responsibility for the colonial and post-colonial economic plunder of the
developing world and those industrial Western nations that do bear such
responsibility," Henry Trofimenko wrote dismissively.[42] The USSR would
never agree to participate, he went on, in undertakings directed at replacing
some forms of neocolonial dependence of the developing countries with
others.

Gradually, too, Washington's foreign policy moved back into more traditional
lines. The process began a few days after the signature of the Soviet–American
statement on the Middle East on October 2, 1977, which proposed a reconven-
ing of the Geneva conference under their joint chairmanship. Under pressure
from Israel and American Jewish leaders, the Carter administration shelved the
document. Its action was seen in Moscow as a disappointment and a humiliation.
The following spring Washington claimed to see Moscow's hand behind recurring instability on the border between Angola and Zaire, even though it had
made no such accusation over similar incidents a year earlier. In May, Brzezinski
visited China, returning with what seemed to the Russians the beginnings of a
U.S.–Chinese alignment directed against them.

The only moment of hope for Moscow in 1979 was the Vienna summit and the
signing of SALT II. But Carter appeared to have doubts about the treaty almost
before he arrived home. He allowed the sudden "discovery" of a Soviet brigade
in Cuba to be used as evidence that Moscow and Havana were testing the United
States. Wayne Smith, who was serving as director of the State Department's
Office of Cuban Affairs at the time, has said that "the brigade had been in Cuba
for a long time, and posed no real threat to the United States. But for domestic
political reasons administration officials portrayed it as new evidence of Soviet–
Cuban aggressiveness so threatening that a U.S. failure to react would be
extremely dangerous."[43] With a new wave of anti-Soviet excitement rising in

Congress, the administration postponed the SALT treaty's ratification. Meanwhile, Washington was continuing to step up its military capability. It reacted to the fall of the Shah in February 1979 by adopting plans already made by the Pentagon under Kissinger for a Rapid Deployment Force to operate in the Persian Gulf. In March (long before Afghanistan) Carter's staff started to prepare the speech that was to declare the Gulf a "vital American interest," to be defended by force if necessary.[44] In mid-December 1979 NATO decided to deploy U.S. cruise missiles and the advanced medium-range Pershing II missile in Western Europe from 1983.

The Kremlin showed signs of surprise over the almost total erosion of détente. The basic factor that had originally prompted it—Moscow's achievement of nuclear parity at the end of the 1960s—was still valid. The Soviets had hoped that American businessmen would have used more influence to keep it alive. The only two episodes in the Third World where Moscow had played a decisive role since the time of the Nixon summits were in Angola and Ethiopia. On the first of these issues the American foreign-policy establishment had been split, and Carter and most Democrats had opposed the Kissinger line of giving covert CIA assistance to two of the factions. In Ethiopia the Soviet Union had responded to an invitation from an internationally recognized government to help it defend its territory from invasion. Had the French not done the same for Zaire in that very continent that very year?

Soviet analysts explained the American retreat from détente as the result of a counteroffensive from a coalition of professionals (academics, politicians, journalists) and special interests, particularly the Jewish lobby, the arms manufacturers, and primitive anti-Communists. Some saw it as an American effort "to overcome American–Soviet parity in strategic arms by establishing regional military superiority."[45] Others considered that the United States was falling back on the old bogey of a Soviet threat in order to reassert U.S. leadership over increasingly dependent allies in Western Europe and Japan.

Détente had been dying for more than two years when the Kremlin found itself confronted by a crisis in Afghanistan. An unexpected military coup had brought to power a Marxist regime that managed to alienate large sections of the population within months of taking over, thanks to a series of excessively sweeping and badly administered reforms. With the regime close to collapse and riven by internal rivalry, the Kremlin was uncertain what to do about a country on its southern border that had been friendly to Moscow for more than fifty years. Its decision in December 1979 to send in Soviet troops to save the revolution must have been finely balanced. On the one hand, it would provide a good chance, certainly the only chance, of preserving a Marxist–Leninist regime, although there was bound to be fierce local resistance. On the other hand, it would provoke a storm of international protest since there could be no easy explanation, as in Angola and Ethiopia. Nevertheless, the intensity of the reaction of the nonaligned movement, which had picked Castro as its chairman in September 1979, seems to have surprised Moscow. More than a hundred countries condemned the Soviet invasion. The Western reaction was more predictable. Moscow appears to have calculated that Western Europe would forget soon, while the Americans were so hostile to détente that Afghanistan would make little difference.

The Kremlin was almost proved right. Neither Chancellor Schmidt of West Germany nor President Giscard of France reacted strongly at first. But Moscow had underestimated the force of symbolism in Western politics. With the Olympics scheduled to be held in the Soviet capital in the summer of 1980, critics of Moscow's invasion had the perfect focus around which to mobilize reaction, complete with references to Hitler's Olympics in Berlin in 1936. French and West German leaders came under pressure from the American president and from right-wing newspapers in their own countries to support an Olympic boycott. (The athletes did not always fall in line. British, French, and Italian sportsmen and women competed in Moscow.) In the Kremlin the boycott was greeted with mixed feelings. It was regarded by most Russians, and even some dissidents, as an insult and a blow against greater contact with the West. The KGB probably welcomed it as a way of restricting the expected awkward influx of Western visitors.

Yet even after the Olympics the Kremlin continued to hope that the bedrock of détente—U.S.–Soviet arms control negotiations and an expansion of East–West trade—would continue. Before Reagan's election, Soviet commentators were recalling that the last serious Republican candidate, Richard Nixon, had been anti-Communist before he entered the White House, but had become "realistic" afterward. After Reagan's victory, Moscow offered him a summit meeting, and even when the White House started to accuse Moscow of being involved in the guerrilla war in El Salvador, the Kremlin sent conciliatory signals. Only later did the Russians begin to realize that the Reagan administration's strategy was a reversion to the containment policies of the early Cold War—an attempt to restore U.S. military superiority, win the arms race, cut back on East–West trade, and weaken the Soviet economy by increasing the burden of defense spending.

The imposition of martial law in Poland in December 1981 was the occasion for a dramatic tightening of American sanctions on the Soviet Union. Even the basic transport links between the United States and the Soviet Union—airline and maritime services—were disrupted. Reagan told Congress he would not seek congressional approval of SALT II. Negotiations on a new long-term grain agreement were postponed, and the issuing of licenses for the export of high-technology items was reduced. There were only two sources of comfort for the Kremlin in all this: in deference to the powerful farm lobby, Reagan permitted the flow of grain shipments to Russia to continue, and indeed, in 1982, to reach the highest total in history. Second, the row between the United States and Western Europe over American efforts to block Western trade with the

Soviet Union raised new doubts in Europe about the United States. Reagan's image as a primitive Cold Warrior aroused dormant West European fears of U.S. unreliability and increased the already growing trends toward greater European independence.

The focus of the trade row was the $10 billion pipeline which would carry natural gas three thousand miles to Western Europe for Austria, Belgium, France, and West Germany—the largest East–West deal ever made. Major components, including the steel pipe and the gas turbines, were to be provided by Western firms. To Reagan the pipeline was a symbol of Western blindness, of capitalism's willingness, in Lenin's phrase, to dig its own grave. The pipeline would accelerate the Soviet Union's growth by tapping new energy sources for Soviet industry. It would allow the Soviet Union to increase its earnings of hard currency, thus financing further imports from the West. It would give the Russians access to advanced technology, and would increase Western European dependence on Soviet energy.

Moscow reacted to the U.S. campaign by fierce attacks on Reagan in the Soviet press, and by encouraging the Europeans to break ranks with Washington. It denied U.S. claims that it was heavily dependent on Western trade and could therefore be damaged by the embargo. It pointed out that it could and would develop the pipeline on its own, if the sanctions were maintained. On this last point the Kremlin surely meant what it said. In his memoirs, published in 1978, Brezhnev described how thirty years earlier the Americans had stopped deliveries of equipment for a power station on the Dnieper in the area where he was then a regional party official. "The Cold War set in. It went on for many years, actually two decades. This was not the first or unfortunately the last time the capitalist powers tried to pin hopes on our difficulties, and attempted to dictate their will to us and interfere in our domestic affairs. The calculation was a simple one: with no choice in the matter, the Soviet Union would have to ask for the machinery and the sheet-steel; with nowhere to turn to, the Communists would submit and fall to their knees . . . so what: did we perish or fall back? Was our advance checked? No! The wise men across the ocean miscalculated in their policies, something it is useful to remind people of today, inasmuch as it is both instructive and topical."[46] Brezhnev went on to say that in spite of the boycott, work on the power station accelerated, and the machinery produced by local workers was more reliable and powerful than that of their American counterparts. The entire world could see the "boundless reserves" of the socialist economy and "the vast might of a country which, should the need arise, is able to regroup its forces and concentrate them on the main objectives."[47]

If the first two of these points sound bombastic, the third one comes close to the mark. By virtue of its centralized command of all decisions, the Politburo can indeed concentrate resources on high-priority objectives. There was no reason to think that the Russians would not go all out to defeat the boycott, as they had in the past, and as other smaller countries have done in the face of international

sanctions. When Reagan, under pressure from Western European governments, lifted his pipeline sanctions in November 1982, the Kremlin naturally
proclaimed a victory for common sense.

It was not enough to modify Moscow's view that better relations with
Washington were unlikely. In September 1982 the Kremlin's chief spokesman,
Leonid Zamyatin, had called the Reagan administration "the most militaristic
and reactionary" American government since the Second World War.[48] Soviet
officials suggested that the Kremlin was debating whether to write off the
administration and wait for the next presidential election, or whether to make
another effort at improving relations. By the end of October the debate
appeared to have been resolved in favor of those who argued for a harder Soviet
line to match U.S. toughness. Brezhnev appeared at a conference of the
command personnel of the Soviet Army and Navy, held at the Kremlin, and
made one of his fiercest attacks on Washington in many years. He accused
Washington of conducting an "aggressive policy which is threatening to push the
world into the flames of nuclear war. The adventurism, rudeness, and egoism of
this policy arouse growing indignation in many countries, including those allied
with the United States."[49] He promised to "spare nothing" to keep the Soviet
armed forces up to the mark. Then he turned to China with another plea for
normalization of relations with Peking. The message seemed to be that Moscow
was looking for a new modus vivendi with China, partly in order to take
advantage of Peking's own waning expectations of American concessions on
Taiwan, but also as a signal to the Americans—a kind of "China card"—that
Moscow could take other foreign policy initiatives if Washington was bent on
confrontation.

Three weeks later, at his first Central Committee meeting since becoming
party leader, Andropov developed the same line, albeit in slightly different
language. His references to China were markedly warmer. He talked of "our
great neighbor," promised respect for China's legitimate interests, and said
there was a "need to overcome the inertia of prejudice."[50] Toward the United
States his approach was less abusive than Brezhnev's final statements but equally
firm. IIe called for a revival of détente but only on the basis of reciprocity and
equality—"We did not introduce sanctions against anyone, we did not denounce
treaties and agreements that were signed and we did not interrupt talks that were
started."

After showing eagerness for a dialogue with the United States at the start of
the Reagan administration, the Kremlin became resigned to the fact that
business with Washington was probably impossible, even though negotiations
with the Reagan administration on arms control were underway. Talks on
intermediate-range missiles in Europe had begun in Geneva in November 1981,
and on strategic arms six months later, but little progress had been made by the
summer of 1983. As Alexander Bovin, *Izvestia*'s influential political commentator and a close friend of Andropov, had put it glumly a few weeks before

Brezhnev's death, "It is now difficult to do business with the Americans. They are dodging, resorting to subterfuges, are saying one thing and doing another. They show a lot of ambition and conceit, but little responsibility. But what can be done? Partners are not chosen. They are given by destiny, by history, and we have to talk to them and conduct negotiations."[51] Andropov appeared to echo this view.

CONCLUSION

During the Brezhnev era Soviet relations with the United States moved in an almost complete circle—from the suspicions of the Cold War to détente and back again. The effort to control the nuclear arms race and remove it from the other competitive aspects of the relationship between the two superpowers peaked in the early 1970s and then collapsed, as the Reagan administration launched a vigorous drive for superiority. The Soviet attempt to develop normal trading links with the United States backfired, and by the end of Brezhnev's time Washington was imposing the fiercest economic sanctions that any U.S. administration had imposed since the 1940s. Meanwhile, the "technology gap" between the Soviet Union and the United States remained as wide as it was when Brezhnev came to power. Any hopes that the Kremlin might have had of catching up with the United States were clearly unrealistic.

But the Soviet Union of the early 1980s was not the same as twenty years earlier. Under Brezhnev it had opened itself up to foreign trade as never before. Its foreign trade minister, Nikolai Patolichev, had written in 1978: "Today it would perhaps be difficult to find an economic sector in the Soviet Union which is not connected with foreign trade, to some extent, or does not receive effective practical aid in its further development. To put it figuratively, foreign trade has become an important artery in the blood circulation of the Soviet Union's economic organism."[52] While this made the Soviet Union more vulnerable to outside pressure, there were factors that discounted it. The United States was no longer able to impose its views so effectively on its Western European allies. They were prepared to continue trading with Moscow even if Washington was not. For Brezhnev, who had invested heavily in the process of détente, this was a vital element. It cushioned the blow when Washington reverted to a policy of containment. It also provided an extra retrospective justification of détente by allowing Brezhnev to present it to any doubting colleagues as a way of bringing out differences within the Western camp.

There was no way of concealing Soviet disappointment with Washington's reversion to a hard-line policy of confrontation. It reversed a process that Moscow had thought was irreversible. The Kremlin's sense that the new "correlation of forces" in the world had forced Washington to become "realistic" was undermined. The decline of détente left a legacy of bitterness and uncertainty that Andropov had to deal with as best he could.

5

WESTERN EUROPE: IS THERE A SOVIET THREAT?

Russia is inextricably woven into the history of Europe—not only as an adversary and danger but also as a partner—historical, political, cultural and economic.

Willy Brandt[1]

After a decade of dramatic ups and downs in U.S.–Soviet relations and heightened Western interest in the Soviet Union's Third World role, it is easy to forget that Europe is still the most sensitive arena of Soviet foreign policy. The United States is the Kremlin's overriding global concern because of the nuclear threat it poses and its rivalry as a superpower. But once the focus moves to traditional notions of territorial security, Europe is Moscow's main worry. Initial Soviet fears about the United States after the Second World War centered on what the Americans might do in Europe and to Europe, particularly in Moscow's Eastern European buffer zone. These fears have remained remarkably constant. The two most serious foreign crises of Brezhnev's period in power were in Europe, Czechoslovakia in 1968, and Poland in 1980–81. As his time came to an end, the focus of Soviet–American arms-control talks was the threat of nuclear war in Europe.

Although Brezhnev added new dimensions to Soviet foreign policy, particularly in the Third World and China, he did not change the basic European focus of Soviet thinking. While Soviet concern about China has risen enormously during the past twenty years, prompting the deployment of a garrison of half a million Soviet troops close to the Chinese border, it is not as intense as Russian worry over its western flank. The Kremlin is less concerned about the potential threat from China than about latent instability in Eastern Europe and NATO power in Western Europe. However unpredictable and violence-prone the Chinese may seem in Moscow's more obsessive moments, the Russians know well that the Chinese are no military match for them. Three-quarters of the Red Army is guarding the opposite flank.

For almost forty years the Kremlin has maintained two objectives in Europe. One is the containment of Germany, either by means of its neutralization (the option originally preferred) or its division. The other is the safeguarding of pro-Soviet control in Eastern Europe. If there was any doubt about Moscow's determination to adhere to these goals after Stalin's death, Khrushchev dispelled it with his military suppression of the Hungarian rebellion in 1956 and his endorsement of the building of a wall through Berlin in 1961.

Under Brezhnev the Kremlin's dual policy was taken several stages farther. First, West Germany and the other NATO nations were persuaded to recognize the German Democratic Republic (East Germany) and the postwar frontiers of Eastern Europe. For the Russians, who value the legitimacy conferred by international agreements, this was an important gain. In return they had to make a number of concessions on the human rights front as part of the general opening of Eastern Europe to Western influences. They also had to give up the "Berlin card." No longer was it possible to use Soviet control of the access routes to Berlin as a device for raising the temperature of East–West relations. Any confrontation in Berlin would jeopardize the whole edifice of stability and East–West accommodation on which the new treaties were based. As Willy Brandt put it after coming away from his second summit meeting with Brezhnev in 1971, the Soviet leader wanted to "unburden" Moscow's relations with Western Europe.[2]

The second stage of the process of *Ostpolitik* was a dramatic increase in Western trade with the East, with West German firms taking the lead. Long-term economic agreements were signed for Western credit to be used in financing huge energy and raw material projects in the Soviet Union with part of the products to be exported to the West. The massive gas pipeline deal, which the Reagan administration fiercely opposed, was only the most conspicuous symbol of a host of smaller agreements. Although Moscow's initial priority in looking for Western credit, technology, and manufactured goods was economic, Brezhnev soon saw the political value of the deals. In a sense he managed to create the kind of restraining web of new relationships with West Germany that Kissinger at one time hoped to do with the Soviet Union, when he first espoused détente. But U.S.–Soviet trade never developed to the point where there was a guaranteed majority within the American foreign policy elite in favor of détente, either because of its benefit to the economy or as a workable lever over Soviet actions. In volume terms U.S. trade was high, but this was primarily because of large sales of grain. Soviet–West German trade, by contrast, had a much broader political consensus. Throughout Brezhnev's period it was axiomatic in West German politics that détente was valuable. The opposition parties, the Christian Democrats and Christian Socialists, argued over the political concessions the ruling Social Democratic party–Free Democratic party coalition were sometimes said to be making. But there was no stomach for a halt in trade with the Soviet Union or for the sanctions that Washington imposed. Between 1970 and 1975 Soviet–West German trade had quadrupled. After 1975 it went up by half as much again.

It was the developing strains between West Germany and the United States that marked the third stage of Brezhnev's relations with Western Europe. As policy differences widened within the Western alliance, Moscow was confronted with increasingly complicated diplomatic and political choices. Those who argue that Moscow simply wants to "split NATO" and therefore exults in any tension among members of the alliance underestimate the complexity of Moscow's preferences. To put it at its crudest, an independent nuclear-armed West Germany, which was no longer under American control or supervision, might well be worse for the Soviet Union. Similarly, those who see a "Soviet threat" to Western Europe have to look at the range of possible Soviet goals for Europe, options we will examine later. Here, in this initial outline of Soviet relations with Western Europe, it is enough to draw attention to the two key features of the period. First, the Kremlin has made no effort, directly or indirectly, to use force in Western Europe or Berlin since 1962. Although the Soviet military arsenal in Eastern Europe facing west is a formidable war machine and has been continually built up, NATO has also been increasing in strength. The difference between the two alliances' military postures—with NATO relying more heavily on nuclear weapons and less on conventional ones—has not upset the essential balance between them for at least twenty years, nor has there been any crisis in which either side seemed ready to risk armed conflict. Soviet activity in Western Europe has been exclusively diplomatic, economic, and political. Second, Western Europe has been almost the only region where Brezhnev's foreign policy can claim to have had some success. With the possible exception of Africa, every other area has produced disappointment or defeat.

The improvement of relations between Western Europe and the Soviet Union was not a Soviet initiative. The policy that Brezhnev inherited from Khrushchev was to insist on Western recognition of East Germany as the precondition for any relaxation of tension. At the Twenty-Third Party Congress in March 1966 Brezhnev talked of West Germany in traditional terms: "Today West German imperialism is the United States' chief ally in aggravating world tension. West Germany is increasingly becoming a seat of war danger where revenge-seeking passions are running high. . . . The policy pursued by the Federal Republic o Germany is increasingly determined by the same monopolies which brought Hitler to power."[3] In a declaration in 1966 calling for a European Security Conference, the Warsaw Pact as a whole also stressed that the West must acknowledge the territorial and political status quo in Europe. When the Bonn government, led by a grand coalition of the CDU and SPD, urged Eastern Europe to recognize West Germany in return for Western economic loans and development credits, it was rebuffed.

The Russians found it hard to abandon a policy of moral and ideological confrontation with West Germany, since they regarded it as the successor state to Hitler's Germany. It was only the advent of an SPD government in 1969 under the leadership of Willy Brandt, a man with impeccable anti-Fascist credentials, that convinced them to soften their view. The change of Soviet policy reflected in the 1970 Moscow treaty in which the two countries renounced the use of force, and in a similar treaty between West Germany and Poland, encountered opposition from East Germany's party leader, Walter Ulbricht, because they did not guarantee East Germany's recognition. It may well have met criticism from senior members of the Soviet Politburo, fearful of the implications of Brezhnev's new policy of reconciliation with West Germany. On his visit to Moscow in 1970, Brandt found Kosygin surprisingly anxious about neo-Nazism in West Germany, while Brezhnev "overestimated" West Germany's importance.[4] This was perhaps natural to men of the war generation, for whom, as Brezhnev told Brandt, "A turn to the better between us is no simple or easy thing. A grim past separates our states and peoples."[5] Marshal Grechko conceded that a complete new system of indoctrinating the Red Army would be necessary, with a modification of West Germany's image as the enemy.[6] It required Ulbricht's gentle removal into retirement as party leader in 1971 for the Kremlin to be able to go ahead with the Four-Power Berlin Agreement and the deal by which Bonn finally recognized East Germany in 1972. Ulbricht could hardly have survived for as long as two years from the beginning of Brandt's *Ostpolitik* if he had not had allies within the Kremlin while Soviet policy was under review.

From Moscow's point of view there were several advantages in the *Ostpolitik* compromise. It would make West Germany less likely to become a nuclear power. It would restrain any revanchism. It would stabilize East Germany by giving it international recognition. It would reduce military tension in Europe at a time when tension was high on the Chinese border. It would facilitate trade. It could become a model for eventual Soviet–American détente. One can easily guess the counterarguments from conservatives who feared the dangers posed to internal security by reduced tensions, greater Western penetration, and the need to adjust entrenched propaganda themes.

Once converted, Brezhnev worked with the energy of a zealot to develop the radical new policy. At times he seemed to be making an almost personal crusade out of what was soon called his *Westpolitik*. He told the West Germans that it was not just a question of developing trade, but of "a moral and political rapprochement between peoples."[7] On his visit to Bonn in 1973, he said he could not speak about the war except with pain. He wanted West Germany as an ally against any repetition of the past, and as a partner over and above the purely bilateral issues. He approved a significant concession in the treaty signed by the two German states, which kept open the theoretical possibility of German reunification. The point was repeated in the Final Accords of the Conference on Security and Co-operation in Europe, signed at Helsinki in 1975. The Soviet draft calling for acceptance of the "immutability" of Europe's frontiers was changed to "inviolability," a diplomatic nuance that might seem trivial. To the Russians it meant that the frontiers could be changed by peaceful means.

Even if Moscow failed to get de jure recognition of the territorial status quo in Eastern Europe, its de facto acceptance was of enormous importance. This is why the Russians were prepared to swallow the even bigger concession implicit in the very title of the conference. The West's insistence that it be called a conference on co-operation as well as security was shorthand for the long list of promises on human rights that the Russians had to make, and that came to be known under their conference heading as "Basket Three." There was to be a freer flow of information and ideas between the two halves of Europe, easier travel, a better chance for divided families to be reunited, and more cultural exchanges. The extent of Soviet commitments was not immediately apparent, but as East–West tensions grew again in the late 1970s and the Soviet Union found itself constantly on the defensive at the conferences that reviewed the way the Helsinki promises had been violated, some observers in the West wondered why Moscow did not repudiate the whole Helsinki process. But this view underestimated the importance the Russians attached to the West's recognition of the territorial status quo. They were prepared to suffer the damage to their pride and image that Western governments inflicted on them by holding up their hypocrisy on human rights, since the Soviets considered that the benefits they gained for their security outweighed the attacks. Brezhnev's personal stake in the Helsinki conference had been immense. On his seventy-fifth birthday, in 1981, *Pravda* called him "the main architect of détente" and described the conference as "a brilliant success for the cause of peace." "Is it possible to forget," *Pravda* continued, "how warmly he was congratulated by the heads of many states at the climactic ending of the conference?"[8]

West Germany is the linchpin of the Kremlin's policy in Western Europe by reason of its economic weight, its history, and its geographical position on the frontier of the Warsaw Pact countries. But Brezhnev also lavished great attention on France, in visits to Paris and while entertaining French presidents in Moscow. He pressed for détente with Italy, Britain, and the other West European states, skillfully adjusting the warmth of Soviet political overtures to the state of economic relations in the hope that the respective countries' governments and industrialists would compete eagerly for Soviet business.

France, in fact, was the first country to arouse Brezhnev's interest in détente. President Charles de Gaulle's offer to recognize Poland's postwar boundaries as early as the mid-1960s, his independence from the United States, and his vision of a Europe "from the Atlantic to the Urals" that would exclude American influence intrigued Moscow. But de Gaulle's views were too unorthodox at the time and too far from the NATO consensus for the Russians to imagine that they would catch on in the rest of Europe. West Germany could exert greater influence in NATO councils. Détente with Bonn meant more for Moscow, both in itself and as a potential model for the rest of the alliance.

Moscow's preference for German-led détente with NATO rather than Gaullist independence may seem a paradox. It reflects the Kremlin's intricate assessment of its contradictory hopes for Western Europe, as measured against the most likely probabilities.

At this point one must turn to Moscow's preferred options for the future. The various Western conjectures can be summed up under three separate headings.

1. Military invasion

2. A peaceful transition to socialism after Western European Communist parties come to power

3. Promotion of a nonaligned, though still capitalist, Western Europe

THE INVASION THEORY

Defense against a possible Soviet invasion of Western Europe has been the bedrock of NATO policy for more than thirty years. Whether this would be a Soviet dash across the north German plain to Hamburg, the seizure of West Berlin, or an attack on northern Norway, Western military planners have worked on the assumption that the Russians might invade at any time, if Western deterrence is not strong enough. For the last twenty years, NATO spokesmen have argued that their deterrence must be nuclear because of the Warsaw Pact's preponderance in conventional weapons, particularly tanks. The pattern of Warsaw Pact deployments has given rise to fears that the Soviet Union and its allies could be planning an attack. Since the beginning of the cold war, Soviet policy has aimed at being able to pose a substantial military challenge to Western Europe. Originally, this was partly in order to compensate for Moscow's inability to deter the United States by a direct attack on American territory. It wanted to keep Washington's Western European allies as a potential hostage in any developing crisis. Later, with the acquisition of its own intercontinental ballistic missiles in 1957, this rationale was reduced. But by then West Germany had been incorporated into NATO, the West was strengthening its conventional forces, and the Soviet Union had become afraid of instability in

Eastern Europe, such as it had seen in Hungary, Poland, and East Germany. NATO's weakness in battle tanks and its reliance on defense in depth after a forced retreat on the central front in Germany hardly suggested any NATO intention to launch an attack. But the Russians were concerned by the possibility of a crisis developing in Eastern Europe which the West might be tempted to exploit. This was the period of Dulles with his talk of "rolling back" communism in Eastern Europe. After the experience of the last war, and Stalin's failure to prepare an adequate defense, Soviet military planners and the political leadership put a high priority on forward defense to avoid another invasion of Soviet-controlled soil. They also believed they maximized their deterrence by demonstrating to potential opponents that they would suffer quick and heavy destruction if they threatened to attack. Soviet military training, with its emphasis on fast, armored, forward movement and rapid bridge building, and the deployment of several divisions in East Germany, were designed to give Moscow the theoretical option of a preemptive conventional strike against West Germany if East–West relations worsened dramatically.

How serious was this option in military terms? For most of the last twenty years it has been the accepted wisdom among Western politicians that the Warsaw Pact is far stronger than NATO. When the Nixon administration took office in 1969, NATO's conventional forces were "vastly inferior," Kissinger claimed in his memoirs.[9] This was not borne out by the International Institute of Strategic Studies' (IISS) survey of the military balance for 1969–70. It cited the Warsaw Pact's troop strength in Northern and Central Europe as 925,000 compared with 600,000 for NATO, with an extra 100,000 if French forces were included.[10] The mobilization of first-line reserves and the movement of other reinforcements could aid the Warsaw Pact in the initial stages of a crisis because the USSR can move up troops faster than the United States. But if the crisis developed gradually enough to permit full reinforcement, NATO would outnumber the Warsaw Pact, since the NATO countries maintain larger armies. On the issue of tanks, the IISS argued that NATO's superiority in antitank weapons and in tank armaments made up for the Warsaw Pact's larger number of tanks. NATO had superior firepower in conventional artillery. The difference in each side's arsenal made it hard to come to a firm conclusion on whether either had an advantage, but any numerical superiority that the Warsaw Pact had in particular categories of weapons needed to be measured against the ratio of four or five to one that an attacking force is usually assumed to require if it wants to be reasonably sure of victory.

The key issues were the amount of time for reinforcement and the seriousness of Moscow's likely willingness to attack, given that NATO planned to use nuclear weapons if conventional defenses were breached. In the second half of the 1970s NATO ideas about the Warsaw Pact's probable tactics became more alarmist. The perceived scenario changed from a massive Warsaw Pact attack with prior reinforcement and considerable warning time to one postulating an unreinforced surprise attack by the forces already in place, consisting of possibly half a million men. In the late 1970s public concern about nuclear weapons began to revive in the West, along with doubts among Western policymakers as to whether the United States would actually risk an all-out strategic nuclear exchange with the Soviet Union for the sake of Western Europe. In response to these doubts and the perceived gap in conventional forces between the Warsaw Pact and NATO, Carter urged a summit meeting of NATO government leaders in Washington in May 1978 to increase spending on conventional defense by 3 percent a year in real terms. This became agreed NATO policy.

By 1982 respected voices among Western military specialists, including firm supporters of NATO, were beginning to suggest that the West's conventional forces might be strong enough to deter the Warsaw Pact on their own. In an article arguing that NATO should accept the principle of "no first use" of nuclear weapons, Robert McNamara, McGeorge Bundy, former national security advisor to Presidents Kennedy and Johnson, George Kennan, and Gerard Smith, the chief U.S. SALT negotiator between 1969 and 1972, declared that "there has been some tendency over many years to exaggerate the relative conventional strength of the USSR and to underestimate Soviet awareness of the enormous costs and risks of any form of aggression against NATO." Americans would have to accept a share in any new level of conventional effort that the policy of "no first use" might require, "yet it would be wrong to make any hasty judgment that those new levels of effort must be excessively high."[11]

Jonathan Dean, who was the ambassador in charge of the American delegation to the Mutual and Balanced Force Reduction (MBFR) talks in Vienna from 1978 to 1981, has written that "despite the concerns of recent years over trends in Soviet and Warsaw Pact forces, NATO forces in Central Europe today have important advantages in specific areas. NATO air forces maintain an impressive edge over Pact forces in many categories including payload. NATO pilots have logged more flying hours and are better trained. NATO has about twice as many modern fighter-bombers as the Warsaw Pact."[12] While the Warsaw Pact had a manpower advantage in Central Europe of about 175,000 ground and airforce personnel, Dean argued that this level had not markedly increased since the 1968 invasion of Czechoslovakia. The Warsaw Pact's almost three-to-one lead in main battle tanks (19,500 to 7,000) was countered by NATO's decision to concentrate its resources on armed helicopters and antitank guided-weapons launchers, in which it has a four-to-one lead. Dean argues that Soviet tank strength is less impressive in practice than it may appear on paper. Soviet conscripts have a low level of education and mechanical aptitude which decreases their usefulness in a highly mechanized force. The pronounced centralism of the Soviet system creates difficulties in training the commanders of small units to show initiative. Over half the Soviet units in Central Europe are equipped with the older, less advanced T-62 tank. "Western force analysts," Dean says, "professionally avoid qualitative estimates. But it is probable that the quality of Soviet ground forces in Central Europe, clearly the best in the Warsaw Pact, is considerably lower than that of West Germany's Bundeswehr.''

Dean's sober and conspicuously nonalarmist assessment of Warsaw Pact power is all the more significant since it comes from a man who has been so closely involved in negotiations on the issue. He concludes his analysis by pointing out that NATO has the advantage of defending its own soil from prepared positions on relatively favorable terrain, and with greater knowledge of its own area and higher military morale. NATO also benefits from the general requirement that the potential attacker must have considerable overall superiority to ensure success.

Besides the general view that NATO's defenses had tended to be underestimated, specialists also argued that the Soviet military "threat" rested on certain weaknesses that the West had overlooked. Thirty-one of the fifty-eight Warsaw Pact divisions in Central Europe are non-Soviet (fifteen Polish, ten Czechoslovak and six East German). One new factor was the widespread realization of Eastern Europe's instability, as seen in the Polish crisis, and the notion that Polish forces and possibly East Germany's might not be totally loyal to the Soviet Union in a conflict. Defection rates among East German border guards, one of the most highly indoctrinated sections of the East German military, cast doubts about their reliability in any conflict with the West. As for the turmoil in Poland, how many divisions could Poland offer the Warsaw Pact if its army was still holding down its own people?

Another argument arose from the poor performance of Soviet weapons during the Israeli invasion of Lebanon in 1982. U.S.-made Israeli jets shot down almost ninety Syrian MiG's in two days of combat without a single loss, and used advanced air-to-ground missiles to destroy nineteen Soviet-supplied surface-to-air missile launchers with the loss of only one jet. The Russians tried to explain the imbalance by suggesting that the Syrian operators were insufficiently trained. This was probably true, but it also raised the question whether Soviet and Eastern European forces might be less well equipped to handle sophisticated weapons than their NATO counterparts—as Ambassador Dean argued in the article quoted above.

In 1982 NATO was making plans to deploy in Europe more sophisticated versions of the precision-guided missiles used by the Israelis in Lebanon. These missiles would have a system of multiple warheads, so that one missile could destroy seven tanks. The United States was so confident of NATO strength that it was developing a new strategy, code-named "Air-Land Battle", which would shift NATO away from a static defense toward a strong emphasis on counterattack. NATO forces would penetrate deeply and rapidly into Eastern Europe and perhaps the Soviet Union in order to destroy the second and third waves of Warsaw Pact forces that might move forward after their forces' initial surprise attack.[13]

Even before these weapons became available, the International Institute of

Strategic Studies argued in its review of the military balance in Europe that "the overall balance continues to be such as to make military aggression a highly risky undertaking."[14] Michael Howard, one of the West's leading military strategists and a vice-president of the institute, told its annual conference in 1982 that the chances of a conventional Soviet attack on Western Europe were "absolutely minimal."[15]

Howard moved beyond the issue of Soviet capabilities to the much less discussed, but equally relevant, question of intentions. "What do the Russians have to gain by it? They can live with the West as it is."[16] Obviously, Soviet spokesmen deny any desire to attack the West. Vikenty Matveyev, *Izvestia*'s columnist, put it negatively: "Why should we grab Western Europe—and add another lot of problems to what we've got already?"[17] Between the two of them, these comments probably sum up the political restraints that Moscow feels. Sudden invasion, after all, even if it were successful, would have to be followed by the occupation of a defeated Western Europe, its industry largely shattered and its people hostile and resistant. As long as peaceful relations between Western Europe and the Soviet Union remain good and détente continues, even in a modified form, it seems inconceivable that Moscow would prefer the unknown consequences of attack and the problems of occupation. It has found it hard to maintain control over Eastern Europe for almost forty years. To add another unwilling region appears to make no sense.

A COMMUNIST WESTERN EUROPE

At first sight the vision of a peaceful transition to Communist rule in Western Europe by means of the region's Communist parties might seem to be the Soviet leaders' fondest dream. Spared the uncertainty and human cost of a military invasion, the Kremlin could look forward with satisfaction and relief to the prospect of cooperative comrades at the helm of government in Paris, Rome, Bonn, and London.

Not so, at least to judge from Moscow's awkward relations with the "Eurocommunist" parties over the last fifteen years. The Italian Communist party, the largest one, criticized the Soviet Union's invasions of Czechoslovakia and Afghanistan and its role in the Polish clampdown. It suggested that the imposition of martial law in Poland marked the final bankruptcy of Eastern European socialism. Its leader, Enrico Berlinguer, condemned the "permanent and grave limitations of freedom" in Eastern Europe and argued that the flight from politics by young people there and in the Soviet Union showed that the system had exhausted its capacity for renewal.[18] Worst of all from Moscow's point of view, the Italian party began to equate Soviet foreign policy with that of the United States, a move that an outraged article in *Pravda* called "truly sacrilegious."[19]

The *Pravda* statement was the strongest attack on any foreign Communist party, apart from the Chinese, for more than twenty years. It marked another chapter in a story of progressive alienation between Moscow and the majority of Western Communist parties that the Kremlin was powerless to stop, but grudgingly had to come to terms with. Brezhnev's references to them between 1966 and 1981 in his five-yearly reports to the Congress of the Communist Party of the Soviet Union produced a gradually more open admission of the differences between them. In 1981 the Soviet party leader had to concede that "in none of the now existing socialist countries have the forms, methods, and ways of the socialist revolution been a mechanical repetition of outside experience. . . . As I see it, unless one ignores the actual facts, one cannot speak of any 'uniformity.'"[20] Pleading for understanding, Brezhnev even made what amounted to a surprisingly frank apology for the state of Soviet socialism: "Critical judgments of separate concrete developments in our country are sometimes voiced in some Communist parties. Far be it from us to think that everything we had was ideal. In the USSR socialism was built in incredibly difficult conditions. The party hewed its way through virgin land. And nobody knows better than we do what difficulties and shortcomings occurred along the way, and which of them have still to be overcome."[21] This was a far cry from the notion of the Soviet "model" as a guide for others to follow.

If Brezhnev pinned little hope on the Italian Communists being helpful to the Soviet Union if they entered government, he had no greater faith in Western Europe's second largest party, the French, whose policy has always been less critical of Moscow than that of the Italians. Their only road to power lay through a coalition with the Socialists, led by Mitterrand. The Kremlin had worked comfortably with de Gaulle and Georges Pompidou, and in the 1974 election it subtly indicated its support for Mitterrand's right-wing opponent, Valéry Giscard d'Estaing. On the eve of the poll the Soviet ambassador in Paris initiated a highly publicized courtesy call on Giscard.

Seven years later the Russians made their feelings even plainer. Giscard had pleased them by meeting Brezhnev in Warsaw in May 1980, the first East–West summit since the invasion of Afghanistan. The visit was turned into an election issue by a critical Mitterrand. Two months before the election *Pravda* called Giscard a restrained and careful politician who had strengthened France's international prestige, while Mitterrand was attacked for the "Atlanticist orientation" of his foreign policy.[22] *Pravda*'s assessment of the French Socialist leader was right. The appointment of four Communists as cabinet ministers, the first in the government of any major Western European country for more than thirty years, made no impact on the victorious Mitterrand's foreign policy, which soon emerged as more pro-American and pro-NATO than Giscard's.

The Kremlin was thus faced with two probable scenarios for Western European Communists in power. Either, like the French, they would be impotent and unable to diverge from the generally anti-Soviet line of non-Communist governments, or, like the Italians, they would be effective but independent of Moscow. Some Western skeptics might ask whether the Italian party's line was not window dressing for electoral reasons, and suspect that once in power it would emerge as Moscow's loyal ally. The history of nationalism within the Communist movement suggests otherwise. In the case of the Chinese and the Yugoslavs and almost every other party that has come to power without the aid of Soviet tanks, splits have only widened once the party ruled.

The Kremlin must sometimes wonder whether the coming to power of Communists in China has not damaged Soviet interests more than if the Nationalists had won the civil war. A Communist Western Europe might be worse. The region's level of economic development and rich industrial base would overshadow the Soviet Union materially in a way that a backward China cannot. Moscow could no longer claim to be the world's most advanced socialist power. Its pride and self-esteem would be gravely wounded—a plight that leaders as insecure as those in the Kremlin would hardly welcome. But perhaps the most serious effect would be in Eastern Europe. No parties there, with the exception of the Albanian (and it acted only for power-political reasons in order to find a counterweight to Moscow), have been tempted to follow the Chinese approach to the building of communism. A Communist Western Europe, by contrast, would exert an immense attraction for Eastern Europeans, where Communist reformers have frequently tried to marry socialist economic theories with the traditions of Western bourgeois liberalism. A victorious Berlinguer, in company with similar comradely governments in the rest of Western Europe, might spark off the final democratic explosion in Moscow's shaky Eastern European zone.

WESTERN EUROPE, CAPITALIST AND NONALIGNED

Dream or nightmare, the chances of a Communist Western Europe are minimal in the near future. Somewhat more likely is the prospect that Western Europe, while retaining its present capitalist system, will loosen its links with the United States. Whether it does, and what alternative foreign and defense policy it would then adopt, are questions that have exercised the Kremlin for some time. Would Western Europe try to build up its own defense forces to substitute for the presumed withdrawal of the American military umbrella, or would it move to a unilateral reduction in armaments? Would it remain basically in agreement with the United States, or adopt a position of nonalignment between the super-powers?

Soviet attitudes to these different and remote scenarios have been contradictory and confused. They have varied according to whether Moscow considered West Germany or the United States offered the greater threat. In the early postwar period the Kremlin tried hard to prevent West Germany from joining

NATO or becoming a nuclear power. It failed on the first point but succeeded on the second, largely because the Western side was also worried about the long-term implications of a nuclear West Germany. France, Britain, and the United States were happy to see West Germany in NATO because they thought it would be easier to control her. They were less happy to see her go nuclear. The onset of détente did not remove Moscow's doubts about West Germany. As recently as 1970 Brezhnev indicated that she was considered a potential rogue elephant that needed to be checked. He accepted a continuing role for the United States in Europe, partly in order to exercise some supervision over West Germany. He put no time limit on the Four-Power Agreement on Berlin, thus preserving some symbolic aspects of the wartime alliance. He also recognized the United States as a permanent partner in the European Security Conference.

At other moments the Russians have seemed more fascinated by the possibility of an independent West Germany balancing between East and West. They may have hoped for a repetition of the kind of policy that Germany adopted in 1922 when it signed the Treaty of Rapallo with the fledgling Soviet Union. A gesture of independence that outraged France and Britain, the treaty rejected Lloyd George's plan for a European alliance that would have included Germany but excluded the Soviet Union. During the early days of *Ostpolitik*, Brezhnev may have looked forward to something on the lines of Rapallo, although he was probably too much of a realist to expect it. In his talks with Brandt in 1970 he merely urged West Germany to follow de Gaulle's example and become "more independent" in its foreign policy. He wanted it to take a position in the world that corresponded to its economic and technical weight, but he was careful to add that Moscow was not trying to improve its relations with Bonn at the expense of Bonn's relations with the United States.[23]

West German right-wingers were certainly suspicious of Brandt's policy, as was Kissinger, who successfully managed to link *Ostpolitik* with Soviet–American issues. "We were determined to spare no effort to mute the latent incompatibility between Germany's national aims and its Atlantic and European ties," he wrote in his memoirs.[24] "Ostpolitik was embedded in a matrix of negotiations . . . that set limits beyond which it could not go without an allied consensus."[25] When Brandt was replaced by Helmut Schmidt in 1974, the Russians had to modify any lingering hopes of persuading Bonn to move away from the Common Market and NATO. Schmidt's views were tied more firmly to the Atlantic Alliance.

The Kremlin increasingly saw Bonn's main value as an advocate of détente within the Western camp, a kind of sheet anchor preventing the West from drifting back into the reactionary thinking of the Cold War and a policy of sanctions and confrontations with the Soviet Union. Schmidt seemed to accept the role, as first the Carter administration and then Reagan adopted a harder line with Moscow. He referred to himself as an "interpreter" of Soviet views to Washington and vice versa. It was a tricky line for Moscow to foster because it knew that if West Germany became too outspoken, it would lose its influence in Washington. The Americans might listen to a critical friend like Schmidt, but they would ignore a maverick or an irritating rival like de Gaulle.

As long as Schmidt was in power, the Russians could be reasonably satisfied with their relations with Bonn. After the downturn in détente in the late 1970s and Giscard's defeat in 1981, they had no other partner to turn to. Mitterrand was uninterested in developing a special relationship with Bonn. The Thatcher government in Britain largely echoed the Reagan line. Whereas Harold Wilson and to a lesser extent James Callaghan had occasionally shown interest in playing a big-power role, harking back to the days of Harold Macmillan in the early 1960s, who had seen himself as an "honest broker" between East and West, Margaret Thatcher spurned any dialogue with Moscow. Schmidt was the only honest broker the Kremlin had. When his government was replaced by Helmut Kohl's in October 1982, Moscow was naturally uneasy. The Kremlin had become used to the SPD after thirteen years of rule.

If Moscow has been ambivalent about whether West Germany or the United States poses the greater long-term danger, it has been consistent in trying to block Western European integration. For years it refused to have any dealings with the European Commission in Brussels, hoping that the Common Market would fall apart in dissension. When the United States overcame its fear of the economic competition a united Western Europe would provide, and saw its main value as strengthening the region's anti-Soviet cohesion, Moscow was concerned for the same reason. The next step in Western European cohesion was likely to be military, it feared. Stalin had tried to stop the formation of the European Defense Community in the early 1950s. (The EDC was blocked by the French, and then suppressed by NATO.) Khrushchev hoped to block Kennedy's idea of a multilateral nuclear force manned by the British, French, and Germans. (It too was blocked by the French.) The Soviet concerns were always the same—that West Germany would gain an enhanced military role, and that Western Europe would become a powerful military entity in its own right in addition to the Americans. Moscow thought this could be forestalled if Western Europe did not unite economically and politically.

NATO's decision in December 1979 to install medium-range American Pershing missiles in West Germany and cruise missiles there and in other Western European nations was a bitter blow to Moscow. The strategic implications of having nuclear missiles on German soil that could strike the Soviet Union were profoundly disturbing. Equally worrisome was the political demonstration that in spite of European concern over Washington's abandonment of détente, the main Western European governments were uniting behind a new military strategy. When the Western peace movement launched a strong campaign against the missiles, the Russians obviously welcomed the new surge of opinion against NATO's move, but they acted clumsily in response. Throughout 1981 when the European peace demonstrations were at their height, the

Kremlin continued to deploy its new mobile SS–20 missiles, which were also a focus of the peace marchers' concern, because they were targeted on Western Europe. If it had announced a moratorium at that time, it could have done much to persuade the peace movement that the Soviet Union wanted to halt the arms race. It was not until March 1982 after deploying some 300 SS–20s that Brezhnev declared a unilateral halt. The Kremlin's delay might have been caused by the Russian preoccupation with the turmoil in Poland and its implications for the Soviet Union's sense of security. More likely, it was another example of the Kremlin's preference for overinsuring itself militarily rather than relying on political measures in the West. However much it may have been pleased by the anti-NATO mood in the West, the Kremlin considered it too tenuous a development to have much effect on the NATO missile decision. Moscow decided to build up its SS–20s regardless.

On two other European issues, however, Moscow did show signs of restraint, partly in order not to upset détente and turn Western European opinion against it. One was its cautious handling of the Polish crisis throughout 1980 and 1981. The Russians watched with growing alarm as the independent trade union movement, Solidarity, gained in strength. They consulted frequently with the Polish party leadership, but ultimately allowed the Polish comrades to find a way of resisting Solidarity on their own. The other area of restraint was Yugoslavia. As Tito lay dying, the repetitive theme of Western speculation was that the Russians would exploit the country's weakness as soon as he was gone. In the event, Moscow did nothing, and three years after Tito's death Yugoslavia was back in obscurity, once excitement about Soviet policy had waned. Hardly anyone in the West could name even one of Tito's successors.

Some decision makers in the West have convinced themselves that the "highest objective of Soviet strategy is to separate Western Europe from the United States."[26] They see it as being done not necessarily by military invasion. Reagan's then chief arms control advisor, Eugene Rostow, argued in 1981 that "the preferred means to achieve this end is not a massed tank attack, but a form of classical Chinese warfare in which victory is achieved without fighting, after the victim's generals draw the reasonable inferences from the superior deployments of the victor. The scenario would follow these lines: the subliminal radiations of the Soviet intermediate-range nuclear arsenal would induce panic in Europe while the growing long-range arsenal would paralyze any possibility of an American strategic response. Presto and checkmate. The Japanese, Chinese, and many other nations would follow suit."[27]

This lurid image, a combination of two favorite code words, "appeasement" and "nuclear blackmail," is also sometimes labeled "Finlandization." Unless Western Europe maintains a strong military defense against the Soviet Union, it is argued, the region will slide into a form of neutralism. Those who use this argument take it for granted that neutralism is a bad thing. Taking their assumptions a stage farther, many expect that Western Europe's "neutralism" would in practice be pro-Soviet. Finland's position is put forward as the sinister model for this unhappy state of affairs.

In Finland itself the label is angrily resented as an inaccurate parody of the country's situation. Finland's neutrality rests on the Treaty of Friendship, Co-operation and Mutual Assistance signed with the Soviet Union in 1948 (since renewed until 1990). Article I states that if either Finland or the Soviet Union is attacked through Finnish territory by Germany or a German ally, "Finland will, true to its obligations as an independent state, fight to repel the attack . . . within the frontiers of Finland . . . and if necessary with the assistance of, or jointly with, the Soviet Union." This assistance can only be given "subject to mutual agreement." Article II requires the parties to confer if there appears to be a threat of attack. The other six articles pledge that neither side will join an alliance directed against the other, will not interfere in each other's internal affairs, will work to improve economic and cultural relations, and so on.

Only once since the treaty was signed has the Soviet Union ever sought to activate it. In 1961 Khrushchev called for consultations under Article II during the East–West tension that arose after the building of the Berlin wall. Finland's President Kekkonen cut short his holiday and persuaded the Soviet leader that consultations were unnecessary. After Brezhnev took over, the Kremlin made no such move again. Its influence on Finland's internal politics has been minimal, and its wishes, when they have been expressed, have been made known with subtlety—but little effect. (One might contrast the public American "warnings" against the inclusion of Communists in government in Italy and France issued by the Ford administration or, in the case of a neutral nation, the American ostracism of Sweden's Olof Palme after he criticized the Vietnam War.) Shortly before the Finnish Center party met to nominate a successor to Kekkonen in November 1981, *Pravda* obliquely backed one of the two contenders. The party nominated the other one. At the same time the small pro-Moscow wing of the predominantly Euro-Communist Finnish People's Democratic League (as the Communist party is known) was attacking the Center party's main opponents, the Social Democrats, and their leader, Mauno Koivisto. When it later became clear that Koivisto would win the presidential election, Moscow changed its line. Five days before the vote, Brezhnev sent a telegram to Koivisto, expressing satisfaction at his willingness to develop Soviet–Finnish relations.

The main proof of Finland's independence is that it remains a multiparty capitalist democracy. Although it does a considerable trade with its Soviet neighbor, as geography and common sense dictate, its total trade with COMECON is less than with the Common Market. Its stand on foreign policy shows genuine nonalignment. Finland called for the withdrawal of Soviet troops from Czechoslovakia in 1968 and from Afghanistan in 1980, and criticized American policy in Central America. The only sign of deference to Soviet sensitivity has been some government pressure on the media not to criticize domestic Soviet affairs, particularly the treatment of dissidents. Against this background, the concept of "Finlandization" is an empty myth. One might ask why its advocates select Finland and do not talk about "Austrianization" as a possible model for Western European nonalignment. Austria's neutrality, also expressed in a treaty signed by the Soviet Union, does not even have the consultation clauses of the Soviet–Finnish document, let alone the notion of mutually agreed joint defense in the case of a German attack. Nor do the Austrian media show any reluctance to criticize internal Soviet affairs.

There is no reason to think that Western Europe or West Germany (better placed than Finland by virtue of geography and relative economic and political power vis-à-vis Moscow) would not choose Austria's neutrality rather than Finland's, if it ever decided to be nonaligned. The Soviet Union would clearly welcome this rather than see West Germany remain in NATO or become a major nuclear power. But Western European nonalignment, if it ever comes, is not likely to be a result of "panic," as Rostow imagines, but of a rational calculation of self-interest, democratically expressed. It is hard to see why its foreign policy would be pro-Soviet, when that of Austria is not.

Conclusion

The three options usually assumed to be the Kremlin's objectives for Western Europe—invasion, a peaceful transition to socialism, and nonalignment—can be ruled out for the present. From the Kremlin's point of view, a military invasion of Western Europe is neither desired nor likely. A Communist Western Europe is unlikely and hardly a desirable goal. Only the option of an independent, disunited, and nonnuclear Western Europe, no longer allied with the United States, offers Moscow definite benefits. But the chances of its happening are too remote for it to be the top priority of Soviet strategy.

Moscow's goals are short-term and humdrum. The major one is to preserve the remnants of détente, preferably with the United States, but if necessary with Western Europe alone. In this way the Kremlin can reduce some of its anxiety over Eastern Europe and benefit from continuing trade and technology deals with the capitalist West. An economically depressed Western Europe with a high rate of inflation may take the gilt off the capitalist system, but is of less value to Moscow, which wants a healthy business partner. In the immediate future Moscow is not expecting positive developments in Western Europe. Its chief hope is that things will not become worse. It does not want Western trade sanctions to be tightened, or American medium-range missiles installed. Until the late 1970s Western Europe had been the most successful region for Brezhnev's foreign policy. By the early 1980s the mood had changed. Here, as elsewhere in the world, Moscow had little opportunity to think of advance. Its efforts were aimed at preventing retreat.

6

EASTERN EUROPE: UNUSUAL EMPIRE

I took the train of socialism and left at the station of independence.

Poland's Marshal Jozef Pilsudski[1]

As Poland's sixteen-month-long experiment with independent trade unions moved toward its climax in 1981, television viewers in the Soviet Union were suddenly treated to a new phenomenon. Night after night the evening news program showed rows of somber-looking Soviet workers at factory meetings, listening gravely to the latest bad tidings from Poland. The meetings ended, according to the television news reader, with the adoption of open letters to the workers of Poland. The letters were published in the following morning's Soviet papers over a period of several days in September 1981. They invariably had the same tone, a mixture of sorrow, alarm, indignation, and puzzlement. How could the Polish working class allow the crisis to continue? "Dear comrades," said a letter from the workers' collective at the Metallurgical Combine in Magneto-gorsk, "The whole Soviet people is watching events in your country with great concern and anxiety. The enemies of socialism are raising their heads more and more clearly. . . . We find it amazing and strange that Polish workers, the vanguard of the Polish people, can tolerate all this mischief at the expense of your country's destiny and be so slow to react."

Then it went on in a refrain that appeared in every other similar letter: "Poland's independence was won by the sacrifice of the lives of 600,000 Soviet

citizens and the best sons of Poland. The economy of the People's Republic of
Poland was created and is developing thanks to the Soviet Union's help. Many of
our specialists took part in the construction and management of scores of Polish
metal works. . . ."[2]

It would be naive to suggest that these factory meetings were spontaneous
affairs. They ended abruptly about a week after they first appeared on television, and clearly had a political purpose, partly to put more pressure on the Poles
and partly to unite Soviet public opinion behind the Kremlin's thinking. But it
would be equally naive to imagine that they did not reflect the feelings of Soviet
citizens. No foreigner who was in the Soviet Union during the Polish crisis found
much sympathy with Solidarity. Popular attitudes appeared to correspond to
those expressed in the open letters. Russians could not understand Poland's
apparent chaos or the seemingly endless strikes that could only lead to wanton
disaster in an economy that, most Russians were sure, provided a higher
standard of living than they themselves enjoyed. What was this Polish madness?

Mixed in with it was anger that the Poles were throwing away the socialist
gains that the Soviet Union had helped them establish after the Second World
War. This last emotion, it is fair to assume, was the predominant one of the
Kremlin. For the leadership, the issue of safeguarding the Soviet Union's
geopolitical postwar gains was the overriding factor. Power had been won, and
power had to be maintained. Yet like ordinary Soviet citizens, Brezhnev and his
colleagues probably also felt angry and perplexed over apparent Polish ingrati-
tude. Of course we will have to wait awhile for an insider's account of the
Kremlin's exact thinking during the various stages of the Polish crisis. But it is
worth going back to the Czechoslovak crisis of 1968, the first Eastern European
upheaval during the Brezhnev era. Although the issues in Poland were different
from those of the "Prague Spring," the Kremlin's emphasis on security had not
changed in the thirteen years between them.

One of the Czech participants in the tense talks in Moscow that followed the
Soviet invasion was Zdenek Mlynar. Now an exile in the West, he has described
the speech that Brezhnev gave to the virtually captive Czechs shortly before they
were asked to sign the protocol legalizing the presence of Soviet troops.
Brezhnev did not waste time, Mlynar recalls, on the "counter-revolutionary
forces" or the "interests of socialism," but directly blamed the Czechoslovak
party leader, Alexander Dubček, for conducting domestic policies without
seeking Brezhnev's prior approval.[3] "I believed in you and I stood up for you
against others. Our Sasha is a good comrade, I said. And you disappointed us so
terribly." As the pace of the Czechoslovak reform movement developed,
Moscow came to believe the Dubček leadership could not be depended on to
protect matters of the utmost importance to the Soviet Union—the results of the
Second World War. Mlynar goes on: "Brezhnev spoke at length about the
sacrifices of the Soviet Union in the Second World War: the soldiers fallen in
battle, the civilians slaughtered, the enormous material losses, the hardships

suffered by the Soviet people. At such a cost the Soviet Union had gained security, and the guarantee of that security was the postwar division of Europe and, specifically, the fact that Czechoslovakia was linked with the Soviet Union 'forever.' According to Brezhnev this was a logical and justifiable result of the fact that thousands of Soviet soldiers sacrificed their lives for Czechoslovak freedom as well, and Czechs and Slovaks should therefore honor their graves, not defile them. Our Western borders were not only our own borders but the common borders of the 'socialist camp.' The Soviet Politburo had no right to allow the results of that war to be jeopardized for it had no right to dishonor the sacrifices of the Soviet people. . . .

"Brezhnev pretended to be almost astonished; it was so simple, how could we fail to understand? Words like 'sovereignty' and 'national independence' did not come up in his speech at all, nor did any of the other clichés that officially justify 'the mutual interests of the socialist countries.' There was only one simple idea behind everything he said: during the war our soldiers fought their way to the Elbe, and that is where our real Western borders are today." Mlynar's revealing description provides the most graphic proof that Moscow's primary interest in Eastern Europe since the war has always been security.

Eastern Europe straddles what has for centuries been the historic invasion route for foreign armies attacking Russia. None was bloodier or more devastating than the Nazi invasion. It was obvious that after the war the Russians would want to create, if they could, a series of buffer states in Central Europe to shield themselves against the more advanced industrial nations who had so often sent their armies east. While liberating Eastern Europe from the Nazi yoke, the Russians imposed their own system. Heinrich Mann, the brother of the great anti-Nazi writer Thomas Mann, called the Soviet occupation zone of Germany "free but conquered."[4] Bulgaria, Hungary, and Rumania had been part of the Nazi axis. There was a sense in which the Russians were also their conquerors. Even victims of Nazi aggression suffered. The Soviet Union incorporated parts of Poland and Czechoslovakia, as well as of once-hostile Rumania. Only in the case of Poland was new territory (taken from Germany) added as partial compensation for what it had already lost to Russia at the beginning of the war when Stalin occupied the eastern parts of Poland in agreement with Hitler. After the war Stalin enforced in Poland and the rest of Eastern Europe a revolution that dispossessed the middle class and any other forces considered hostile to socialism, regardless of their wartime role. For the Russians to expect that gratitude would be the dominant and lasting emotion in Eastern Europe was extraordinarily shortsighted. Yet gratitude is what they claimed to expect as late as 1981.

It has become normal in much Western parlance to talk of a "Soviet empire." At one of his first cabinet meetings, President Reagan reportedly ordered that reference to the Soviet empire should be the normal usage.[5] The phrase conceals more than it reveals, since the Soviet empire, if it is one, is of a unique type. No part of the world in which the Soviet Union has influence comes closer to being a collection of colonies than Eastern Europe, yet the differences between it and the former empires of the Western European powers are huge. With the exception of the three Baltic states and Bessarabia, which Moscow annexed, the states of Eastern Europe are politically sovereign. This is not just a semantic nicety. However much control Moscow exerts in practice, in law the states of Eastern Europe are independent—a fact that has always made every Soviet intervention embarrassing for Moscow and has required all kinds of elaborate justifications that other imperial powers could ignore. Second, there has never been any significant Russian settlement in Eastern Europe. Moscow has treated the various Eastern European states as military outposts with Soviet garrisons, security police, and a Soviet embassy, but no large or visible presence of administrators ensconced in every segment of the economy and society. In spite of the geographical contiguity of Eastern Europe, the Soviet Union remains remarkably cut off. The traveler who crosses by rail from the Soviet Union to Poland encounters barbed wire and watchtowers on the Soviet side of the frontier; it is as though Poland was already "the West," an alien and threatening culture against which Russia feels it must defend itself.

And in a sense Poland is. For the third and perhaps most important difference between Eastern Europe and the other recent European empires is the reversal of the normal wealth gap. If Moscow is the metropolis and the Eastern European countries the colonies, then this is a unique case where the colonies are richer. The point is important in human terms, for it explains why the Soviet Union has tried to restrict travel by Eastern Europeans to the Soviet Union and by Soviet citizens to Eastern Europe. If too many Russians discovered for themselves that Eastern Europeans live at a significantly higher standard than they do, grumbling and outright dissent on economic grounds might well increase in the Soviet Union. For Eastern Europeans to see how poor their Russian neighbors are would only increase the sense of cultural superiority that most Eastern Europeans already have. There are any number of accounts by Eastern European Communists of their shock and disillusionment when they first visited the Soviet Union, the Mecca of their ideological dreams. They had to convince themselves that its underdevelopment was the result of inherited backwardness, capitalist encirclement, and war, rather than an inherent effect of Soviet-style socialism itself. For less committed Eastern Europeans, direct experience of Soviet conditions might be less shocking, but it could reinforce their feeling of psychological distance from the country that dominates their lives.

Nevertheless, in spite of the relatively limited amount of travel between the Soviet Union and Eastern Europe, by comparison with the amount of travel by Western Europeans and Americans to each others' countries, the general picture of an economically backward Soviet Union and a more advanced Eastern Europe is understood by most people. It tends to feed prejudices and resentment on both sides. Each side believes it is subsidizing the other and being forced to delay its own development. Who is right? Surprisingly, perhaps, the Russians—at least in recent years—have the better case. Estimates by several Western economists suggest that since the early 1970s, if not earlier, Moscow has been paying more than it has earned from Eastern Europe. Paul Marer argues that Moscow began to incur a net cost in the mid-1960s.[6]

In the immediate postwar period the Soviet Union behaved in Eastern Europe like a classic asset-stripper. It took reparations, extracted raw materials (uranium from Czechoslovakia and Hungary, coal from Poland) at low prices, and dismantled factories. The largest burden, about seven-eighths, was shouldered by East Germany, but Rumania, Hungary, and Poland all suffered. After Stalin's death, what Marer calls "uncompensated resource transfers" ceased. With Eastern Europe's increasing industrialization, the Soviet Union became the region's major supplier of primary products and principal net importer of machinery, consumer goods, and other manufactures. As the terms of trade between these items altered, Moscow began to pay more for its imports than it was getting for its exports. The disadvantages of this trade with Eastern Europe becomes clearer if one calculates the potential benefits that Moscow could have incurred either by being more self-sufficient or by trading with the West. Another Western economist, C. H. McMillan, argues that the consumer goods that Moscow imports from Eastern Europe could have been produced at less cost in the Soviet Union than it takes to pay for them by the exporting of underpriced raw materials.[7] Alternatively, the Soviet Union could exchange its energy exports in the West for higher quality imported goods.

Moscow began to try to rectify the balance in the early 1970s, first by a series of ad hoc measures. It encouraged Eastern European countries to invest in developing new energy and raw material sources in the Soviet Union on the grounds that they would benefit from the eventual supply. It began to demand hard currency payments for goods not specified in existing agreements, and insisted that the goods it bought from Eastern Europe should be of a higher quality—in other words, that Eastern Europe stop treating the Soviet market as a dumping ground for shoddy goods it could not expect to sell in the West.

After the quadrupling of the world price for oil in 1974, the Russians made a major long-term revision in COMECON (Council for Mutual Economic Assistance) prices. Instead of maintaining fixed prices for raw materials over several years, each year's prices came to be based on the average world price for the previous five years. Although this still allowed Eastern Europe to import Soviet energy at prices lower than those of the world market, it significantly increased Moscow's revenues and improved the terms of its COMECON trade. Some idea of the benefit that Eastern Europe gained from the old price system can be seen in the following figures. In 1974 Moscow exported approximately 60 million tons of crude oil and petroleum products to Eastern Europe at the price agreed in 1970—approximately $16 to $20 per ton, depending on the grade—for a total revenue of $1 billion to $1.2 billion. In the same year it sold approximately 40 million tons of oil in the West at the world price of $70 a ton for a total revenue of about $2.8 billion. Yet even with the adjustment of COMECON prices, the Soviet Union appears to be spending more on Eastern Europe than it earns.

It is worth stressing the region's net economic cost to Moscow. It illustrates that the Soviet relationship is neither colonial in the classic nineteenth-century sense of the word nor neocolonial in the twentieth-century pattern of the West's relationship with the Third World. The more accurate picture is one of military domination and political hegemony. The fact that the Soviet Union is prepared to tolerate the economic price of maintaining Eastern Europe only emphasizes how high a value it puts on the other advantages that this region provides.

The military benefits are primary and can be simply stated. Eastern Europe gives Russia a massive buffer zone to the West by moving the de facto security border of the Soviet Union right up to the Elbe. Control of the region is denied to any other great power, in particular to Germany, which has been the most immediate enemy of the Soviet Union in this century. The creation of a Communist East Germany divided Germany and lessened the potential threat still more. Politically, Eastern Europe gives Moscow several benefits, first as a world power, and second as the missionary leader of an ideological community. Because of its control of Eastern Europe, the Soviet Union can stand with the United States as one of the only two alliance leaders in the world. It also gains status as the head of a major political system. Eastern Europe symbolizes the extension of Soviet-style socialism beyond the borders of the Soviet Union, offering the prospect that other states may one day join the system. If before the war Stalin's strategy was to build "socialism in one country," his postwar strategy, based on the secure control of a buffer zone in Eastern Europe, was to build "socialism in one region." Eastern Europe provided the first opportunity to start to make the Soviet system universal.

Under Stalin, Moscow's concern with security far exceeded the priority given to ideology. The extension of one-party Communist rule over each of the Eastern European states was a relatively slow process in the first two years after the war. It accelerated after East–West tensions mounted with the announcement of the Truman Doctrine in 1947 and after Tito's break with Moscow in the following year. The forced collectivization of agriculture on the Soviet model did not get going until the 1950s and even by the time of Stalin's death in 1953 it was still patchy. By the end of 1953, collectives covered 8 percent of the land in Poland, 25 percent in Hungary, and 40 percent in Czechoslovakia. In the Soviet zone of Germany, Stalin followed a two-track policy—imposing a Communist revolution but also offering to withdraw Soviet troops in return for a similar Western withdrawal and the creation of a united but demilitarized Germany. When his successors pulled Soviet troops out of Austria in 1955 in favor of neutrality, they gave a reminder that Moscow had been and still was prepared to consider a similar solution for Germany.

Throughout Eastern Europe Stalin was preoccupied by fear of nationalism, particularly among the Communist elites themselves. In each country he was determined to exert control over the army and the party. Each state was forced to conclude a bilateral defense treaty with the Soviet Union. The army command was thoroughly purged, and officer commissions were given to party members who had trained in the Soviet Union. In Poland and Hungary, Soviet officers even occupied the senior posts in armies that were national only in name; they functioned as little more than branches of the Red Army. Within the Communist parties, Stalin suspected anyone who had not spent the war years in the Soviet Union. After the split with Yugoslavia, several people were executed and hundreds more were purged on suspicion of being "Titoist agents" or "national deviationists."

Stalin's death brought an end to the era of terror and a tentative relaxation of Moscow's central control. The founding of the Warsaw Pact in 1955, although primarily a reaction to West Germany's incorporation into NATO, provided the semblance of a multilateral political organization instead of direct Soviet hegemony. With the recall of the senior Soviet officers, Eastern Europe's armed forces were "renationalized" under local leadership. Khrushchev's reconciliation with Tito suggested that Moscow would tolerate "national Communism," at least in certain circumstances. His denunciation of Stalin at the Twentieth Party Congress in February 1956, and the rehabilitation of thousands of his victims, aroused the hopes of intellectuals that a new and more liberal chapter was opening. But the upheavals in Hungary and Poland later that year, and Moscow's contradictory reaction, posed what was to be a recurring factor for doubt in Eastern Europe right up to the present day.

The Kremlin showed that it would set limits to political reforms, up to and including the use of force, if it felt it had to stop them. The problem was that there was no clear definition of where the limits lay. In Hungary, when popular demands for a more pluralistic system led to an upsurge of nationalism and calls for Hungary's withdrawal from the Warsaw Pact, the Russians moved in with force. In Poland the Russians were poised to do likewise but were persuaded to hold off, thanks to assurances from the reformist new party leader, Wladyslaw Gomulka, that Poland would remain loyal to the Soviet connection and that the leading role of the party would not be weakened.

The confusion left by Moscow's dual reaction to the 1956 events was not removed by Khrushchev's subsequent policy. He concluded agreements regulating the status of Soviet forces in East Germany, Hungary, and Poland and promising that they would not interfere in internal affairs. He agreed to a Rumanian demand to withdraw Soviet troops in early 1958. In Czechoslovakia there were no Soviet troops at all.

But the main thrust of Khrushchev's policy after 1956 was in the economic field. Severe problems had been caused by the forced collectivization of agriculture, begun in the later years of Stalin and continued after his death, and by an excessive investment in heavy industry at the expense of consumer goods.

Khrushchev promoted a loosening of the Stalinist command economy under which every decision had been centrally planned. Lower level units, even down to factories themselves, were to have some right to set prices and decide on investments. At the same time he tried to find a more rational division of labor within COMECON. Established by Stalin, COMECON had remained essentially a paper organization until 1961, when Khrushchev proposed that it become a general body for joint international planning and specialization. This was in many ways a courageous venture. Khrushchev had already run into resistance the previous year when he tried to persuade Albania to give up its Stalinist ambitions to build its own heavy industry and concentrate on agriculture instead. The Albanian leader, Enver Hoxha, denounced Khrushchev publicly at a meeting of eighty-one Communist and workers' parties in Moscow in astonishingly virulent terms. In anger Khrushchev withdrew all Soviet technicians from Albania, and the split between the two countries was never healed. In spite of this damaging dispute, which lost Moscow the use of a valuable submarine base on Albania's Adriatic coast, Khrushchev repeated his arguments for a shift away from heavy industry toward agriculture, this time with Rumania. The result, though couched in more moderate terms by the Rumanians, was almost the same. Rumania remained within the Warsaw Pact but embarked on a new and more assertive course in foreign policy.

By the time Khrushchev was ousted, the Kremlin appeared to have accepted that the Eastern European parties must try to win legitimacy for themselves on the basis of economic progress and some concessions to local nationalism. Many criticisms were made of Khrushchev's period in office, but his policies in Eastern Europe were not among them. Brezhnev and his colleagues continued the broad lines laid down by Khrushchev. If there were any lessons for Eastern Europe to be drawn from his conduct of affairs, they were that a limited amount of ideological experimentation would be tolerated by the Kremlin, provided that certain conditions were met. First, there must be no threat to a country's membership in the Warsaw Pact. Second, the Communist party must retain its leading role. Any concessions to pluralism must not affect the Communist party's ability to stay in control of the political process. Third, the local leadership must express due deference to the Soviet Union and take its advice. A fourth factor was geography. Countries like East Germany, Czechoslovakia, and Hungary, which were on the edge of Moscow's buffer zone in Central Europe and therefore liable, in Moscow's view, to Western attack, would be more closely watched than those like Poland and Rumania which were not in the front line. Rumania was able to develop some autonomy in foreign policy, partly because its internal policies remained under tight democratic centralism, but also because it had no border with the West.

Much also depended on the posture of the Western powers, and the degree of suspicion which the Kremlin had about the West's intentions. For most of Khrushchev's period in office the "Western dimension" played a minor role.

Although there was much bellicose noise from Washington about "liberating" Eastern Europe and "rolling back communism"—which helped to heighten Soviet anxiety during the run-up to the crisis of 1956—the West's passivity when the Hungarian uprising occurred showed that the mood in Western capitals was realistic. It was accepted, albeit reluctantly, that Eastern Europe was in the Soviet sphere of influence.

By the mid-1960s the mood had shifted. Western politicians were again interested in seeing Eastern Europe change. For the United States the area remained "a target in search of a policy," as one Western analyst put it.[8] But instead of expecting to see Communist rule in Eastern Europe collapse suddenly, the hope was that the region could gradually be weaned away from Moscow's control. Like the Russians, Western strategists were also putting security above ideology. It was no longer a question of overthrowing communism, but rather of encouraging the local Communist regimes to distance themselves from Moscow, in the way that Yugoslavia and, more recently, Rumania had done. Some called it "bridge-building." Others like Zbigniew Brzezinski, who was later to become President Carter's national security advisor, called it "peaceful engagement." Willy Brandt, who became West German foreign minister in the mid-1960s, called it "change through rapprochement."

The new strategy seemed to make more political sense. It was a slow evolutionary process, which could feed on the clear longing among most Eastern Europeans for closer contact with the West. It also made economic sense. The Eastern European economies were beginning to experience a slowdown in their growth rates. Their planners were arguing that now that the great postwar wave of migration from the countryside to the cities was almost over, future growth would have to be more capital-intensive. By importing advanced Western technology they could accelerate the process. In the West politicians and businessmen were becoming aware of the attractions of the Eastern European market. Pressures mounted for a relaxation of the restrictions that had been imposed on the exports of many industrial goods to Eastern Europe during the Cold War under what was a strategy of offensive economic warfare against the Soviet Union and its allies. Between 1960 and 1968 Eastern Europe's imports from the Common Market countries almost tripled from $935 million to $2,434 million. Much of the trade was financed by credits from the Western trading partners.

Although France under de Gaulle was the first country to develop the new strategy, West Germany's *Ostpolitik* made a greater impact. It was, in fact, the major factor that differentiated the Brezhnev era from earlier Soviet foreign policy in Eastern Europe. Twenty years after the end of the Second World War the German problem was still the major piece of unfinished business on the European agenda. To a degree that very few Westerners appreciated, Germany was still seen in Moscow as a bigger threat than the United States to the Soviet Union's western flank. Germany, after all, was a permanent feature of Europe and would always be there, even if one day the Americans withdrew. Since the beginning of the century Germany and Russia had had a love–hate relationship. On the eve of the First World War, almost half Russia's imports came from Germany. During the depression German exporters who could find no markets in the West turned eagerly to Moscow and helped to strengthen the fledgling Soviet Union. But there were also two wars, the second of which cost twenty million Soviet lives. Eastern Europe was the ground on which Russia and Germany seemed fated to compete.

The endless crises over Berlin under Stalin and Khrushchev were symbols of Moscow's determination to keep Germany weak. Both leaders would have preferred a neutral Germany. What they feared was a rearmed and united Germany. With the building of the Berlin wall in 1961, Moscow signaled the final rejection of its hopes of a neutral Germany and its determination to ensure the permanence of the country's division. Even after that, its fear of Germany remained. When the West talked in the early 1960s of a multilateral nuclear force in French, German, and British hands, the Russians made it clear that they thought this was a greater danger than American nuclear weapons on West German soil. Better an American than a German finger on the nuclear button.

The notion of a threat from West Germany was not without value in Eastern Europe. It helped to bond the region together and legitimize Soviet control through the Warsaw Pact. In East Germany it allowed Walter Ulbricht to justify his harsh internal policies. In Poland the regime used the population's strong anti-German feelings as a channel for diverting their almost equally strong anti-Russian feelings. It was more prudent to focus Polish nationalism in an anti-German direction than allow it to turn against the Soviet Union.

Under Khrushchev the German issue, at least in its impact on Eastern Europe, was stable. Contact between West Germany and the region was sparse. West Germany had no diplomatic relations with any of the Eastern European states. For even though, much to Ulbricht's annoyance, Moscow had exchanged ambassadors with West Germany in 1955, the Russians made it clear that their allies would not be allowed to follow suit. If the West was trying to keep East Germany isolated, the East would do the same with West Germany.

In December 1966 a grand coalition of the Christian Democrats and Social Democrats came to power in West Germany and promptly stirred up the waters. The new government's offer to open diplomatic relations with Eastern Europe and expand West German trade links revealed major splits in the Eastern European facade. Rumania accepted with alacrity. Hungary, Bulgaria, and even Czechoslovakia were favorably inclined. East Germany and Poland were opposed. Ulbricht was worried about being bypassed. Gomulka wanted to insist that West Germany give up its claims to prewar German territory and recognize the Oder–Neisse line as Poland's western frontier. As for the Russians, they hesitated. What were they to make of this German diplomatic offensive toward Eastern Europe, backed by the offer of hard currency and long-term capital investment to countries that responded sympathetically? Would this not reduce Eastern Europe's dependence on Moscow, and create new forms of contact between East and West that could slip out of Moscow's control?

Swayed by Ulbricht and Gomulka and their own natural caution, the Russians came down against the initial West German overtures and forbade their allies (with the exception of Rumania, over which they had virtually lost control) to open diplomatic relations with Bonn. But time would show that they were trying to stem an unstoppable tide. As Philip Windsor has argued, "a nexus had been established between Germany, détente, and the individual development of Eastern European society."[9] As détente itself developed, and contacts between Washington and Moscow began to supersede West Germany's smaller scale *Ostpolitik*, Eastern Europe would increasingly become subject to the ebb and flow of East–West relations as a whole. The first victim of this new nexus was Czechoslovakia. Thirteen years later it would be Poland.

The Czech crisis took the Soviet Union unawares. Brezhnev himself had flown to Prague in December 1967 at the request of Antonin Novotny, the rigidly conservative party secretary who had led the country since just after Stalin's death. Unlike any other Eastern European leader, Novotny held the two jobs of party secretary and head of state, a monopoly of power that symbolized the outdated authoritarianism of his regime in one of the most traditionally democratic countries in the region. Brezhnev was suspicious of Novotny, who had been known to express sorrow at Khrushchev's overthrow.[10] Although Novotny had invited Brezhnev to help him against rising opposition within the Czechoslovak leadership, Brezhnev washed his hands of the affair. He told the Czechs to sort it out themselves—*Eto vashe dyelo* (It's your business).[11]

Brezhnev's relaxed attitude at this stage suggests that Moscow felt it was time for the Czechoslovak leadership to modernize and saw no danger in it. But within two months of Novotny's replacement by Alexander Dubček, Soviet anxieties were evident. We have seen how Brezhnev justified the subsequent invasion by his fear that the Prague Spring would undermine Soviet security and weaken the common borders of the socialist camp.

That fear was already expressed by Brezhnev in March in a speech to a party conference in Moscow. The Soviet party leader had just returned from a meeting in Dresden with Dubček and the other Eastern European party leaders, where concern was expressed over the developments in Prague: the call for a modification of censorship and an increase in the role of Parliament; talk of a "socialist market economy" and greater inner-party democracy. Brezhnev saw all this as playing into the hands of the West, and perhaps as actually masterminded by the West. "An acute ideological struggle is now in progress. The front line of this struggle, its watershed so to speak, lies between socialism and capitalism. . . . Imperialism has attempted to weaken the ideological-political unity of the working people in the socialist countries. It banks mainly on nationalist and revisionist elements. To put it briefly, the ideological struggle in our time is the sharpest form of the class struggle. In it there can be no political indifference, passivity or neutrality with respect to the aims pursued by the enemy."[12]

Having laid out the dangers inherent in the situation, Brezhnev wanted to strengthen the determinaton of the party to resist them. Almost every previous crisis in Eastern Europe had been a crisis within the Communist party. The Prague Spring was no exception. In societies where one group had enjoyed a monopoly of power, it was natural that that group would have the monopoly of the problem and be seen as having the monopoly of the solution. In March 1968 Brezhnev still hoped that Czechoslovakia's Communists would block the dangerous trends themselves, provided they were aware of the weakness in their own ranks. "Anti-Soviet organizations created by the imperialists are looking for morally unstable, weak and politically unsure people. Enmeshed in their traps are persons prone to self-advertisement and ready to assert themselves as loudly as possible—not by working for the good of the country but by any politically dubious means. . . . These renegades cannot count on remaining unpunished."

Stripped of its epithets, Brezhnev's words were the language of power. Reinforcing the sense that security is the Soviet Union's ultimate concern, Brezhnev's analysis was basically nonideological and un-Marxist. There was no discussion of the balance of forces in Czechoslovak society or of the way in which twenty years of Soviet-type socialism had affected the interests of different classes. Brezhnev's concepts were based on personalities. It was a tangled muddle of conspiracy theories and talk of the need for leadership and discipline.

Locked into this style of thinking and brought up on a tradition of monolithic rather than graduated responses to crises, Brezhnev and his colleagues did not take long to decide that they might have to intervene by force. Exactly when Moscow worked out a contingency plan for an invasion is not known for certain. Zdenek Mlynar, who was closer to events than any other surviving informant who has gone on record, says that Brezhnev revealed that the option was prepared in May 1968. But the Soviet leader added, "At that time it seemed that it wouldn't be necessary."[13] The decision followed a meeting between Dubček and the Soviet leadership in Moscow on May 4, and separate visits to Czechoslovakia in the middle of May by Marshal Grechko, the Soviet minister of defense, and Alexei Kosygin, the prime minister, who each assessed for themselves the way the reform movement was spreading.

After May, the Kremlin had a two-track policy. It continued to put pressure on the Czechs to stop the reforms, but it was also preparing for invasion. Military maneuvers in June and July helped to test the ground. Ideological justifications for violating Czechoslovakia's sovereignty were prepared. A letter written to the Czechoslovak leadership by the party leaders of the Soviet Union, Bulgaria, East Germany, Hungary, and Poland at a summit meeting in mid-July in

Warsaw for the first time raised the arguments that Western commentators were to label "the Brezhnev doctrine" of limited sovereignty—"we cannot agree to have hostile forces push your country away from the road of socialism and create a danger of Czechoslovakia being severed from the socialist community. This is something more than your own concern. It is the common concern of all the Communist and workers' parties and states united by alliance, cooperation and friendship. It is the common concern of our countries, which have joined in the Warsaw Treaty to ensure independence and peace and security in Europe, and to set up an insurmountable barrier against the intrigues of the imperialist forces, against aggression and revanchism."[14]

The Warsaw letter was followed by three further efforts to order the Czechs to slow down the reforms. At Cierna, on the border between the two countries, nine members of the Soviet Politburo met their Czechoslovak counterparts at the end of July. The fact that almost the entire Soviet Politburo attended the meeting suggests that Brezhnev wanted to reach a collective decision, because the Politburo was divided. Two weeks later the leaders of the Warsaw Pact gathered in Bratislava for the last alliance-wide confrontration with the Czechs, and shortly thereafter Brezhnev sent a personal letter to Dubček, pleading for him to take decisive action against the reforms. But Dubček failed to act, at least to Moscow's satisfaction. In the early hours of August 21 the Warsaw Pact tanks moved in.

The timing of their move may have been linked to the imminence of special congresses to be held by the Slovak party on August 26 and the Czech party on September 9. The congresses would have confirmed the reforms and dropped from power most of their opponents. Draft statutes for the congresses published on August 10 provided for strictly limited tenure for party officials and secret elections for office, both of which were novelties in the Soviet political system.

There were several other developments that would have worried hard-liners in Moscow—the icy reception given to Ulbricht in Prague by contrast with the warm reception for Marshal Tito of Yugoslavia and Rumanian President Nicolas Ceausescu in August, the projected reforms that would have led to a "socialist market" economy, the appearance in Czechoslovakia of scores of West German businessmen, which could have suggested an eventual weakening of COM-ECON, and the reinvigoration of the normally subservient non-Communist political parties amid talk of a revived multiparty system.

If the forthcoming congresses were the final factor that helped to precipitate the Soviet move, the line-up of forces within the Soviet leadership can only be sketchily estimated. Three months after the invasion Brezhnev reportedly told Bohumil Simon, who led the Czechoslovak delegation to the anniversary of the October Revolution, that he had been against it. "If I hadn't voted in the Politburo for military intervention, what would have happened? You almost certainly would not be sitting here. And I probably wouldn't be sitting here either."[15] Mlynar argues that Brezhnev and his colleagues were pushed into the decision by the threat of a putsch in the Kremlin by anti-Brezhnev forces backed by Marshal Grechko and other Soviet marshals.[16] At all events the Soviet Politburo interrupted their vacations and returned to Moscow on or around August 17 or 18. Brezhnev, according to Mlynar, forestalled a putsch by rapidly taking the initiative and uniting with the "hawks" in favor of the invasion. Mlynar admits that he does not know who the hawks were. They may have included Alexander Shelepin, who was removed from the Politburo a few years later, and Pyotr Shelest, the party secretary of the Ukraine. They probably did not include Mikhail Suslov, who took a moderate line at Cierna because of his concern over the effect of invasion in advance of the international Communist conference which he was organizing.[17] But evidence is contradictory. The Czech prime minister, Oldrich Cernik, told a government meeting that Shelepin had reservations about the invasion.[18]

What can be calculated with some degree of certainty is the list of arguments for and against the invasion. The primary one was the Soviet fear that events in Czechoslovakia were drifting out of the party's control, and that Dubček and his colleagues had shown neither the will nor the determination to control them. There was no prospect that the situation would improve. On the contrary, the longer they were allowed to develop, the less reversible the reforms would be. Sooner or later the reforms would give Czechoslovakia a form of ideological independence that would encourage the extremists to call for the country's departure from the Warsaw Pact, and the establishment of, at best, an alternative model of socialism, at worst, even a Western kind of social democracy, as had happened in Hungary in 1956. Even Tito warned of this latter possibility. Visiting Prague in the second week of August, the Yugoslav leader warned Dubček not to weaken the influence of the party and underestimate the danger of "social democratism."[19]

The second Soviet argument in favor of invasion was concern about the Prague Spring's effect on the rest of Eastern Europe, and even in the Soviet Union itself. This was a kind of domino theory. Gomulka had been one of the earliest to warn the Kremlin of the dangers posed by Czechoslovakia. In March 1968 he was being challenged by Polish reformists. Ulbricht was also scared. In the Soviet Union, too, the Czech events were being followed eagerly by intellectuals, who saw in them the logical development of de-Stalinization which had been abruptly halted in the mid-1960s but which they hoped to see revived.

Finally there must have been a strong view in the Kremlin that Moscow could simply not afford another defection. In the last eight years they had lost Albania and China and seen Rumania become increasingly independent. To lose Czechoslovakia would be to risk the loss of the whole of Eastern Europe and the entire buffer zone they had managed to set up at the end of the war.

Fear was the common factor behind all these arguments. In 1956 Khrushchev intervened in Hungary when the crowds were already in the streets shouting anti-Soviet slogans and the government was announcing its intention to leave the

Warsaw Pact. By contrast, Czechoslovakia in August 1968 was calm. Most people were on holiday. There was no hard evidence for any of the dangers that Brezhnev and his colleagues claimed to see. That was the measure of the difference between their cautious style and Khrushchev's self-confidence. Where he took chances, they overinsured. Where optimism allowed him to wait, insecurity made them preempt.

The public justifications for the invasion were little different in 1956 and 1968. While the West has made much of the so-called Brezhnev doctrine, the same argument was used by Khrushchev over Hungary. On his first visit to the country since the invasion he said at Tatabanya in April 1958, "If provocateurs or enemies of the workers attempt a putsch or counterrevolution in any Socialist country, then I tell them here and now that all the Socialist countries and the armed forces of the Soviet Union will be ready at all times to give the provocateurs the answer they deserve."[20] Under Brezhnev the formula was made less conversational and given more theoretical backing, but the brutal message was the same. It was spelled out most clearly in a commentary in *Pravda* in September 1968. "In connection with the events in Czechoslovakia the question of the relationship and interconnection between the socialist countries' national interests and their international obligations has assumed particular urgency and sharpness. . . . It is impossible to ignore the allegations being heard in some places that the actions of the five socialist countries contradict the Marxist–Leninist principle of sovereignty and the right of nations to self-determination. Such arguments are untenable primarily because they are based on an abstract, non-class approach to the question of sovereignty and the right of nations to self-determination.

"There is no doubt that the peoples of the socialist countries and the Communist parties have and must have freedom to determine their country's path of development. However, any decision of theirs must damage neither socialism in their own country nor the fundamental interests of other socialist countries nor the worldwide workers' movement which is waging a struggle for socialism. This means that every Communist party is responsible not only to its own people but also to all the socialist countries and to the entire Communist movement. . . .

"It should be stressed that even if a socialist country seeks to take an 'extra-block' position, it in fact retains its national independence thanks precisely to the power of the socialist commonwealth and primarily to its chief force, the Soviet Union, and the might of its armed forces. The weakening of any link in the world socialist system has a direct effect on all the socialist countries which cannot be indifferent to this. . . . The Soviet Union and other socialist states, in fulfilling their internationalist duty to the fraternal peoples of Czechoslovakia and defending their own socialist gains, had to act and did act in resolute opposition to the anti-socialist forces in Czechoslovakia."[21]

On the opposite side of the balance sheet the arguments against invasion were remarkably weak. The main one was its likely effect on the rest of the world's Communist parties. But of the parties in power who supported Moscow in the dispute with China, the only one who might complain was Cuba, and Moscow felt it had enough leverage in Havana to contain a major protest. The other parties, such as those in the West, were a long way from any prospect of power. Their views were of relatively little account.

Then there was the question of potential Czech resistance. The Hungarian uprising had cost hundreds of lives. Czechoslovakia was probably different. The Czechs had no traditional enmity for Russia, and little stomach for a fight. The Russians had the advantage of surprise and it would be better to act quickly before outright anti-Soviet nationalism took to the streets as had happened in Budapest. Finally came the West's reaction. What effect would the invasion have on détente, and the talks with the United States on reducing strategic arms, which were soon due to begin? The Russians probably calculated that the effect, if any, would be short-lived. The Americans were in an election year, and the country was torn apart over Vietnam. The chances of a strong response to an invasion of Czechoslovakia were small, and arms control talks could in any case hardly begin to make progress until after the election. Besides, it might be valuable to remind the West that Moscow would not tolerate any deviation in its Eastern European sphere of influence.

The Kremlin's calculations about the likely reaction in the West proved correct. Most Western politicians' condemnations of the invasion were ritualistic in tone. President Johnson's overtures for a summit meeting in Moscow to discuss arms control were only briefly delayed. By the end of November the White House was already asking again if the president could come to Moscow.[22] The invasion reinforced the view that any change in Eastern Europe would be slow in coming, and the West could do little in the immediate future to hasten the process. In contrast to the reaction a decade later, when the West used the Soviet intervention in Afghanistan and the pressures on Poland as a device for strengthening Western cohesion, no sanctions were taken over Czechoslovakia. None were even proposed. The incoming Nixon administration, with Henry Kissinger as national security advisor, put Eastern Europe low on its list of priorities. Although the new men in Washington talked of linking Soviet conduct to the pace of the forthcoming strategic arms limitation talks, Czechoslovakia was not one of the issues that they proposed to link. Washington was more concerned about the incipient Soviet competition in the Third World. Indeed, there was a strong feeling that stability under Soviet control in Eastern Europe was preferable to continual upheaval, which might lead to an unpredictable confrontation between East and West.

Kissinger's chief advisor on Communist affairs, Helmut Sonnenfeldt, expressed the mood most clearly in a briefing to American ambassadors based in Europe. Although his remarks were made in 1975, they reflected the administration's line from its assumption of power in 1969. "The Soviets' inability to acquire loyalty in Eastern Europe is an unfortunate historical failure, because Eastern Europe is within their scope and area of national interest," Sonnenfeldt argued, according to a State Department summary of his words.[23] "It is doubly tragic that in this area of vital interest and crucial importance it has not been possible for the Soviet Union to establish roots of interest that go beyond sheer power. . . . It must be in our long-term interest to influence events in this area—because of the present unnatural relationship with the Soviet Union—so that they will not sooner or later explode, causing World War III. This inorganic, unnatural relationship is a far greater danger to world peace than the conflict between East and West."

Sonnenfeldt made a cursory nod in the direction of Eastern European hopes for greater autonomy. The United States should "respond to the clearly visible aspirations in Eastern Europe for a more autonomous existence within the context of a strong Soviet geopolitical influence." But the Sonnenfeldt thesis patently played down any strong effort at pressing for liberalization in Eastern Europe. Ever since 1945 Western policy had been torn between the contradiction of recognizing the reality of Soviet power in Eastern Europe and the wish to reduce it. The invasion of Czechoslovakia seemed to reinforce the incoming Nixon administration in favor of realism.

In West Germany the invasion had a similar effect. Chancellor Kurt Kiesinger referred mildly to "the Czechoslovak adventure," and there was a brief delay in Bonn's talks with Moscow on a treaty renouncing the use of force between the two countries.[24]

In July 1969 the talks picked up again, and when the elections in September brought Willy Brandt into power they noticeably accelerated. The Brandt government accepted the Soviet argument that West Germany must finally come to terms with Europe's postwar frontiers. Between 1970 and 1972 Bonn reached agreements with the Soviet Union, Poland, and the German Democratic Republic. In 1973 even Czechoslovakia, whose hard-line Communists had been most suspicious about the effect of West German influence, agreed to exchange embassies. In 1971 the Soviet Union and the three Western powers came to an agreement regulating access to West Berlin.

This flurry of diplomacy, completing the unfinished business of the Second World War, was based on a historic compromise. The Russians finally gained West German acceptance of the territorial status quo in Eastern Europe, including the existence of a second German state. The Russians wanted détente with the major continental power in Western Europe to improve the general climate between the two halves of Europe at a time when tension was high on the Soviet Union's border with China. The Russians did not relish tension on both flanks at once. The price of these achievements was not excessive. Moscow would no longer be able to rely in its propaganda on a simple devil-image of West Germany. It would have to accept an increase in contact between Eastern Europe and the West. It formally gave up the opportunity to put pressure on

West Berlin at moments of East–West stress, as Brezhnev's predecessors had frequently done.

On points of detail Moscow made a few minor concessions. In the Berlin agreement Moscow had to accept that the Federal Republic and West Berlin could enlarge their links. The treaty between the two German states recognized a special relationship between them on the lines of Brandt's concept of "two states within one nation." The East German leader, Walter Ulbricht, found this point particularly galling, and when he tried to block it, he was gently eased out of power with Moscow's blessing. The Kremlin was not willing to have the whole deal sabotaged by a stubborn ally, especially as the special German relationship had benefits as well as costs. While it kept open the possibility of an eventual reunification of Germany—a prospect that might be unsettling one day—this glimmer of light could be alluring for West Germans and keep them half turned toward the East rather than be totally integrated into the Western camp.

The Brezhnev conception of détente in Europe reached its full flower at the Conference on European Security and Co-operation in Helsinki in 1975. The Russians and their Warsaw Pact allies had proposed the idea of a conference shortly after the invasion of Czechoslovakia. As with the bilateral treaties with West Germany, the aim was to ratify the European status quo at a conference that would take the place of the full-scale peace conference originally planned to meet at the end of the war, but which had never been held. The West reacted with initial skepticism, but after the signing of West Germany's treaties with the East suspicions eased. In return for agreement to attend the conference, the West put forward a series of demands for a "freer flow" of information, people, and ideas between the two halves of Europe. Soviet concessions were modest and largely semantic, and the Western diplomats who negotiated the conference document expected no more than a very gradual relaxation of the East's restrictions. But the document for the first time put on paper Soviet acceptance of some liberalization in its sphere of influence.

Underpinning the new détente in Europe was a massive increase in economic exchanges between West and East. Trade tripled between 1969 and 1974, and Western investors increasingly looked East at potential projects in which the Eastern partners would repay Western loans either with energy supplies or with industrial goods. The West began to see beyond the alleged political and military threat the East was said to represent. The Soviet Union was located in a vast reserve of energy for a hungry world. Eastern Europe had a pliant labor force, no independent trade unions, and the advantages of nearness—which made it a better bet for multinational companies than most parts of the Third World. At the back of it all was the Soviet Union. There was no chance of Eastern European countries defaulting on debts, for the Soviet Union with its stockpiles of gold would be sure to bail them out. Buoyed by these certainties, Western lenders poured the money in.

It was indeed remarkable how soon after the invasion of Czechoslovakia tensions in Eastern Europe eased. When Polish workers in the Baltic ports struck in the winter of 1970, Moscow reacted with coolness and restraint. It approved a change of party leadership and with a generous hard-currency loan showed it supported the first secretary, Edward Gierek, in his policy of reversing unpopular price rises. In Hungary, too, the Kremlin backed the party's decentralization of the economy and the reform of prices, known as the "new economic mechanism." The new policy must have had the backing of Andropov who joined the Politburo in 1967. As Soviet ambassador in Hungary between 1954 and 1957, and then for ten years head of the Central Committee's department for liaison with the socialist countries, he was one of the Kremlin's most experienced analysts of Eastern Europe. He presumably understood better than many of his colleagues the diversity of the region and the possibilities of tolerating limited economic experiments. Of course Moscow continued to insist on political orthodoxy and loyalty to the Soviet Union's international line. There could be no talk of alternative models of socialism. In foreign policy Hungary and Poland were as outspokenly anti-Chinese as the Russians were. With the adoption of a "comprehensive program" in COMECON in 1971, Moscow ensured that its Eastern European allies pledged to coordinate their national plans and collaborate on long-term investment projects.

The lesson from the first half of the 1970s was clear. The political climate in Eastern Europe depends on the level of tension between East and West. When tension is low, conditions are at their most relaxed, and the Soviet Union is able to feel indulgent. At the Twenty-Fifth Party Congress in February 1976 Brezhnev was more cheerful about the state of his Eastern European union than at any party congress before or since. "The ties between socialist states are becoming ever closer with the flowering of each socialist nation and the strengthening of their sovereignty. . . . This process of a gradual drawing together of socialist countries is now operating quite definitely as an objective law. Of course much depends on the policy of the ruling parties and their ability to safeguard unity, to combat isolation and national exclusiveness, to honor the common international tasks and to act jointly in performing them. . . . A few parties, as we know, have particular views on a number of questions but the overall tendency is unquestionably characterized by a growing cohesion of socialist countries. We value this tendency highly and shall, as before, promote it in every way."[25]

The sharp rise in world oil prices in the second half of the decade, and the worsening of Eastern Europe's terms of trade with the West forced a slowdown in the region's growth rates. Eastern Europe found itself importing inflation from the West. But there is no evidence that Moscow saw any dangerous political consequences from this. The fact that on top of it Moscow told its allies that it would be charging higher prices for its own oil exports suggested that the Soviet Union believed their allies could afford the necessary belt-tightening. Indeed, there were benefits to be gained. The economic crisis caused Rumania to increase its trade with the Soviet Union, and become more conciliatory.

Relations with Yugoslavia also improved for similar reasons. Recession in the West took the glitter off the apparent success of the capitalist economies and was a useful tool for the Soviet propaganda machine. When Western doubts over Yugoslavia's future grew loud during Tito's long final illness in early 1980, the Russians reacted calmly. Neither then nor in the period that followed did they see any advantage in trying to destabilize Yugoslavia. Since the original split with Tito in 1948, the country's strategic importance had declined.

The first sign that the recession might have adverse political effects in Eastern Europe came in Poland in the summer of 1980. The strikes in Gdansk which led to the birth of the Solidarity movement surprised Moscow as much as anyone else. They were soon to lead not only to the severest internal crisis in any Eastern European country since 1968, but also to a grave threat to Brezhnev's policy of détente with Western Europe. Brezhnev had made this so-called *Westpolitik* one of the major elements of his period in office. The need to preserve it became a significant restraint on Soviet policy throughout the crisis.

The initial Soviet reaction to the strikes was one of appeasement, and an almost exact replay of the line taken during the strikes on the Baltic coast ten years before. It approved the change of leadership in the Polish party, and the new government's efforts to buy off the workers with wage increases, which Moscow backed with the provision of extra economic aid and emergency food exports. But Moscow also saw the ideological dangers of the strikers' demands for independent trade unions and the fear of a "contamination" effect in other countries. On the sixth day of the strike it resumed jamming of Western broadcasts in the Soviet Union for the first time since 1973.

Signs that the Kremlin was divided over how to deal with Poland came from a member of the Polish party's Central Committee, Ryszard Wojna, who said in early September, "The Soviet comrades are watching and listening to the current process in Poland with eyes and ears well open. . . . Some comrades do not like our ideas but others are watching our efforts with great interest."[26] Wojna's comment reflected an aspect of the developing crisis that in retrospect may seem absurdly optimistic. There was a view in Poland that the Kremlin might actually see some value in the compromises that Solidarity and the party were intermittently trying to work out. Serious thinkers, including party members and experienced dissident activists, such as Jacek Kuron from KOR (The Committee for Workers' Self-Defense), argued that a "Poland of social movements" would benefit everybody, including the Soviet Union. The strikes of 1980 were, after all, the fourth case of major working-class unrest in the postwar period. Surely experience showed that the old system of central control by a party monopoly was a recipe for continually recurring upheavals. A Poland with new institutions would be a more stable Poland. Poland was already to a large extent an exception in Eastern Europe, with its system of private agriculture and a powerful Roman Catholic Church. A social contract between the party and an independent trade union movement which could pull Poland out of its economic chaos would make the country a more reliable ally for the Soviet Union.

Although this optimistic view was not shared by all Poles, reporters in Poland found few who agreed with the West's wholly negative view that the Soviet Union was bound to intervene by force sooner or later to squash the Polish developments. Most Poles rejected this determinist line.[27] Instead, they placed the responsibility for events upon themselves. If Poles could restrain themselves, the Russians would hold off. If they failed to find their own Polish compromise because of popular impatience and official stubbornness and brought economic collapse and political catastrophe on themselves, then the Russians would almost be justified in intervening. Throughout the crisis the West stuck to its line, interpreting virtually every Soviet move in the light of allegedly imminent invasion and thus blinding itself to other possible outcomes, including the one that was eventually chosen. Although few Poles predicted martial law itself, they came closer than the West to foreseeing a Polish rather than a Soviet denouement.

Admittedly the Kremlin gave the invasion-watchers some grounds for their belief, at least in the early stages. In October a Soviet naval task force was deployed in Gdansk during a one-hour general strike. At the end of the month and during the beginning of November, Soviet forces conducted extensive exercises in the western part of the country bordering Poland. On November 24 *Izvestia* warned that a threatened rail strike could affect Poland's "national and defense interests" by disrupting rail links across the country that brought supplies to the twenty Soviet divisions in East Germany.[28] On November 29 the Soviet media (reprinting an article from the Czechoslovak party paper *Rude Pravo*) for the first time compared the Polish events to the "counterrevolution of 1968" in Czechoslovakia. New military maneuvers were underway on Poland's borders with the Soviet Union, East Germany, and Czechoslovakia, and Soviet reservists were called up in the Carpathian, Byelorussian and Baltic military districts. The Soviet Union closed a portion of the East German–Polish border in a restricted zone up to fifty miles wide, instead of the usual three miles. On December 2 the United States declared that several Warsaw Pact countries had placed their forces on alert. The Soviet ambassador in Washington, Anatoly Dobrynin, was warned of severe consequences if Moscow intervened by force.

There is little doubt that the Soviet Union was preparing a military option it could hold in reserve. But Brezhnev seemed determined to go for a political solution. At the end of October in Moscow, when the new party leader Stanislaw Kania flew in for a hastily summoned meeting, Brezhnev approved the compromise under which Solidarity was officially registered as a legal trade union movement. At the height of the invasion scare, he took a cool line at an emergency summit of the Warsaw Pact on December 5 which was held in the Soviet capital. Whereas during the crisis of 1968 the hawks had been Poland and East Germany, this time the East Germans were joined by the Czechs. The three states have sometimes been called the "iron triangle" defending the western approaches to the Soviet Union, and this time the weak link was Poland. The East German interior minister Erich Mielke used the Warsaw Pact summit to accuse the Polish leadership of supporting anti-Soviet views by failing to stop antisocialist remarks appearing in Poland's unofficial press. The Russians reportedly said little.[29] Three days later Brezhnev left on a long-planned trip to India.

Whether the Soviet Politburo came close to a political decision to launch an invasion can only be guessed at. Five days after the Warsaw Pact summit, Soviet Defense Minister Marshal Ustinov called for heightened vigilance by the Soviet armed forces because the West was trying "to damage the positions of the socialist nations, especially of socialist Poland."[30] An article by Alexei Petrov (a pseudonym often used for high-level statements) in *Pravda* attacked the West for denying Poland's right to call for military help if necessary.[31] But these statements may have been felt to be the least Moscow should do so as not to appear to be backing off in the face of Western warnings. If nothing else, Moscow wanted to put pressure on the Poles by keeping them guessing about a possible invasion.

The arguments for and against it were different from those that the Kremlin considered before going into Czechoslovakia twelve years earlier. Because of its severe economic crisis and the barely suppressed nationalism of all Poles, the country was far less stable than Czechoslovakia had been. West Germany's treaty in 1970, recognizing Poland's takeover of prewar German territories in Silesia and Pomerania, had removed one of the main grounds for Poland's anti-German stance. Polish nationalism could now be turned against the country's other traditional enemy, the neighbor to the east. The Polish crisis was a working-class revolt. Whereas the Czech events had been mainly a crisis within the party and the intelligentsia, the Polish masses were involved. It was a confrontation between the party and the people. The party was losing authority and splitting into factions. Ideologically, the concept of independent trade unions in a Communist country was a dangerous notion which could have enormous implications if it was allowed to take root.

Against an invasion there were powerful arguments to consider. There was no guarantee that the Polish Army would not resist. Even if the Soviet Union eventually suppressed resistance, there could be a dangerous period of several months during which East Germany would be virtually cut off and at the mercy of a possible internal revolt of its own, with or without Western encouragement. The Soviet Union's vital rail links to East Germany would be vulnerable to saboteurs. There was a danger of protracted war on two fronts, Poland and Afghanistan. Once the Soviet Army established control, it would have to face the problem of Poland's near-bankruptcy. The invasion of Czechoslovakia had left the population apathetic and angry. An occupied Poland would require Soviet subsidies on an even more massive scale. But the most important change since 1968 was the international climate. At that time détente in Europe had barely begun. Moscow was highly suspicious of Western intentions in Eastern Europe, and saw the West's overtures for rapprochement as a device for potential destabilization. East Germany was still unrecognized. By 1980 Moscow felt more reassured. Since the recognition of Europe's postwar boundaries in West Germany's bilateral treaties and the Helsinki Conference, Moscow had successfully maintained Eastern Europe's ideological cohesion. The potentially liberalizing effects of détente had been held in check. The threat now was not so much that of a slippage of Soviet control within Eastern Europe as of a big increase in armaments in Western Europe. NATO's decision, in December 1979, to install 108 Pershing–II missiles in West Germany raised the prospect of an American first strike on Soviet territory with minimal warning time. The Russians must have considered what value its Eastern European buffer zone would have if the West could simply leap over it with a lightning attack from Western Europe. The Russians still hoped the decision to deploy the new missiles could be reversed by the growing protest movement in Western Europe. Those hopes would surely be dealt a death blow if the Russians moved into Poland with force. The strong series of Western statements must also have been a factor. The West had said little in advance of the invasion in 1968. Western politicians were determined not to be caught out a second time.

After the December invasion scare, Soviet policy toward Poland seemed to be based on a longer perspective. The hope was that the Polish party could win the battle against Solidarity by a process of attrition. Soviet commentaries looked for signs of splits within Solidarity, or between Solidarity's leaders and the rank and file. They called on Polish communists to take the lead in the battle against radical elements. The Russians apparently calculated that, although the Solidarity trade union movement was a dangerous new factor, the Polish events would have little appeal to the rest of Eastern Europe as long as the economy was in chaos. This seemed to be borne out in East Germany and Hungary where visitors found little popular sympathy for the Poles. Official Soviet and Eastern European commentaries stressed the anarchy, chaos, and food shortages in Poland, and played on widespread prejudices that Poles were inherently lazy and disorganized.

On the other hand, if the Polish economy collapsed completely, there was danger of massive public disorder and riots. The Russians accordingly offered some aid, on the grounds that it was best to keep Poland between the two dangerous extremes of collapse and full recovery. As the debate mounted in the West over whether or not to call in the huge Western loans to Poland, Moscow also found it useful to draw the public lesson that Poland's troubles were caused by overdependence on the West. It drew a contrast between Moscow's allegedly disinterested aid and the West's economic strings.

At the Soviet party congress in February 1981, Brezhnev warned that "the pillars of the socialist state in Poland are in jeopardy" and gave the ambiguous pledge that "we will not abandon fraternal, socialist Poland in its hour of need."[32] But he added that the Polish comrades were redressing the critical situation. At a meeting a few days later with Kania and the new Prime Minister General Jaruzelski, Brezhnev called on the Poles "to turn the course of events," meaning that they should take control at last. When the Warsaw Pact began its spring maneuvers, known as Soyuz–81, in Poland, the GDR, Czechoslovakia, and the Soviet Union on March 17, there was no reason to link them directly to the internal situation in Poland, which was quiet.

The calm was broken on March 19 when two hundred policemen broke up a sit-in by members of Rural Solidarity, the peasants' union, in the prefecture of Bydgoszcz. Several Solidarity members were injured in what appeared to be a deliberate act of provocation. Tempers were aroused and the union called a national strike. Hard-liners in the Polish Politburo, including Stefan Olszowski, a former foreign minister, called for the declaration of a state of emergency. Kania and Jaruzelski refused. The Soyuz–81 maneuvers continued beyond the appointed deadline, and alarm mounted in the West again.

In a rare flash of insight the White House warned of "indications that the Polish authorities may be preparing to use force" or that the Soviet Union might be intending to move in. With the benefit of hindsight some observers have argued that General Jaruzelski's appointment as prime minister in February was the first step in a planned program of militarization which was intended to end with martial law. General Leon Dubicki, who defected to the West the following August, said that from March onward the army was conducting special screenings to weed out soldiers who might be reluctant to enforce martial law.[33] In the event, the unlimited general strike was never called. A last-minute compromise worked out between Solidarity's leader, Lech Walesa, and Mieczyslaw Rakowski, the deputy prime minister in charge of negotiations with Solidarity, averted the crisis. The Soyuz–81 maneuvers came to an end, and Brezhnev let it be known that he would like to visit Bonn sometime soon.

This important signal from the Soviet party leader was dramatic evidence of his anxiety about détente and the key role he attached to West Germany. Ronald Reagan's first two months in office had alarmed the Russians. Complacent Soviet expectations that Reagan would be "another Nixon" who would drop his emotional anti-Communism in favor of realism once he entered the White House were rapidly being revised. The new president had insulted Moscow in his first press conference and gone on to announce a massive increase in arms spending. The hard-line American view made the Russians think again about West Germany. If the Americans were determined to reject détente, then at least there might be a chance of preserving it in Europe if West Germany could be persuaded to do so. The argument against a Soviet intervention in Poland had become even stronger now that West Germany was seen as the main focus of Soviet diplomacy.

Brezhnev's hint that he wanted to visit Bonn created a significant hostage to fortune. The Soviet leader must have known that the visit could not be arranged immediately, and that he was therefore foreclosing any Soviet move into Poland until it was over. The West clearly had an interest in delaying it for that very reason. The Russians proposed July, while the Germans held off until November. Was Brezhnev's gamble in putting détente with West Germany above his concern over Poland a pure calculation of international priorities, or had he by then decided that martial law administered by the Poles themselves would be a workable solution? Was he confident that a Soviet invasion was unnecessary and that the Polish crisis could be contained by other means?

It is an intriguing possibility, but one that cannot yet be proved. On the one hand there were no more suspicious moves by Soviet forces after March. On the other hand there were signs that the Russians were not yet happy with General Jaruzelski. They were still toying with the aim of strengthening the party leadership by engineering Kania's replacement by Olszowski. On a visit to Prague in April to attend the Czechoslovak party congress Brezhnev asked that the other party leaders stay away. The Polish delegation was headed by Olszowski, with whom the Soviet leader was able to talk alone. Two weeks later Mikhail Suslov became the first Soviet Politburo member to visit Poland since the crisis began. The joint statement at the end of his talks laid out clearly the Soviet Union's fears. It called for the party to oppose anti-socialist efforts to create "dual power" in Poland, i.e., any alternative to the party's monopoly. Suslov's greeters at the airport did not include Jaruzelski.

The most obvious clue to Moscow's doubts came in early June in a letter from the Soviet party's Central Committee to its Polish counterpart. The letter suggested that Kania and Jaruzelski, whom it named, had shown themselves unable to deal with the crisis. At this stage the Russians were still concentrating on the need to preserve orthodox control within the party in the face of challenges for greater accountability by the leadership to the rank and file, secret elections, and the right to recall Central Committee members who lost local branches' confidence. The Russians were looking for orthodox solutions. The notion of an army general in charge of the party had "Bonapartist" overtones. In the event, the special party congress, which many Western analysts, mindful of Prague 1968, assumed that Moscow would prevent, took place in July. It was a damp squib. Secret elections were held, Kania was confirmed in office, but the new Central Committee was not noticeably radical. Most Poles considered the party had become irrelevant in the search for a solution to the country's problems, and in a sense they were right. Suslov's concept of "dual power" was close to the mark.

The more significant event was the two-part congress of Solidarity held in Gdansk at the beginning and end of September. Its appeal to the workers of Eastern Europe to set up their own free trade unions produced a furious reaction in Moscow, including the special meetings in Soviet factories mentioned at the beginning of this chapter. It challenged the Polish government to join in working out an economic program to save the country, and threatened to set up its own factory committees to handle the distribution during the forthcoming winter emergency. Although Walesa staved off radicals challenging him for the union's leadership, the congress marked a shift toward an angrier, more radical and riskier mood.

Whether or not the Kremlin engineered Jaruzelski's appointment as party leader on October 18, Brezhnev signaled his support in a telegram of congratulations that referred to Jaruzelski's "great prestige." Among many Poles Jaruzelski did enjoy prestige. His refusal to let the army fire on workers in December 1970 and again during the Gdansk strikes in August 1980 was remembered and respected. If there was one party figure who commanded some trust, it was he. But he also commanded support—though perhaps not yet trust—in the Kremlin, precisely because he was seen as the best man to restore party control in a deteriorating situation.

Unlike Czechoslovakia in 1968, when the Russians had doubts over the Dubček leadership's loyalty to the Soviet Union and the maintenance of central party control, the Polish crisis was seen in the Kremlin as a test of the party's skill and determination to defeat a rival center of power, Solidarity. Jaruzelski was part of a group of generals who were soldiers or junior officers during the war and received advanced military training in the Soviet Union. They were upwardly mobile, career-oriented, and loyal to the system. For Jaruzelski, the army's role was to protect the party against distortions and be, in a sense, its conscience. The Russians were banking on the fact that in a clash between the elite and the workers' movement, Jaruzelski would back the elite.

From the moment of his appointment, Soviet media criticism of the Polish party ceased. From that moment, too, planning for martial law began. On October 23 the army was sent into the countryside to help local authorities to cope "with the threat to internal life."[34] It stayed a month, ostensibly helping with food distribution and investigating corruption, but also gaining useful experience and contacts for the subsequent imposition of martial law. In November similar task forces went out to the towns and cities. On October 28 General Florian Siwicki, who had commanded the Polish forces that went into Czechoslovakia in 1968, was named a deputy member of the Politburo, thus increasing the convergence of army and party. Arrest lists were printed with the names of several people who turned out no longer to be in the country on December 13, the day that martial law was declared—a clear sign that the authorities were planning ahead. Marshal Kulikov, the commander-in-chief of the Warsaw Pact, arrived in Warsaw on November 24 with the pact's chief of staff to talk to Poland's leaders. He is believed to have returned shortly before December 13 and stayed for several days after the imposition of martial law.[35]

The evidence suggests that Jaruzelski had decided to prepare for martial law by October at the latest. All that was needed was the political decision and an appropriate pretext to launch it. Jaruzelski and the Kremlin found it in the form of tapes of a meeting of Solidarity leaders in Radom which called for total confrontation with the government. On December 10, after a period of relative Soviet media silence, Tass charged that counterrevolutionary forces in Poland were openly calling for the violent overthrow of the government.

When the deed was done, Tass welcomed martial law with enthusiasm as a step that is "of course Poland's internal affair." "Tass is authorized to state that the Soviet leadership . . . has received with a feeling of satisfaction W. Jaruzelski's statement that the Polish–Soviet alliance has been and remains the cornerstone of Polish state interests, a guarantee of the inviolability of the Polish frontiers and that Poland has been and remains an unbreakable part of the Warsaw Treaty, a member of the socialist community of states." When Jaruzelski visited Moscow the following March, Brezhnev said that if Poland's Communists had given way to counterrevolution, "the destinies of Poland, stability in Europe, and the world at large would have been jeopardized."

Although earlier in the spring Western observers had briefly discussed the chance that Poland would impose a state of emergency, the swiftness and completeness of the move caught them by surprise. The initial reaction was angry but resigned. Some observers, particularly in the big banks with outstanding loans to Poland, welcomed it. A West German banker told the *Financial Times*, "What I am saying may be a bit brutal, but I think the Polish government was no longer in a position to govern the country. I now see a chance for Poland to return to a more normal working schedule and this could be a good thing for the banks."[36]

The Reagan administration, which had been expecting a Soviet invasion, behaved as though this is what had happened. Prompted by its own hard-line instincts and pressure from the leaders of the Polish–American community in the United States, it imposed economic sanctions. It also used the event to drum up Western support for a tough stance against the Soviet Union in an effort to bring West Germany back into line with mainstream NATO policy and to discredit the Western European peace movement. The moves served only to heighten the strains within NATO. The Russians could well argue, as martial law gradually weakened Solidarity's power and the West wrangled over its own sanctions policy, that they had seen control restored successfully in a wayward ally by the use of a technique that other Eastern European states might one day come to use.

CONCLUSION

The Kremlin still views Eastern Europe as more than just a sphere of Soviet influence. Ever since the Second World War it has regarded it as an integral component of the Soviet Union's security. For centuries the area was the historic invasion route for Russia's enemies. Since 1945 it has been transformed into a Soviet-dominated buffer zone. Security always took primacy over ideology, and some economic and political diversity could be tolerated, provided that it did not threaten or undermine the stability of a particular state or the region as a whole.

Eastern Europe is not an empire in the classic sense of the term. On paper its states are politically sovereign—which means that every Soviet intervention has caused an international outcry and required awkward Soviet efforts at justification. There has been little Russian settlement—which means that the cultural gap between Russia and its supposed allies is still wide. Above all, in contrast to other empires, Eastern Europe's standard of living is higher than that of the metropolis. Indeed, since the start of the Brezhnev era, as a result of subsidized raw material prices, Moscow had been putting more money into the area than it was getting out. This only showed how determined the Kremlin was on keeping control of the area as a vital security buffer for the Soviet Union itself. Time and time again the Kremlin engineered or encouraged the replacement of party leaders in Eastern Europe in whom it had lost confidence. In 1956 and 1968 it invaded allied territory in order to restore orthodox control.

With hindsight, the Polish party's confrontation with the independent trade union Solidarity in 1980 and 1981 can be seen to have marked a new stage in the Soviet Union's relations with Eastern Europe. Some features were the same as those of previous crises. Moscow still valued its security and the preservation of the Warsaw Pact above all other considerations. However much of an economic and political burden Poland was, the Kremlin was not prepared to abandon it with the risk of unraveling its buffer zone in Eastern Europe. Moscow also made it clear, as it had already done when it invaded Czechoslovakia in 1968, that it would set limits to the development of political pluralism in Eastern Europe. It could accept the existence of alternative institutions, such as the Roman Catholic Church, and relics of a capitalist structure, such as private agriculture. It could tolerate a certain amount of local nationalism. But it would not permit any lifting of censorship or any significant power-sharing by a ruling Communist party.

The new factor was the Kremlin's acceptance that an Eastern European army could perform the internal policing function that in previous crises the Red Army had taken on. The Polish crisis was a new kind of upheaval, which must have been profoundly disturbing to the Soviet Union. Although there had been previous workers' revolts in Eastern Europe since the war, none had been so widespread as Solidarity's challenge. It was both nationwide and national. None had produced so well-articulated a set of political demands, founded on the concept of a trade union movement, independent of the party. None had made such a deep criticism of the party that claimed to represent the interests of the working class and now found its very legitimacy and historic relevance under attack. And the challenge did not come from workers who could be said to be living with a prewar consciousness. They had all been brought up in People's Poland.

Solidarity showed that, at least in Poland, the effort to satisfy workers by means of economic improvements and "consumer socialism" had failed. For

Andropov, who had encouraged similar efforts in Hungary, this was an important lesson. With the prospect that the 1980s would see a further decline in growth rates throughout Eastern Europe, the Kremlin will have to face the possibility of Solidarity-style protests in other countries. The most difficult new factor is that in handling these protests it may have to take greater account of Western Europe than ever before. As long as Western Europe, and West Germany in particular, has a strong current of public opinion in favor of détente, the Soviet Union will think twice and three times before alienating it. The Reagan administration's hard-line policies have worried many West Europeans and strengthened the growing tendency for a more independent European voice. A hard Soviet line in Western Europe, designed to strengthen the Warsaw Pact, has the effect of strengthening NATO too. Thanks to the Polish crisis, Moscow is aware that its policies in Eastern Europe can no longer be carried out in isolation.

7

AFGHANISTAN

We knew that the decision to bring in troops would not be popular in the modern world, even if it was absolutely legal. But we also knew that we would have ceased to be a great power if we refrained from carrying the burden of taking unpopular but necessary decisions, extraordinary decisions prompted by extraordinary circumstances.

Alexander Bovin
Izvestia's senior political columnist, 1980[1]

"There's a bandit over that wall right now," Yuri Volkov announced. Sitting on the veranda of one of the high-walled villas, which the middle class of Kabul built for themselves in easier times, his visitor looked up startled. "You won't recognize him, though," Volkov went on. "Who knows who is a bandit out there? He may be carrying a machine gun under his coat. Sometimes they may even veil themselves to look like women."[2]

A genial man with bushy eyebrows and a stiffness in one leg, Volkov had become one of the Soviet Union's veteran experts on Afghanistan after several tours of journalistic duty there. On the very morning that he received his visitor, one of his Afghan staff had anxiously reported the arrival of a "night letter," a hand-delivered message threatening her with death if she continued working with Russians. By then Soviet troops had been in the country for almost two years, and it was clear that they were hopelessly bogged down. They and the Afghan government forces they were trying to help were confined to Kabul and the other main towns and a few isolated garrisons elsewhere. Ninety percent of

116

the countryside was in the hands of the resistance. Soviet and Afghan convoys were frequently ambushed, and Soviet troops knew that if they ever fell into rebel hands, they were likely to be executed on the spot. Repeated bombing raids on suspected rebel strongholds had not blunted the resistance of the *mujaheddin*, the so-called "warriors of God."

It was a bleak balance sheet two years after an invasion in December 1979 that had prompted worldwide surprise and immediate disapproval. For the first time since the end of the Second World War the Russians had dispatched large numbers of combat troops outside the Warsaw Pact area. The death of President Hafizullah Amin within hours of the intervention, which the Russians claimed he had asked for, looked suspiciously like a deliberate assassination. Nonaligned governments in the Third World as well as Euro-Communists joined the more predictable protest from Western governments and asked why this had happened.

The Soviet leadership tried to deal with the second point by claiming that Amin had been killed by other Afghans—as Brezhnev put it in a statement in *Pravda* on January 13, 1980, when "the people under the leadership of the People's Democratic Party, headed by Babrak Karmal, rose against Amin's tyranny and put an end to it." In an effort to pretend that he had not been installed by the Russians, Karmal claimed that he had returned secretly to the country before the Soviet intervention to help to coordinate the alleged uprising. As for the charge that the invasion was illegal, Brezhnev said that "the Afghan leadership repeatedly asked the Soviet Union for assistance" in suppressing a counterrevolution, as it was entitled to do under the Afghan–Soviet Treaty of Friendship, concluded in December 1978. "It was no easy decision for us to send Soviet military contingents to Afghanistan," Brezhnev said. Their only task was to help the Afghans in resisting the aggression from outside which was being supplied and backed by the United States and China. In an angry attack on the concept of international law he argued, "When the world's first socialist state was born in 1917 our people did not ask anybody's permission. Today too they decide for themselves what laws to live by."[3]

Brezhnev's claim that the intervention was justified by foreign aid to a counterrevolution did not deal with the Euro-Communist complaint that the Soviet Union should have gone to the United Nations with its evidence rather than take unilateral military action. Neither then nor subsequently did the Russians offer serious evidence of significant foreign interference. The story that Amin's death had nothing to do with the Soviet intervention was too fantastic for anyone to take seriously. Why was no enquiry into the circumstances of his death ever permitted? Karmal and his supporters even argued that Amin had all along been a CIA agent, although this was a line that the Russians wisely did not use much themselves. But the Russians were concerned that Amin might turn out to be "another Sadat" who would eventually ask them to end all involvement in Afghanistan.

For the most part the Russians blurred the issue of Amin's downfall. They continued to justify the dispatch of some 85,000 combat troops on the grounds that (a) it was a legal response to an invitation by a sovereign government; and (b) the first foreign intervention came from the West and China and not from the Soviet Union. Occasionally, however, a more subtle and honest Soviet viewpoint was heard. Alexander Bovin, *Izvestia*'s political columnist, admitted that things were complicated.[4] "What kind of revolution is it that has to be supported with the help of Soviet troops? What kind of new rule is it against which not only landlords but peasants, too, are rising up in arms? These questions are quite legitimate." The primary reason he gave was the impatience of the revolution's activist supporters. "It has been inherent in all revolutionaries in all eras to be impatient, wanting to make the ideals of the revolution come true as quickly as possible, to jump from the past into the future. 'War communism' in the Soviet Union and the 'great leap' in China—given all differences—have a similar psychological basis. . . . Psychologically understandable impatience, plus the absence of experience, has clearly led to a scope of reforms and a pace of their implementation which went beyond the confines of the possible. . . . That the feudal lords and reactionary clergymen came out against the reforms doesn't surprise anyone. Power and wealth were taken away from them, and they resisted. But the truly dramatic nature of the revolution lies in the fact that the leftist extremes have divorced a part of the masses from the new power, enabling the former nobility to scare people with talk of 'godless Marxism' and to bring a noticeable part of the peasantry under its sway." Bovin pointed out that peasants "do not lend themselves easily to revolutionary transformation." He also conceded that the April 1978 revolution was not a mass movement. "It is true that the crisis of the revolutionary regime did not reach such a sharp point as, say, in Iran where the revolution began with spontaneous mass action." But what was the "political vanguard" supposed to do? Should it sit idly by or give history a push by taking power in an army coup? "By leaning on the army they chose to take political power and in the process of social transformation to involve millions of people in the revolution. If there were failures, difficulties and mistakes in the course of this process, it by no means follows from this that there was no need to take power. It follows that this power had to be used with greater wisdom, flexibility and caution."

Bovin claimed that the regime could have handled the incipient counter-revolution if the situation had not been "complicated" by foreign support for the rebels. "At the same time, the seven purges which Amin carried out in the army substantially undermined the combat ability of the armed forces." Amin was unreliable, although Bovin stopped short of making the charge that he was working for the CIA. "Amin maneuvered, assuring Moscow of his friendly feelings towards the Soviet Union and demanding that the latter bring in troops to Afghanistan, while trying to establish contacts with the rebels and ensure American support."

The Soviet Union "was forced to make a choice; we had either to bring in troops or let the Afghan revolution be defeated," he said. To justify the former decision, Bovin then used the argument of great-power prestige which is a major factor in Soviet decision making, though rarely admitted. "We knew that the decision to bring in troops would not be popular in the modern world, even if it was absolutely legal. But we also knew that we would have ceased to be a great power if we refrained from carrying the burden of taking unpopular but necessary decisions, extraordinary decisions prompted by extraordinary circumstances."

Although the Bovin article was unusual in its frankness, it did not produce a clear answer to one key question. If the Russians had allowed the Afghan regime to founder, what sort of government did they expect to follow it? At one point Bovin said the country would have been turned into "a kind of Shah's Iran," paving the way for a "massive American presence in a country which borders on the Soviet Union." At another point, he suggested that the counterrevolution would have given victory to "religious zealots" and resulted in a huge bloodbath—a scenario that sounded more like Khomeini's Iran. The Russians were not sure which of these scenarios was the more likely. In either case, they calculated that the new regime would have been nationalistic and anti-Soviet, and whether or not it aligned itself with the United States, it would be more hostile to the Soviet Union than the previous regime or even the pre-1978 regime.

Some Western commentators have argued that the Russians were also afraid of a kind of "contamination effect" from the resurgence of Islamic nationalism in Iran and Afghanistan on to the Muslims of Soviet Central Asia, who are an expanding section of the overall Soviet population. In 1982 there were 44 million, roughly 18 percent of the population. Their birth rate is higher than that of the Russians, and by the end of this century the proportion of Muslims will be between 20 and 25 percent. Most preserve Islamic cultural traditions, performing circumcision, celebrating religious marriages and burials, and observing the fast of Ramadan. Intermarriage with non-Muslims is rare.

Islam is more persistent than any other religion in the Soviet Union, and in recent years there appears to have been an increase in the influence of *tariqas* or secret societies based on the Sufi brotherhoods, which are outside the officially recognized Muslim establishment. While there are only 300 working mosques left in the Soviet Union compared with 24,000 before 1917, Sufi orders can be found in all parts of the Soviet Union. They represent a kind of "parallel Islam" which runs clandestine mosques and schools teaching Arabic. Some of their activities are centered on the holy places, which are often the tombs of heroes who died fighting against the Russians.

Although it is impossible to gauge the current strength of these groups, they do not appear to pose a direct political challenge to Soviet rule. There is no Muslim samizdat literature or open protests such as those that have become common among Jews and other European minorities in the Soviet Union. It is also debatable whether Soviet Muslims consider themselves a homogeneous group. Ethnic, geographic, and linguistic divisions within them are powerful obstacles to unity, just as they are among the Muslims of the Arab world. They may feel different from Russians, but that is a long way from uniting and taking action against Soviet rule. Soviet spokesmen argue that the relatively high level of urban and industrial development in Central Asia, the enormous advances in education and medicine, and the encouragement of local languages have produced a broad consensus in favor of Soviet rule. No independent observer can deny that the standard of living for most Central Asians and for Azerbaijanis in the Soviet Union is higher than it is in the neighboring areas of Turkey, Iran, and Afghanistan. From a material point of view there is no "contamination effect" from across the border, nor any solid evidence yet of a resurgence of nationalism in Soviet Central Asia.

Yet it is possible that the advances already made may produce a destabilizing factor in the long term. A frustrated intelligentsia is often a more revolutionary catalyst for channeling discontent upward against an alien system than a downtrodden peasantry on its own. If the Soviet system does not find ways of allowing more political power to the new Central Asian elites, it might in time find itself with a problem on its hands. Whether their discontent would be directed toward greater power for the republics within the Soviet Federation, or more career opportunities for non-Russians in the central apparatus in Moscow, or whether it would go toward the extreme of demanding independence cannot be predicted. The problems may be easily containable. Professor Alexander Bennigsen, one of the leading Western students of Islam in the Soviet Union, has argued that "Communism and Islam can co-exist, with Communism as a frame and Islam as a kind of inner essence. This is a twist on the 1920's declaration by Stalin which called for a proletarian essence within a national framework."[5]

The Soviet invasion of Afghanistan was primarily aimed at limiting damage abroad. The Russians were trying to stop the collapse of a Marxist–Leninist regime in a neighboring country. They were afraid of the consequences of its fall, believing that whatever successor regime came to power would be at best an unknown and probably uncontrollable quantity, at worst anti-Soviet. In either case it would not be like the prerevolutionary Afghan governments, officially nonaligned, but in practice tolerant of the Soviet Union and receptive to its influence. Failure to rescue the Afghan regime would also have been a severe blow to Soviet pride and prestige. The Kremlin had supported the Afghan regime heavily soon after it came to power. Not to have defended it later would have seemed a sign of weakness, it believed.

What of the argument that the Soviet move was motivated by expansionism and was an outward-looking strategic move, bringing the Soviet Union a step nearer both to the Persian Gulf and also to the Indian subcontinent? It requires only a cursory look at the map to see the absurdity of the first of these claims. The Iranian oil province of Khuzestan is nearer to Soviet Azerbaijan and Turkmenistan than to any part of Afghanistan. The invasion brought the Russians no nearer to the oil fields of the northern part of the Persian Gulf than they were already. Even if the Russians decided to march on the gulf from Afghanistan, a Pentagon official has pointed out that they would need five days to cross the 347 passes, bridges, and other vulnerable choke-points on the way "even without opposition."[6] As for the oil fields of the southern part of the gulf and Saudi Arabia, these are separated from Afghanistan and Iran by water. The flying time for paratroop battalions from Afghanistan to these fields would be a few minutes shorter than from the Soviet Union, but it is surely ludicrous to imagine that the Kremlin would undertake an operation as risky as the invasion of Afghanistan simply to save a minute or two of aircraft fuel.

The only strategic advantage of the invasion for the Russians is that it brought them closer to the Indian subcontinent, as well as to the Pakistani ports on the Arabian Sea. In theory they have acquired a potential new asset by occupying Afghanistan. In practice it is an asset of limited extra value. Soviet political influence in India has been strong for most of the last fifteen years. Any perception in India that the Soviet Union was a military threat would only weaken Moscow's carefully built-up political position. As for Pakistan, the Kremlin must have had to calculate that the invasion of Afghanistan might produce the result that in fact ensued—a strengthening of Pakistan's dependence on the United States and an increase in American military aid.

Long before the invasion, Afghanistan had had a unique relationship with the Soviet Union. A direct neighbor of the Soviet Union, it was more closely tied to Moscow than any other country in the Third World except for socialist states such as Angola, Cuba, and Ethiopia. In the late 1940s, at the start of the Cold War, the United States had devoted lavish amounts of economic aid to Afghanistan, as it did to all Russia's neighbors. But after turning down an Afghan request for military assistance because this clashed with plans to build up Pakistan's forces, the Americans found their influence reduced. The Soviet Union became the country's biggest supplier of aid as well as its main trading partner. For years the Russians made it clear that they were less interested in Afghanistan's political system than that its foreign policy should not be anti-Soviet. Khrushchev visited the country as the king's guest in 1955. In his memoirs he recalled nothing of the country's social system. His only interest was that "we have earned the Afghans' trust and friendship, and it hasn't fallen into the Americans' trap."[7]

In 1963 the king embarked on a course of constitutional liberalism promising a series of political reforms. But they were only partially implemented, and in 1973 his cousin, the former Prime Minister Muhammad Daoud, took power in a coup. The coup was planned and organized by the Parcham wing of the Marxist People's Democratic Party of Afghanistan (PDPA), which allied itself with

Daoud in the hope that he would initiate social change and land reform. Moscow piled on more economic and military aid, building roads and helping in oil exploration, mining development, and irrigation projects. Four ministries were given to Parcham leaders. But two years later Daoud began to betray his Parcham allies and abandon the reforms. Religious conservatives and political liberals were also purged. Pressure on Daoud to effect the purges came from the Shah of Iran who was determined to expand his power across the region. His aim was to eliminate what he saw as excessive Soviet and Marxist influence in Afghanistan. The shah offered unprecedented amounts of aid, particularly for water-sharing and iron-mining projects which would link the two countries closely. His secret police, SAVAK, operated freely in Afghanistan.

Daoud's attack on the Left came to a climax in April 1978. The two wings of the PDPA, the Parcham and the Khalq, organized street demonstrations to protest against the murder of a popular radical. These were the first public demonstrations in five years, and they attracted large numbers of educated young people who could find no jobs in an economy suffering from lopsided development. Worried about the explosion of popular feeling, Daoud arrested the senior Marxist leaders, including Babrak Karmal, Nur Muhammad Taraki and Hafizullah Amin. But Amin managed to smuggle out instructions for a coup to the young army and air force officers whom he had been recruiting for just such an eventuality for the last few years. The next day a rebel tank column moved on the city center, and after several hours of fighting, stormed the Presidential Palace and overthrew Daoud. The coup was thus triggered directly by Daoud's offensive against the Left, and indirectly by the Shah. One American student of the region, Selig Harrison, commented: "Put in perspective, the 1978 Afghan coup emerges as one of the more disastrous legacies of the Shah's ambitious effort to roll back Soviet influence in surrounding countries and create a modern version of the ancient Persian empire."[8] There is no firm evidence to suggest that the coup was engineered by the Russians or to doubt the version given by Taraki at a press conference in Havana in September 1979, where he told journalists that "when the revolution took place President Carter and Comrade Brezhnev were equally surprised."[9]

The coup was not considered an unmixed blessing in Moscow. According to Vladimir Kuzichkin, a former KGB major who defected from the Soviet embassy in Tehran in 1982, the KGB anticipated problems with the new regime. It also argued that Moscow should back Karmal over any other potential leader.[10]

The first few months under the new government were quiet. It took care not to alienate Islamic sentiment, and published many of its early, mildly reformist proclamations in the name of Allah. The official media used Uzbek, Turkoman, and Baluch languages for the first time. There was broad popular acceptance of the regime, which was carefully balanced between the two wings of the PDPA. The Parcham ("Flag") group was identified with the cosmopolitan life of the

Dari-speakers in Kabul and had good contacts at the university. Babrak Karmal, its leader, was an eloquent speaker who had spent several years in parliament. The Khalq ("Masses") under Taraki and Amin was dominated by Pushtun speakers from tribes and communities in eastern and southern Afghanistan. Their opposition to the Daoud government, with which Parcham had originally collaborated, gave them a more clandestine and conspiratorial style and meant that suspicion between the two groups was strong. In July 1978 the rivalry came to a head. The Khalq group took over supreme power. Babrak Karmal and five Parcham colleagues were given ambassadorships abroad. From then on the regime's program became more radical and impatient. It changed the colors of the country's flag from Islamic green to red. It issued decrees expropriating large landowners, eliminating rural debt, reducing the customary bride price for marriages, and introducing compulsory education for both sexes. Had these reforms remained on paper as had similar-sounding ones from earlier governments, no Afghan would have been surprised. But this time eager teams of city-based revolutionary cadres backed up by a newly radicalized police force and the army fanned out into the villages, haranguing landlords and insisting that women take off the veil.

Rapid social transformation is hard in any country. In Afghanistan it was almost impossible. Because the country had never been a colony of any of the imperial powers, it had no tradition of local administration. The authorities in Kabul had never been able to make much headway in collecting taxes or imposing legislation in the villages. Local tribal and religious leaders were strong. Peasants did not see the world in class terms so much as in terms of tribal loyalties. Country people also had a long tradition of carrying guns, a relic of a history of resisting outside forces. For young Marxists to come into the countryside and try to disrupt age-old social relations overnight was bound to be catastrophic. Khalq's arrest and execution of a growing number of religious and tribal leaders who resisted the reforms began to provoke open counterrevolution. The changing regional climate also put pressure on the revolution. The victory of the Islamic forces in Iran in February 1979 and the expulsion of the Shah gave a powerful psychological boost to Muslim feelings in Afghanistan. Pakistan had a history of tense relations with Kabul over the disputed issues of Baluchistan and Pushtunistan and started to give help to Pushtun tribesmen coming over the border from Afghanistan. China openly criticized the revolution. Perhaps encouraged by Carter's national security advisor, Zbigniew Brzezinski, who visited Peking in 1978 with the request that China start taking more forceful action against the Soviet Union "in parallel" with Washington, the Chinese began to give limited military training to the rebels. But none of this altered the fact that the main resistance to the regime was spontaneous, widespread, and locally based.

The Soviet Union had watched the first few months of the unexpected revolution with closer interest than it had done in the case of two earlier embryonic socialist revolutions, those of Cuba and Chile. Afghanistan was a neighboring country in a zone of far greater strategic sensitivity to the Soviet Union than Latin America. They knew its army leadership relatively well. The revolution was led by an orthodox Communist party with whom they had good links. Nevertheless, Soviet identification with the PDPA government was not overwhelming and the Russians cannot have been happy with the outcome of the power struggle which sent Babrak Karmal into virtual exile. Moscow had always been closer to Parcham than to Khalq.

By the spring of 1979 Moscow was already faced with the dilemma that eventually recurred in a starker form on the eve of their invasion. Should they cut their losses and withdraw support from an unpopular regime that was becoming increasingly unstable, or should they help to prop it up? The revolt had spread to most of Afghanistan's twenty-eight provinces. The first serious sign that the counterrevolution might be successful occurred on March 22 when Pushtuns and Shias seized Herat. In a violent pogrom, scores of Khalq officials and Soviet civilian and military personnel were murdered. It took the government three days to recapture the city with armored and air force units. The uprising in Herat suggested that the regime's control of the cities could be doomed. Since almost all Khalq's support was urban, the message was grim.

Shortly after the Herat trouble, Hafizullah Amin took over the prime ministership, and in effect supreme control of the country, from President Taraki. To assess the events, Moscow sent a high-level delegation headed by General Alexei Yepishev, the chief of the main political directorate of the Soviet Army and a known hard-liner. The Russians decided to increase their involvement. By early summer they had sent in 5,000 advisors, including 1,500 military specialists. These were deployed throughout the Afghan armed forces, down to company level. Soviet units helped to fly the MI–24 helicopter gunships and MiG–23 fighters armed with rockets.

Soviet policy now seemed to be firmly committed to a military solution. But the revolt inside Afghanistan only gained in strength. The tough Soviet strategy of using air power to strafe and bomb villages suspected of harboring rebels alienated more of the population. It led to a collapse of army morale, and prompted several counterattacks by rebel forces in the cities. Aqsa, the secret police, which was under Amin's control as prime minister, was conducting a policy of preventive detention that led to the arrest and torture of thousands of suspected counterrevolutionaries.

With the situation going from bad to worse, the Russians—even though they had helped to contribute to the problem—began to consider another tack. Perhaps a slight softening of the regime might help. This appeared to be the thinking of President Taraki, whose public pronouncements in the summer of 1979 differed from those of the more hard-line Amin, who had now also assumed control of the Ministry of Defense. On his return from the Summit Conference of the Non-Aligned in Havana in September, Taraki was invited by Brezhnev to make a stopover in Moscow.

There were reports that Babrak Karmal and other Parchamites in exile joined the talks. Taraki went back to Kabul, apparently with the recommendation that he seize control from Amin. In fact, the opposite happened. On September 14 in a gun battle in the Presidential Palace, known as the People's House, an unknown number of cabinet officials and senior party men were killed. Two days later Taraki was reported to have resigned, and on October 9 Radio Kabul announced that he had died of an "illness." It is unclear whether Taraki actually died in the gun battle or was wounded or captured. At a press conference in Kabul four months later, a Major Jandad, described as the former chief of Amin's bodyguard, said that Taraki was put under house arrest and then suffocated with a cushion on October 8. The Russians signaled their unhappiness with this turn of events by their hesitant public reaction to the change of leadership. The Soviet prime minister, Alexei Kosygin, pointedly avoided stopping at Kabul when he flew home from a visit to India a few days later.

Foiled in their effort to soften the regime's line and remove Amin, the Russians did not give up. The invasion that took place at the end of December was essentially designed to achieve what Taraki's small-scale coup had failed to do. Between October and December roughly four thousand Taraki loyalists in the army and civilian posts had been arrested by Amin. To remove him the Russians could no longer hope to avoid intervening directly themselves. Taking advantage of Amin's repeated calls for Soviet help against the rebels, the Russians began to send in thousands of combat troops in the last two weeks of December. After some hours of shooting in Kabul on December 27, Amin was said to have been tried and executed. A new PDPA government, led by Babrak Karmal, was installed. So far, the invasion was a success.

But like the first military escalation in the spring of 1979, full-scale invasion was soon seen only to have made matters worse. The Islamic nations criticized Moscow, and Castro's influence as chairman of the Non-Aligned Movement evaporated. Inside Afghanistan the Soviet forces failed to gain ground against a resistance movement whose numbers were swollen by the sense of outraged nationalism that the invasion provoked.

Two years later a visitor found the Russians in Kabul taking a wearily optimistic line, a kind of socialist version of the "white man's burden." They claimed that as agents of a process of modernization and economic development they would win the support of a grateful Afghan people. "You cannot expect quick results in a country which is still in many ways in the fifteenth or sixteenth century," said Vasily Sovronchuk, one of the senior political advisors in the Soviet embassy.[11] "Here in embryo is the history of our own revolution," he went on. "It took us at least five years to consolidate our power and win through in Russia, and ten years in Central Asia." He referred to the so-called "Basmachi" revolt in Central Asia. For ten years well-armed ground forces fought against the effort to extend Bolshevik control to Turkestan, or what is now Soviet Kirghizia, Turkmenistan, Tadzhikistan and Uzbekistan. Eventually, by the end of the 1920s, the Bolsheviks had won by a combination of military repression, unwavering determination, and economic development.

The difference in Afghanistan was that the Russians were promising an eventual withdrawal, although they did not expect it soon. "I don't see any prospect of a Soviet withdrawal without a political settlement," Sovronchuk emphasized. "We have to do our revolutionary duty. The Afghan government would never agree to being left alone to face the massive international conspiracy against it. Any revolution is of an irreversible character. It cannot be turned back, even in as backward a country as Afghanistan. The peasant population here is overwhelming and Muslim influence is very strong. That is the negative side. The positive side is that Afghanistan has an experienced party with seventeen years of struggle, much of it underground. They can never be defeated. A process is underway which is the same as in Vietnam, Nicaragua, Angola, and Ethiopia."

Sovronchuk's perspective of a long, bleak struggle was justified by the grim state of the war. Soviet military tactics since the invasion provide strong evidence that the Kremlin views the war as a frustrating sideshow rather than a springboard for further moves to the south. In the first two years Moscow did not increase the number of its combat troops. In spite of their failure to defeat the Muslim rebels, the Russians chose not to send in extra troops. Although many Western commentators cheerfully referred to Afghanistan as "Russia's Vietnam," the comparison is unjustified. Indeed, the Russians appear to have learned from the Americans' mistakes in Southeast Asia. They saw that a massive escalation of their troop strength would not help in dealing with armed guerrillas who had the support of the rural population and intimate knowledge of difficult mountainous terrain. The first increase in their contingent came two years after the invasion, with the dispatch of an extra 15,000 men to boost the 85,000 originally sent at the end of 1979. Another 5,000 came later. While new Soviet barracks have been built, the Russians have not equipped their air bases in Afghanistan to support strategic aircraft on long stop-overs by lengthening runways, expanding petrol storage facilities, or building more hard-stands for parking reserve squadrons. Their air base improvements have been geared to the short-term purpose of providing better operational facilities for helicopters and fighter aircraft used against the guerrillas.[12]

Soviet restraint in not significantly reinforcing itself in Afghanistan was important in view of the miserable military and political situation the Kremlin faced. By the end of 1982, Soviet and Afghan forces only controlled Kabul, the capital city, and a few of the major towns. Kandahar, the country's second city, was the site of major fighting with rebel forces on several occasions, and the Karmal regime could only tentatively exert its authority during daylight hours. Herat was the target of frequent rebel attacks, and only Jalalabad and Mazar-i-

Sharif were relatively quiet. The regime had less control of the countryside than the Americans had at the height of their involvement in Vietnam. In the autumn of 1981, officials admitted that half the country's schools were closed and that the program of land reform was operating in only a quarter of the country.[13] The contingent of some one hundred United Nations aid officials, most of them concerned with rural development, had not been allowed to travel outside Kabul for over a year because of guerrilla attacks and roadblocks. Senior Soviet advisors were under constant threat of kidnap or assassination. Total Soviet control of Afghanistan's airspace was slowly being eroded as the rebels acquired Western-supplied, ground-to-air missiles. Several Soviet efforts to drive the rebels from strategic rural areas, such as the Panjshir and Kunar valleys in eastern Afghanistan, failed, with the Soviet forces either coming under heavy fire or else finding that the rebels returned as soon as the Russians retreated from places they thought they had "pacified." Added to this catalog of military gloom was the withering away of the Afghan army through a combination of desertion, wounding, and death.

In response to this grim military picture, Soviet strategy became one of trying to hold to a military stalemate in the hope of an eventual political stabilization. The Russians calculated that the rebels at least could never win. They had neither the ideological commitment nor the political unity of classic liberation movements. On the contrary they were divided into roughly seven groups, some Islamic fundamentalists, some tribally based, and some secular modernists.

One advantage for the Kremlin was the absence of an articulate antiwar movement in the Soviet Union, another contrast with the American experience in Vietnam. The number of Soviet troops in Afghanistan is only a sixth of the American contingent at its peak in Vietnam. The chances of a young Soviet conscript ending up in Afghanistan are small. More important, the exact nature of the war is suppressed in the Soviet media. Although the press is full of justifications for the intervention, there is hardly a mention of Soviet casualties. Nor does the press, except on rare occasions, focus on individual acts of heroism or show pictures of identifiable soldiers. Soviet leaders do not publicly award decorations for bravery, visit the front, or console bereaved families. When they fight or when they die, the Red Army is composed of faceless men.

A report in *Krasnaya Zvezda* admitted that the war is "at times very, very difficult," but it went on: "Not a single soldier or officer with whom we met for a short chat has even mentioned the difficulties. They are in a fighting mood."[14] Other reports in the same paper have written about the loneliness and nostalgia of Soviet conscripts in their Afghan barracks—"memories, memories . . . you cannot help noticing how the inmates of the room keep glancing at their bedside tables. On each stand small framed photographs, here a woman's portrait, there a group. These are the people waiting for them in the homeland. Wives, children, parents."[15] One need not imagine that ordinary Soviet citizens' private reactions to the war are as stiff-upper-lipped as these morale-boosting reports would like to suggest. But there is little chance that private grief would ever lead to demands for the recall of the troops.

No official casualty figures exist, but the best Western estimates do not put them very high. Professor John Erickson, one of the foremost authorities on the Soviet military, has argued that the total number of Russians dead in the first eighteen months of the invasion did not exceed fifteen hundred, including motor accidents, accidental shootings, and disease. U.S. embassy sources in Kabul put the battle casualty figure over the first twenty-one months at between two and three thousand dead. Even if these figures are low, the impact of Soviet deaths is too well concealed and cushioned to have any political impact. A society that has been able to muffle the fact of millions of deaths in the purges of the 1930s and 1940s is not going to break apart over deaths in Afghanistan. Moreover, there appears to be no crisis of legitimacy among the Soviet public over the invasion. In its psychological dimension, the invasion is not so much Russia's Vietnam as Russia's Ulster. Russians talk about it as the English talk about Northern Ireland—only rarely. It is a geographical neighbor yet psychologically remote, a strange, unruly part of an otherwise placid community; "ours," yet not really part of us, a tedious battleground with no end in sight, but bearable because the death rate is and probably will remain low. "Even when it was a monarchy, I always felt Afghanistan was a satellite, almost like Tadzhikistan," Vasily Aksyonov, one of the country's best writers, said shortly before he emigrated to the West.[16] He opposed the invasion, but it seemed to leave him untouched. Would the invasion have the same effect on the young generation as Czechoslovakia had had on young Russian intellectuals in 1968, he was asked. If it did, it would not be an ideological shock as 1968 was, he thought. It would be a shock to people's concept of state power. People would wonder what had happened to Soviet might if the authorities had to send so many troops to help a friendly neighbor.

Aksyonov's view illustrates why the Soviet Union is unlikely to admit or accept defeat in Afghanistan. It was concern over prestige, as well as security issues, that took the Russians into this country to shore up the revolution, and it is prestige and security that prevent them from withdrawing. They are looking for a political settlement that will allow them an honorable departure, provided the revolution's future is guaranteed. In the meantime the military stalemate is no great price to pay while they try to achieve a negotiated arrangement with Afghanistan's neighbors. The Russians hope to persuade Pakistan to cease supplying the rebels with arms and offering them sanctuary. If that could be done, it would weaken the rebels' military position. At the same time, the Russians hope to convince the new, urban, educated elite of Afghanistan that the Soviet Union and the Karmal regime represent the forces of modernization, whereas the rebels stand for feudalism and reaction. In this way time would work in favor of the Soviet Union, as it held the towns and hoped the rural revolt would fade away. About 9,000 Afghans are enrolled on scholarships at Soviet educational institutions besides an unknown number at military training schools. On their return home, they will be expected to staff the Party, the army, and other elite organizations.

Whether that strategy would work seems doubtful. Even if the rebels were vigorously discouraged by Pakistan, the border is too wild and mountainous to police effectively. Arms supplies would continue to come in. By now, many of the rebels' weapons are captured from the Afghan Army or brought over by deserters. The Karmal regime has shown no sign of broadening its domestic political base enough to persuade the rebels that it would negotiate seriously or share power with them. Meanwhile, the West's pressure on Pakistan not to achieve an accommodation with Afghanistan has continued and the covert military help to the rebels has increased under the Reagan administration. Its strategy has been to give the rebels enough help to prevent the Russians winning but not enough to enable the rebels to win. Some officials in the Reagan administration seemed to relish having the Russians tied down for years in Afghanistan.

The Soviet invasion may therefore be seen in some Western quarters as a benefit rather than a threat to the West. The propaganda disadvantages that Moscow has suffered remain considerable. Even if some Soviet troops are getting potentially valuable combat experience, the cost of tying down close to one hundred thousand men in a corner of Southwest Asia cannot be discounted. The Afghan issue has made it easier to find support for the Rapid Deployment Force and an enhanced American presence in the Persian Gulf area. It may also have acted as a restraint when the Russians were calculating their moves over Poland. If politicians can learn from mistakes, the Afghanistan invasion is more likely to have reinforced Soviet caution in the future than to have encouraged the Kremlin to project its forces into uncertain territory again.

CONCLUSION

The Kremlin sent its forces into Afghanistan to defend a revolutionary regime whose popular support was draining away. Although Moscow had lived comfortably with a non-Communist Afghanistan as its neighbor for decades, it was afraid that the defeat of the Afghan revolution might lead to an outcome that would be worse than the prerevolutionary status quo. With the collapse of the Shah's Iran a few months earlier, the Kremlin feared an Afghanistan that might either be ruled by fanatical Islamic nationalists or become a new outpost of American power. In either case it would be anti-Soviet, the Kremlin believed.

The Kremlin did not see its invasion as the first step in a general Southwest Asian offensive toward the Persian Gulf and the Indian subcontinent. Nor was it particularly worried over the loyalty of its own Muslim population in Soviet Central Asia. The primary purpose of the invasion was to keep Afghanistan within broadly the same foreign policy position that it had maintained for the past twenty-five years—official nonalignment plus close cooperation with the Soviet Union.

The army coup that brought a Marxist regime to power in April 1978 was not organized by Moscow, but it prompted the Kremlin to increase its political and economic support. When popular resistance mounted against the regime's revolutionary decrees, the Kremlin increased its involvement still further and began to introduce military advisors. By December 1979 when the Kremlin took the decision to intervene massively with its own troops, it saw itself faced by an issue of prestige as well as security. Having supported the revolutionary regime from the beginning, it felt that Soviet prestige and its image required it not to reverse policy in midstream and abandon a Marxist–Leninist ally, particularly on the very borders of the Soviet Union. With the Carter administration already backing off from the SALT II treaty in Washington, and preparing a Rapid Deployment Force for the Indian Ocean and the Persian Gulf after the shah's collapse, the Kremlin was less concerned about the invasion's impact on détente than it might have been had the Afghan crisis happened in the early 1970s.

Although it initially hoped for a quick victory, the Kremlin has adjusted its perspective and is now prepared to accept a military stalemate rather than send in even more troops. It is aiming at a political settlement between Afghanistan and Pakistan which will, it hopes, make it harder for the resistance movement to operate from Pakistan. The best hope seemed to be the United Nations mediation effort which got underway in 1982. By the spring of 1983 the UN undersecretary-general, Diego Cordovez, was reported to have obtained provisional agreement on a plan for a phased Soviet withdrawal of combat troops within a fixed time period in return for an end to Pakistani support for the resistance. Pakistan was finding the presence of close to three million Afghan refugees a growing political and economic burden. The UN plan would also allow for the continuation of a pro-Soviet, communist-led regime, though probably not one headed by Karmal. It would permit Moscow to maintain a military presence but not combat troops, for some years to come.

Andropov seemed to be pressing for this compromise, which would give Moscow much of what it wanted. At Brezhnev's funeral he made a point of meeting with Zia ul-Haq, the President of Pakistan. At the end of March 1983 he held talks with the UN secretary-general, Perez de Cuellar, in Moscow. As a former KGB leader, Andropov was better briefed than most of his colleagues on the real difficulties facing the Russians in Afghanistan. But the chances of a political solution were still bleak. The UN plan required a major effort of political will by Pakistan and the backing of the United States. Even if both countries agreed, the resistance itself might refuse to accept a deal made over its head.

8

ASIAN
ANXIETIES

We Europeans are totally different from the Chinese.

Leonid Brezhnev, 1972[1]

China's reemergence on the world stage in the 1970s was the second most significant development of the entire Brezhnev era. If Moscow's advance to strategic nuclear parity with the United States was the greatest single achievement, leading to détente and some increase in Soviet self-confidence, China's new position negated much of the advantage that parity had brought. From being a tiresome ally in 1964 China became a major security threat in Soviet eyes, adding to the long-established challenge posed by the West. The Soviet Union felt threatened on two separate fronts, in Europe and the Far East.

Only in the first few weeks of the Brezhnev period, and then again during its last months, was there any flicker of optimism for Sino–Soviet relations after years of failure and gloom. As head of the Central Committee's international department, which dealt with China and the other socialist countries, Andropov was one of Moscow's China experts in the 1960s. He headed delegations to Peking in 1963 and 1965. From almost the first day of his administration, he demonstrated that he hoped to continue the search for a new and better basis for relations with Peking, which Brezhnev had tentatively started in 1982. By sending their foreign minister to Moscow for Brezhnev's funeral, the Chinese leadership also showed they wanted to reduce some of the earlier tension. After two years of arguments with the Reagan administration over Taiwan, the

131

Chinese were ready to distance themselves from Washington and find a more independent role. A position of pragmatic Chinese nonalignment between the two superpowers would be an important strategic shift but would not eliminate Moscow's security concerns in the Far East. The Kremlin was bound to remain wary of Chinese intentions and keep part of its military arsenal deployed in the Far East, even after a thaw in Sino–Soviet relations.

It was far from certain that such a thaw could be achieved after the wide disagreements that grew up during Brezhnev's rule. In 1964 the two great nations of the Communist world were at odds on several fronts. They differed over numerous party issues, from the role of the Communist party of the Soviet Union, and its right to expel any other party from the movement, to the question whether war with imperialism could or should be avoided. They differed over foreign policy. How far should the national liberation struggles be pushed? Was détente with the United States worth pursuing? They differed over state issues such as the level of Soviet aid to China and the just delimitation of their mutual borders. And they differed particularly over nuclear weapons after Khrushchev signed the limited Test Ban Treaty with Britain and the United States in 1963.

Long though the list of disagreements was, and however angrily each was treated in the other side's polemics, the Sino–Soviet dispute in 1964 was still expressed in political terms. It had no military dimension. At the time of Khrushchev's removal, the border between the Soviet Union and China was lightly defended on both sides. It was Khrushchev's successors—indeed within little more than a year after his fall—who took the momentous decision to start a military buildup in the Far East. In the 1950s and early 1960s the China "problem" had been largely a political and ideological issue, but under Brezhnev it began to be perceived in the Kremlin as a threat to national security. Unwilling to accept China as an equal power, the Kremlin attempted to apply military pressure. Although it stopped short of sending troops across the border, Moscow's saber-rattling between 1965 and 1969 confirmed the paradox that was to become increasingly evident in a world with several Communist states. Moscow was more likely to invade a neighbor with a Communist government than one with a capitalist one.

Its decision to turn the confrontation with China into a military issue brought no improvement. Not only did it fail to win political concessions from China, or make a negotiated settlement of the differences any easier, it also required massive investment in Soviet arms and a consequent distortion of the Soviet Union's economic growth. It heightened Chinese fears of Moscow, confirmed their enmity, and eventually spurred the reconciliation between China and the United States, which left the Soviet Union infinitely worse off.

Moscow's predominant concern over Peking colored Soviet policy in the whole of the rest of Asia, in India, Indochina, and Japan. The results were mixed. By the end of the Brezhnev era Soviet influence in Asia had grown in only one of the continent's regions, Indochina. In India and Japan it remained static. In China it no longer existed. Taken as a whole, the record of Soviet relations in Asia during the last two decades is far from the conventional Western image of global expansion. In Asia it is a story of diminishing influence.

CHINA

The origins of the Sino–Soviet dispute go back almost forty years. Some observers even date it to the mid-1920s when Stalin urged the Chinese Communist party to form a united front with the nationalist Kuomintang. Whether one takes the earlier or later period, the dispute has lasted long enough to destroy the once current notion of a Sino–Soviet "split." The world has been accustomed to tense Sino–Soviet relations for so many years that it seems hard to believe that the public emergence of a "split" in the early 1960s was greeted with skepticism. Some Western politicians maintained for years afterward that the "split" was a cunning Communist plot to get the West to "lower its guard." In fact, it can be seen that to talk of a split is to reverse the truth. The normal state of relations between the Soviet and Chinese Communist parties has been one of suspicion, tension, and dispute. One might profitably talk of a Sino–Soviet Cold War. Where there has been a period of relative harmony, such as from 1953 to 1956, it was a rare time of détente.

This echo of the usual phraseology of U.S.–Soviet relations is no glib analogy. The disparities that underlie the relationship between the Soviet Union and the United States are similar to those that separate the Soviet Union from China. The fact that both nations are ruled by Communist parties does not outweigh the reality that proud nation-states with a missionary ideology in a period of rapid socioeconomic advance are bound to have different interests. Each emerged from the human destruction of the Second World War with its main geographical rival temporarily weakened by defeat. In Asia, the collapse of Japan left China the predominant power, even though civil war delayed China's resurgence for four more years. In Europe, the collapse of Germany left the Soviet Union as the strongest continental power.

Although their interests differed, was it inevitable that these newly powerful neighbors should clash? Numerous analysts have given reasons why they did. Some rely on personalities: Mao's feeling of superiority to Khrushchev as a revolutionary, and Khrushchev's abrasive, provocative style. Some put it down to traditional racial antagonism. Some talk of the two countries' different economic needs, and the Soviet Union's unwillingness to give sufficient aid to China. Some mention the historic asymmetry between the two countries, the fact that the Soviet Union was a postrevolutionary, "satisfied" power at a time when the Chinese Revolution had just begun. Some see the problem as that of rival nationalisms clashing over common territory.

While most of these factors were certainly issues in the Sino–Soviet dispute at one time or another, it is not clear that they were causes. The real causes were the different power relationships between them, and between each one of them and the United States. China's advance toward great-power status was almost bound to lead to awkward questions within a few years of the Chinese Revolution.[2] Either China would have to accept a permanent condition of economic, military, and hence political dependence on the Soviet Union, or it must seek independent growth. The choice of the second option, which was probably never in doubt, was hastened by Moscow's unwillingness to concede China political parity in the Communist movement. Just as détente between Moscow and Washington broke down in the 1970s over American reluctance to adjust to a relative decline in power and accept parity with the Soviet Union, détente between Moscow and Peking broke down over a similar issue a decade and a half earlier.

The rivalry between the Soviet Union and China was exacerbated by the role of the United States and the different postures that Moscow and Peking adopted toward it. Although the Second World War had left China and the Soviet Union as the dominant Asian and European powers, it had also faced each of them with a challenge from an extracontinental state that was not part of the European or the Asian landmass. A newly outward-looking United States was eager to share power in Europe with the war-ravaged European nations and replace the old European-dominated order in Asia with one dominated by itself. It had also embarked on a global campaign against communism.

The notion of a superpower triangle is considerably older than is usually appreciated.[3] Long before it was widely recognized at the time of Washington's opening to China in 1971, the idea that each of the three major postwar powers would try to play off one rival against another was in operation. In 1949 the Chinese Communists were still too weak, and American suspicions of them too strong (after the so-called "loss" of China as a result of the defeat of the Nationalists) for Mao to have any alternative but to rely on Moscow. His tentative overtures to Washington to establish a working relationship were turned down except on condition that he remain aloof from Moscow.[4] The American hope was to turn China into a kind of Asian Yugoslavia—a degree of isolation to which Mao was not attracted.

By the mid-1950s Mao was ready for a new approach to the Americans. This time he was rebuffed for different reasons. Washington was intrigued by the possibility of a dialogue with Khrushchev who was already hinting to Western leaders in 1954 that the Soviet Union and the West should jointly beware of China.[5] The Geneva summit conference and the Austrian State Treaty in 1955 had suggested that the Soviet Union under its new leader might—as the West saw it—be tamed. The Americans were more interested in the benefits that would flow from better relations with Moscow than with those that might come from Peking. Some American analysts may have guessed that there could be a useful side effect. By playing the "Moscow card" and ignoring China they would be widening suspicions between the two Communist powers.

This indeed happened. In his report to the Twentieth Party Congress in February 1956, Khrushchev stressed that the fundamental principle of Soviet foreign policy was peaceful coexistence between states of differing social systems. To Mao this was not only a doctrinal lapse but a sign of weakness in the face of American imperialism. When the Soviet Union tested its first intercontinental ballistic missile in 1957, but soon afterward refused to help China liberate Taiwan, Mao was confirmed in the view that the Russians were being unnecessarily timid. Chinese requests for access to Soviet nuclear technology were turned down, and Peking resolved to become an independent nuclear power.

Visits by Khrushchev to Peking and Washington in 1959 demonstrated that in this phase of triangular contacts Moscow's relations with the United States were already warmer than those with China. His Washington trip produced an atmosphere of mutual goodwill, symbolized by talk of a "spirit of Camp David," President Eisenhower's retreat in the Maryland mountains where the Soviet leader was entertained. His Peking visit failed even to provide a communiqué.

For the next five years Sino–Soviet relations continued to worsen. In 1960 Khrushchev withdrew all the Soviet technicians from China and cut back on trade. In 1962 he was neutral during the Sino–Indian war. In March 1963 China, for the first time, declared that the Russo–Chinese border treaties of the nineteenth century were "unequal" and should be renegotiated. In July 1963 Soviet agreement to the nuclear Test Ban Treaty with Britain and the United States was openly denounced by China, which saw it as directed against itself.

Although the increasingly public argument between Peking and Moscow was worrying other Communist parties, many of whom pleaded for a truce, Khrushchev was determined to have a showdown. He pressed for the early convocation of an international conference of Communist parties at which Mao was to be brought to book.

After his fall in October 1964, Khrushchev's successors recognized that they had inherited a deteriorating international situation. Relations with the United States were uneasy in spite of the Test Ban Treaty. Relations with China were causing a blight in the Communist world and creating irritating complications for Soviet policy in Africa, the Middle East, and Asia where Moscow constantly found itself accused of weakness by the Chinese. For Brezhnev and his colleagues, policy toward the United States had to have priority. There was no prospect that they would abandon peaceful coexistence and accept China's militant posture toward imperialism. But they did hope for some modifications of the tone of polemics with Peking, so that the quarrel could at least remain a bilateral matter and cease to poison the rest of their foreign policy. Brezhnev and his colleagues were willing to make some initial overtures to Peking. As a first step, they halted the anti-Chinese propaganda and delayed plans for the international conference.

However, two new developments made it unlikely that any reconciliation would succeed. One was the detonation of China's first atomic bomb, by coincidence on the day after Khrushchev was overthrown. Whatever strategic implications Moscow may have seen in the event, it was a dramatic symbol of China's developing potential for self-reliance. The other factor was the growing tension between North Vietnam and the United States, marked by the clash between ships of the two countries in the Gulf of Tonkin. Until this point China's ability to create serious obstacles to the Soviet Union's hopes of achieving a modus vivendi with the United States had been strictly limited. None of the areas where Moscow and Washington had recently come near to confrontation—Berlin, the Congo, Cuba, and the Middle East—were places where China had much influence. Vietnam was a different case. Here was a national liberation struggle which was being closely watched by uncommitted nations in the Third World and could lead to fully fledged war with the United States, and over which Moscow had less control than Peking. Vietnam threatened to tear apart all Moscow's contradictions of trying to deal with the United States while simultaneously posing as the responsible champion of the fight against imperialism. Vietnam could also play China off against the Soviet Union and obtain aid from both.

Like the new Kremlin leadership, the Chinese leaders saw Khrushchev's downfall as a potential turning point. Chou En-Lai offered to come to Moscow for the anniversary of the October Revolution, presumably in order to sound out Khrushchev's successors. In his formal anniversary speech Brezhnev restated the essential themes of Khrushchev's foreign policy, but he and his colleagues used their private talks with Chou to offer China a resumption of scientific and cultural cooperation and trade. They proposed a summit meeting with Mao and suggested the two sides should coordinate their foreign policies. The Chinese response was negative. Chou left Moscow without any agreement and a few days later an article in *Red Flag* said that Moscow would have to change its policy first.[6]

Three months later the Kremlin made another attempt to neutralize the damage done by the dispute with Peking, and to prevent it spilling over into the escalating crisis between Vietnam and the United States. Brezhnev and his colleagues had welcomed Lyndon Johnson's victory over the hard-line Republican, Barry Goldwater, in the U.S. presidential election in November 1964, but it soon became clear that the administration was preparing a massive increase in American involvement in South Vietnam. Johnson himself later revealed that already in September 1964 he had ordered the Pentagon to make plans for air strikes on North Vietnam.[7] All that was needed was the right pretext for implementing them.

In February 1965, Soviet Prime Minister Alexei Kosygin flew to Hanoi. (His delegation included Yuri Andropov.) It was a delicate mission, for North

Vietnam at the time was closer to Peking's side in the ideological dispute with Moscow. Moscow had a number of aims: to assess Hanoi's intentions and military strategy; to prevent any further loss of influence in the case of escalation on the battlefield; to isolate the issue of support for Vietnam from the Sino–Soviet dispute; and to encourage negotiations.

If the mission was delicate when Kosygin arrived, events soon made it trickier. On February 6, the day before he was due to address a rally in Hanoi, the forces of the National Liberation Front in South Vietnam attacked the American air base in Pleiku. Like all important military decisions, the order for the attack probably came from Hanoi, but it is hard to be sure whether Kosygin was aware of it in advance. It may have been meant to trap him into increasing Soviet support for North Vietnam and the NLF.

At all events the United States responded with the unprecedented step of launching its planned bombing raids on North Vietnam. The move was bound to seem a direct challenge to Kosygin. In the discussion that preceded it, the Americans had focused mainly on whether bombing of North Vietnam would encourage China to bring in troops. It was assumed—mistakenly—that Kosygin's visit to Hanoi "promised only more trouble."[8] Johnson argued in his memoirs that the Soviet leaders "may have concluded that Hanoi was about to win, and that, having removed Khrushchev, they should move in to share credit for the anticipated victory."[9]

The Soviet reaction was more complex. First in Hanoi and then in Peking, where he met Mao on his way home to Moscow, Kosygin proposed joint action by the Soviet Union and China.[10] There should be a unified system of military supplies to Hanoi. Moscow asked for access to a southern port in China and staging rights for air transport via China to Vietnam. While preparing for war, Moscow also hoped for peace. Shortly after Kosygin arrived back in Moscow, the Soviet Union proposed to Britain that as co-chairmen of the Geneva Conference on Indochina (which had originally met in 1954) they should call for negotiations.

The idea was rejected not only by Britain and the United States but also by North Vietnam and China. Kosygin's talks in Peking had been no more successful on the ideological front. Peking reopened its anti-Soviet polemics, attacking the Soviet leadership for pursuing "Khrushchevism without Khrushchev."[11] Still Moscow attempted to achieve unity of action with Peking, at least on the question of Vietnam. In April it proposed that the leaders of North Vietnam, China, and the Soviet Union should meet. Hanoi accepted but Peking declined, accusing Moscow of trying to lure Vietnam and China into a trap "so that you could speak on behalf of Vietnam and China in your international maneuvers, strengthening your position for doing a political deal with imperialism."[12] In a clear reference to the triangular nature of great-power politics, Peking went on: "You should not oppose socialist China by allying yourself with U.S. imperialism."[13]

There was one subsequent high-level meeting that summer when Brezhnev met Deng Xiaoping at the congress of the Rumanian Communist party. It produced no breakthrough. Shortly afterward Moscow began to increase its military deployment on the border with China. Although Brezhnev continued to say publicly that the two sides should look "for ways of settling disagreements and strengthening friendship and cooperation between the Soviet and Chinese peoples and between our parties and countries," the Kremlin had decided to alter the military balance on the Sino–Soviet border in its favor.[14]

Moscow's reasons for this momentous decision have never been stated publicly. But they are not hard to guess. In 1963 Mao had, for the first time, begun to question the border treaties signed between Tsarist Russia and Ch'ing Dynasty China, calling them "unequal" and subject to revision. In an interview with visiting Japanese Socialist party members in Peking on July 10, 1963, Mao said, "About a hundred years ago, the area to the east of Baikal became Russian territory, and since then Vladivostok, Khabarovsk, Kamchatka and other areas have been Soviet territory. We have not yet presented our account for this list."[15] Mao's sweeping territorial claims on some one and a half million square kilometers of Soviet land were bound to be unsettling, even though at secret consultations that began in February 1964 China said it was not demanding the recovery of the land.[16] All it wanted was a Soviet admission that the treaties were unequal. Once that was done, the two sides could negotiate a new treaty, using the old ones as a basis. The Russians were uneasy about this procedure for three reasons. They feared that an admission of the illegality of their occupation of these large tracts of land could be a precedent for future claims by states in Europe, particularly Rumania, Poland, Czechoslovakia, and West Germany. Second, they were afraid that the Chinese might not fulfill the other part of the bargain, which called for negotiations. A third difficulty was the Chinese insistence that most of the several hundred islands in the Amur and Ussuri rivers belonged to China, on the ground that the Sino–Soviet frontier ran along the deepest point of the channel rather than, as the Russians argued, on the Chinese bank. In spite of the basic disagreement revealed during the "consultations," the Russians proposed in September 1964 that negotiations proceed to the stage of "talks." China made no reply to the Soviet note.

By the time of Khrushchev's departure the border issue had thus been added to the long list of disputes between the two countries. After a year of tentative efforts to improve relations, most of which had been rejected by Peking, the Kremlin took stock. China's increasingly frequent references to the unequal treaties and her rapid development of nuclear weapons technology persuaded Moscow that the argument with Peking was no longer purely a matter of politics and ideology. Soviet national security could also be at stake. It was not necessary for the Russians to think that a Chinese attack on the Soviet Union, in order to regain the disputed territories, was imminent or likely. It was enough to feel that such an attack was a future possibility. Ever since the Second World War, Soviet strategy had been to overinsure militarily on every threatened land frontier. By 1965 the Kremlin had come to the view that the border with China was a vulnerable area.

Two of Siberia's major cities, Vladivostok and Khabarovsk, lay in the region under dispute. In addition, the Trans-Siberian Railroad, which is the only lateral land route from central Russia to the Pacific, runs within twenty miles of the Chinese border for most of the last eight hundred miles of its length. Any cut in the line would block overland supplies to eastern Siberia and interrupt the main source of oil to the Pacific Fleet. Under the circumstances, the strengthening of the Soviet military defenses in the area "reflected prudence more than paranoia," in the words of one Western expert.[17]

Most countries' military deployments are based on a worst-case analysis of enemy intentions. After several years of tension, China had come to be seen in Moscow as a long-term military threat. In some ways it combined several of the dangers the Russians saw in their other two main adversaries, West Germany and the United States. Like West Germany, it was a powerful historical rival on the Eurasian landmass which had unsatisfied territorial grievances. Like the United States, it was a nuclear-armed great power which was competing for influence around the world. What made China more threatening than West Germany was that it had a direct two-thousand-mile border with the Soviet Union. What made it more threatening than the United States was its numerically superior population, which an anxious Kremlin saw as a potential invasion force, a new kind of "Yellow Peril." Added to all that was the fact that China was not so much an ideological adversary like West Germany and the United States, but an ideological rival within the Communist movement. If the Russians feared that Western capitalist attitudes and aspirations were a perpetual influence on the people of Eastern Europe, China provided a potential pole of attraction for the region's party leaderships. To Moscow, the latent nationalism of Eastern European Communist parties was more threatening than the nationalism of the people, since it was the party that provided the first line of defense for Moscow's European buffer zone. China's rejection of united action over Vietnam, coupled with similar, though less dramatic, rivalry in Africa, also convinced the Kremlin that Peking opposed any form of partnership in the competition with capitalism.

The first major move by the Soviet Union to improve its Far Eastern defenses was the signing of a new defense treaty with Mongolia in January 1966. Soon afterward, Soviet troops, which had not been garrisoned in Mongolia since 1957, began to return. By early 1967 nearly one hundred thousand men had arrived.[18] During 1966 Moscow supplied its Far Eastern forces with sophisticated missiles and surface-to-surface rockets with nuclear warheads. Between seven and eight Soviet divisions were moved from central Asia to positions east of Lake Baikal, reinforcing the fifteen to seventeen regular divisions already there.[19]

If there were any doubts in Moscow over their assessment of a hostile China, they must have been removed by the events of 1966 and 1967 when China entered the xenophobic upheavals of the Cultural Revolution. In March 1966 China refused to attend the Twenty-Third Party Congress, thus effectively breaking off party relations with Moscow. Mass demonstrations were held outside the Soviet embassy in Peking in August and the following January. Soviet students in China were expelled.

During 1967 Soviet political and military leaders, including Kosygin, frequently addressed Soviet troops in the border areas, calling on them to be vigilant in the "new, dangerous stage" of the Chinese Revolution. In November 1967 in his speech on the fiftieth anniversary of the Russian Revolution, Brezhnev warned that any attempt at a surprise attack against the Soviet Union "wherever it may come from—the north or the south, the west or the east—will encounter the all-conquering might of our glorious Armed Forces."[20]

At this stage the Soviet buildup on the Chinese border can legitimately be described as defensive. There is no evidence that the Russians were preparing for an attack. However, there are signs that the buildup was intended to exert political pressure within China and was linked to efforts at destabilization, particularly in the Xinjiang area which had been a hotbed of local dissent for several years. In 1967 broadcasts by Radio Tashkent in Uighur, the language of the ethnic Muslim minority in Chinese Xinjiang, were doubled. Soviet-based Muslim guerrillas were reportedly encouraged to raid Chinese border posts in Xinjiang.[21] The Russians hoped to take advantage of the internal ferment caused by the Cultural Revolution and strengthen forces in the leadership that were opposed to Mao. In the first six months of 1968 the Soviet press published several articles designed to encourage Mao's opponents. "The struggle against Mao Zedong's group is the struggle for restoring friendship and cooperation with the Chinese Communist party to the positions of scientific socialism. This is practical international aid to those forces in China who remain loyal to Marxism–Leninism and resist Maoism," said an article in the theoretical journal *Kommunist*.[22]

Whatever chance there might have been of countering China's negative view of the Soviet Union, it was badly damaged by the Soviet invasion of Czechoslovakia which turned out to have important repercussions on the Sino–Soviet dispute. Moscow's self-proclaimed right to intervene in other Socialist countries, by force if necessary, clearly implied that Moscow might feel impelled to do the same against China. Peking had endorsed the use of Soviet military might in Hungary in 1956, but by 1968 its experience of the Russians was different. The Soviet Union was incomparably stronger and its resort to force against a Socialist ally, even at a time when it should have been worried about its image in the world, showed that there were no potential limits to Soviet action. In March 1966, in a private discussion with Japanese Communists, Mao had already talked of a possible Soviet invasion of China. The Czech events brought the speculation to life.[23] Two days after the invasion Chou, for the first time, used the phrase "social-imperialism" to describe the Soviet Union, thus publicly putting the Soviet Union on a par with the United States. On October 1 he went further, talking of a possible attack by the Soviet Union on China, with or without U.S. help: "We must heighten our vigilance, intensify our preparedness against war, and be ready at all times to smash any invasion launched by U.S. imperialism, Soviet revisionism, and their lackeys, whether individually or collectively."[24]

In spite of Chou's parallel reference to the Soviet Union and the United States, he and Mao had for some time taken the view that Moscow had become China's principal enemy and a greater long-term threat than the United States. The view was not yet universally agreed upon by the entire Chinese leadership, but the invasion of Czechoslovakia helped to reinforce it. Nor was it clear what Peking's counterstrategy should be. Should it respond to the new overtures that Washington was beginning to make and seek American help against the Soviet Union, or should it prepare to defend itself against the Soviet Union on its own? The first option involved a dramatic shift in both Chinese and American policy.

On March 2, 1969, there occurred a startling event in the unfolding saga. Chinese troops ambushed a Soviet patrol with machine-gun fire on a frozen island (known as Damansky in Russian and as Zhenbao in Chinese) in the Ussuri River about two hundred and fifty miles from Vladivostok. More than twenty Soviet soldiers were killed. Although both sides accused the other of provoking the clash, most analysts accept that the initiative was Chinese. Two explanations have been offered for it. The first puts the responsibility on Lin Biao, who was keen on the eve of the Ninth Party Congress in China to dramatize the need for the military to assume a greater role and even take control of internal power. The second sees it as an initiative by Mao and Chou to emphasize the case, at home and abroad, that the Soviet Union had become China's main enemy, and that the invasion of Czechoslovakia was matched by Soviet aggression against China.[25]

The Russians reacted energetically with a combination of military power and vigorous diplomacy. Two weeks later a Soviet force of approximately battalion strength, armed with tanks and artillery, took revenge and attacked a Chinese force on the same island. In Moscow thousands of demonstrators smashed windows in the Chinese embassy. Demonstrations spread to other Soviet cities. The Soviet media denounced China, and the Soviet ambassador in Washington, Anatoly Dobrynin, informally enlisted U.S. aid, telling Kissinger that China was everybody's problem.[26] The Soviet poet, Yevgeni Yevtushenko, published a luridly anti-Chinese piece, evoking ancient Russian fears of the Mongol invaders:

> You can see in the murky twilight
> The new Mongol warriors with bombs in their quivers
> But if they attack the alarm bells will ring
> And there will be more than enough fighters
> For a new battle of Kulikovo

Behind this increase in anti-Chinese diplomacy and propaganda, a major debate was apparently underway in Moscow. Several options were studied. One was a new try at a negotiated solution with Peking. A second was the continental containment of China by a broadened set of political and diplomatic means. A third was a preemptive military strike. During the spring and summer Moscow started on the first of these options. In April, it proposed that the joint committee on navigation on border rivers resume its meetings. This was a less sensitive issue than the wider question of the border zones, and in August an agreement was signed. In June, Brezhnev publicly called for "a system of collective security in Asia." Although the concept was left vague, it appeared to be aimed against China. In May, Kosygin had visited Pakistan to put strong pressure on President Yahya Khan to join an economic grouping with Afghanistan, Iran, India, and the Soviet Union. A senior Soviet Foreign Ministry official toured Burma, Laos, Cambodia, and Japan. Feelers were even extended to Taiwan. Moscow also urged Western European nations to delay any recognition of China.

At the same time the military option remained alive. Soviet maneuvers were held on the Chinese border, and on May 9 the defense minister, Marshal Grechko, who had taken a leading role in the Czech invasion, listed China along with West Germany and the United States as one of the Soviet Union's major enemies. Further fighting broke out along the Amur River and in Xinjiang in May and June. In June Soviet bomber units flew mock exercises against targets in northwest China.[27] Soviet activity did not go unnoticed. On August 15, New China News Agency charged Moscow with preparing for war and urged the Chinese people to do the same.[28] In August a Soviet diplomat, for the first time, sounded out the Americans on how they might react to a Soviet attack on China. They replied publicly with a statement that it would be a matter of "deep concern."[29] The most intriguing mention of attack came on September 16, when Victor Louis, a Soviet journalist based in Moscow, wrote in the *London Evening News* that Marxist theoreticians were discussing the possibility of a war between China and the Soviet Union. He talked of a possible Soviet air strike against the Chinese nuclear test site at Lop Nor and claimed that there were anti-Maoist forces in China who might ask other socialist countries for fraternal help. Louis referred back to the Czech events "which confirmed that the Soviet Union is adhering to the doctrine that socialist countries have the right to interfere in each other's affairs in their own interest or in those of others who are threatened."

Whether Moscow came close to an actual attack on China in 1969 must be doubted. The chances of a successful "surgical" strike at all Chinese nuclear facilities and missile emplacements cannot have been high. China's resistance against the Japanese invasion must also have been a warning that she would be a hard enemy, even for a technologically superior invader. Ten years later, when China's invasion of the Soviet Union's ally, Vietnam, gave Moscow better political justification for an attack on China, Brezhnev and his colleagues held back.

The invasion talk in 1969 at least had a political effect in spurring negotiations between the two sides. On September 11, on the way home from Ho Chi Minh's funeral in Hanoi, Kosygin diverted his aircraft and flew to Peking for a hastily arranged meeting with Chou. The two men reached agreement on a resumption of border negotiations, which formally opened in Peking on October 20. The Chinese made a significant concession by dropping their demand that the Russians acknowledge the "unequal" treaties as a precondition for opening full-scale negotiations. However, they required the Russians to evacuate the disputed areas before negotiation of an agreed frontier. The Russians insisted on a reaffirmation of the status quo.

In retrospect the crisis of 1969 can be seen to have been the peak period of military tension between the two countries. The subsequent border talks rumbled on for ten years until they were broken off by China after the Soviet intervention in Afghanistan and then renewed in October 1982. Since 1969 there have been no more border clashes of comparable magnitude. Having come so close to war, the two sides looked over the brink and drew back.

We can now ask whether the Soviet strategy of military escalation after 1965 and talk of a preemptive strike in 1969 was a mistake. Earlier in this chapter it was argued that the policy failed to ease the political crisis. It increased Chinese fears of Moscow and encouraged the rapprochement between Peking and Washington. Could these developments have been avoided? Was Moscow's failure a blunder, or was a U.S.–Chinese reconciliation probable anyway?

The record suggests that there is little that Moscow could have done short of a political climb-down of the kind that no superpower finds it easy to make. Most of the initiatives for a negotiated resolution of the dispute came from Moscow and were either rejected or ignored by Peking. The increased military deployments on the Soviet side of the border were defensive precautions which any military establishment would have been likely to make, given the adversary's border claims and the hostility shown by its propagandists. The chaos of the Cultural Revolution was not caused by the dispute with the Soviet Union, but it clearly fueled Moscow's feeling that it was dealing with an unpredictable opponent. Although Moscow's militarization of the Sino–Soviet dispute added a dramatic new dimension, the heart of the conflict was political. Only if Brezhnev and his colleagues had been able to go against all their inherited assumptions and show willingness to deal with Peking as an equal could the conflict have been resolved.

In the absence of any such concession by Moscow, Mao's position was that China had to cultivate the lesser enemy in order to deal with the greater one. Once it was decided that the Soviet Union was the main enemy and that the United States would withdraw from the landmass of Asia, Moscow had little chance of preventing Peking's détente with Washington. Equally, the United

States was attracted by the concept of détente with Peking as a way of putting pressure first on Vietnam and second on Moscow. As Kissinger put it, "As for the Soviets we considered the Chinese option useful to induce restraint; but we had to take care not to pursue it so impetuously as to provoke a Soviet pre-emptive attack on China."[30]

Soviet military pressure on China certainly made it easier for Mao to sell the rapprochement with Washington to his colleagues. It also excited American interest and dramatized the extent of Sino–Soviet hostility. But the decisive event, as we have seen, was the Ussuri River clash, which was provoked not by Moscow but by China. It was only after this that Moscow seriously considered preemptive military action.

Once détente between the United States and China began, Moscow's main effort was to try to contain it. The Kremlin found itself fighting a rear-guard action against an American initiative, just as it was to do later in the Middle East. The versatility and imaginativeness of Kissinger's diplomacy left Moscow flat-footed and offbalance. Brezhnev and his colleagues reacted with almost naive gullibility to Kissinger's opening to China. At the beginning they failed to realize the implications of his triangular diplomacy and the degree to which it was aimed against them. They were convinced that Soviet policy had shown itself to be restrained and responsible by contrast with that of China. They seemed to assume that this would be appreciated by the Americans who would therefore prefer to have closer relationships with themselves than with Peking. In January 1970 Kissinger reports that Dobrynin asked about the U.S.–Chinese talks that were going on in Warsaw. "He hoped I understood that this was a 'neuralgic' point with Moscow. Would I brief him? This constant Soviet fretting about China is as inexplicable to me now as then. . . . The incessant inquiries could yield no positive benefit. If the Soviet Union had a real reason for concern, it was unlikely to receive a truthful reply; it was more likely to remind us of our strategic opportunity."[31]

The announcement in July 1971 that President Nixon would soon visit China stunned the Kremlin. But Brezhnev and his colleagues made no change in their own strategy. They showed no sign of modifying their attitude to Peking or making concessions in order to try to deflect Mao from pursuing links with Washington. They still hoped to convince Washington they were a better partner, in deed as well as word. Moscow could offer Washington concrete benefits, they told the Americans. As Brezhnev put it later, Nixon went "to Peking for banquets, but to Moscow to do business."[32] Kissinger remarks cheerfully, "There was no reason to disabuse the Soviets of their belief."[33]

Even after the U.S.–Chinese opening had become stabilized, Russian policy on China consisted of little more than waiting and seeing. Moscow continued to try to persuade the United States and Western Europe that Peking was a false friend. It hoped vaguely that some unpredictable rift would destroy the West's marriage of convenience with Peking. It increased its forces on the border with

China. It wondered whether matters would improve once Mao died. In the meantime it would keep the border talks going and maintain state-to-state relations with China on as correct a footing as possible. On only two points did Moscow hint at a softening of its line. In 1971 it offered to agree that the border could be drawn along the main channel of the Amur and Ussuri rivers rather than on the Chinese bank, with the one exception of Bear Island near the Soviet city of Khabarovsk. In the same year Brezhnev proposed a nonaggression treaty with China—which Peking rejected.

Moscow's best hope of a split in the Chinese leadership which might benefit the Kremlin was represented by the defense minister, Lin Biao. He opposed many of the changes introduced by Mao at the end of the Cultural Revolution, particularly the opening of relations with the United States. He was not in favor of a reconciliation with Moscow, but wanted a more even-handed policy between the two superpowers. With the collapse of his challenge in September 1971, any chance of a softer Chinese line toward Moscow receded.

Brezhnev officially acknowledged this in March 1972 when he conceded, as Mao had long demanded, that Sino–Soviet relations be governed by "peaceful coexistence" rather than by "proletarian" or "socialist internationalism," as would be normal between socialist states. In separate speeches Kosygin and Brezhnev revived the idea of a collective security system in Asia. Arguing that almost two-thirds of the Soviet Union is in Asia, Brezhnev said that collective security "must in our view be based on such principles as renunciation of the use of force in relations between states, respect for sovereignty and the inviolability of borders, non-interference in internal affairs and the broad development of economic and other cooperation on the basis of full equality and mutual advantage."[34]

Although Brezhnev promised in December 1972 that the system could have China's "full participation," the Russians had little expectation that Peking would be interested.[35] In the meantime the idea was to forge a better position for the Soviet Union in Asia, regardless of Peking. Over the year, until the end of 1973, Soviet troop strength along the border increased by a third, rising to forty-four divisions.

Sino–Soviet relations rumbled on with a series of ups and downs but with no basic improvement for several years. Tension was relatively high on the border after March 14, 1974, when three Soviet officers and their helicopter were captured on the Chinese side of the frontier between Xinjiang and Soviet Central Asia. They were released suddenly in December 1975 in what appeared to be Peking's first use of a "Moscow card." The release took place three weeks after President Ford had made what Peking felt was a disappointing visit to China, and seemed to be a signal of Chinese anger with Washington. It was only a minor tiff, however, in Peking's relationship with the United States.

After Mao's death, just as the Chinese had accused Brezhnev and his colleagues in 1965 of continuing "Khrushchevism without Khrushchev,"

Moscow—after an initial lull in the polemics—talked of "Maoism without Mao."[36] This slogan masked Moscow's realization that in fact things had changed for the worse. In moving away from the policies of Mao's final years and those of the Gang of Four, Chinese activity had become more calculating and considered. China was stronger internationally and less isolated. It talked less of revolution and more of modernization.

The opening of diplomatic relations between China and the United States produced a brief signal from Peking that it might be willing to improve its relations with Moscow as well. Although it announced that it would not renew the 1959 Sino–Soviet friendship treaty when it ran out in a year's time, this was hardly unexpected. To have renewed the treaty would have required more goodwill on both sides than was likely at the time. Nevertheless, Peking offered to discuss Sino–Soviet relations without preconditions. This was a noticeable softening of the previous Chinese line. In September 1979, talks between deputy foreign ministers began in Moscow. It is not clear whether Peking seriously intended to explore a compromise with Moscow or whether the overtures to the Soviet Union were another card intended to warn Washington that it must not take China for granted. During the summer Peking had told the Carter administration that it was unhappy with the completion of the SALT negotiations, which culminated with a Carter–Brezhnev meeting in Vienna in June, American even-handedness on trade relations with Moscow and Peking, and American criticism of the Chinese invasion of Vietnam.

The announcement of the forthcoming Sino–Soviet talks prompted a change in U.S. policy. The United States said it would give China most-favored-nation trading status, even though a comparable deal with the Soviet Union was not ready. U.S. Secretary of Defense Harold Brown arranged to visit Peking to discuss military relations. But if Peking's use of the Moscow card had encouraged the United States to adapt its policy, Peking's "Washington card" produced no such flexibility from the Kremlin. Soviet decision making is a slower and more cumbersome process, and the Russians perhaps thought the issues were too important for a hasty change of line.

At the Sino–Soviet talks in September, no agreement was reached, even on the agenda. The only positive conclusion was that the talks should resume in Peking. Three months later Soviet troops entered Afghanistan and the Chinese called off the talks. The Soviet invasion dramatically accelerated the impetus of U.S.–Chinese relations. Washington agreed to sell China "dual-use" technology (civilian goods with a military potential) and military support equipment, and was allowed to install a sophisticated electronic listening post in Xinjiang from which Soviet nuclear tests could be monitored.

In spite of these changes, signs of a debate over future attitudes to Moscow continued to be seen. Early in 1980 the Chinese announced that Mao had been incorrect in his commentaries in 1963 and 1964 which described Soviet economic policy as "revisionist." Chinese specialists increasingly acknowledged that the

Soviet Union had made impressive economic and technical progress. With the apparent dropping of the ideological dispute with Moscow, Peking's differences with the Soviet Union were reduced to foreign policy and state relations.

The election of a new American president with a strong attachment to a non-Communist Taiwan produced another Chinese signal. Deng Xiaoping called for Moscow to take "concrete actions" to open the way to better relations, such as a reduction of Soviet troops in the Far East and Mongolia down to the level maintained under Khrushchev.[37] Moscow took its time to respond. At the Twenty-Sixth Party Congress in February 1981, Brezhnev laid out the Kremlin's considered view of China. He took obvious comfort from the Chinese's own reassessment of the Cultural Revolution as "a most cruel feudal-fascist dictatorship." "We have nothing to add to this assessment," he said. China's experience over the last twenty years was "a painful lesson showing what any distortion of the principles and essence of socialism in home and foreign policy leads to."[38] But Brezhnev was still too cautious to expect that this rather patronizing view of China as a prodigal son could be followed by rapid repentance. Time would show to what extent the present Chinese leadership managed to overcome the Maoist legacy, he said. "Unfortunately there are no grounds yet to speak of any changes for the better in Peking's foreign policy. As before, it is aimed at aggravating the international situation and is aligned with the policy of the imperialist powers. That of course will not bring China back to the sound road of development. Imperialists will never be friends of socialism."[39]

Although Brezhnev claimed it was China's fault that relations were still frozen, he put even greater blame on the United States, Japan, and NATO for trying to use China against what he argued were its own best interests. Six months later Moscow sent Peking a diplomatic note proposing a resumption of talks on the border dispute and overall relations.[40] In February 1982 the Soviet prime minister, Nikolai Tikhonov, gave an interview to a Japanese journalist in which he said that Moscow "would not back away from concrete steps" toward improving relations, provided this was not one-sided.[41] A month later, in a speech in Tashkent, Brezhnev said the Soviet Union was ready to agree on measures to improve relations on the basis of mutual respect. He declared pointedly that Moscow had never doubted China's sovereignty over Taiwan, and said Moscow and Peking should discuss "possible measures to strengthen mutual trust in the arena of the Soviet–Chinese frontier."[42]

While rejecting Soviet overtures in public, the Chinese used a number of unofficial exchange visits between Soviet and Chinese academics, experts, and diplomats during 1982 to test Moscow's seriousness. Apparently satisfied that Moscow was genuinely interested in China and had lost its faith in any early renewal of Soviet–American détente, Peking responded favorably. It accepted a resumption of the Sino–Soviet talks which had been broken off after the Soviet invasion of Afghanistan. When the Soviet deputy foreign minister, Leonid

Ilyichev, arrived in Peking in October 1982, he was told that Peking's three main demands—for a Soviet withdrawal from Afghanistan; for a Vietnamese withdrawal from Kampuchea; and a major scaling down of Soviet troops on the border—were no longer preconditions for substantive talks. They were negotiable. A month later the Chinese foreign minister, Huang Hua, attended Brezhnev's funeral, becoming the highest Chinese official to visit the Soviet Union for almost twenty years. Shortly after his talks with Gromyko, Viktor Afanasyev, a member of the Central Committee and editor of *Pravda*, told Japanese reporters that China and the Soviet Union might agree to reduce their troops in the border area.[43] In March 1983 the two countries reached a new trade agreement that would increase commercial exchanges by about 170 percent. Andropov, it seemed, was determined to make a fresh start with China.

However Sino–Soviet ties develop over the next few years, there can be no return to the relationship of the 1950s. China will never allow itself to be so dependent on Soviet economic aid again. In spite of some lessening of its initial enthusiasm for Western and Japanese technology and capital since the mid-1970s, it will continue to look primarily to the West and Japan for outside economic help. It will not accept any ideological guidance from the Soviet Union. It will insist on the independence of its party line, and repudiate the notion of a "leading center" in the world Communist movement.

The most that Moscow can hope for is peaceful coexistence. Out of that might come some coordination of foreign policy in the Third World and—less probably—vis-à-vis the West. China's stance on the Middle East, which was closer to Moscow's line than that of Washington in 1982, might be a model. If a firm basis for good relations with China is to be achieved, Moscow has to throw off the assumptions of twenty years of policy and practice. The Politburo will have to overcome the vested interests in the Soviet hierarchy who consider a certain level of conflict with China useful in keeping public opinion mobilized in support of foreign policy and in justifying the present diversion of resources toward military use.

At the back of it all is a deep-seated national and racialist suspicion of China that is rooted in the popular Russian consciousness. This pervades both orthodox and dissident opinion, and can be found in the writings of such anti-Soviet exiles as Andrei Amalrik and Alexander Solzhenitsyn. Under Brezhnev the Soviet leadership viewed its Maoist counterpart in China as irrational, unpredictable, and unstable—in the words Kissinger attributed to Brezhnev in a conversation the two men had in 1973, "treacherous, arrogant, and beyond the pale."[44] It will not be easy to move from this attitude to one that recognizes that the central necessity in Sino–Soviet relations is for Moscow to accept Peking as an independent equal.

VIETNAM

Vietnam was the one area where the Sino–American rapprochement in 1972 and 1973 produced a significant shift in Soviet policy. In the later stages of the war, Soviet interest in promoting a strong Vietnam as a counterpoint to China became evident. By the end of 1974 the Russians were also more willing to see the United States humiliated, even at the risk of provoking American anger against Moscow. This was a subtle difference from the Soviet attitude at the beginning of the Brezhnev era.

In 1965, when U.S. bombing of North Vietnam began, Moscow had been anxious to prevent it from prejudicing its hopes for détente with the United States. It had sought a negotiated settlement while also realizing it had to compete with Peking in aiding Hanoi. As Foy Kohler, the American ambassador in Moscow, put it in a telegram, "[The] Soviets are interested in working out some sort of modus vivendi which could take heat out of the situation while not undercutting their own position in Commie world as loyal socialist ally."[45] With the collapse of any chance of negotiation, the Russians had sent in massive amounts of aid to Hanoi. According to U.S. Defense Secretary Melvin Laird, Moscow had supplied 65 percent of Hanoi's military equipment up to 1968.[46] Yet the Russians continued to act as intermediaries between Washington and Hanoi, relaying each side's overtures for talks. The start of the Paris peace talks in 1968 was welcomed by Moscow as a way of isolating the American conflict with Vietnam from the mainstream of East–West business.

Four years later Peking and Moscow were both disclaiming any major interest in Vietnam. The announcement of Nixon's visits to Peking and Vietnam caused alarm in Hanoi. Kissinger deliberately orchestrated the timing of the two visits to create a feeling of isolation in Hanoi and encourage the two major Communist powers to outdo each other in being conciliatory to Washington. When Kissinger visited Moscow in April 1972 to arrange the final details of the summit, Brezhnev told him that its postponement "would only help China."[47] Kissinger points out that the Soviet leader still did not understand the nature of triangular diplomacy, assuming that anything that helped China would be opposed by the United States. Brezhnev also expressed embarrassment at Hanoi's spring offensive which had just been launched. He complained that Hanoi wanted to cancel the summit. Although Hanoi was using a massive amount of Soviet equipment, including two hundred Soviet-made tanks and new 130-mm artillery, Brezhnev claimed this had been delivered up to two years earlier. Even when on May 9 the United States mined the harbor of Haiphong, damaging Soviet ships and killing some Soviet citizens, the Russians protested but did not cancel the summit. Brezhnev's policy came under criticism from some of his colleagues, as their oblique public comments make clear. Marshal Grechko warned of the "growing aggressiveness of imperialism, and primarily American imperialism," while Andropov declared that the Soviet Union had no illusions and "was not exaggerating the possibilities of cooperation" with the United States.[48] The Ukrainian party secretary, Pyotr Shelest, is believed to have expressed the strongest opposition to the Nixon visit. A few days before Nixon's arrival, he lost his job in the Ukraine.

At the summit itself, apart from the symbolism of having the Soviet leadership greet the American president in Moscow, the Russians gave away nothing of substance from Hanoi's point of view. Brezhnev, Kosygin, and Podgorny lectured Nixon in turn. Brezhnev was particularly emotional, attacking Washington's "cruel" bombing and virtually comparing U.S. policy to Hitler's. He told Nixon, "It was certainly difficult for us to agree to hold this meeting under present circumstances. And yet we did agree to hold it. I want to explain why. We felt that preliminary work prior to the meeting warranted the hope that two powers with such economic might and such a high level of civilization and all the other prerequisites could come together to promote better relations between our two nations."[49]

Although Kissinger concedes that the Russians made no promises over Vietnam at the summit, he argues that Hanoi's sense of isolation and betrayal affected its morale. It is true that when Washington's talks with Hanoi began again two months after the Moscow summit, the North Vietnamese negotiator, Le Duc Tho, started to modify his position. He dropped his side's old demand that Washington's client in Saigon, South Vietnam's President Thieu, should resign in favor of a coalition government. As the talks proceeded, it became clear that Hanoi had made a fundamental change of strategy. It was no longer pressing for a simultaneous U.S. withdrawal and a decisive shift of power toward the Communists. It was separating the two processes—first, get the Americans out, then after an interval of perhaps a year or two, achieve the political victory that would lead to Communist rule in the South and unification with the North.

There is no evidence that Hanoi's strategic shift was caused by Soviet diplomatic pressure or threats to withhold arms supplies. It is more likely that the reason was the failure of Hanoi's spring offensive. Disappointed, the North Vietnamese leadership appears to have calculated that it was becoming too costly to try to defeat the Americans on the battlefield. Better to let them withdraw, as an increasing number of Americans were demanding that they should, and then deal with Saigon later. Perhaps Hanoi calculated that if it were to ask the Russians for more weapons to enable it to launch another offensive, Moscow would not have given them. The Moscow summit had demonstrated a remarkable degree of Soviet eagerness for a long-term accommodation with the United States.

By the end of 1974 the Kremlin's eagerness had lessened. The experience of détente was chastening. Nixon and Kissinger were demanding that Moscow show "restraint" in the Third World, but were showing none themselves. They had helped to destabilize the Allende government in Chile. They had moved into Egypt in a successful effort to replace Soviet influence after the war of October 1973. They were developing their relationship with China in a way that, as Moscow by that time could not help seeing, was directed against it. Equally important, the Americans had failed to deliver on one of the main promises of détente. After months of negotiations in which the Americans insisted that the Russians permit a substantial number of Soviet Jews to emigrate to Israel every year, the Americans had refused to give the Soviet Union "most-favored-nation" treatment in trade and had imposed a ceiling on U.S. credits. It mattered little to Moscow that in this instance the villain had not been the Nixon administration, but the United States Congress which acted against the wishes of the White House. As the Kremlin saw it, the United States was seeking to humiliate the Soviet Union and was an unreliable partner.

Kissinger admits that the Nixon administration in 1972 was linking trade concessions with Soviet "restraint" on Vietnam.[50] Two years later Moscow reversed the linkage. With the trade concessions unfulfilled, it abandoned any restraint. There was now an extra reason for showing boldness over Vietnam. China's new links with the United States gave Moscow a powerful incentive to encourage Hanoi to ally itself firmly with the Soviet Union. At the end of December, as the CIA's chief strategy analyst in Saigon later disclosed, Moscow decided to give all-out military aid to Hanoi for what turned out to be the final offensive of the war.[51] The initiative for the assault came, as it had done throughout the war, from the North Vietnamese. Launched in mid-December after months of preparation, the winter/spring campaign was not expected to be a total victory. But shortly after it began, a North Vietnamese spy in Thieu's entourage leaked a copy of his plans and perspectives. This enabled Hanoi to aim its assault on towns where the South Vietnamese least expected it. In late December General Viktor Kulikov, chief of the Soviet armed forces, flew to Hanoi to join the North Vietnamese Politburo in its discussions. After his visit, seaborne shipments of Soviet war matériel to North Vietnam quadrupled. Although it had decided to give Hanoi massive backing, Moscow continued to make one important concession to détente. Its public references to the defeat of Washington's ally in Vietnam remained discreet. As its North Vietnamese ally swept through the South, forcing its U.S.-sponsored adversary into panic and retreat, the news was kept off the front pages of the Soviet press.

Brezhnev and his colleagues could well feel satisfied. The United States had been pushed out of Indochina. Soviet aid to Hanoi had been decisive, and there was every likelihood that a victorious North Vietnam, united with the South, would remain a firm Soviet ally against Peking. Hanoi's triumph had changed the balance of power in Southeast Asia and produced a double benefit for Moscow—a military defeat for the United States, which affected its global credibility as a superpower, and a psychological defeat for China, since Moscow had become Vietnam's major ally.

But Soviet hopes of a close peacetime relationship with Vietnam were short-lived. Moscow soon found, as it had done with numerous non-Communist clients in the Middle East and Africa, that the supply of arms did not produce a ready payoff. In the immediate aftermath of Hanoi's victory, Soviet suggestions that Vietnam join COMECON, sign a Treaty of Friendship, and provide the Soviet fleet with base rights were turned down.[52] Hanoi continued to hope for good relations with Peking and even with Washington, and was reluctant to become totally aligned with Moscow.

Hanoi's shift toward the Soviet Union in 1978 occurred only after China and the United States had rejected it. The decisive events were China's support for Kampuchea's attacks across the border against Vietnam and Brzezinski's long and ultimately successful campaign to persuade the Carter administration to make the normalization of relations with Peking its highest priority. Brzezinski was confirmed in this view on a visit to Peking in May 1978, when he and Deng Xiaoping agreed that China and the United States had common interests in opposing what they saw as Soviet influence around the world.

The Brzezinski line took some time to win through. Carter was initially in sympathy with the State Department Asia specialists who hoped to open relations with Vietnam as a way of promoting détente between Hanoi and the non-Communist states of Southeast Asia and to prevent it moving too close to Moscow. The issue was complicated by Hanoi's demand for economic compensation for the war and by uncertainty surrounding the fate of the American troops and airmen missing in action. But on September 29, 1978, in New York the U.S. assistant secretary of state for Asian affairs, Richard Holbrooke, and a senior Vietnamese diplomat, Nguyen Co Thach, agreed to normalize relations after Hanoi dropped its claims for aid.

By then military tension between Vietnam and the Peking-backed Pol Pot regime was increasing. Chinese propaganda was describing Vietnam as a Soviet puppet or, in their own words, "an Asian Cuba." In November Hanoi signed a friendship treaty with Moscow that included clauses calling for mutual consultations in the event of war and pledging each side to take "appropriate effective measures" to repel any threat against the other. The Carter administration cited the treaty as the reason for a halt in the process of U.S.–Vietnamese normalization. But the real reason was the acceleration in its talks with Peking on the establishment of diplomatic relations. In his memoirs, Carter revealed that he decided several months before the treaty "to postpone the Vietnam effort until after we had concluded our agreement in Peking."[53]

There is little doubt that during the negotiations on the friendship treaty Moscow learned of Hanoi's plan for the invasion of Kampuchea which was launched a month later. Soviet leaders were reported to have expressed reservations, and in February 1979 Soviet diplomats in several capitals told other governments that they wished the Vietnamese had not invaded. They indicated they favored the negotiation of a coalition government under Norodom

Sihanouk.[54] Although the Russians probably hoped that Pol Pot's international isolation would minimize criticism of Vietnam's action, they were concerned at its effect on the members of the Association of Southeast Asian Nations (ASEAN). They later gave public assurances to Thailand and the United States that Vietnamese troops would not invade Thailand.

Why did Moscow sign the friendship treaty with Vietnam if it had doubts about the planned invasion? The treaty's language was the same as that contained in the Soviet pact with India in 1971, which had been designed to deter Peking from any thought of attacking India during the Bangladesh crisis. Moscow and Hanoi hoped that the new pact would deter China from retaliating when Vietnam went into Kampuchea. They were wrong. On February 17, 1979, China launched a multipronged attack along the entire border with Vietnam. Moscow responded with a major airlift of military supplies to Hanoi and in early March a Soviet naval task force assembled in Vietnamese waters. But Moscow promptly hinted that it would not intervene itself. A Soviet government statement a day after the invasion said that Moscow would honor its obligations under the friendship treaty, but Vietnam was "capable of standing up for itself this time again."[55]

As the Chinese advance continued, Gromyko slightly toughened the line, demanding that "the Peking leadership stop before it is too late—I repeat these words, before it is too late."[56] Moscow's allies, East Germany and Hungary, announced through their official news agencies that volunteers were offering to go to the help of Vietnam. But when Brezhnev spoke four days later on his return to Moscow from a rest at his dacha on the Black Sea he did not repeat the warnings. While demanding that China withdraw, he gave no hint of any Soviet action if they failed to comply.

Military observers called the seventeen-day Chinese invasion a draw in which neither side was the victor on the battlefield. Vietnamese resistance was stronger than expected, but Vietnam suffered heavy casualties and massive physical damage and was left overstretched militarily. However, Hanoi was not prevented from extending its political control over Kampuchea and Laos. The Soviet Union took advantage of its position as Vietnam's only outside defender to begin regular port calls by Soviet ships. Soviet submarines for the first time sailed in and out of the old and largely destroyed American base at Cam Ranh Bay. The combined result of Chinese and American policy had been to push Hanoi into Moscow's arms and to give the Soviet Union an incentive for staying in the region. There was no change in the strategy as Carter gave way to Reagan in 1981. Washington let Peking call the tune in Southeast Asia. China kept up military support for Pol Pot in his guerrilla campaign against the new Hanoi-backed regime in Phnom Penh and put pressure on ASEAN not to recognize it. The United States endorsed Peking's line, happy to see the Soviet Union on the diplomatic defensive, even though the area remained unstable with its economic rehabilitation under stress.

JAPAN

If Indochina was an area where Moscow felt it was worth being bold partly in order to develop a bulwark against Peking, Soviet relations with Japan showed the opposite pattern. As China reemerged onto the international stage in the early 1970s, taking an active anti-Soviet line, it seemed to some Western commentators that Moscow would seek to woo Japan. If Moscow could not seriously expect to win Tokyo to its side, it might at least hope to persuade the Japanese not to agree with China against the Soviet Union. In the event, Moscow made little effort, and by the early 1980s Japan was giving in to heavy American and lesser Chinese pressure to increase its military spending against a perceived threat from the Soviet Union.

Moscow's diplomatic passivity surprised many observers but the reasons are clear. They confirm just how unyielding the Soviet Union is on the basic priority of its foreign policy, the defense of Soviet territory. In maintaining that goal, the Soviet Union is determined to be totally self-reliant, is suspicious of allies, and is unwilling to concede a single square kilometer of Soviet land.

Land is the central element of the historical dispute between the Soviet Union and Japan. The two main issues are the island of Sakhalin, sometimes known as "East Asia's Alsace-Lorraine" because of its fluctuating ownership, and the Kurile Islands which stretch from Hokkaido to the peninsula of Kamchatka. Sovereignty of Sakhalin was conceded to Russia in 1875 in the Treaty of St. Petersburg, but it was seized by Japan after the Russian defeat thirty years later.

The Second World War gave Moscow a chance to win territory back. At the Yalta Conference in February 1945, where Stalin came under heavy Western pressure to enter the war against Japan, Sakhalin was promised to him. No decision was taken on the Kuriles, which had been ceded to Japan in 1875 by the same treaty that gave Sakhalin to Moscow. In August 1945 Soviet forces occupied all of them. Although only a minority of Japanese irredentists still claim the northern and central islands in the Kurile chain, Soviet occupation of the southern ones, Kunashiri, Etorofu, Shikotan, and the Habomai archipelago, has remained a constant irritant in Soviet–Japanese relations.

The issue of the islands, known in Tokyo as "the northern territories", has continually prevented signature of a post-Second World War peace treaty. In a joint declaration signed with the Japanese government in 1956, the Soviet Union promised to transfer two of the smaller islands if Tokyo agreed to a peace treaty surrendering the main two. But four years later, Gromyko insisted that even the smaller islands would be returned only after all U.S. forces had left Japan. The only subsequent hint of flexibility by Moscow came in the communiqué after Japanese Prime Minister Kakuei Tanaka visited Moscow in 1973, which referred to "unsolved questions" remaining from the Second World War. Tanaka's visit came shortly after he had been to Peking. But Moscow never spelled out what concessions it might make, and the standard line now remains, as *Izvestia* put it bluntly in September 1981, "There is no territorial issue between the USSR and Japan." Any attempts to claim Soviet territory were "a hopeless venture."[57]

In seeking to delay or prevent the growth of Japanese relations with China, Moscow preferred to rely on traditional methods—blunt diplomatic statements of Soviet concern and vague warnings of unspecified retaliation. As China and Japan began a three-year negotiation for a peace and friendship treaty, Gromyko visited Tokyo to discourage the Japanese. Shortly afterward *Pravda* publicly warned Japan not to sell military technology to China.[58] For a time the Japanese hesitated to sign the treaty in which Peking was insisting on a clause binding each side to oppose efforts by any nation to establish "hegemony" in the region. This was clearly aimed against the Soviet Union.

Brzezinski's trip to Peking in May 1978 tipped the balance. He persuaded the Chinese and the Japanese to go ahead with the treaty. Brzezinski's aim, as it became clear when President Carter met the Chinese leader, Chairman Hua Guofeng, in Tokyo in July 1980, was to forge an alliance of China, Japan, and the United States against the Soviet Union.[59]

The Soviet response to the Sino–Japanese treaty was to build up its military forces on the disputed islands. But as with so many other increases in Soviet power, it was not a unilateral Soviet initiative so much as a reaction to outside pressure. "The diplomatic move by Japan toward China was integrally involved in projecting Soviet power further into the region," as a senior Western specialist has argued.[60]

Was it likely that Moscow would ever give up the southern Kurile Islands in the interests of improving relations with Japan? To expect that it might would be to underestimate Soviet preoccupation with security and the strategic import- ance that Moscow attaches to the islands. The Soviet Union has become increasingly concerned about maintaining access to the Pacific Ocean, both for its navy and its merchant fleet. Of the three main shipping routes to Vladivostok only one passes close to Soviet territory. It is this northerly route past the tip of Sakhalin that the Kurile Islands are able to guard. To give up the islands would amount to the renunciation of what the Kremlin considers a vital link in its chain of defenses.

The Soviet leadership must have asked itself what the benefits of a retreat would be. How could it rely on any assurances that Tokyo might offer in return for the islands? In the early 1970s in the period of East–West détente, Moscow had approached the Japanese with several offers for long-term partnerships in developing the natural resources of Siberia. While many of these offers were taken up, producing an outpouring of more than $1.5 billion in credits from Japan, most of the money was spent on exploratory work. Few projects were completed. Although in some cases there were sound technical reasons for the postponement or cancellation, the major obstacles were political. China and the

United States persuaded Japan that an improvement in the Soviet Union's transport network in Siberia and the development of critical resources there could pose a strategic threat.[61] Before China's advent on the international scene, Moscow had always considered Japan to be an obedient client of the United States, a kind of economic giant but political dwarf. China's new pressure on Japan merely confirmed the Soviet assessment. American efforts under the Carter administration to warn Japan against investing heavily in the coal and oil deposits of Siberia were a precursor of equivalent pressure brought by the Reagan administration on Western Europe.

Faced with the prospect of a strategic triangle in the Pacific ranged against it, Moscow adopted its time-honored posture of bolstering its defenses and maintaining self-reliance while calling for comprehensive regional talks. At the Twenty-Sixth Party Congress, Brezhnev said it would be useful to elaborate a set of "confidence-building measures" in the Far East, "where such powers as the Soviet Union, China, and Japan border on each other. There are also U.S. military bases there."[62] The Brezhnev offer was clearly aimed at reminding the other major Pacific nations that the Soviet Union has legitimate interests there. Whether the Kremlin seriously believed the offer was likely to be taken up in the heavy atmosphere of anti-Soviet feelings in the Pacific must be doubted.

INDIA AND PAKISTAN

The Indian subcontinent provided the Soviet Union with its most successful foreign policy arena during the Brezhnev era. For several years Moscow was in effect the "crisis manager" for the region. Thanks to an American posture of general passivity, punctuated by bursts of incompetence in action, the Soviet Union was able to enjoy a superpower role almost unchallenged. It used its power for the most part responsibly and with restraint.

The first superpower involvement in the region had come from the United States, which persuaded Pakistan to sign a defense pact and join the Central Treaty Organization (CENTO) in 1954. Pakistan agreed to allow the United States to use its airfields for U–2 spy-plane missions across the Soviet Union. In return Pakistan received new American armaments, which served mainly to embolden it in making territorial claims on parts of Indian-held Kashmir. The U.S. arms pact with Pakistan opened the door to Indo–Soviet friendship and cooperation and stimulated a massive increase in Soviet interest in India. In the Sino–Indian border war in 1962, Moscow remained conspicuously neutral in what was one of the most dramatic public signs of its foreign policy differences with China, and also proof of its eagerness to keep on good terms with India.

The war produced a flurry of new American concern over China and renewed interest in India, which soon became the recipient of billions of dollars of U.S. military hardware. It was not long before India and Pakistan, each armed mainly by the United States, went to war over Kashmir. When the war ended in a stalemate three weeks later, it was the Soviet Union that took the initiative for a diplomatic settlement. The new post-Khrushchev team had been in power for just over a year. During that time the effort to reach a reconciliation with China had failed, and it made sense to extend the Soviet role in South Asia by trying to have good relations with Pakistan as well as India.

Kosygin invited the leaders of the two countries to a conference in Tashkent in Soviet Uzbekistan. Welcoming them as "our southern neighbors" the Soviet prime minister sought to suggest that South Asia, because of its closeness to the Soviet border, was a natural sphere of Soviet influence. The Tashkent agreement, by which each side withdrew its forces and promised to normalize relations, was a diplomatic triumph for Moscow and the model for the Soviet-sponsored border settlement that the Kremlin later tried to achieve in the Horn of Africa and would have liked to bring about between Iran and Iraq.

Although Moscow subsequently supplied Pakistan as well as India with new arms, it continued to push for a system of peaceful cooperation in the region. In 1968 Kosygin proposed an economic conference of Afghanistan, India, Iran, Pakistan, and the Soviet Union to find ways of expanding trade and transport links in the area. Out of this a regional security system was expected to grow, based on a series of treaties renouncing the use of force and respecting international frontiers.

Pakistan refused to attend. In spite of two visits by President Yahya Khan to Moscow, the Russians were unable to persuade him to loosen his ties with China. When the Pakistan election of December 1970 raised tensions between the central government in West Pakistan and the Awami League, led by Mujibur Rahman and based in East Pakistan, Moscow was drawn to the East Pakistani side, which was calling for autonomy and a new state of Bangladesh.

As the crisis mounted in 1971 Yahya Khan arrested Rahman and decided to crush the Bangladesh movement by force. India was under pressure to intervene on behalf of the millions of refugees who had fled there. While China and the United States gave diplomatic support to Yahya Khan, Moscow called for a peaceful political settlement. Then came the stunning announcement of Kissinger's secret trip to Peking, organized by Yahya Khan, and the invitation for Nixon to visit China. Moscow suddenly began to fear a shift of power in South Asia that might undermine its position.

In August 1971 Moscow achieved a minor counterblow when it signed a twenty-year treaty of friendship with India. The clause calling for each side to take appropriate effective measures in the case of attack was meant to deter China. The Indian prime minister, Indira Gandhi, flew to Moscow to discuss the looming war over Bangladesh, but was told by Moscow that it could support her only on the issue of Bangladesh, not on any incursions into West Pakistan. The Soviet Union described the Bangladesh struggle as a war of national liberation.

The Indian invasion in support of the rebels in December gave the Soviet Union almost total political success. It vetoed three United Nations ceasefire resolutions backed by the United States and China. When the Americans sent a naval task force to the Bay of Bengal, Moscow sent its own ships and told New Delhi it would not allow the U.S. to intervene. Once India's goals had been achieved, when the Pakistanis surrendered in Bangladesh two weeks after the start of the war, Moscow supported India's immediate ceasefire.

The crisis emphasized Soviet preeminence in the region and was an almost exact replica in reverse of American activity in the Middle Eastern wars. Here it was Moscow that successfully warned other powers to keep out and manipulated the timing of the ceasefire, while its superpower rival was made to look impotent and ineffective.

In spite of this one-sided Soviet triumph, Moscow did not follow it up with a major commitment of resources toward expanding its influence in the subcontinent. Nor did it ask for naval bases in India. It acted cautiously and urged the South Asian countries to settle their border disputes by negotiation. It backed the agreements between India and Pakistan after the 1971 war. It invited the Pakistani leader Zulfikar Ali Bhutto to Moscow in 1974 and pressed him to settle his frontier disagreements with Afghanistan. If tension continued in the subcontinent, it was not Moscow's fault. The Soviet Union did what it could to create a regional détente throughout the 1970s.

Moscow's mistake came at the end of 1979 when it invaded Afghanistan. Iran and Pakistan bitterly opposed the move. India was unhappy but chose to retain its good relations with Moscow. After the high hopes of the Tashkent agreement, the Soviet Union ended the Brezhnev period with its preeminence in the subcontinent still intact, but its diplomacy on the defensive.

CONCLUSION

The Soviet Union, it is often argued in the West, is on the offensive in Asia. As evidence for this view observers cite the massive Soviet military buildup on the Chinese border in the second half of the 1960s, Soviet military aid to North Vietnam in its war with the United States and later for its invasion of Kampuchea, and the gradual expansion of the Soviet Pacific Fleet in the waters off Japan, and the invasion of Afghanistan.

Each of these developments was important, but it does not follow that they were all connected as parts of a deliberately planned and comprehensive whole. Nor can they be seen simply as Soviet initiatives, rather than as reactions to outside events. The alternative view is argued here that the Soviet Union had and has no "strategy for Asia." Its military confrontation with China was an aggressive attempt to intimidate and subordinate a powerful neighbor and ideological rival. As such, it had the same hallmarks of overreliance on military strength, clumsy and unimaginative diplomacy, and failure to accept the right of sovereign, socialist nations to remain independent that have characterized Soviet relations with Eastern Europe. But it was not a move toward a determined expansion of Soviet influence so much as a misguided effort to preserve a position that was slipping. Under Brezhnev the Kremlin gave a military dimension to the Sino–Soviet conflict which previously had been only political, economic, and ideological. Blame for the breakdown must rest on both sides. The Russians were unwilling to grant China political parity within the Communist movement. They could not adjust to the rise of an independent Communist-led China. The Chinese were unwilling to accept the changed context of the competition between capitalism and socialism in a nuclear world. They sneered at Moscow's efforts to combine peaceful coexistence with the United States on a global scale with its wish for a united stand behind North Vietnam in its local struggle against American intervention.

In the 1970s the entire strategic environment in Asia was altered by the American opening to China. The full significance of the new Sino–American relationship took some time to be appreciated in Moscow, and it left the Kremlin perplexed and uncertain, fighting a rear-guard action to prevent NATO's Western European partners from striking up as close a relationship with China as Washington had done.

In Vietnam the Soviet role was subsidiary. Although it became Hanoi's major outside arms supplier, it never controlled North Vietnam's decision making, either on the battlefield or in the five years of peace negotiations. Moscow was encouraged to support Hanoi, partly by the subtle North Vietnamese pressure on both Peking and Moscow to match each other's aid in the 1960s, and then in the early 1970s by the Kremlin's desire to gain a stake in Indochina in order to thwart an increase in Chinese influence. Although Moscow was the only superpower with any significant position in Indochina after the American retreat in 1975, it still did not control Hanoi's actions. The Vietnamese invasion of Kampuchea was not a Soviet-initiated move but the culmination of increasing Kampuchean–Vietnamese border tensions that were largely provoked by the Kampuchean leader, Pol Pot. When China subsequently invaded Vietnam in February 1979, the Russians sent military supplies but made no direct intervention to defend their ally.

The gradual growth in the Soviet Pacific Fleet has been in almost exact proportion to the expansion of the Soviet Navy as a whole. The only component of the Pacific Fleet that grew faster in the 1970s was its submarine fleet, whose mission is not directed at Asian states but at strategic targets in the United States. In terms of its conventional ships, the Pacific Fleet was the last to receive modern equipment.[63] Its mission is to defend the regional waters that wash Soviet Siberia, particularly the sea of Japan, but its ability to support offensive activity is limited to eighteen amphibious ships and two naval regiments totaling 4,000 troops.[64] The Pacific Fleet has only one carrier, with twelve aircraft and twenty helicopters which are geared mainly for antisubmarine warfare. The buildup of troops on two of the disputed Kurile Islands followed signature of the Sino–Japanese treaty of friendship. It cannot have provoked the treaty.

It is true that Soviet interest in the Pacific has been increasing. Under Brezhnev the Politburo took several key decisions to try to develop the vast resources and empty space of Soviet Siberia. Investment in a second Trans-Siberian Railroad, the Baikal–Amur Main Line, roughly two hundred miles north of the old one that runs close to the Chinese border, was described by Moscow as "the construction project of the century." Efforts to encourage the extraction of Siberia's enormous reserves of oil, gas, coal, iron, copper, and gold, either with or without Western and Japanese help, made sound economic sense. With the reduction of Japanese interest in these projects, largely as a result of Chinese and American pressure on Tokyo, the Soviet Union will have to reconsider how far and fast to push scarce financial and labor resources toward developing Siberia. On paper the marriage of Japan and the Soviet Far East seems like an economist's dream. A day's boat ride separates an overpopulated Japan, hungry for raw materials, from a Siberia that is empty of people but replete with natural resources. Far from contemplating an invasion of Japan, Moscow has been eagerly urging Japanese capitalists to invade Siberia—so far, with only limited success.

When Andropov succeeded Brezhnev in November 1982, he inherited a record of general frustration in Asia. Moscow's sense of encirclement seemed more soundly based than when Brezhnev took over in 1964. The prospect of any softening of Japanese or American suspicions was bleak. Japanese military spending was increasing. China was determined to remain independent.

Only in Indochina was the Soviet position better than in 1964. But the relatively strong Soviet presence might in retrospect turn out to have been the peak of Soviet success. If tension eases between Vietnam and ASEAN, it is probable that Hanoi will recommence the search for good relations with the United States, Japan, and Western Europe which it was making in 1977 and 1978. Soviet influence in Indochina is a function of the Chinese effort to keep the Pol Pot forces engaged in Kampuchea. The consolidation of a pro-Vietnamese government in Phnom Penh would hasten the day when the Soviet Union finds itself less wanted by Vietnam. In the Indian subcontinent, by contrast, the Soviet position would be enhanced by a settlement of the Afghan crisis and a with-drawal of Soviet troops. But this looks unlikely. There is little prospect of a negotiated solution to the civil war. As long as India remains broadly loyal to its traditional but cautious friendship with Moscow, the Soviet Union will retain its influence as the major diplomatic partner of the region's largest state. But the benefits of this partnership will probably be as limited in the future as they have been for the last twenty years. Throughout Asia, taken as a whole, Soviet influence in the Brezhnev years did not increase. It declined.

PART TWO

The Periphery

9

APPROACHES TO
THE THIRD WORLD

*Comrades, among the important results of the party's
international activity in the period under review we
can list the visible expansion of cooperation with
countries that have liberated themselves from colonial
oppression.*

Leonid Brezhnev
February 1981[1]

Now we'll have to feed them too.

Overheard in a Moscow bus queue on the day
that Soviet troops invaded Afghanistan

The Brezhnev era began on a note of considerable skepticism in the Kremlin
about the potential benefits that Moscow could expect from the Third World. If
the language was not exactly as blunt as that of the anonymous bus passenger
quoted above, the indictment laid against Khrushchev by his colleagues on the
day of his downfall was similar in sentiment. Mikhail Suslov told the Central
Committee in Khrushchev's presence that he had been indiscriminate and
profligate in the promises he had made to other nations.[2] He had awarded
Nasser and his Defense Minister Abd al Hakm Amer the decoration of "Hero of
the Soviet Union," which was inappropriate for foreigners and non-
Communists. He had committed the Soviet Union to helping Iraq construct a

163

railway line six hundred kilometers long at a time when the USSR itself was only able to extend its own rail network by that amount each year. He had seen fit to order Soviet engineers to build a stadium in Indonesia where extreme poverty was endemic.[3]

The attack on Khrushchev was in part a search for a scapegoat, since the charges against him only highlighted excesses in a general policy that his colleagues had all approved. The real issue was the leadership's frustration with the disappointing results of a decade of active Soviet involvement in the Third World. Moscow had greeted the decolonization process in Africa and Asia in the 1950s with eager optimism. As always, it saw things from a double perspective. One was the issue of Soviet state security; the other was ideology. Khrushchev welcomed the newly independent countries into what he called the "world camp of peace forces" opposed to the capitalist West.[4] Although many of them called themselves neutralists, Khrushchev and his colleagues expected them to take the Soviet side on most international issues. The second issue was how to accelerate the transition of those countries to socialism, since none of them, with the exception of North Vietnam, had achieved independence as a result of action by local Communists. India, Indonesia, Ghana, and Egypt were brought to political sovereignty by representatives of the "national bourgeoisie."

The fact that Moscow was primarily interested in the new nations' foreign policy was clearly shown by its actions in India and Egypt. To the chagrin of the Communist party of India, on a tour of India in 1955 Khrushchev praised Nehru's domestic and foreign policy. A year later he warned the CPI that if Moscow was forced to choose between Indian communism and progressive bourgeois nationalism, it would choose the latter.[5] At the same time with its sale of arms to Egypt and its aid for the Aswan Dam project, even though Egyptian Communists were suffering persecution, Khrushchev acted in marked contrast to Kremlin policy under Stalin, which had attacked Nehru and Nasser as reformists and reactionaries.

By the end of 1970 when eighty-one Communist and workers' parties met in Moscow to discuss strategy, the Kremlin faced a complex set of pressures and imperatives with regard to the Third World. Relations with the United States had gone sour with the U–2 incident and the cancellation of the Paris summit meeting. A Soviet effort to take an independent role in the Congo crisis, outside the framework of the United Nations, had been repulsed with the acquiescence of most UN members. China was accusing Moscow of being insufficiently militant toward the United States and of not recognizing that the transition to socialism would of necessity be violent. The Moscow conference ended with a compromise statement and the adoption by the Soviet leadership of a new attitude to the national bourgeoisie in the Third World. The Kremlin invented the concept of "national democracy"—halfway between "bourgeois democracy" and "people's democracy"—under which states could create the conditions for taking the "non-capitalist road to development." By strengthening the state

sector of the economy, minimizing Western economic influence, and guaranteeing freedom of action for "democratic forces," i.e., the local Communist
parties, states could move to socialism while jumping the stage of capitalism that
earlier Marxist theories had considered essential. In foreign policy a "national
democratic" state would fight against imperialism and its military blocs and
bases on foreign territory, and uphold its political and economic independence
by resisting new forms of colonialism.

The new theory was a transparent attempt to explain how developing countries could adopt progressive policies without a major input from a Communist
party. It justified the notion that local Communist parties should work with a
broad coalition of other progressive forces, but left open the question whether
the Communists should try to take the lead. A further complication arose two
years later when the new Cuban leader, Fidel Castro, reprimanded the Communists who were attempting to gain important positions in the revolutionary
movement. Moscow had a difficult choice. It could either condemn Cuban
socialism as unscientific, as it was already doing with "African socialism" and
"Arab socialism," or else change its theory.

It chose the latter course. Cuba was described as a "revolutionary democracy," typifying the new possibility that "the representatives of the radical petty
bourgeoisie during a true people's revolution can go over to the side of the
working class and socialism."[6] Even countries without a working class or a
Communist party could be revolutionary democracies if they were led by urban
petty-bourgeois intellectuals, students, or army officers who were sympathetic
to socialist ideas. The role of the proletarian vanguard, which had to be taken by
the working class under orthodox theory, was now said to be taken by the Soviet
Union. "At present the socialist world system both materially, morally and
politically carries out on an international scale the functions of the proletarian
vanguard," as one of Moscow's leading theoreticians put it.[7] Two lessons arise
from this hasty and unconvincing effort by Moscow to construct new theories for
the Third World. It showed that the Kremlin was still anxious to encourage
social and economic transformations that would somehow reinforce the unstruc-
tured emotional socialism of Third World leaders. It also showed that Moscow
was willing to be utterly pragmatic in deciding whether to declare a Third World
leader a "revolutionary democrat." Khrushchev awarded the Algerian leader,
Ben Bella, the decoration of "Hero of the Soviet Union" in May 1964. Nasser's
award of the same decoration came shortly afterward.

Khrushchev's enthusiasm for this new theory was not shared by all his
colleagues, as Suslov's remarks on the day of his overthrow make clear. Over the
next few months army coups toppled three "revolutionary democrats," Ben
Bella in Algeria, Sukarno in Indonesia, and Nkrumah in Ghana, and strengthened the hand of the Kremlin's skeptics who had always doubted the reliability
of the Third World as an ally of the Soviet Union. In foreign affairs Third World
leaders tended to adopt a posture of nonalignment, reserving the right to

criticize the Soviet Union. Domestically, it was clear that many of their regimes rested on a narrow power base that could easily be undermined, giving way to a reactionary alternative.

Faced with this disappointing balance sheet after a decade of decolonization, Brezhnev and his colleagues modified their policies. First, there was to be less money available for the Third World. A *Pravda* editorial of October 27, 1965, said that the socialist countries had to develop their own economies before "increasing aid to other detachments of the liberation struggle." The people of the Third World must shoulder the main burden of development themselves. In the first two years after 1965 Soviet aid deliveries to the Third World declined. Soviet spokesmen also made it clear that they would take a much longer perspective on the time needed for the construction of socialism. One of Moscow's senior development economists summed up the new realism: "The failure and setbacks of some African countries which have tried to introduce socialist measures show . . . that it is impossible to introduce socialism by decree. . . . The advance to socialism requires planned systematic work and the gradual creation of the economic and social base of the new social system."[8]

During the second half of the 1960s and early 1970s there was a subdued quality about Soviet involvement in the Third World. Moscow now looked to trade as the main way of expanding Soviet influence abroad. It attempted to develop new partners in Latin America, sub-Saharan Africa and Southeast Asia. It adopted a more strictly commercial attitude to aid, which picked up again in 1968 after a two-year drop, but grew slowly from $355 million in 1969 to $505 million in 1975.[9] Prestige projects received less support, while Moscow favored schemes that could produce a reasonable economic return. Soviet aid conditions hardened. Although the basic terms for Soviet project loans remained the same (repayment over twelve years at an interest rate of 2.5 percent, starting the year after completion of the project) Moscow gave a larger proportion of its loans in the form of commercial credits which carried a higher rate of interest, between 4 and 6 percent. More Soviet aid was tied to the interests of the Soviet economy, with clients paying back in the form of raw materials, labor-intensive goods, or semitropical and tropical fruits that the Soviet consumer would never otherwise see.

Aid was increasingly concentrated on six countries close to the Soviet border (Afghanistan, Iran, Iraq, Pakistan, Syria, and Turkey). The message was clear. Regardless of their internal political systems, Moscow hoped to buy goodwill or what it preferred to call "good neighborliness" with its economic aid. By 1970 the three earlier major recipients of Soviet aid, India, Indonesia, and Egypt, had been reduced to one. The anti-Communist coup in Indonesia in 1965 led to an abrupt drop in Soviet aid. India repaid the Soviet Union more in 1970 than it was receiving in new disbursements. Only Egypt remained as a large beneficiary of Soviet help.

The Six-Day War in the Middle East in 1967 gave a new dimension to the

Soviet aid program. Spurred on by demands from Egypt and Syria to have their arsenals replenished, Moscow increasingly projected itself as an arms merchant in the Third World. In 1969 arms deliveries for the first time exceeded the amount dispatched by the Soviet Union in economic aid. By the end of the 1970s arms exports had risen dramatically. Recent figures calculated by the CIA claim that Moscow provided $6,615 million worth of weapons to the Third World in 1979 compared with $1,720 million worth of nonmilitary aid.[10]

Under Brezhnev the continual dilemma over whether to support internal revolutionary forces or forge state-to-state relations with repressive regimes was usually resolved in favor of the latter. During the Brezhnev era Moscow supplied arms to the Shah of Iran, to Uganda's Idi Amin, and to Iraq's Saddam Hussein. It expanded trade with Argentina while the clampdown on that country's Left was at its height.

In spite of its rhetorical support for revolution, Moscow did little to promote social upheavals in the Third World. All the revolutionary changes of the last two decades took place without Soviet involvement in the overthrow of the old regime—Cuba, Nicaragua, Iran, Afghanistan, Ethiopia, and the collapse of the Portuguese empire. Only in the case of Afghanistan, Angola, and Guinea-Bissau had Moscow even had any previous direct contact with some of the new leaders. Kissinger's view that the Soviet Union "tends to fill any vacuum" is not borne out by events.[11] After the departure of Washington's clients in Nicaragua and Iran, Moscow made no immediate effort to replace the United States. It has eschewed any role in the vacuum of authority in Chad. With the exception of Afghanistan, Moscow's interventions in Third World civil wars have always been on the side of the group that had majority support in the international community—the MPLA in Angola, the federal government in Nigeria, and the Communists in Vietnam. When wars have broken out between Third World states, as in the conflict between Ethiopia and Somalia, Iran and Iraq, and India and Pakistan in 1965, Moscow initially tried to promote a mediated settlement.

Sadat's expulsion of Soviet advisors, and the switch by Guinea, Somalia, and Sudan back to pro-Western policies in the 1970s, taught the Kremlin some hard lessons about the problem of dealing with powerful and independently minded clients. Countries with Marxist–Leninist regimes like Vietnam and Cuba were not much easier to control. In spite of Moscow's arms supplies during the Vietnam War it was Hanoi that took the key decisions as to when to launch its military offensives and whether to take account of U.S. truce proposals.

In the Middle East this lesson was repeated with the most poignancy from Moscow's point of view. At least the Vietnamese were not losing. In the Arab conflict with Israel, Moscow found itself continually being asked to arm clients for wars whose timing Moscow could not easily control and which they invariably lost. In mid-May 1967 Moscow's actions helped to contribute to the Six-Day War when it encouraged Egypt to take a more threatening posture toward Israel after tension mounted on the Syrian–Israeli border. The main Soviet aim was to divert Israeli attention away from Syria and confront it with a joint Egyptian–Syrian stand. But Moscow then found itself unable to control Nasser's actions, and in spite of strong Soviet appeals to Cairo to show restraint, the Egyptian leader mobilized his forces to the point where Israel launched a preemptive attack.

The Arab defeat left Moscow increasingly reluctant to see another war with Israel. Once again, however, it slipped into a contradictory position. It preferred Egypt and Syria to look for a political path in attaining their territorial objectives, but it also saw that unless it answered their requests for new weapons it would lose influence as their patron. The result was that Moscow pressed the Arabs to recognize Israel's right to exist while giving Egypt enough arms to deter another Israeli attack but not to start a war. It was this Soviet restraint that finally led an angry Sadat to expel the Soviet advisors from Egypt in July 1972.

The further difficulty for Moscow was that although it preferred a political settlement, it knew that any serious negotiations would inevitably increase American influence and diminish its own, since it had no diplomatic leverage in Israel. The Arabs would turn to Washington for help, as they increasingly did after 1973.

The result was that in the Arab world Soviet influence has shown no significant gain since 1964. On the central issue, the Arab–Israeli dispute, Moscow has found itself pushed to the sidelines. It lost all influence in Egypt after 1973, and failed to gain any in Jordan despite Israel's occupation of the West Bank in 1967 or in Lebanon despite Israel's invasion in 1982. Only in Syria has it managed to retain a toehold. Even the Palestine Liberation Organization, to which Moscow has given diplomatic and military support, has shown interest in seeking American backing for its views, rather than relying on the Soviet Union. Beyond the front-line states Moscow's influence has wavered in response to events over which it had little or no control. In Iraq the Soviet position slipped when it condemned the war with Iran. In Libya Qadaffi's Islamic fervor prevented the Kremlin from turning its massive arms sales to political account. In Saudi Arabia and the Gulf, with the exception of Kuwait, Arab conservatism prevented Moscow from even opening diplomatic relations. The one clear asset that Moscow gained in the Arab world during Brezhnev's tenure was the use of the port in South Yemen, a costly benefit when measured against the vast Soviet expenditure of diplomatic energy in the Middle East over the last twenty years.

Latin America during the Brezhnev era provided a clear pattern of evidence that the Soviet Union puts support for revolution low on its list of priorities. Three different trends emerged. The Kremlin showed a consistent reluctance to challenge the United States in its own hemisphere. Second, it failed to give material backing to the numerous urban and rural guerrillas operating in most Latin American countries during the two decades. In the two cases where revolutionary governments came to power during the Brezhnev period—whether by the ballot box in Chile or by armed struggle in Nicaragua—Moscow gave rhetorical backing, but little else. Third, Moscow demonstrated continual eagerness to develop beneficial trade relations with the major Latin American states regardless of their repressive regimes. Its breaking of diplomatic relations with Chile after the military coup against Allende was the exception, not the rule. At the height of the campaign against the Left in Argentina, which was not very different from the terror used by Chile's President Augusto Pinochet, Moscow was successfully cultivating Buenos Aires as a source for imports of grain and meat. It agreed to train Argentinian officers and blocked UN discussion of human rights violations there. It supplied the Peruvian military government with the first surface-to-air missiles in Latin America.

The one practice of revolutionary solidarity that Brezhnev maintained was support for Castro's Cuba. This was a legacy inherited from Khrushchev, which it would have been difficult, though not inconceivable, for Moscow to reject. Nevertheless, the Kremlin had several clashes with Castro because of its unwillingness to support the continental guerrilla movements, and at one stage in the mid-1960s the Soviet leadership threatened to reduce oil supplies to Cuba and abandon their commitment to defend it against U.S. attack. As with Vietnam, they found that Cuba was an ally whose value to them was double-edged, since it threatened to obstruct and complicate their relationship with the United States. Luckily for Moscow, Latin America was quiet for most of the 1970s. When Central America erupted at the end of the decade, the Kremlin demonstrated that it still stood by the policy principles laid down in the early 1960s. In spite of a propaganda effort to suggest that Moscow was sending arms to the guerrillas in El Salvador, Washington was never able to produce solid proof. Far from reacting to the arrival in the White House of a fiercely anti-Soviet president in January 1981 by seeking a confrontation, Moscow made a number of efforts to be conciliatory. It offered several signals that it would rather have a renewal of détente than any clash over developments in Central America.

In Africa Brezhnev and his colleagues adopted a kind of leopard-spot approach, selecting a few countries for support and ignoring the rest. For the first ten years of their power they neglected sub-Saharan Africa and only revived their interest when the Portuguese dictatorship was overthrown and independence for Portugal's African empire became imminent. Their policy was essentially reactive. Their moves were prompted from outside. It was the collapse of the empire that reminded them of Angola's potential, and the awareness of growing American involvement in the struggle for power that led them to join in themselves. The Soviet and Cuban involvement only began after South Africa's incursion turned most African governments in favor of the MPLA, while rising criticism in the United States Senate made it almost certain that Washington would not openly intervene with force. (At the end of 1975 the Senate cut off funds even for covert intervention.) Moscow thus obtained international legitimacy and the near certainty of victory on the ground. The restraints that usually hold the Kremlin back had fallen away.

But those who saw the Kremlin's success in Angola as the probable start of a more activist Soviet policy in southern Africa were wrong. For several years Moscow had given small amounts of arms to the Southwest Africa People's Organization (SWAPO) which was conducting a guerrilla war against South Africa's illegal occupation of Namibia. With Angola now secured as a sanctuary for SWAPO, an interventionist Kremlin might have been tempted to exploit the general international odium against South Africa by stepping up military supplies in the Namibian guerrilla war to the point where SWAPO could win a military victory. Giving in to African pressure, Moscow made some increase in its aid and logistical support to SWAPO, but the Kremlin was well aware that the military balance was even less in favor of its clients than it was in the Arab–Israeli dispute. It deliberately prevented any serious escalation of the war on the part of its allies. Over the next few years the decisive increase in the conflict came not from SWAPO's side but from South Africa, which repeatedly invaded Angola while Moscow watched passively.

Even in Zimbabwe the more advanced military struggle by the two guerrilla movements against white minority rule failed to alert the Kremlin to the need to review its approach. Moscow continued to back only one of the movements, ZAPU, a mistake that cost it dearly when the other movement, Robert Mugabe's ZANU, won the elections in 1980 that followed the Lancaster House Conference and the ceasefire.

The Horn of Africa produced the crisis where the Russians were next involved after their Angolan triumph, but here, too, the Russians were slow to take a military role. The area's strategic proximity to the Indian Ocean was of concern to Moscow because of U.S. Polaris submarine patrols, and it had carefully cultivated Somalia in order to win the use of naval facilities at Berbera. The overthrow of Emperor Haile Selassie in Somalia's neighbor, Ethiopia, in 1974 created new uncertainties with which the Russians were slow to grapple. When they switched to Ethiopia's side four years later, it was after a number of efforts to prevent Somali–Ethiopian tensions from becoming an East–West issue or provoking a border war. As in Angola, they sought to support the side that enjoyed majority backing in the Organization for African Unity and at the United Nations.

The exception came the following year when a new revolutionary regime in Afghanistan began to founder through a combination of its own mistakes, lack of popular support, and a growing movement of armed resistance. After the Russians invaded and set up a different government, it was tempting for some Western politicians to link Soviet responses in Ethiopia and Afghanistan and detect a new militancy in Soviet policy. Zbigniew Brzezinski added the fall of the Shah of Iran to produce the concept of a geographical "arc of crisis" which the Soviet Union was alleged to be eager to control. Under his thesis, a range of countries stretching from the Horn of Africa to Pakistan had become targets of opportunity whose fragile political and social structures could produce chaos that the Russians would exploit. Other Western politicians such as Reagan saw the chaos itself as caused by the Soviet Union—"Let's not delude ourselves. The Soviet Union underlies all the unrest that is going on."[12]

Western concern about the area stemmed from a number of specific trends— the rise of the Organization of Petroleum Exporting Countries (OPEC), the withdrawal of British forces from the Gulf in 1971, the internal strains provoked by massive inflows of petro-dollars into traditional societies, and the resurgence of militant Islamic nationalism, most notably in Iran. But there was little evidence from Soviet actions to support the idea that Moscow was making a high priority of seeking to dominate the area, or would be successful if it tried.

In Iran Moscow hoped for more influence after the Americans were expelled, but in the face of Khomeini's fiercely anti-Soviet views chose to wait rather than take firm action. In December 1980 Brezhnev announced a set of proposals for the Persian Gulf that were designed not so much to enhance Soviet influence as to prevent the area from moving further under Washington's. He called for agreement on a set of obligations under which the Soviet Union, China, Japan, the United States, and other Western powers would pledge not to set up military bases and would guarantee free use of the international sea lanes.

By the end of the Brezhnev era the Kremlin had evolved a complex and contradictory set of relations with the Third World. On the military side its partners could be divided into three different kinds. First were those countries that had produced "progressive" regimes either by means of an internal left-wing coup, such as Ethiopia, Afghanistan, and Grenada, or as a result of a successful liberation struggle, as in Angola, Mozambique, and Indochina. Echoing the vagueness of Khrushchev's earlier talk of "national democracies" and "revolutionary democracies," Brezhnev described them for the first time at the party congress in 1976 as "socialist-oriented states." At the party congress in 1981 he listed them in more detail as "states that have opted for socialist development. Development along the progressive road is not, of course, the same from country to country, and proceeds in different conditions. But the main lines are similar. These include the gradual elimination of the positions of imperialist monopolies, the local big bourgeoisie and the feudal elements, and the restriction of foreign capital; the securing by the people's state of commanding heights in the economy, a transition to planning in the development of production, and encouragement of the cooperative movement in the country- side; the enhancing of the role of the working masses in social life, and gradually reinforcing the state apparatus with national personnel who are faithful to the people; and an anti-imperialist foreign policy. Revolutionary parties expressing the interests of the broad mass of the working people are growing stronger there."[13]

In none of these countries did the change to a "socialist-oriented" regime take place as a result of Soviet initiative. The changes were prompted by internal developments. But once the revolutionaries were in power, Moscow answered the call to help defend them or, as Brezhnev put it in 1981, "We are against the export of revolution, and we cannot agree to any export of counter-revolution either."[14]

The second category of customers for Soviet arms were Middle Eastern states, such as Iraq, Libya, and Algeria, that could afford to pay cash. In these countries Moscow still hoped to gain political influence in return for supplying arms. As Moscow found itself facing increasing difficulties in "front-line" Arab states—forced out of Egypt and with declining influence in Syria—it developed more interest in the radical Arab oil exporters. But its interest focused less on their hard-line attitudes to Israel than on their geographical positions in the strategic rivalry with the United States—Libya and Algeria on the Mediterranean where Moscow wanted anchorages for its fleet, and Iraq, a useful counterweight against an Iran which was until 1979 still dominated by the United States.

The third category was countries of less geographical or political importance which might nevertheless become one-time or regular customers for Soviet arms. By breaking the previous Western monopoly of the arms trade, Moscow could win a small political point at Washington's expense, even if the Kremlin did not have serious hopes that these states would become allies. Examples were Peru, Kuwait, and Jordan, which all turned to Moscow for particular arms deliveries in the 1970s. Coupled with these arms sales went a Soviet program for training officers and technicians, either on weapons courses in the Soviet Union or by sending Soviet military instructors to the Third World.

With the increasing prevalence of military regimes in the Third World, the Kremlin saw a political value in developing links with men who might one day be in power. Between 1955 and 1979, 45,600 citizens of developing countries went to the Soviet Union for military training.[15] In 1978, the last year for which figures are available, 12,070 military instructors from the Soviet Union and its Warsaw Pact allies were working in some two dozen countries of the Third World.[16] (This was in addition to 21,850 such instructors and combat soldiers from Cuba.)

Where possible, the Kremlin insisted on repayment for its aid. Even close allies such as Angola were expected to pay—in Angola's case, with hard currency derived from its sales to the United States of oil extracted under a joint production venture with the Gulf Oil Corporation. Vietnam helped to pay back a small part of its estimated $3 billion debt to the Soviet Union by sending seven thousand citizens to work on construction projects and in factories in the Soviet Union. The Soviet media angrily criticized Western reports that these were "migrant workers," and said instead they were trainees who received the same pay as equivalent Soviet workers. The fact remained that they were helping to relieve a chronic Soviet labor shortage.[17] Bulgarians and other Eastern Europeans have also been reported to be working on projects in the Soviet Union in what has been described by Soviet sources as "a new form of economic integration."[18]

On the economic side, Soviet aid commitments in the Third World were equally patchy. The largest number of Warsaw Pact and Soviet economic technicians in 1979 were concentrated in a few countries, mainly in the Middle East—Algeria, Libya, Iraq, and Syria. Much of the cash aid was concentrated on two countries, Cuba and Vietnam, which the Soviet Union could not afford to abandon because of their historical, strategic, and symbolic importance in resisting the United States. Neither of them would ever be able to pay Moscow back in full. Other aid went to less important "socialist-oriented states," even though the Kremlin knew from bitter experience that they could not be relied upon. Egypt, Somalia, and the Sudan all changed their foreign policy without changing their leadership. "The link between the character of the class forces in power and foreign policy does not, of course, manifest itself automatically," one Soviet study pointed out accurately in 1975. "Foreign policy, particularly any specific action of the liberated countries, is influenced by the economic development level, geographic location, traditions, economic relations, the volume and sources of foreign aid, the internal situation and other factors."[19]

Another problem for the Kremlin is that foreign aid is not supported willingly by most Soviet citizens. There is widespread grumbling and resentment among ordinary Russians over the amount of aid, which is assumed to be partly to blame for the shortage of consumer goods at home. The Soviet Union's global involvement is seen as a drain on the country's prosperity. The Soviet media refer to Moscow's "selfless" aid to Third World countries, but little effort is made to involve the public in individual aid-giving or to appeal to their own instincts of generosity. Unlike East Germany, where schools and factories regularly collect money for Vietnam, the southern African liberation movements or Nicaragua, the Soviet Union confines its aid transfers to government-to-government projects.

Moscow provides few funds for international humanitarian appeals such as disaster and famine relief. In aiding refugees or the victims of war, it prefers to select a few people for health treatment or education in the Soviet Union rather than send money abroad for the short-term needs of larger groups. Even on occasions such as the relief of starvation in Kampuchea, which became a focus of worldwide attention at the end of 1979 and where the Soviet Union sent larger amounts of aid than the West, Moscow made little effort to trumpet its activity, apparently out of concern at the domestic reaction. "Sacrifice is no way to resolve the complex problems of world economic development," in the words of a magazine article by Yuri Krasin, the prorector of the Academy of Sciences of the Central Committee.[20] In the coded way that public discussion of Soviet policy usually has to be conducted, Krasin directed his remarks at the working class of the capitalist countries, but they applied equally well to Soviet workers. The problems of developing countries could not be solved "through economic sacrifices by the working class. . . . Anyone who propounded such belt-tightening austerity theories and programs would not meet with understanding in the working class and would find himself isolated."[21]

Moscow is also skeptical about aid to the Third World because it has seen that most nations remain tied to the capitalist market. During the 1970s Soviet specialists became increasingly disappointed with the scale and pace of internal economic change in Third World countries. In the first place this meant that the Soviet Union had less leverage than it had hoped for in preventing aid recipients from defaulting on their debts to Moscow, whether these were cash debts or less definable political obligations. Egypt had been paying off part of its $5 billion military and economic debt by exports of cotton and textiles between 1973 and 1976, but when Moscow refused to consider Sadat's request for a ten-year grace period and a rescheduling of repayment over thirty or forty years, the Egyptian leader unilaterally declared a ten-year moratorium. Moscow found there was nothing it could do. Had Egypt done this to a Western country, the full might of the International Monetary Fund, the World Bank, and private banking sanctions would have been brought to bear. Moscow has no such control over international financial institutions.

In addition, Moscow has little leverage to push countries toward socialism. A study of Soviet policy in Africa under the editorship of Yevgeni Tarabrin, deputy director of the Africa Institute of the Academy of Sciences, pointed out that "it is extremely hard to develop economic ties and run government-owned enterprises in countries where private capitalist, small-commodity, and semi-natural economies predominate. . . . Individual enterprises built in African countries often receive financial support from private credit banks, lack the necessary economic and technical leadership, and are left to themselves in a hopeless fight against overseas companies engaged in a similar line of business."[22] This was true, the study added, even of "socialist-orientated states" in tropical Africa which are "building a new society while remaining outside the world system of socialism and continuing to be dependent on the capitalist market."[23] Under the Soviet definition, Africa has more socialist-orientated states than any other continent—Angola, Benin, Cape Verde, Congo, Ethiopia, Guinea, Guinea-Bissau, Madagascar, Mozambique, São Tomé, and Tanzania.

The implication of the Tarabrin study left Moscow with two bleak alternatives. It either took countries almost entirely under its wing, as it had done with Cuba and Vietnam, and thus risked a perpetual drain on its resources, or else it left them to the mercy of the international economy with the probability that any internal trend toward socialism would be aborted.

It was perhaps no wonder that Soviet specialists began to take a longer perspective about the likelihood of change in the Third World. Yuri Krasin appeared to postpone the notion of worldwide socialism forever: "It would be utopian to expect some mythical universal justice in the solution of the problem of developing countries."[24] Others revised the long-standing theory of "two world economies" and increasingly spoke of a single world economy dominated by the capitalist system. They classified the developing countries in terms of their economic indicators rather than their political profiles.[25] There were the poorer states where prefeudal or feudal forms still predominate and which do not produce for export; the relatively developed states that produce raw materials, export some industrial goods, and even invest abroad (they can be "progressive" like India or "conservative" like Indonesia or Morocco); and the reactionary oil-rich monarchies, ruled by state monopoly capital, which spend enormously for domestic development as well as investing abroad.

Shifting its policy, Moscow proceeded not to encourage developing countries to break their links with the capitalist-dominated world economy, but to find a more equitable international division of labor. At the Fourth Session of the United Nations Conference on Trade and Development (UNCTAD IV) in Nairobi in May 1976, the Soviet foreign trade minister, Nikolai Patolichev, attacked Chinese proposals that the Third World develop self-reliance and form new producer cartels on the pattern of OPEC. He said it should operate in the world economy and "with due regard for the interests of both commodity producers and consumers."[26] At the Twenty-Fifth Party Congress Brezhnev talked about "global problems such as raw materials and energy, the eradication of the most dangerous and widespread diseases, environmental protection, space exploration and the use of ocean resources," from which the Soviet Union "cannot remain aloof."[27] These have also affected Third World countries, regardless of their social system. Under this new tolerance of the existing world economy, Soviet specialists envisaged a kind of global cooperation in which the more advanced capitalist countries would invest in Soviet raw materials while the socialist bloc with its less advanced technology dealt with the developing countries. In return for exporting their primary products, the developing countries would obtain foreign capital and know-how in building up their infant industries. There was nothing radical in this notion, which Brezhnev expounded at the party congress in 1976: "A specific feature of our times is the growing use of the international division of labor for the development of each country, regardless of its wealth and economic level."[28] This provided new possibilities "for successfully fulfilling economic taks and saving time, enhancing production efficiency and speeding up scientific and technical progress."[29]

Soviet economic approaches to the Third World now tend to divide into three. With the world's poorest states, Soviet aid is concentrated on geological surveys to help to discover and extract raw materials. With the oil-rich countries Moscow looks for sales of Soviet goods and equipment in return for hard currency. With the middle-rank countries, it proposes to set up industrial enterprises whose products might in part be exported to the Soviet Union or to Third World countries. The factories could be owned by the host country or be joint ventures with Soviet capital. The benefits for the Soviet economy are obvious. (In 1978, according to Soviet figures, almost 24 percent of its imports from the developing countries came from Soviet-aided factories.)[30] In 1977 the Soviet Union and India signed several contracts to supply Indian equipment from Soviet-aided plants to Bulgaria, Cuba, Egypt, and Turkey. Moscow has even begun to go into joint ventures with Western capital in the Third World. It started a pipeline in conjunction with an Anglo–American asphalt group in Nigeria and contracted with an American firm to build a thermal electric plant in Argentina.[31]

In addition to the obvious implication that Moscow was more interested in short-term economic gains than any destabilization of the international economic system, its approach was also hard to distinguish from that of Western capital. The Russians tried to argue that their capital, being government-owned rather than private, was superior, since it did not add to the profits of transnational corporations. Because Soviet capital took part in joint ventures for only a limited period before being bought out by the local partner, they also claimed it was less self-interested. But from the point of view of the developing country, there was little to choose between the two. It was hardly surprising that developing countries saw the Soviet Union as merely another advanced industrial country that took a hard-headed attitude toward the Third World.

Demands grew for the Soviet Union to join the North–South dialogue. In 1974 Foreign Minister Andrei Gromyko said the Soviet Union would resist efforts to separate the national liberation movement from "its natural ally, the community of socialist states." "We shall never accept, either in theory or practice, the false concept of the world being divided into 'rich' and 'poor' countries, which equates the socialist countries and certain other states that have extracted so much wealth from countries under colonial yoke."[32] Moscow also opposed efforts to have all the advanced countries, including the Soviet Union, pledge a fixed portion of gross national product in economic aid. Its own aid was "not a compensation for damage inflicted or an atonement for past wrongs. It is aid by a friend and ally to the struggle against the common enemy—imperialism, colonialism and neo-colonialism."[33]

CONCLUSION

By the end of the 1970s the mass of contradictions in Soviet approaches to the Third World nations seemed to be dispiriting the Soviet leadership. Politically, it continued to claim that the Soviet Union was their "natural ally." Economically, it bargained with them in as firm and ungenerous a way as any Western nation. When the nonaligned movement met under Castro's chairmanship in Havana in 1979, Moscow failed to persuade it to come out firmly on the Soviet side. Three months later, it completely overlooked the nonaligned nations' likely objections and invaded Afghanistan, proving more dramatically than ever that Soviet security interests override the Kremlin's concern about its national image.

Soviet attitudes to the Third World have of course changed over the last twenty years. As a world power with a global interest in competing with the United States, it sees Third World nations as part of the terrain of competition. Moscow's primary purpose is a strategy of denial—to prevent their being used by the United States for military purposes. Its secondary aim is to set up its own network of naval and airfield facilities to protect its ocean-going submarines and merchant fleet and to enable it to defend new revolutionary allies. Although Moscow played a decisive role in only one of the successful recent revolutions and liberation struggles in the Third World, it feels a historic responsibility to prevent them from being reversed. This does not mean that it will always take action to do so. But it now feels more able to play a role, provided the circumstances are judged to be right.

While this set of Soviet aims gives the impression of a new "interventionism" that was less evident twenty years ago, it is balanced by a new realism on both the political and economic fronts. Moscow is aware that the former colonies—what it calls the "newly-free countries"—are still tied to the capitalist economic system, and cannot easily be turned into permanent Soviet allies except at considerable cost. It has experienced a series of disappointments either because progressive governments were overthrown or because they switched their foreign policies from broad alignment with the Soviet Union and turned toward the United States. Moscow will continue to give all Third World nations broad rhetorical support and, in a few special cases, military aid. But its central posture toward most Third World nations will hover between those two extremes. It will trade with those who are interested. It will sell arms to those who can pay. It will provide economic aid on tough commercial terms to state enterprises. And it will hope—without much conviction—that this will somehow win it friends.

Moscow's heavy involvement in the export of weapons to the developing countries is more a sign of weakness than of strength (as well as a factor in intensifying the arms race in the Third World and contributing to increased instability). Arms are one of the few commodities with which the Soviet Union can compete with the West. By contrast, Moscow has few economic products to offer the Third World. It is the West that controls the terms of world trade, organizes the international capital market, and arranges most of the transfer of technology. The Soviet Union has failed and probably will continue to fail to make a deep penetration of the Third World. It is this lack of depth that has made it easy for such countries as Egypt to ask the Russians to leave. In spite of considerable Soviet economic as well as military aid to Egypt, Sadat was able to expel the Russians without suffering a major economic dislocation. Allende, on the other hand, found it almost impossible to reorientate the Chilean economy away from Western influence. Even a country like Angola, which has moved much farther than Chile toward political alignment with the Soviet Union and is totally dependent on it and Cuba for military help, is still deeply linked to the West through the international economy. Vietnam, one of the closest Soviet allies, joined the International Monetary Fund before it joined COMECON, the economic grouping of socialist states that Moscow leads.

A second limiting factor on the growth of Soviet influence is the increasing reluctance of many Third World countries to be drawn into the superpower confrontation. A few countries, particularly in Latin America, an area of historical U.S. dominance, have improved their relations with Moscow as a deliberate way of asserting a balance. But no country has been willing to shift completely to the Soviet side unless the pressures on it from the United States have been extreme, as in the case of Cuba. For its part, the United States has also been having problems. It found increasing difficulty in persuading even friendly countries to accept American bases. In the Persian Gulf conservative states have been reluctant to be drawn into too direct a military link with Washington. They prefer the American presence to remain "over the horizon." As long as Third World countries continue these trends toward nonalignment, or at the least some distancing from the superpowers, the growth of Soviet influence is bound to remain as retarded as it has been until now.

10

THE MIDDLE EAST

*The Russians were unable to comprehend the domi-
nating role of nationalism in the Arab world.*

Mohammed Heikal, 1978[1]

As Israeli forces besieged an Arab capital for the first time in July 1982, and the United States prepared to send marines to Beirut, observers noted the Soviet Union's remarkable passivity. During the previous two Middle East wars, the Kremlin had hinted, albeit in a cautious way, that it might intervene militarily on the Arab side. This time it made no such suggestion even though one of its clients, the Palestine Liberation Organization, was surrounded by the Israelis. It called on the Arabs to show greater unity in the face of the Israeli onslaught. It criticized Israel in ritualistically fierce terms. But its strongest warning to Washington, a private message sent by Brezhnev to Reagan and paraphrased by the news agency Tass, was the statement that if American troops went in to supervise a PLO retreat, "the Soviet Union will adjust its policy in accordance with this fact."[2] When the troops went in a few days later, the Kremlin's "adjustments"—if there were any—were invisible to the naked eye.

Any analysis of the Kremlin's options in the face of Israel's overwhelming military superiority in Beirut might well have concluded that there was little that Moscow could do. But its use of bluff had been stronger on previous occasions and now seemed unusually weak. Was this, observers asked, a sign that Brezhnev's health was finally collapsing at the age of seventy-five? Had the

Kremlin lost the physical and mental energy needed to hammer out a response to an admittedly awkward situation? Or was the Kremlin's passivity a reflection of its lack of favorable options and its unwillingness to become involved in yet another crisis in the Middle East where it was almost certain to lose out once again?

The last of these potential explanations is probably the correct one. By 1982 the Soviet position in the Middle East was extremely weak. Its influence was confined to Syria and South Yemen. Short of a direct invitation from the Lebanese government to intervene—a most remote possibility—the only available point of entry into the Lebanese situation was via Syria, whose forces were in the Bekaa Valley in central Lebanon. Yet these were already performing badly against Israeli air attack, and there was no reason for the Kremlin to expect that this would change, or even that a better Syrian performance in the Bekaa could affect the outcome in Beirut.

Contrary to the conventional wisdom in the West, the Kremlin has always tended to act in the Middle East with restraint. If Soviet policy during the Beirut crisis was passive, this was different only in degree from its posture on other occasions. The Kremlin's involvement with Egypt in the mid-1950s—the first serious move in the Middle East that the Soviet Union made—took place after the United States had rejected Nasser's overtures and as a result of an invitation from the Egyptian leader whom Moscow had initially called a reactionary. Brezhnev and his colleagues vastly extended the Soviet presence, not only in the states directly confronting Israel, but also in North Africa and along the Red Sea. Yet their record continued the general theme of restraint that marked Khrushchev's activity in the area.

With few exceptions, the Soviet Union has not tried to stir up local tensions. In the wars between Ethiopia and Somalia or Iran and Iraq it either sought to prevent them by finding a diplomatic settlement or adopted a hands-off policy. The Soviet Union discouraged the three most recent Arab–Israeli wars and has imposed limits on its arms deliveries, often at the risk—as in the case of Egypt—of incurring Arab displeasure. On the central aspect of the Arab–Israeli dispute, the existence of Israel, Moscow has consistently urged the Arabs to recognize the Jewish state. Most important of all, it frequently put its hopes for détente with the United States above the chance of local advantage in the Middle East.

Yet this cautious policy produced few dividends, and by the early 1980s the balance sheet of Soviet gains and losses looked bleak. Overall East–West détente was shaky, and in the Middle East, Moscow had completely lost the strategic position it had briefly enjoyed in Egypt in the 1960s. The United States had successfully maneuvered to have the Russians ousted from that country. Repeated Soviet offers to act as a partner with Washington in the settling of the Arab–Israeli dispute had been rejected. Neither in providing the Arabs with the machinery of war nor in gaining a role in the area's international diplomacy had the Russians been able to turn the situation to their own benefit. They supplied the Arabs with aircraft and weapons but never seemed able to use this as leverage in the vital decisions about going to war. The Arabs mainly ignored their advice. When it came to negotiations, the Russians' lack of influence on Israel denied them any real chance to act as a mediator. From the moment of its first involvement in Egypt in 1955, the Kremlin faced a recurring dilemma: Should Moscow seek to work with the Western powers as joint arbiters of events in the Middle East, if the West would permit it? Or should it develop its own policy and do its best to undermine Western positions? The history of Soviet involvement in the Middle East in the last quarter-century suggests that the Russians never resolved this dilemma. They swung back and forth between the options without ever developing a strategy. They were never moderate enough for those Americans who were willing to concede them a role, nor militant enough for the Arab radicals.

The Soviet instinct was to be cautious and avoid so-called "adventures" because war in the Middle East always carried the risk of Arab defeat, which would mean a blow to Soviet prestige, a need for Soviet intervention, escalation, superpower confrontation, and possible failure. Yet at the back of it all was the danger that a moderate state might switch toward the United States and "do a Sadat." Internally, the Arab states were unpredictable. Nationalist regimes, however anti-imperialist they sounded in their foreign policy rhetoric, showed no signs of happily tolerating local Communist parties. In Iraq, Egypt, and the Sudan, local Communists were victimized or murdered. This in itself did not cause the Russians much concern except fleetingly in the 1960s, when Khrushchev came under some criticism from his more ideological colleagues, such as Mikhail Suslov.[3] If the Russians had hoped that nationalist regimes that had embarked on the "non-capitalist road to development" with a heavy state involvement in domestic industry would evolve toward socialism, they were disappointed. This stage—in reality state capitalism rather than socialism—did not preclude a foreign policy switch back to the West, as happened in Egypt, where the door to foreign investors was reopened in the mid-1970s.

Soviet policy, and indeed the whole of Soviet strategy, in the Middle East began and continued as damage-limitation. The primary goal was to prevent the region from becoming a safe asset for the West in its policy of encircling the Soviet Union. This meant that Western political and economic influence should be challenged where feasible. As a subsidiary goal, in order to counteract the West's military deployments, the Soviet Union wanted to deploy its own fleet in the Mediterranean in a forward defense role. For this, the acquisition of naval base and storage rights and access to port facilities would be useful.

TURKEY AND IRAN

At the time of Khrushchev's downfall none of the Soviet Union's three distinct border zones looked as unpromising or difficult as the Middle East. In view of China's break with Moscow and Eastern Europe's continuing problems, this may seem a cavalier statement. But Eastern Europe, in spite of the still relatively recent uprising in Hungary, the tension in Poland, and the building of the Berlin wall, was at least an acknowledged Soviet sphere of influence. The early postwar Western effort to "roll back" communism had failed, and no one seriously imagined that the area posed a strategic threat to Moscow. China's split was a political and ideological cataclysm, yet here again it was a row within the Communist geopolitical family. There was no prospect of a link between the West and China. Any suggestion that China, which had broken with Moscow partly because Mao considered Khrushchev too soft on capitalism, would one day invite Richard Nixon to China and to a limited extent join hands with Washington would have been ridiculed.

The Middle East, by contrast, was an area of deep Western penetration. This zone, known in Russia as the Near East, straddles the Soviet Union's long southern flank and is thousands of miles from the United States. Yet looking from the Kremlin, Khrushchev's successors saw that Turkey and Iran, two of the Soviet Union's neighbors, were closely linked with Washington. In 1964 Afghanistan was the only country that was not a potential threat to the Soviet Union. Turkey was a member of NATO. Iran was a military ally of the United States, a customer for American weapons and host to a growing American military and intelligence community. Over the horizon in the eastern Mediterranean cruised the U.S. Sixth Fleet with its aircraft carriers and Polaris submarines providing a powerful nuclear threat to the industrial heartland of the Soviet Union. Washington's strong strategic position in the Middle East developed from the American policy of containing the Soviet Union on its own doorstep, which had already begun before the Second World War ended.

Soviet policy in the region at the end of the war had been confined to Turkey and Iran. Although both countries had had long-standing disputes with the czars, revolutionary Russia had little to do with them. In 1920 after the Turkish attack on western Armenia, which had been within the boundaries of the Russian Empire, Lenin ceded the cities of Kars and Ardahan to Turkey. This arrangement was confirmed by the Soviet–Turkish friendship treaty in 1921. The Soviet–Iranian friendship treaty of the same year stabilized relations between the two countries, although with greater potential benefits for the Soviet Union. Under article six, the Soviet Union was authorized to dispatch troops into Iran if a third power tried to use Iranian territory to threaten Russia.

In the Second World War, Turkey and Iran expressed sympathy with the

Nazis and aroused concern, not only in the Soviet Union, but also among the Western allies. Churchill made repeated efforts to persuade Turkey to enter the war on the allied side, hinting that otherwise he would support the Soviet position on their territorial disputes. It was not until after the Yalta Conference early in 1945 that the Turks finally declared war on Germany. Iran was jointly occupied by Soviet and British troops in 1941 and by American troops the following year, although under the treaty concluded between Britain, Iran, and the Soviet Union the allies agreed to withdraw their troops within six months of the end of hostilities with Germany.

Toward the end of the war Stalin made two attempts to gain allied agreement on permanent, internationally guaranteed concessions for the Soviet Union from its two southern neighbors. He asked that the Soviet Union have joint control of the Bosporus and the Dardanelles, which govern passage into the Black Sea. If the British had rights to defend the Straits of Gibraltar and the Suez Canal, and the Americans to defend the Panama Canal, Moscow felt entitled to have similar rights over the waterway through which all its southern traffic had to pass. Britain and the United States rejected the Soviet demand and were able to use it as a device for strengthening the already strongly anti-Soviet feelings of the Turkish Army. In 1947 the U.S. Congress allotted $100 million to spend on building military bases along Turkey's border with the Soviet Union and improving the country's strategic highways. Turkey joined Greece in proposing a Western-orientated Mediterranean bloc that would "embrace Turkey, Greece, the Arab countries, and Israel."[4] In 1952 Turkey was coopted into NATO, subordinating its land and air bases to the Supreme Allied Commander in Europe. A year later, recognizing the fait accompli, Moscow tried to normalize its relations with Turkey and formally renounced any Soviet claims on Kars and Ardahan.

In Iran, too, Stalin hoped for some postwar advantage. In 1944 he suggested that the Iranian railways and a free port on the Persian Gulf should be operated under international trusteeship, with the clear aim of giving Russia an assured economic outlet to the Persian Gulf. The Americans rejected the plan, arguing that, as a State Department paper put it, "British policy for more than a hundred years has been pointed towards preventing any other great power, and especially Russia, from gaining a foothold on the Persian Gulf. . . . If we proceed on the assumption that the continuance of the British empire in some reasonable strength is in the strategic interest of the United States, it might be considered wise, in protection of vital British communications in this important area, to discourage such a trusteeship."[5]

The other dominant issue in postwar Iran was access to the country's vast oil reserves. Here the main competition was between Britain and the United States, with oilmen from each country, backed by their respective governments, scrambling for concessions. In September 1944 the Russians entered the picture by staking a claim to oil rights in the northern provinces, which their troops were occupying. Their interest in the oil was probably not as great as their wish to establish the principle that affairs could no longer be organized on their borders by other countries without any reference to Soviet wishes. George Kennan, the American ambassador to Moscow and at that time the architect of Western containment of the Soviet Union, wrote to Washington "that the basic motive of recent Soviet action in northern Iran is probably not the need for the oil itself but apprehension of potential foreign penetration in that area. . . ."[6] The Americans reacted to the move with subtlety and skill. They persuaded the Iranian government to abandon the negotiations on oil concessions and concentrate on a speedy withdrawal of all foreign troops, confident that in a postwar Iran American oilmen would be able to renew their demands. Disappointed in their hopes for a free port in the south, the Russians then overplayed their hand in the north. They encouraged the creation of two Left-dominated autonomous republics in Azerbaijan and the Kurdish area of Mahabad, and refused to withdraw their troops. It was only after the Iranian government agreed to give the Soviet Union a joint share in a special Soviet–Iranian oil company that the Russians finally pulled out in May 1946. Five months later the Iranian parliament annulled the agreement and sent in troops to crush the autonomous republics.

The episode showed that the Russians could be persuaded in certain circumstances to retreat, if they felt the diplomatic cost of not doing so would be too high. In fact, their actions poisoned the well of Soviet–Iranian relations for several years afterward. When the CIA overthrew the nationalist prime minister, Dr. Mohammed Mossadeq, in 1953, in an American-organized coup after eighteen months of worsening U.S.–Iranian relations, the Russians and their allies, the pro-Soviet Tudeh party in Iran, took no action. Dr. Mossadeq had been one of the prime movers in the campaign to resist foreign oil concessions and evict all foreign troops at the end of the war. Perhaps the Russians continued to harbor resentment against him, or else—more probably—they were unable to understand that Third World nationalism was directed against all major outside parties. They expected anti-Western movements to be automatically pro-Soviet.

The Brezhnev era saw little progress in Turkey and Iran. Shortly after Khrushchev's removal, the Kremlin had launched a good-neighbor policy toward both countries. Gromyko visited Ankara in May 1965, and over the next two years the Soviet and Turkish prime ministers exchanged visits. Moscow provided aid for several major industrial projects and trained technical cadres. When Turkey invaded Cyprus in 1974, Moscow avoided criticism. By 1979 the amount of aid given to Turkey far exceeded that given by Moscow to any other non-Communist country over the previous twenty-five years. In spite of the military coup in September 1980 and the suppression of all left-wing activity, Moscow continued to maintain close political and economic relations with Turkey. Yet none of this weakened Turkey's membership in NATO or reduced the threat to Moscow from U.S. installations on Turkish soil.

Moscow made a similarly fruitless effort to use a policy of "good neighborliness" to woo Iran away from the Western camp. The Shah was invited to make his first trip to Moscow in 1965. The Soviet Union agreed to build a steel mill in Isfahan which Iran would pay for by supplying natural gas. A year later Iran even bought military supplies from the Soviet Union in the first Soviet arms deal with a member of a Western military alliance. The deal consisted mainly of trucks, troop carriers, and small arms. Although Soviet relations with the Shah remained generally good throughout the 1970s, they did not stop Washington's massive penetration of Iran with its own economic investment, military aid, and military advisors, as well as American electronic spy stations close to the Soviet border.

When mass demonstrations against the Shah developed in early 1978, Moscow was as surprised as Washington. It gave the subsequent Khomeini regime a cautious welcome, stressing the Iranian revolution's "anti-imperialist" character. It approved the expulsion of the Americans, Iran's withdrawal from CENTO, and the nationalization of various Western firms. But it found it difficult to believe the new regime was really leftist, or likely to offer Moscow better relations than it had had with the Shah.

The seizure of American diplomats as hostages left the Russians in a quandary. At the United Nations they joined in condemning the action as a violation of international law. They were worried that similar actions could take place against their own diplomats. (Their fear appeared justified. Crowds twice threatened the Soviet embassy in Tehran, forcing Moscow to protest to the Khomeini regime.)

At the same time, the Russians did not want to alienate Khomeini's supporters by appearing to discount the strongly felt Iranian sense of grievance against the United States. Partly in the hopes of minimizing Iranian opposition, and in order to win favor with Iran by posing as its friend in the face of mounting Western sanctions, Moscow soon toned down its disapproval of the hostage taking. The Russians sought to warn Iran that the United States was the greatest threat to Iranian independence. They joined Iran in condemning the American effort to rescue the hostages by force. At the Soviet party congress in February 1981, Brezhnev expressed Moscow's general confusion over Iran when he called its revolution "a specific type. However complex and contradictory, it is essentially an anti-imperialist revolution, though reactionary circles at home and abroad are seeking to change this."[7]

The West's sanctions against Iran and Moscow's neutrality in the war between Iran and Iraq helped to improve the Soviet position in Tehran. In 1981 trade between the two countries reached a record high, but the Russians still felt frustrated by the slow pace of any political rapprochement with Tehran. The Iranians were restricting the number of Soviet diplomats in Iran, broadcasting anti-Soviet propaganda, and lumping the Soviet Union with the United States as a dangerous power. Iran strongly criticized the invasion of Afghanistan and periodically aided the Afghan rebels. Although the expulsion of the United

States from Iran had been an unexpected boost, Moscow was concerned that it would one day slip back into the Western camp. In 1983 these fears gained ground, when Nureddin Kianuri, the leader of the now banned Tudeh party, was arrested and forced after torture to confess to espionage for the Soviet Union. Fifteen hundred other members were due to stand trial. Eighteen Soviet diplomats were expelled from Iran, and the authorities began to say that the Soviet Union was a "greater Satan" than the United States. Trade overtures to the West increased.

The Arab–Israeli Conflict

Apart from Turkey and Iran, the only issue in their southern border zone in which the Russians took some interest during the immediate postwar period was the creation of the state of Israel. Seeing it as a device for undermining British imperial interests, they supported Israel's foundation. Speaking in the United Nations General Assembly on May 14, 1947, Andrei Gromyko, then the Soviet ambassador, said that the sorrow and suffering that the Jews had undergone during the Second World War were "exceptional" and "indescribable." "The fact that no Western European state has been able to ensure the defense of the elementary rights of the Jewish people, and to safeguard it against the violence of the Fascist executioners explains the aspirations of the Jews to establish their own state. . . . It would be unjustifiable to deny this right to the Jewish people."[8] Gromyko went on to argue that the rights of the Arabs in Palestine must also be preserved and that no unilateral solution should be imposed. The Soviet Union's preferred solution was for a single Arab–Jewish state with equal rights for Arabs and Jews. But if the worsening of relations between Arabs and Jews made this impossible, Moscow would support the partition of Palestine into two autonomous states. In a move that would later seem ironic, Gromyko arranged for Czechoslovakia to provide arms to the Jewish militia, the Haganah.[9]

Although Moscow became critical of Israeli policy two years later, Moscow took little further action on the Arab–Israeli dispute until after Stalin's death in 1953. Between January 1949 and January 1954 the Soviet delegate abstained on all votes connected with Israel at the United Nations. Two things changed thereafter. One was the general feeling among Stalin's successors that Moscow should give aid and diplomatic assistance to the group of Third World states that had emerged from Western colonialism and were resisting Western efforts to reintegrate them into anti-Communist military pacts. The Soviet Union had already focused its attention in Asia on Afghanistan, Burma, and India. Now it became more interested in the Arab states. The other factor was the upsurge of nationalism in Egypt.

Turkey and Pakistan had agreed to military cooperation in 1953 and Pakistan had offered the United States the use of air bases. Washington had its eye on

Iraq, Iran, and Egypt as future members of a pact. But when Gamul Abdel Nasser emerged as Egypt's prime minister in April 1954, he soon made it clear that he would oppose any efforts to replace the Anglo–Egyptian links, which the Free Officers' coup had managed to sever, by new military links with the United States. The Soviet Union had concluded several trade agreements with the new Egyptian regime, but the Kremlin was still not resolved on any dramatic new initiative in the Middle East to take advantage of Nasser's anti-Western moves. East–West tensions in other parts of the world had subsided, and the Kremlin appeared more interested in improving relations with the West.

The initiative for a switch in Soviet policy came from Nasser who asked the Russians to supply him with arms in April 1955. Nasser had originally hoped to get arms from the United States. His army was weak and could not prevent humiliating Israeli raids against Palestinian guerrillas in the Gaza strip. His request for arms interested American Secretary of State John Foster Dulles, who thought he might enlist Egypt's new leader in the anti-Communist crusade. But for Nasser, as for many other Arab leaders after him, the prime enemy was not communism, but fear of Israeli expansionism. When Dulles coupled his offer with a condition that Egypt accept U.S. advisors, Nasser, who had just expelled the British, hesitated. The delay gave the British time to dissuade Dulles from the whole idea. So Nasser turned to Moscow instead. In the words of Mohammed Heikal, Nasser's colleague and friend, the Russians were "sucked into the Middle East by events. It was not they who had started the great offensive but Egypt who had forced it upon them."[10]

Moscow took six weeks before deciding whether to agree to the Egyptian request. After negotiating with the Egyptians on the types and quantities of weapons that Cairo wanted, the Russians decided to funnel the arms through Czechoslovakia to avoid upsetting the Americans. As Heikal puts it, "[T]he arms deal transformed the situation in the Middle East. It was no longer possible for the area to be regarded as a Western preserve, forbidden territory to intruders. The breaking of the West's arms monopoly was a signal to all Arabs that an alternative policy was available, and a very attractive one it looked to many of them."[11] Although Moscow's arms deal with Egypt widened Soviet and Arab options at a stroke, it was not intended primarily as the thin end of a Soviet military wedge. Khrushchev's main interest was to prevent more countries joining the recently formed and Western-sponsored Baghdad Pact. He knew that the West's military involvement in the Middle East was far greater than his own. It would be hard for Moscow to match it. On a visit to London in April 1956 he called for a joint Eastern and Western arms embargo to the Middle East. Prime Minister Anthony Eden rejected it.

The Czech arms deal was enormous. Though never publicly admitted, it appeared to include at least one hundred tanks, eighty IL–28 jet bombers as well as self-propelled guns, armored personnel carriers, and several naval vessels. In practice these gave Cairo a weapons advantage over Israel. But the exact details of Israel's own arsenal and its expected deliveries were also unclear at the time, and it cannot be stated for certain whether Moscow intended to give Egypt military superiority. At all events, once the 1956 Suez crisis arose after the United States refused to finance Egypt's Aswan Dam project (which the Russians agreed to do three years later) Moscow acted with caution. Nasser did not tell the Russians before he nationalized the Suez Canal Company—the move that precipitated the crisis—nor did he consult with them about the danger of British and French military action for fear that they might tell him to draw back.[12]

As British pressure on Egypt mounted during August, the only hint of Soviet action in Egypt's defense was a piece of Khrushchevian bluster. He told British Ambassador Sir William Hayter at a reception in Moscow that if a war started, Soviet sympathies would be with Egypt and Soviet "volunteers" might be sent. In fact, it was not until six days after the Anglo–French bombing of Egyptian targets on October 31 that the Russians made any threats of intervention. Their initial statements had merely called on the United Nations to restrain Britain, France, and Israel. On November 5 Bulganin sent notes to Britain, France, Israel, and the United States. While the first three notes talked vaguely about the future survival of the Israeli state, and asked Britain and France how they thought they could survive a potential rocket attack, no one took them seriously. The Soviet Union had only one type of rocket in large quantities, with a range of 450 miles. Longer-range rockets had been tested but not deployed. The significant note was the one to Eisenhower in which the Russians proposed that the United States and the Soviet Union act together militarily to stop the fighting. At the same time the Soviet Union submitted a draft ceasefire call to the United Nations. Eisenhower rejected the plan for American and Russian forces to go in, but put pressure on Britain and France to accept the ceasefire. Soviet rhetoric became stronger after the ceasefire was accepted. A declaration by the official news agency Tass raised the issue of unilaterally dispatching Soviet volunteers if British, French, and Israeli forces did not withdraw. The Tass statement bore all the hallmarks of an empty gesture, designed to retain prestige in the Arab world. The Russians appeared to want to gain credit for compelling the withdrawal of foreign forces from Egypt, when the main pressure on Britain and France had come from the United States.

Eleven years later when the Six-Day War occurred, circumstances in the Middle East had altered. This time Egypt, far from being the victim of a coordinated military campaign by Israel and two of its war allies, played a major role in laying the groundwork for the war. Moscow also was more heavily engaged in the Middle East. It was no longer a relative newcomer to the area. In the years since Suez, Syria and Iraq had moved in a strongly anti-Western direction and Moscow had become a major arms supplier to both countries. A tripartite pact concluded between Syria, Iraq, and Egypt in 1963 may have encouraged the Russians to think that an anti-imperialist progressive bloc could be formed. In 1963 Moscow sent Egypt its most up-to-date model T-55 tanks, the first time it had given contemporary battlefield equipment. Khruschchev's removal in 1964 had no impact on the continuing Soviet arms deliveries to the three states. Yet the formidable Soviet supply operation did not include significant numbers of ground-attack aircraft and tactical rockets. According to one of the most detailed Western analyses of the Russians' military deliveries, Moscow gave the Arabs "sufficient weapons for defending themselves and engaging in limited offensive action but not to allow contemplation of a successful first strike or total victory."[13]

Politically and militarily, this was a disastrous combination since it provided the Arabs with the illusion, though not the reality, of superiority over Israel. The 1967 crisis began with a gradual escalation of tension on the Syrian–Israeli border. Moscow announced that Israel was trying to overthrow the left-wing Ba'athist government in Syria. It felt that the best way to defend Syria was to encourage the Egyptians to come out in open solidarity with the Damascus regime. Moscow sent repeated warnings to Egypt of an imminent Israeli invasion of Syria. It is not certain whether the Russians really believed their own warnings about Israel, or whether they merely hoped that a firm display of Egyptian–Syrian unity would provide a propaganda victory.

Moscow began to show some concern when Nasser ordered his armed forces into Sinai and asked the UN to remove their troops from the strategic Red Sea bastion of Sharm el-Sheikh. The United Nations Secretary-General U Thant chose to remove the entire United Nations Emergency Force from Sinai, thus leaving the Egyptian and Israeli armies in potentially direct confrontation. Four days later Egypt closed the Straits of Tiran to Israeli ships. The crisis left the Russians in a quandary. They had to support Egypt publicly, but they also knew that it was no match for Israel in an all-out war. In a statement put out by Tass the day after the closure of the Straits of Tiran, the Russians appealed for restraint. While criticizing Israel, Tass said, "It is the firm belief of the Soviet government that the peoples have no interest in a military conflict in the Middle East. . . . It is only the forces of imperialism, with Israel following in their wake, that can be interested in it."[14] This was about as direct a signal of Soviet reluctance for war as could be expected. Privately, the Russians warned the Egyptians to be cautious. Kosygin told the visiting Egyptian minister of war, Shams el Din Badran, "We are going to back you. But you have gained your point. You have won a political victory. So it is time to compromise, to work politically."[15] Before dawn on May 27 the Soviet ambassador to Cairo awoke Nasser with an urgent appeal from the Kremlin not to initiate hostilities. Nasser denied that he had any such intention.

Over the next week tension increased as Jordan and Iraq joined the unified Egyptian–Syrian command and Israel formed a government of national unity. On the morning of June 5, 1967, the Israeli air force launched surprise attacks on the Arab air forces, dealing them crippling blows. Moscow's concern about the effect on superpower relations was immediately apparent. In the Kremlin's first use of the Moscow–Washington hotline since it was set up four years earlier, Kosygin urged Lyndon Johnson to put pressure on Israel for a ceasefire. He also made it clear to the Egyptian ambassador in Moscow that Moscow would not intervene militarily. The Russians were "frozen into immobility by their fear of a confrontation with America," Nasser later complained.[16] In spite of the Arabs' losses of aircraft, Moscow made no effort to resupply them during the war.

At first Moscow wanted the United Nations to promote a ceasefire and an Israeli withdrawal, but as it became clear that time was on the side of the advancing Israeli forces, it called simply for an unconditional ceasefire. Fighting stopped on the Egyptian front after the Israelis had swept through Sinai to the Suez Canal, but as Israel continued to advance over the Golan Heights in Syria, Soviet anxiety increased. The Russians were afraid that the left-wing government in Damascus might be overthrown. Moscow announced that it was breaking diplomatic relations with Israel and threatened to take further sanctions if it did not immediately halt the war.

Moscow's most important communication was reserved for Washington. The Soviet leadership told Johnson that Moscow might have to take "an independent decision" involving "necessary action, including military."[17] Unlike Khrushchev's threat of unilateral action in 1956, the Kremlin's statement in 1967 came while the fighting was still going on. Was the statement meant primarily for the Americans or the Israelis? Was it designed to convince the Arabs that Moscow would not let them down? Was it aimed to satisfy critics of the Kremlin's cautious line in Peking or among hard-liners in Moscow itself? Would the Russians have implemented the threat if their bluff had been called?

The Americans subsequently intervened with the Israelis to insist on a termination of hostilities and the crisis abated. The Russians could and did claim that their threat of unilateral action had worked, while the Americans argued, with some plausibility, that the Russians could not have carried out their threat. They were stronger than in 1956 and had sent about seventy naval vessels from the Black Sea into the Mediterranean during the crisis. This certainly gave them more military credibility than Khrushchev had had in 1956 when he talked vaguely of a strategic rocket attack on Britain and France. But the 1967 fleet had little amphibious-landing or nonnuclear-war-fighting ability. Nevertheless, Johnson said the United States would resist "Soviet intrusion" in the Middle East and ordered the Sixth Fleet to sail nearer to the Syrian coast.[18]

The Arabs' catastrophic defeat prompted the biggest debate in the Kremlin on policy toward the Middle East since Khrushchev had fallen. Had Moscow done enough to help the Arabs and could it have done more? What should it do next? The Russians were engaged in aiding and arming a friendly region in another part of the Third World, Vietnam. There, in the face of a massive American bombing campaign, an anticolonial guerrilla war led by a disciplined Marxist–

Leninist party was determinedly continuing. Could lessons be learned from that for the different circumstances of the Middle East?

In the immediate aftermath of the war Moscow found itself under criticism from China and the Arab radicals. They charged Moscow with standing by while its friends and allies were sacrificed. Even President Tito of Yugoslavia, who had good reason to question the use of Soviet military power in other circumstances, was worried about Soviet softness in the face of Israel's attack on his good friend, Nasser. While the war was still going on, Tito had persuaded Moscow to summon a meeting of the Warsaw Pact and invite him to attend. There he argued that if the socialist camp appeared to be doing nothing to defend one of the leading nonaligned countries, the Third World would gain a miserable impression indeed.

Worse than the charge of inaction was the suggestion that Moscow had wittingly or unwittingly colluded with Washington. This was prompted by Soviet use of the hotline to the White House during the war and two messages from Kosygin to Nasser in which the Soviet leader passed on information from the Americans. Heikal reports that there was a "widespread conviction in the Arab world that the Soviet Union's policy of détente had led it into what amounted to collusion with the Americans. Opinions differed over whether the Russians were dupes of the Americans or were too frightened to be able to come to the help of their friends."[19] On June 12, the day after the war ended, Algerian President Houari Boumedienne flew to Moscow to express the Arabs' feelings of bitterness. He asked the Soviet leadership to explain its policy. "The worldwide national revolution is receiving successive blows from American neo-colonialism and your friends feel that the slogan of peaceful coexistence has turned into fetters restricting your movements. We sincerely wish to know where the dividing line lies," he said.[20] The Russians promptly replied, "What is your view of nuclear war?"[21]

Boumedienne's visit was not a success. The Kremlin was still assessing the war. On June 20 and 21 the Central Committee of the Soviet Communist party met to hear a report from Brezhnev on the war. The debate appears to have revolved round several issues, including the impact of East–West détente on the Soviet Union's freedom of action. There was some discussion over whether the Soviet Union could afford the economic cost of a large-scale reequipping of Egypt's armed forces, or whether it might not be better to encourage the Arabs to maintain the struggle by means of guerrilla warfare. The wisdom of basing the Soviet–Arab alliance so heavily on Egypt was queried, with the suggestion that a country like Algeria, which was not in the direct front line with Israel, might be a better bet.

The Soviet Politburo also met on June 21 to decide whether Kosygin, who was then attending the Middle East debates at the United Nations, should meet with President Johnson. Although there is some evidence that Suslov was against the move, the summit was arranged but produced no agreement. Shortly after the

Central Committee meeting, the Moscow city party secretary, Nikolai Yegor-
ichev, and Alexander Shelepin, a Central Committee secretary, lost their jobs.
Both moves were probably linked to disagreements with Brezhnev's line.

The Politburo also decided on a massive resupply of Soviet arms to Egypt.
President Podgorny was sent to the Middle East to explain Soviet thinking. The
Arabs were not entirely satisfied, and after a meeting in Cairo of the leaders of
Egypt, Syria, Iraq, Jordan, and Algeria, the so-called confrontation states,
Boumedienne and President Aref of Iraq were sent to Moscow. Heikal has given
a lively account of what transpired in the Kremlin as Brezhnev pleaded with the
Arabs for patience and urged them to recognize Israel.[22] On the military side,
Brezhnev argued that the Arabs would have to be better prepared and mobilize
their population if they wanted to win a war. He was probably thinking of the
Vietnamese, Moscow's more reliable ally, although he referred only to Israel,
which had a quarter of its people under arms, he said, while only 1 percent of
Egypt's were. He touched delicately on Arab losses. "I am sad because our
reputation was bound up with your reputation. I am sad because the most
modern arms we supplied you with have now been sent to America or West
Germany. We gave you our planes but you had no pilots; we gave you our tanks
but you had no crews."

The heart of Brezhnev's argument was that the Arabs must recognize Israel.
"We want to criticize you a little because without criticism there is no love," he
told the two Arabs. "We are confronted with a dilemma. You feel yourselves
unable to recognize Israel, even indirectly, but we all want to see the Israeli
forces withdraw. Is there not possibly a contradiction here?" The imperialists
wanted the status quo to continue so that Israel's occupation would continue
indefinitely. The closure of the Suez Canal would hurt the Arabs and friendly
countries like India. He understood the enmity between the Arabs and Israel,
but this need not lead to Israel's liquidation. He recalled Soviet history and the
treaty of Brest-Litovsk when Lenin had made realistic but temporary sacrifices.

Then Kosygin joined in: "Revolutionary slogans can work against the interests of the Arabs. Look at China. They are taking a very hard revolutionary
line and say that if you go to war they will help you. But what can they help you
with? Ten articles? A hundred meetings? Revolutionary ideas expressed in
words don't mean anything unless they are backed by real power." The Soviet
leaders' moderate approach did not convince their Arab guests on the issue of
recognizing Israel, although they went home aware of the dilemma the Kremlin
faced as the weaker of the two superpowers.

In an article in *Al Ahram* in August, Heikal threw more light on Soviet
thinking at the time.[23] The Americans had been quicker than the Russians, he
wrote, in escaping from the stalemate caused by the mutual superpower threat of
nuclear war. They had reverted to use of conventional force and support for
counterrevolutionary elements in the Third World. "The United States controlled all the bases of its military alliances throughout the world and used them

as springboards; it relied on the colonies of its allies among the old colonialist powers; its common interests with the counterrevolutionary forces created natural ties between it and the world reactionary ruling class; and it established a naval fleet in every sea and began to launch raids in the spirit of the policy of strength. . . . In the meantime the Soviet Union was unable to take definite action. The United States captured the initiative in the free use of conventional weapons and left the Soviet Union the alternative of resorting to the use of nuclear power, if it could. . . . The Soviet Union finally awoke to this serious fact. The new Warsaw Pact commander Marshal Yakubovsky has declared that the Soviet Union has begun to prepare itself for possible limited wars using conventional weapons. But the problem that will face the Soviet Union is this: Where are the bases and footholds from which the Soviet Union can meet the possibilities of limited wars with conventional weapons?"

The Soviet Union continued to make strenuous efforts to use the United Nations to put pressure on Israel to withdraw, while urging the Arabs to recognize Israel. The effort came to nothing, and the net effect of Moscow's policy after 1967 was to increase its investment in Egypt. On the political front, the Russians tried to encourage Nasser to move farther down the "non-capitalist road" by nationalizing more of the economy and forming a single disciplined political party. This was also the prescription being recommended to Castro in Cuba at the same time. In 1965 the Russians had urged the Egyptian Communist party to dissolve itself and let its members join Nasser's party, the Arab Socialist Union. After 1967 the Russians stepped up their economic aid to Egypt with the aim of strengthening the state sector of the economy, increasing agricultural production and lessening Egypt's trade links with the West.

On the military front, the Soviet Union—at Nasser's insistence—became heavily involved in training the Egyptian armed forces. In addition to the small number of weapons instructors and teachers in military academies who were in Egypt before 1967, Nasser asked for Soviet advisors down to battalion level. He also proposed a mutual defense pact and asked Moscow to give Egypt air support to allow Egyptian ground troops to attack Israel. Counseling patience, the Russians refused. Instead, they called for a complete restructuring of the armed forces and a purging of scores of officers. They made the army more professional and more egalitarian, cutting down the previous sharp cleavage between officers and enlisted men. Pay was improved and only career people were allowed to become officers. The Kremlin wanted to improve the combat potential of the Egyptian armed forces over the long term, but leave itself as far as possible in control of when and whether the Egyptians made war.

Moscow's heavy but ultimately awkward role in Egypt was obviously a matter of considerable interest in Washington. By chance American foreign policy was about to come under the control of a man who would outmaneuver the Soviet Union and inflict on it one of its most humiliating foreign policy defeats. Henry Kissinger was appointed national security advisor by the Nixon administration at the end of 1968. His colleague at the head of the State Department was the gentlemanly William Rogers.

Between them the two men soon came to epitomize what had been a continuing debate in U.S. foreign policy ever since the Soviet Union first showed interest in the Middle East. On the one hand Rogers took the view that it was best to bring the Russians into the diplomatic search for peace; even if peace itself proved elusive, the Russians would be tamed. If peace was achieved, the Russians would have less scope for influence since their leverage, such as it was, rested almost entirely on the supply of arms. Russia, it was conceded, had a stake in the area. Kissinger, by contrast, was less interested in regional issues than in a global confrontation with the Soviet Union. Although the Middle East is considerably closer to the Soviet Union than to the United States, Kissinger saw Moscow as a "meddler."[24] His aim was to exclude the Russians from the area. Whether or not peace between Israel and the Arabs was achieved, the hope was to remove the dispute from the superpower arena by turning it into something like the Greek–Turkish dispute, an argument between two dependent allies of the United States. War between them was less important than the fact that the Soviet Union had no role to play. The device by which to promote this process was to encourage local suspicions of the Soviet Union. In Israel this was an easy task which became even easier as more Soviet Jews emigrated to Israel. In the Arab world it was harder, for several Arab regimes depended on the Soviet Union for military aid and diplomatic support.

Kissinger's strategy was to demonstrate that the Soviet Union was powerless to break the stalemate in the Middle East because it had no influence over Israel. In order to convince the Arabs that this was so, it suited the United States to prolong the stalemate. He had this strategy in mind from the very beginning of his time as a White House advisor. In his memoirs he describes his first meeting with Nasser's foreign affairs advisor, Mahmoud Fawzi, who had come to Washington for Eisenhower's funeral in March 1969. Fawzi explained that the Russians were anxious for peace. "Egypt was eager for progress partly because the Soviets were pressing it in the direction of peace, he said. They seemed to understand that they would not be able to help their Arab friends any other way; in a stalemate Soviet standing in the Arab world was bound to deteriorate. Fawzi's last point was, of course, precisely the strategic opportunity I perceived for the United States. If the Soviet position in Egypt was bound to deteriorate the longer a settlement was delayed, we had no incentive to accept the first Soviet or Egyptian offer."[25] In fact, the stalemate lasted for another three years, and it was not until after Nasser's death in 1970 that Egypt, under his successor Anwar Sadat, adopted the strategy that Kissinger had prepared. By then Sadat's frustration with Moscow had grown, not just because it had no influence with Israel, but because the Russians refused to supply all the weapons that Sadat wanted to launch his war against Israel.

A year and a half before his death in 1970 Nasser had launched the so-called "war of attrition" along the Suez Canal. The aim was to apply continuous pressure on Israeli forces on the east bank of the canal by means of commando raids and artillery bombing. The Israeli response was to step up air raids deep into Egypt. As with the Six-Day War, it turned out to be another one-sided struggle in which the Arabs risked daily humiliation, but found it hard to achieve an honorable way of stopping. Once again the Russians felt themselves forced to aid Egypt, this time with the supply of SAM–3 surface-to-air missiles, which were effective at low altitudes and were manned by Soviet crews, and the dispatch of some one hundred Soviet pilots to protect the new SAM sites. It was Moscow's first commitment of troops in a combat role in a non-Communist country, and it had a significant effect in eliminating Israel's air superiority over the canal.

When Sadat came to power, the Russians continued to increase their supplies, partly in order to maintain the allegiance of the new leader who was already showing signs of wanting to open a serious dialogue with the United States. At a meeting with Brezhnev in March 1971, Sadat specifically told the Soviet leader, "The Americans have started to contact us. They tell us that the Soviet Union can't help us—only the U.S. can do that, and so we will have to trust them and follow their advice."[26] But when Sadat asked for advanced MiG–23 interceptors to counter the American Phantom fighter-bombers acquired by Israel, the Russians delayed. They sent more MiG–21s and doubled the density of Egypt's surface-to-air missile system. In May, after further rousing Soviet doubts by jailing many of the most pro-Soviet politicians in Cairo, Sadat proposed that the two countries sign a Treaty of Friendship and Cooperation.

While the treaty for the first time publicly linked Soviet arms deliveries to the Egyptian aim of reconquering the occupied territories, Moscow obtained an implicit pledge from the Egyptians to consult the Soviet Union before launching a war. By then Sadat had conceived his plan of starting a surprise attack across the Suez Canal. Throughout 1971 and the early part of 1972 Sadat impatiently pressed Moscow for further supplies, but the Russians now had their eye on Nixon's forthcoming visit to Moscow. It was to be the first time an American president had been to the Soviet capital, and coming as it did just after Nixon's visit to Peking in February 1972, the Russians were anxious not to give the Americans any excuse to cancel it. Their aim had long been international recognition of the Soviet Union as an equal partner with the United States, and they saw the summit as an important element in that strategy. It was irritating enough that Nixon had preceded the Moscow visit by his trip to Peking. To have the meeting put off altogether would have been doubly annoying.

On the Middle East the Russians were less interested in Egypt's feeling of humiliation in the face of Israeli strength than in the hope of obtaining a comprehensive peace settlement, with a guaranteed role for themselves as arbiters. On a visit to Washington in September 1971, Gromyko had told Kissinger privately that Moscow was prepared to withdraw its military advisors in Egypt as part of a comprehensive peace settlement. Moscow would also join in an arms embargo to the Middle East provided that the Soviet Union could participate in guarantees. Gromyko added one final condition. The United States must withdraw its advisors from the Soviet Union's neighbor, Iran. Kissinger turned the proposal down, partly because he considered it too extreme, but partly in order to prolong the peace process—"a strategy that would only magnify Egyptian restlessness with Soviet policy."[27] At the Moscow summit Kissinger adopted the same delaying tactics. The communiqué contained a bland call for a peace settlement and military relaxation in the Middle East.

The communiqué infuriated Sadat. He sent Brezhnev an angry seven-point questionnaire demanding to know when the Russians would supply the offensive weapons he wanted. Fobbed off again with a vague reply, Sadat announced in July that he was expelling most of the 15,000 Soviet military personnel in Egypt. Although Sadat later indicated that Russian use of Egypt's Mediterranean ports could continue, the expulsion of the advisors was a public slap in the face and an astonishing climax to Moscow's years of patient investment in the strengthening of Egypt.

The Kremlin reacted publicly to Sadat's action with studied calm and acquiescence. Privately, a major debate went on. Moscow was in a quandary. On the political front, Egypt had proved to be unreliable. Besides expelling Soviet advisors, Sadat had sent his top national security assistant, Hafiz Ismail, for secret talks with Kissinger. Militarily, the Egyptians were no match for Israel, so that perhaps it was as well for the Russians no longer to be involved. Diplomatically, the Russians could see no way ahead. Their overtures to Washington to join in guaranteeing a comprehensive settlement were repeatedly slapped down. The Americans were doing everything to evict the Russians from the peace process.

When Sadat approached Moscow three months later with a request to patch up their relations and resume the arms supply, the Russians were uncertain how to react. It was Marshal Grechko, the defense minister, who argued most strongly that Moscow had no alternative but to comply. As Heikal puts it, the Soviet Union decided to double its stakes.[28] Grechko told his Politburo colleagues that the Arabs ought to be given enough weapons to let them risk a battle, since otherwise they would turn to the Americans. If they won, the Russians could claim credit for the victory. If they lost, the Arabs would have to turn back to the Russians to help rescue them. From October onward Soviet arms poured back into Egypt, including SAM–6 missiles, the latest antitank weapons, and bridging equipment. Sadat was getting the wherewithal for his long-planned crossing of the Suez Canal.

As preparations mounted during 1973, Soviet alarm became evident. During his visit to the United States in 1973, Brezhnev made a final effort to interest Nixon in an overall settlement. On the eve of the war itself, Moscow appeared to be trying to warn both Israel and the United States. Sadat told the Soviet ambassador on October 3 that he had decided to launch an attack.[29] In an astonishing move, the Russians promptly flew all Soviet dependents out of Syria and Egypt. No other Communist country followed the Russians in this highly visible step that almost seemed designed as a last-minute caution to the Arabs and a signal to the West that something was up.

Once the war began, Moscow hesitated. It consulted with Egypt, Syria, and Algeria about a possible ceasefire, but drew back until it could see which way the battle was going. On the third day with the Arabs still in the ascendant, Brezhnev appealed to Jordan and Algeria to join in the war. Moscow also started to resupply Egypt and Syria with arms and equipment, though not as much as they wanted. But as the tide began to turn, with the United States more than matching the Soviet airlift of weapons, and Israel successfully counter-attacking, Moscow urged an immediate ceasefire. It appealed to the Americans to join in pressing each side's allies to hold back. By now it was the Israelis' and Americans' turn to delay in order to give more time for the Israelis to reverse the territorial losses of the first few days of the war. Finally, with the Egyptian position close to disaster after Israel surrounded the Egyptian Third Army on the banks of the Suez Canal, the Russians threatened a unilateral military intervention. Its terms were almost exactly the same as in 1967, with the one important difference that this time the Russians had a greater capability for implementing it by airlifting troops. The intervention was requested by Egypt, and it was intended only as a desperate last resort if the Americans were unwilling to join the Russians in a United Nations-sponsored operation to enforce a standstill.

Unlike the Johnson administration in 1967, which took a similar Soviet threat as a mainly theatrical gesture, Kissinger reacted excitedly. Although he had initially permitted Israel to violate the ceasefire, the prospect of Egypt's total defeat was not what he wanted, since it would minimize the chance of American overtures to Cairo. Nevertheless, Russia's suggestion of strong action to rein-force the ceasefire was more important to him than the ceasefire itself; "We were determined to resist by force if necessary the introduction of Soviet troops into the Middle East."[30] During the night of October 24–25 the United States alerted its 82nd Airborne Division for possible movement and ordered its entire armed forces to adopt a heightened state of alert, unprecedented in the nuclear age. At the same time Washington put new pressure on Israel to observe the ceasefire. The Russians may well have considered that their threat had once again succeeded in forcing Washington to deal with Israel, although Kissinger continued to insist that the Americans acted independently.[31]

Had the Russians seriously intended to use the crisis as a device for introducing their own troops into the Middle East, they would hardly have called so insistently for a United Nations-sponsored ceasefire. Nor, even if they had sent troops, could they have been sure that Sadat would not ask them to leave when the crisis was over, as he had done with the Russian advisors a year earlier. In fact, the Russians consistently denied that they had ever alerted their forces for possible dispatch to Egypt. This denial made it hard for them to rebut the charges from China, Libya, and perhaps some radical critics within the Kremlin that they had colluded with the United States. The October War made it abundantly clear that their overriding priority was to avoid a superpower confrontation in the Middle East.

Extra problems arose after the October War. The ceasefire resolution passed by the Security Council called for negotiations to take place between the parties "under appropriate auspices." This was taken to refer to the United States and the Soviet Union, and was a political gain for Moscow, giving it a position as cochairman with Washington of a forthcoming conference on the Middle East. But before the conference could get down to work, another difficulty had to be settled. The messiness of the ceasefire lines, particularly in the area around the Suez Canal where the Egyptian Third Army was surrounded, made it inevitable that the first task was to disengage the Israeli and Arab armies. As only the United States had contacts and potential leverage with Israel, Kissinger was able to project himself as the lone mediator.

Kissinger himself concedes that the Russians were "so obsessed with getting a piece of the action" by attending the Geneva Conference that they fell in broadly with the American strategy.[32] "The Soviets may not have had brilliant options but they pursued those that gave us the least trouble. Détente did not prevent us from seeking to reduce the Soviet role in the Middle East nor the Soviets from scoring points with the Arabs now and then. But fairness compels the recognition that Moscow never launched an all-out campaign against us. And we took pains not to humiliate the Soviet Union overtly even while weakening its influence."[33] That brief paragraph accurately encapsulates the Soviet difficulty after 1973, which continues today. All that the Russians could do was "to score points" while the Americans were the ones with the dominant influence.

Under the Carter administration the Russians had a brief flurry of hope that they might reenter the picture. By then Kissinger had brought about disengagement agreements between Israel and its two neighbors, Egypt and Syria. The way seemed clear for comprehensive negotiations that would also have to include the Palestinians, with whom the Carter administration recognized that the Russians had some leverage. The new secretary of state, Cyrus Vance, took the view that it was better to have the Russians in peace talks than outside them. In October 1977 he signed a statement with Gromyko calling for a revived Geneva Conference by the end of the year. If the Russians felt that the American effort to squeeze them out of the Middle East was being relaxed, they were soon disappointed. The Soviet–American statement caused a storm in the U.S. Congress and Israel. Within a week the Israeli foreign minister, Moshe Dayan, had persuaded Carter to accept that Israel did not have to agree to the statement as a precondition for coming to Geneva. The American president also reemphasized the original 1967 Resolution 242 of the United Nations, which did not mention the Palestinians. Moscow interpreted Carter's new position as a repudiation of the joint Soviet–American statement. Although the issue of a revived Geneva Conference was delayed still further when Sadat made his historic visit to Jerusalem in November 1977 and the way for Camp David and a separate peace between Egypt and Israel was opened, the Kremlin continued to feel insulted by Carter's sudden change of tack.

By the early 1980s the Soviet position in the Middle East was as bleak, if not bleaker, than it had been when Brezhnev came to power. In 1964 there was still a faint chance that Egypt, the leading power in the Arab world, could become "another Cuba" in the sense of a progressive, nationalist, and anticolonial regime, which could transform itself gradually into a pro-Soviet socialist society. But there were important differences between Egypt and Cuba. In Cuba after the revolution the middle class left. The island's nationalism was strongly anti-American. Religion was not a major political or cultural influence. Cuba's geographical and economic position made her highly dependent on an outside power. When the Americans embargoed, the Russians could gain overwhelming influence by filling the gap. In Egypt circumstances were different. There, as in other parts of the Arab world, the Russians found it hard to make any cultural or political headway against the strong influence of Islam in a society whose elites, however "leftist" they sounded, had been strongly dominated by the materialism of the West, and who, of course, did not go into exile.

Although Arab unity remained a mirage, there was enough common feeling among the different Arab states, particularly in the face of the perceived intrusion of Israel, that differences between progressives and conservatives, radicals and moderates, Left and Right were often overshadowed. No one Arab state could ever be as isolated and vulnerable as Cuba was within the Western hemisphere. Even after Sadat's visit to Jerusalem and the rift in diplomatic relations with most Arab states, Egypt remained within the Arab family. There was no economic or cultural boycott. As far as Moscow was concerned, Egypt was by then already a lost cause.

If its relations with Egypt were the linchpin of Soviet policy toward the Arabs, Moscow had little more success in Syria and Iraq, the other major states that had leftist regimes. Moscow sold both of them arms in massive quantities. It signed treaties of friendship with each of them. It gave copious aid toward their industrialization. In neither case was Moscow able to prevent the estrangement or persecution of local Communists nor, more important, to moderate each country's move toward war—even with their Arab brothers. At the end of May 1976 Kosygin flew to Damascus to try to dissuade Syria from sending regular army units into Lebanon against the Lebanese Left and the Palestinians, only to find that the Syrians had moved in just before he arrived. In 1980 Moscow attempted in vain to halt the Iraqi invasion of Iran, "an absolutely senseless war," as Brezhnev described it.[34]

A principal reason why the Soviet Union was able to exert so relatively little influence over its Arab friends was that—contrary to much Western mythology—Moscow was consistently moderate on the central issue of Middle Eastern politics. It had been one of the first countries to acknowledge Israel's existence as a state, and it repeatedly urged the Arabs to do likewise. Moscow did not modify this line when the Palestinians finally emerged as a political entity with their own voice with the formation of the Palestine Liberation Organization in 1964. At that time the PLO was close to China. It took until 1972 for the Russians to receive the PLO leader Yasir Arafat as an official visitor in Moscow rather than as a guest of the nongovernmental Soviet Afro–Asian Solidarity Organization. When Moscow finally gave the PLO diplomatic status in 1979, numerous non-Communist countries, such as Austria, India, Kenya, Pakistan, and Senegal, had already done so. The Soviet Union urged the Palestinians to pursue a political rather than a military solution.

The Kremlin, it now seems clear, sees little benefit in the continuation of the Arab–Israeli dispute, provided that a peaceful settlement is not a Pax Americana designed to exclude Moscow from any role. When it first became involved in Egypt and Syria in the mid-1950s Moscow may have felt the dispute provided an opportunity for it to gain influence. As long as there was enmity between the Arabs and Israel, Moscow had a chance to become a major regional arms supplier with the prospect that he who sells the weapons calls the tune. The experience of the subsequent twenty-five years proves otherwise. Moscow is still a major arms supplier, but it does so now out of inertia, habit, and fear of being criticized if it does not, and because it can think of nothing else to do. A quarter-century of arms supplies to the Arabs (most of which have not even been paid for) have shown minimal results. First, it is obvious that the Arabs cannot overtake Israel in the arms race or defeat it in war. Second, in the aftermath of each war the Soviet Union has been sidestepped by the United States in the search for ceasefires or a disengagement. Third, the Arab–Israeli dispute continually threatens to become a major source of East–West tension. Fourth, Moscow sees more chance of its retaining a role in the Middle East as part of a comprehensive peace settlement than under conditions of "no war, no peace," because it still clings to the hope that it will be asked to provide superpower guarantees.

Its specific proposals were spelled out in a six-point plan in September 1982. They were an Israeli withdrawal from Arab lands occupied in 1967; the establishment of an independent Palestinian state in the West Bank and Gaza; the return of East Jerusalem to the Arabs with free access to holy places in all Jerusalem; assurances of security for all states in the region, including Israel; an end to the state of war between Israel and Arab nations; and guarantees of the settlement by the five permanent members of the United Nations Security Council or by the Security Council as a whole.[35]

The Mediterranean and the Persian Gulf

During the Brezhnev era the Soviet Union significantly increased its naval deployments in the Mediterranean. After the 1967 war it gained access to Egyptian ports and airfields, but had to abandon the airfields five years later when Sadat expelled the Soviet advisors. The Soviet Navy had to leave Alexandria in March 1976. By then it had gained alternative facilities at Latakia in Syria. The cooling of relations with Egypt encouraged Moscow to place more emphasis on other North African powers, particularly Libya and Algeria. Libya signed a major arms deal in 1975 and agreed to pay in hard currency, but in spite of a massive buildup of Soviet weaponry and Eastern European advisors, Qadaffi declined to allow the Russians to use his ports or airfields. The Soviet Navy began to make courtesy calls in Tunisia and Morocco.

The Kremlin's initial decision to move the Soviet Navy from purely coastal defense to forward deployment had been a response to the threat from American sea-based nuclear delivery systems, particularly the Polaris missile which President Kennedy emphasized on taking office in 1961. The first operational version of Polaris, the A–2, had a range of fifteen hundred nautical miles, putting the heartland of the Soviet Union at risk from the Mediterranean. The second version, the A–3, with a range of twenty-five hundred nautical miles, significantly enlarged the circle of threat and raised the possibility of attacks from the Red Sea and the northern part of the Indian Ocean. Clearly the Soviet Navy, once deployed, could be used as a device for building political influence but the primary purpose of its forward posture was to guard against a perceived strategic threat.

This order of priorities is confirmed by the operational use of the Soviet ships on forward deployment.[36] The Soviet Navy makes few port visits and, when it does, a high proportion of them are made by submarines, which are generally considered to be less effective than surface ships in an influence-building role. Most ships on forward deployment are designated as "antisubmarine" and carry mainly antisubmarine rather than antisurface missiles. All the evidence suggests that the navy's primary aim is to counter the West's seaborne strike capacity rather than to give Moscow the power to interfere with shipping on the high seas or intervene locally on shore.[37]

The Soviet Union's interest in base facilities in the Arabian Sea has to be seen in the same light. While some Western politicians discovered a so-called "arc of crisis" in the later 1970s, running from the Horn of Africa to Afghanistan, in which the Soviet Union was allegedly causing trouble to vital Western interests, Moscow had already seen the region's seas as potentially critical for itself a decade earlier. It began to think of maintaining regular patrols in the area. In the late 1960s, as the British announced plans to withdraw from Aden, the Soviet

Union viewed Aden and Berbera in Somalia as potential bases. After Soviet Defense Minister Marshal Grechko visited Somalia in February 1972, there was a large buildup of Soviet support facilities at Berbera. The People's Republic of South Yemen (Aden) had close diplomatic and economic links with the Soviet Union, but provided no naval facilities in the first years of independence. It was only after Somalia expelled the Soviet Union in November 1977 that Moscow moved its dry dock and other equipment to South Yemen. But the Russians did not deliver as much economic aid as the South Yemeni president, Abdul Fatah Ismail, expected, in spite of a twenty-year treaty of friendship with the Soviet Union. In 1980, after public criticism of the Soviet Union mounted, dissension within the leadership led to Abdul Fatah being voted out of power in the Politburo. South Yemen thus joined the long line of countries in which the Russians were shown not to have total control.

The Soviet Union has kept a vigilant eye on the Persian Gulf. Here, as in the rest of the Middle East, its main interest has been to try to resist the spread of American influence and prevent the United States from increasing its military presence in the area. It has been a hard task. Moscow has found it difficult even to forge diplomatic, let alone economic, links with most of the conservative sheikdoms on the western side of the Persian Gulf and with Saudi Arabia. These have been the exclusive preserves of the West. Its relations with Iran and Iraq, the two powers at the northern end of the gulf, have been bedeviled by local conflicts in which the Russians have never been sure which side to support.

It took almost ten years from the overthrow of the Iraqi monarchy in 1958 for Soviet–Iraqi relations to improve substantially after the Ba'athist coup of July 1968. Moscow agreed to supply experts and machinery to develop the northern Rumaila oilfields in return for some of their eventual output. Yet even while stepping up its involvement in Iraq, including the sale of arms on a large scale, the Russians never closed the door on Iran. It took a neutral line in the border dispute between the two countries in the late 1960s. It kept silent when the Shah occupied three Arab islands in the gulf in 1971. Moscow was also interested in Iraq's neighbor Kuwait, which was to become the only one of the oil sheikdoms to set up diplomatic relations with the Soviet Union. When Iraq seized a narrow strip of Kuwaiti territory in March 1973, the Russians quietly encouraged the Iraqis to retreat.[38] Whether because of Moscow's ambiguous attitudes to Iraq's border conflicts or for other reasons, Iraq never offered Moscow the base facilities in the Gulf at Umm Qasr that the Russians would have liked. Moscow's tentative switch toward Iran in 1982 offered no prospect of access to bases on the other side.

In spite of Moscow's failure to make any significant political headway in the Persian Gulf, it remains fashionable in the West to argue that Moscow poses a threat to the area's oil reserves. The argument rests on two assumptions. The first is that the Soviet Union will soon need vast amounts of gulf oil and will seize it. The second is that the Soviet Union wants to control the oilfields so as to be able to precipitate a crisis by denying this oil to the West. In either case, the allegation that the Soviet Union is preparing to take over the oilfields by force is backed by no evidence and is inherently implausible. Even before President Carter declared that any attack on the Gulf would be regarded as an attack "on the vital interests of the United States of America, and such an assault will be repelled by any means necessary, including military force,"[39] the Soviet Union would have calculated that aggression in the gulf would lead to a superpower confrontation. In view of Moscow's general reluctance to risk such confrontations elsewhere in the world, there is no reason to expect it in the Gulf.

The Soviet Union has urged the other major powers to join in creating "a normal, calm situation" there. In a speech before the Indian parliament in December 1980, Brezhnev proposed that the Soviet Union, the United States, China, Japan, other Western powers, and any interested states should agree on a five-point set of mutual obligations: (1) not to establish foreign military bases in the area of the Persian Gulf and adjacent islands, or to deploy nuclear or any other weapons of mass destruction there; (2) not to use or threaten the use of force against the countries of the Persian Gulf area, and not to interfere in their internal affairs; (3) to respect the nonaligned status chosen by Persian Gulf states and not to draw them into military groupings with the participation of nuclear powers; (4) to respect the sovereign right of the states of the region to their natural resources; (5) not to raise any obstacles or threats to normal trade exchange and the use of sea lanes linking the states of the region with other countries of the world.[40] The Brezhnev proposals (which have never been tested by Western diplomats in serious discussions with the Soviet Union) hardly sound as though they come from a confident, assertive power. They are much more likely intended to prevent a further worsening of the Soviet position. The evidence that the Soviet Union is eager to have access to a large part of the region's oil is shaky.

The first doubts on this issue were sounded by the CIA in 1977. In the crisis that followed the Arab oil embargo, some influential voices in Washington, including that of Defense Secretary James Schlesinger, had been hinting that the United States might want to seize control of the oilfields to prevent the Arabs from attempting to blackmail the West. Although the idea was rejected publicly, policy planners began to suggest that the United States should prepare a Rapid Deployment Force for possible intervention in trouble spots in the Third World, including the Persian Gulf. One rationale for the idea was that the Russian threat to the area was allegedly increasing. Whether they believed their own projections or not, the CIA publicized a study in April 1977 that asserted that Soviet oil production would reach its highest level in the early 1980s and then steadily decline. In the mid-1980s Moscow would be forced to import more than 3.5 million barrels of oil a day.[41] By 1980 these projections had proved embarrassingly inaccurate, underestimating actual output by as much as 1.1 million barrels a day.[42]

Although the CIA revised its estimates upward, it continued to insist that the Soviet Union would become an oil importer. The CIA's projections caused widespread controversy among oil industry experts and even among other U.S. government agencies. In 1981 the Defense Intelligence Agency challenged the findings in a report that said that Soviet output would continue to rise slowly until 1985, then level off in the late 1980s and increase again after 1990.[43] In fact the Soviet Union has been the world's largest oil producer since 1974. It is also a major oil exporter. Apart from gold, oil is its biggest source of hard-currency earnings. In 1980 it sold about 22 percent of its oil abroad, one third of it to hard currency areas.[44] It is true that the Soviet Union has begun a drive to conserve energy and is switching many of its oil-powered factories to coal and gas and is developing nuclear energy. It is also true that it has told its Eastern European allies that it cannot increase its oil supplies above the 1980 level. The squeeze is on the Eastern Europeans who have begun to look urgently for alternative sources of supply, including the Middle East. But to imagine that the Eastern Europeans in their desperation would try to seize the Persian Gulf is pure fantasy. Nor is it any less absurd to think that the Soviet Union, having told its allies to go elsewhere for oil, should suddenly on their behalf invade the Gulf and risk a world war.

The Soviet attitude to Western oil crises has never been as simple as the hawks like to claim. When the Arab oil producers launched their embargo against the West during the October War, Moscow was indeed quick to give it verbal support. It presented the embargo as a dramatic example of the Third World striking back at the transnational corporations and capitalist monopolies. At the same time, however, it made no effort to reinforce the embargo itself. There is evidence that it even increased its own sales of oil to the United States and the Netherlands, despite Arab criticism.[45] The Russians were more interested in OPEC's price increases than in the embargo. As an exporter, Moscow's interest in higher prices was obvious, not only because of the immediate prospect of higher profits, but because the energy crisis would increase Western and Japanese interest in helping to develop the vast Siberian reserves. But higher prices are a two-edged sword. As we have already noted, they benefit the USSR as an exporter to hard-currency areas but are an extra burden to Eastern Europe.

The Arab countries' increasing share in the oil extraction business through the nationalization of some of the multinationals' operations has not helped Moscow significantly. While more Soviet geologists are working in the Middle East than before, their record in comparison with Western oil company technicians has not been impressive. Nor have the Arabs' higher hard-currency earnings significantly increased their imports from the Soviet Union. Most petro-dollars have flowed back to the West.

The oil exporters' higher revenues have tended to increase their independence, leaving Moscow with rather less influence among the radicals as well as the moderates than it had before. Iraq and Libya take more extreme positions than

Moscow on the Arab–Israeli dispute, but the Russians find it hard to express public criticism. At the other end of the spectrum, Saudi Arabia has enjoyed an enormous increase in power and influence in the Arab world since the oil price increase. Saudi oil money is financing a conservative, anti-Communist alliance with Egypt and the Sudan, who have been taking an increasingly hard line against Moscow. The Saudis have made offers of aid to South Yemen and Jordan to reduce or prevent a Soviet role as arms supplier, and may do so in Syria too.[46] Although their aid was rejected in South Yemen, the offer could be renewed. Saudi Arabia has encouraged Bahrain, Kuwait, Oman, Qatar, and the United Arab Emirates to join in a Gulf Cooperation Council as a first step toward creating a coordinated Arab air defense system, based on the purchase of the most advanced American electronic equipment.

Conclusion

Soviet interest in the countries lying along or just beyond its southern flank in the Middle East grew significantly during the Brezhnev era. For the first time, Moscow concluded important political, military, and economic agreements with countries on the outer edges of the region, in South Yemen, Libya, Algeria and Morocco. Its fleet developed from being a largely coastal weapon to a navy with regular patrols in the Mediterranean and the Arabian Sea. It signed treaties of friendship with Egypt, Syria, Iraq, South Yemen, and Afghanistan. It lavished huge quantities of economic aid, favoring the Middle East over all other parts of the Third World. (Of the ten major non-Communist recipients of aid between 1954 and 1979, eight were in the Middle East: Turkey, Morocco, Egypt, Afghanistan, Iran, Syria, Algeria, and Iraq.)

Yet in spite of this impressive outreach, Moscow has suffered some major reverses and is no further forward in the competition with the United States for influence than it was in the mid-1960s. In terms of the strategic military balance it has been forced into retreat. Since 1965 the pattern of superpower dominance in Egypt has been completely reversed. The United States has supplanted the Soviet Union. In Turkey millions of rubles of economic aid and patient efforts at developing good-neighbor relations have not altered Turkey's adherence to NATO. In Iran and the Gulf the Soviet Union has made little headway, even though U.S.–Iranian relations have been at rock bottom for more than three years. Washington has more than made up for its loss of influence in Iran by forging a closer strategic and military relationship with Saudi Arabia and the oil sheikdoms. In Afghanistan the Soviet Union chose to intervene to defend a revolution that it had not engineered, and found itself not only bogged down militarily but roundly condemned by the majority of nonaligned states. The United States was able to use the suspicions aroused by the Soviet intervention to put together a Rapid Deployment Force and obtain access to air and naval facilities in Oman, Somalia, and Kenya. Britain, which had wound down its commitments east of Suez by the end of the 1960s, was beginning to join other NATO countries in contingency plans to help the United States to intervene in the Persian Gulf. Meanwhile, the strategic nuclear threat to the Soviet Union posed by U.S. Polaris submarines in the Mediterranean was about to be enhanced by longer range Trident missiles on submarines in the Indian Ocean. No objective analysts could claim that the last fifteen years have been a period of Soviet success.

The first months of Andropov's rule suggested that the new leader was as bound to the old treadmill of Soviet Middle Eastern policy as his predecessor. He re-supplied Syria with the arms and aircraft lost over Lebanon in 1982 and sent SAM-5 ground-to-air missiles to form a defensive curtain against Israeli air attack all along Syria's Western flank. He urged President Assad to reject the Israeli–Lebanese agreement which had been negotiated by the United States. The aim was to force the Reagan administration to recognise that only a comprehensive settlement, in which Moscow would be allowed a role, could bring a lasting peace. Partial arrangements such as Israel's treaties with Egypt and Lebanon were merely a device to weaken support for the Palestinians, and delay resolution of the central issues. Yet in playing the Syrian card as a means of gaining attention to its interest in a wider settlement, Moscow was once again running the risk of helping to provoke a new conflict, this time between Israel and Syria.

11

LATIN AMERICA

Vast stretches of ocean separate us from the Western hemisphere.

Leonid Brezhnev
May 1982[1]

On October 3, 1958, less than three months before Fidel Castro's guerrilla army swept down from Cuba's Sierra Maestra and overthrew the Batista dictatorship, a Brazilian journalist interviewed Khrushchev about Soviet thinking on Latin America. With no visible enthusiasm and clearly unaware of the momentous victory that was imminent, the Soviet leader talked of the "heroic but unequal struggle of the Cuban people."[2]

His ignorance of what was happening in a small Caribbean island ninety miles from the United States was hardly surprising. Even the Cuban Communist party, the Partido Socialista Popular, took a long time to assess Castro's significance. In the last months of 1958 its policy still called for "national unity" and a democratic coalition of opposition forces to remove Batista. Castro's strategy appeared highly risky. Hedging its bets, the party instructed one of its leaders, Carlos Rafael Rodriguez, and a few activists to join the guerrilla columns in October 1958, but decided to wait before endorsing Castro fully. A victorious Castro entered Havana before the PSP ever clearly defined its position toward him and before the opposition front that it was proposing was established.

If Cuba's own Communists were so slow to appreciate Castro's chances of

207

winning, Moscow's failure was understandable enough. For the Soviet Union, Latin America has always been the remotest continent. Its closeness to the United States and its distance from the Soviet Union were bound to mean that it figured very low in Soviet priorities. Washington's Monroe Doctrine of 1823, which unilaterally denied any European power the right to intervene in the western hemisphere, was left virtually unchallenged by the Russians for the first forty years after the October Revolution. Psychologically, the continent hardly existed for them.

Physical distance was not the only reason. In the decolonization movement of the 1950s, which swept through Africa, Asia, and the Middle East, raising hopes in the Kremlin of a host of new anti-Western and pro-Soviet regimes, Latin America was an anomaly. Most of its nations had been independent of the former colonial powers, Spain and Portugal, for more than a century. Admittedly, many of them were inclined to resent the power and hegemony of the United States, and their grumbling was growing louder. But neocolonialism is a harder enemy to define and oppose than direct political control from a metropolitan power. The spreading of Soviet influence in opposition to the West was a more difficult enterprise in Latin America than in the rest of the Third World. There was also the problem of local Communist parties, which were active in almost every Latin American state. The Soviet Union had to decide whether to support them or the established governments of Latin America whom the Communists opposed. Was Moscow more interested in seeing indigenous revolutions triumph in Latin America, or in encouraging the governments to take up an anti-American line? Was Moscow's priority to minimize U.S. influence globally or to have successful revolutionary allies, given that the former might happen sooner and that successful revolutionaries might be unreliable?

Lenin had inclined to the view that revolution in Latin America was remote. The delegate representing the Mexican Communist party at the Second Comintern Congress in 1920 found that Lenin "was not interested in the socialist movement in Mexico. He realized that it was bound to be very rudimentary. But he was interested in the masses of the people in their relation to the United States, whether there was a strong opposition movement to the United States."[3] Lenin told another delegate that "there were more urgent revolutionary tasks which must have priority. It would be a long time before revolution could succeed in the New World. Conditions might alter in the near future. But American imperialism was on the alert to intervene as it had done in the past."[4]

Lenin's distant approach to Latin America set the tone for his successors for forty years. Occasionally they flirted with the continent's Communist parties, but this tended to cause problems. Moscow found itself embroiled in local party disputes, as in Chile in 1927 when the party split, or embarrassed by its links with the Communists, as when Mexico in 1930 and Uruguay in 1935 broke diplomatic relations with Moscow and asked its representatives to go home because of their connections with the opposition.

Trade with Latin America remained at a low level. Before 1960 the Soviet share of the region's trade never reached 1 percent of the total. It fell a long way behind Soviet commercial dealings with the rest of the Third World. In 1958 the turnover with Asia was eight times and with Africa three times what it was with Latin America.

Castro's revolution in Cuba made no immediate impact on this long tradition of Soviet inertia in the hemisphere. Although the Soviet president, Marshal Voroshilov, sent a letter to the new Cuban president, Dr. Manuel Urrutia, in January 1959 announcing Soviet recognition of the regime, it took more than a year for the first formal contacts between the two governments to occur, with a visit by First Deputy Prime Minister Anastas Mikoyan to Havana in February 1960. For most of 1959 Khrushchev confined himself to taking discreet soundings about the new region. Absorbed by his tour of the United States that summer, the Soviet leader was not primarily interested in the potentialities of the anti-American gadfly that had unexpectedly appeared off the coast of Florida.

The collapse of the brief U.S.–Soviet rapprochement with the downing of the American U–2 spy plane in 1960 changed the picture. As American pressure on Cuba mounted and Castro became increasingly radical, the island began to loom larger in Soviet thinking. Here was a revolution that suddenly, as one American commentator put it, "seemed to disprove the law of 'geographic fatalism' and show that a national revolutionary struggle could be successful in the very shadow of 'United States imperialism.'"[5]

Castro's Cuba was both an opportunity and a challenge. A charismatic leader was defying the United States and had set off a wave of optimistic nationalism among left-wing forces throughout the continent. In spite of his ideological unorthodoxy he was bound to seem attractive to Khrushchev, one of the Soviet Union's most flamboyant and unrestrained politicians. It was natural that when the two men met for the first time during the United Nations session in New York in September 1960 they liked each other. But Castro was also a challenge. Could the Soviet Union afford to support him, at the risk of angering the United States or appearing impotent if Washington really decided to take action against Cuba? Then there was the problem of China, which was already accusing Moscow of being too soft on imperialism. Castro seemed a likely ideological ally of Mao Zedong, and Moscow would have to be careful to prevent him siding openly with the Chinese in the bitter quarrel that was beginning to split the Communist movement. In his memoirs Khrushchev explained the position graphically: "The fate of Cuba and the maintenance of Soviet prestige in that part of the world preoccupied me . . . one thought kept hammering away at my brain: what will happen if we lose Cuba? I knew it would have been a terrible blow to Marxism–Leninism. It would gravely diminish our stature throughout the world, but especially in Latin America. If Cuba fell, other countries would reject us, claiming that for all our might the Soviet Union hadn't been able to do anything for Cuba except to make empty protests to the United Nations."[6]

As the United States became more excited about Cuba, the Russians felt compelled to act. Exactly when Khrushchev took the decision to install Soviet rockets on the island and whether it was primarily Khrushchev's decision alone are unanswerable questions. Khrushchev's overtures to the United States in 1959 had caused doubts and alarm among some of his colleagues, and when he reversed the line after the U–2 incident he may well have been responding to their urging.[7] But Khrushchev typically tended to go to extremes, giving collective decisions a personal, bombastic twist that angered his colleagues and eventually led to the charge of "bragging and bluster" with which they celebrated his departure.[8] He announced in July 1960 that "in case of need, Soviet artillery men can support the Cuban people with their rocket fire should aggressive forces in the Pentagon dare to start intervention against Cuba."[9] At that stage the threat was to fire rockets from the Soviet Union. It was hardly serious, as became clear from Soviet actions during the U.S.-inspired Bay of Pigs invasion of Cuba in April 1961. While the invasion was underway, the Russians did nothing.

It was not until the summer of the next year that the question of placing Soviet rockets on Cuban soil arose. The initiative for the move is disputed. Khrushchev later said he acted in response to a Cuban request, but Castro denied this, saying the proposal "surprised us."[10] On another occasion he said, "Moscow offered them to us. . . . It was not in order to assure our own defense, but first of all to reinforce socialism on the international scale."[11] It seems most likely that Moscow initiated the idea with the primary motive of countering Kennedy's new intercontinental missile program rather than in order to defend Cuba. At the time the decision was taken, American threats against Cuba were not particularly intense.

The Soviet Union announced on September 11, 1962, that it was shipping "up-to-date weapons" to Cuba. On October 22, President Kennedy threatened to blockade all shipments of offensive weapons unless they were withdrawn. Four days later Khrushchev wrote to Kennedy promising to withdraw the missiles if Washington undertook not to invade Cuba. Kennedy accepted. Khrushchev tried to justify the episode in his memoirs as "a great victory for us as we had been able to extract from Kennedy a promise that neither America nor any of her allies would invade Cuba."[12] But there is little doubt that it was seen by Khrushchev and his colleagues as a humiliation. Khrushchev himself admitted that the Russians had made a tangible concession in return for a verbal promise—"[W]e were worried that as soon as we retreated, the Americans might move in on the offensive."[13] The episode had massive repercussions for future Soviet policy. The main lesson learned in the Kremlin was that until the Soviet Union had global parity with the United States, it ran the risk of being outgunned in a crisis. A threat to use nuclear weapons in defense of an ally was nothing but a bluff, if the other side had superiority in conventional forces. The Soviet Union must never expose itself to the danger of having its bluff called by making an impetuous, ill-thought-out move in an area and on an issue where it was overstretched.

As for its effect on Soviet policy in Latin America, the missile crisis showed that Cuba had become a major destabilizing element in the U.S.-Soviet relationship. If Moscow wanted to have good relations with both Washington and Havana, it was going to have to find a more subtle way of managing the complicated new triangle that had emerged since Castro's revolution. Any improvement in Soviet relations with Washington was likely to damage Soviet relations with Havana, and vice versa. At best Moscow would have to be careful in improving its links with Havana in order to ensure that they be seen as purely bilateral and not directed against the United States—provided that Moscow wanted good relations with Washington.

This basic lesson had a subtheme—Cuba's impact on the rest of Latin America. Most members of the Organization of American States (OAS) had turned against Castro soon after he took power. Moscow's links with Cuba were bound to put the Soviet Union in a worse light among governments throughout the region whether or not Moscow was really supporting Castro's foreign policy. Inasmuch as the United States saw itself as the guardian of the status quo in Latin America, any attempt by Castro to support revolutions in the region would be seen by Washington as a threat in which very probably the Russians were implicated. Once again the whole Soviet–American relationship could be affected. Another lesson of the crisis for Moscow was that patron/client relationships in international affairs are highly complicated. A powerful country cannot simply order a weaker ally to do its bidding, particularly when the weaker ally decides to take a militant, international line. The necessity of proclaiming the alliance to be a partnership of equals, despite all the evidence to the contrary, may require the stronger partner to give in to the whims of the weaker one. The tail comes to wag the dog. For almost a decade after the missile crisis Cuba was the Soviet Union's most difficult ally. Among Communist nations, only Yugoslavia, Albania, and China proved more awkward. Cuba was in many ways "the Soviet Union's Israel," as irritating and hard for Moscow to control as Israel became for the United States in the 1970s. A small remote country, heavily dependent on endless flows of capital and arms supplies from its patron, strategically isolated and vulnerable to an oil embargo, it nevertheless often called the international shots,

The first glimmerings of these problems, which were to become major concerns for Khrushchev's successors, were apparent in the aftermath of the missile crisis. The Chinese Communists talked first of Soviet "adventurism" and then of "capitulationism."[14] Castro mentioned "some differences" with the Soviet Union.[15] Khrushchev sent Vice-Premier Mikoyan back to Cuba to try to repair relations. He stayed for three weeks. The next April Castro made his first visit to Moscow (for five weeks), followed by another visit in January 1964. This flurry of extended contacts showed how much the two sides needed each other.

The debate within the Communist movement between the Soviet and Chinese parties over the policy of peaceful coexistence with the capitalist world was at its height. Emotionally, Castro and his comrades from the guerrilla movement felt more sympathy with China. Politically, they had to stay closer to Moscow. At least the dispute gave them room to maneuver between the two sides and bargain with Moscow for the best possible terms for the economic aid that Cuba needed. The Soviet Union could not let Castro side with China publicly or accuse Moscow of being a false friend, since Castro had enormous prestige among nationalist movements throughout the Third World.

By the autumn of 1964, when Khrushchev was removed from power, Castro and the Soviet leadership had achieved an uneasy modus vivendi. The Russians were underwriting the Cuban economy at substantial cost, thanks to a long-term agreement to buy roughly half the island's sugar crop at three times the world price. In return Cuba agreed to abandon the radical economic plans of the minister of industry, Ernesto Che Guevara, who wanted to transform the country as soon as possible into a heavy industrial power equipped with the latest technology. Cuba also agreed to remain at least neutral in the Sino–Soviet dispute. But there was no meeting of minds on the all-important issue of revolutionary change in Latin America.

For the next three years Khrushchev's successors tried to find a way of keeping up with Castro's revolutionary enthusiasm while also developing economic links with Latin American governments. The one thing on which Russia was determined was not to challenge the United States openly again. When American marines landed in the Dominican Republic in April 1965 in order to prevent left-wing officers achieving a nationalist coup, the Soviet Union took no action.

When Cuba hosted a "Tricontinental Conference" in Havana in early 1966, Moscow supported the move as a way of expanding the Afro–Asian People's Solidarity Organization, in which the Chinese had strong influence, into something in which Latin American movements with links to the Soviet Union could balance the numbers. But the Soviet delegation found itself obliged to keep up with the mood of the conference by coming out with calls for "fraternal solidarity with the armed struggle waged by the patriots of Venezuela, Peru, Colombia and Guatemala for freedom against the puppets of imperialism."[16] The chief Soviet delegate, Sharaf Rashidov, a candidate member of the Politburo, said, "[T]he Soviet Union has always supported people's wars, the armed struggle of the oppressed peoples, and has been rendering them every possible support and assistance."[17] Several Latin American governments promptly condemned the Soviet statements. The reaction seemed to surprise the Russians who hastily put out an unconvincing statement that Mr. Rashidov had been speaking on behalf of social organizations in the Soviet Union rather than the Soviet Communist party or government.

It was becoming clear that revolution in Latin America was not the Kremlin's priority. Moscow was engaged on an important trade push in Latin America and could not afford to be embarrassed. In 1966 it granted Brazil and Chile trade credits of U.S. $100 million and $57 million respectively. With Argentina it achieved a precedent-setting deal in the search for grain imports from countries outside NATO, in order to lessen the risk of political pressure from the West. The Russians agreed to provide oil in exchange for Argentinian grain. A year later Moscow started trade negotiations with Colombia, just as a number of leaders of the militant Colombian Communist party were being arrested. It also concluded a trade agreement with the Chilean government of President Eduardo Frei.

Castro's reaction to these deals was outspoken. "The socialist camp is of course independent and has the right to do what it deems fit; that is its business," he conceded in a speech. But he went on, "It is our duty to warn the socialist countries against Frei's hypocrisy and flirtations, since the prostitute will not become a virtuous woman simply because attention is paid to some of her flirtations. Let Frei first prove that his is an independent government." Unless and until Chile broke away from the U.S.-inspired boycott of Cuba, "we Cubans have every right to feel injured by any country that offers technical and economic aid to the Frei regime."[18]

With the approach of the Havana conference of the Organization Latinoamericana de Solidaridad (OLAS) in July 1967, Moscow was determined not to get caught in the same confusion as it had done at the Tricontinental Conference eighteen months earlier. A few weeks before the conference was due to open, Soviet Prime Minister Alexei Kosygin arrived unexpectedly in Havana on his way back from a summit meeting with President Johnson. Although he was the most senior Soviet politician yet to visit the island, his official reception was cool. No communiqué was issued after his talks, which appeared to go badly and led to almost a year of tense relations between the two countries. Kosygin tried to persuade Castro to tone down his line on revolutionary struggle in Latin America. From hints given by Castro later it seems clear that the Russians threatened to reduce economic aid and oil supplies, as well as refusing to guarantee that they would come to Cuba's aid in case of an American attack. On July 26, Castro warned Cubans that they must be ready to fight alone against an invasion.

But Kosygin's pressure had little effect. In response the Soviet Union sent only a low-level delegation to the OLAS conference, which reaffirmed the Cuban line that armed struggle was the surest path to revolution and criticized unnamed socialist countries for supporting the Latin American oligarchies. The Russians responded obliquely but unmistakably by the well-worn method of publishing in the Soviet press articles by foreign Communists that opposed the Cuban position. Castro in turn snubbed the Russians by sending the minister of health instead of President Dorticos to the fiftieth anniversary celebrations of the October Revolution.

The two things that most worried the Kremlin about Castro's line and that of the other Latin American revolutionary movements was their rejection of a peaceful transition to socialism, and their belief that local Communist parties should defer to the guerrilla leaderships rather than the other way round. The argument was dressed up by Régis Debray, a French intellectual who was close to Castro and Guevara, into a substantial modification of Leninist thinking. Under his theory of *foquismo*, a people's war against internal colonialism replaces the class struggle, with a guerrilla band or *foco* providing a spark for a revolutionary army recruited from the peasants. This takes the role of vanguard which is normally supposed to be taken by a working-class party. From Moscow's point of view the trouble was, first, that the guerrilla movements risked provoking American intervention, thus forcing the Kremlin to take a stand; and second, that the downgrading of local Communist parties left Moscow with the fear that it could not control developments. Caution and control, after all, were the watchwords of the post-Khrushchev leadership.

Moscow's approach was expressed most clearly in a major article in *Pravda* in March 1968 by Professor Viktor Volsky, the director of the Latin American Institute in Moscow. Professor Volsky conceded, as he had to, that the victorious Cuban struggle had been led by "revolutionary-democratic strata reflecting the interests and sentiments of the broadest popular masses."[19] But he went on to argue that the "far more complex goals and tasks" of changing society called for leadership by the "vanguard party of the working class, well-armed with Marxist–Leninist theory." He reminded Cuba that although it had chosen socialism without any interference from outside, "this choice became possible thanks to the existence of the Soviet Union." In conclusion he argued that conditions were not identical in the various countries of Latin America. One should not "stereotype revolutionary tactics and elevate any one form of struggle to the status of an absolute." Although the Volsky article appeared to be a compromise, it was meant as a warning to the Castroists not to be intolerant of the Soviet Union's softer and more flexible line.

The Volsky article was prepared at a moment of maximum tension between Havana and Moscow. The Russians had won a minor victory three years earlier when Castro agreed to transform his loosely structured movement known as the Integrated Revolutionary Organization (ORI) into a conventional Communist party, but there was still friction between Castro's guerrilla comrades and the veterans of the old, prerevolutionary Cuban Communist party (the PSP). In January 1968 it was unexpectedly announced that several of these veterans had been arrested for activities against the government. They were accused of trying to enlist Soviet support and encouraging the Russians to intervene and appoint their leader, Anibal Escalante, in Castro's place.

Whether the Soviet Politburo supported the alleged plotters and knew of their extensive contacts with Soviet officials and journalists in Cuba is not known. Castro himself never made this accusation. But it is very likely that the Kremlin sympathized with some of the criticisms made by the Escalante group. In an extraordinary speech to the Cuban party's Central Committee, Raul Castro, Fidel's brother, read out notes of some of the plotters' alleged conversations. They sound like the authentic voice of Castro's Soviet critics. "The main leaders of this revolution and this party do not have a Communist background. The majority were anti-Communists. The party is rife with petit bourgeois elements. There is a leftist adventurist deviation, which is in command. They consider Cuba the hub of the world. From here we give advice to the whole world and we don't accept it from anyone. At the Twenty-Second Congress of the Soviet Communist Party, the Cubans made speeches telling the Soviets what they had to do. We suppose the Soviets laughed and said, 'Ah! These boys.' "[20] Two months later Cuba and the Soviet Union signed a new trade protocol in which the Russians had clearly driven a hard bargain. In a speech to a local audience Castro complained of Cuba's dependence. "That can become a weapon and at least create a temptation to use it against our country."[21]

If Cuban–Soviet relations in the spring of 1968 seemed to be at a low point, with hindsight it can be seen that Castro's major differences with Moscow were, in fact, coming to an end. On the Russian side the failure of the plot against Castro, whether or not it had the backing of the Politburo, was a reminder that Castro was too difficult to remove. On the Cuban side there was an even more powerful impetus to patch things up with Moscow. On October 8, 1967, in a wooded canyon leading down to the Rio Grande in Bolivia, Castro's guerrilla companion, Che Guevara, was captured and shot dead by Bolivian soldiers. Guevara had been the most passionate exponent of the idea of starting a guerrilla campaign in South America designed to repeat on a continental scale the success of Castro's band in the Cuban Sierra Maestra. He had arrived in Bolivia several months earlier with the aim of creating the conditions for a revolution by mobilizing a passive peasantry. The area he chose turned out to have few inhabitants. Those there, far from opposing Bolivia's military regime, had become accustomed to it. Guevara's band found it hard to win recruits, not least because they were foreigners, white, and intellectual, with no knowledge of local people, language, or conditions. Their efforts were doomed. Guevara's death was a heavy personal and ideological blow for Castro. The path to revolution by means of the armed struggle appeared to be blocked, and more and more analysts of the Cuban Revolution, even those who were sympathetic, began to talk of Cuba as an exception in Latin America. The Cuban model could not be imitated.

This was the argument the Russians had used consistently. Guevara's failure was seen by them and their ideological allies among Latin America's Communist parties as a vindication of the alternative road to revolution, using a broad mass movement and a national coalition of unity to take power by peaceful means. As the impact of Guevara's death sank in during 1968, Castro's drive and inclination to stand up to the Russians softened. When the Russians sent their troops into Czechoslovakia in August 1968 to snuff out the reform movement within the

Communist party, Castro passed the test of loyalty to Moscow by supporting the invasion.

But his line was critical and showed that his revolutionary instincts were stronger than Moscow's. Castro considered the Czechoslovak reform movement to be counterrevolutionary and tainted by "bourgeois liberalism." But it was wrong of the Russians to find a group of anonymous Communists to invite their army in as though this legalized the invasion. "The sovereignty of the Czechoslovak state was violated . . . in a flagrant way. From the legal point of view this cannot be justified." The invasion could only be explained in political terms, he argued, asking militantly, "Will the Warsaw Pact divisions also be sent to Vietnam if the Yankee imperialists step up their aggression against that country and the people of Vietnam request that aid? . . . Will they send the divisions of the Warsaw Pact to Cuba if the Yankee imperialists attack our country, or even in the case of the threat of a Yankee imperialist attack on our country, if our country requests it? We acknowledge the bitter necessity that called for the sending of those forces into Czechoslovakia; we do not condemn the socialist countries that made that decision. But we, as revolutionaries and proceeding from positions of principle, do have the right to demand that they adopt a consistent position with regard to all the other questions that affect the world revolutionary movement."[22] Subdued by the death of Guevara, Castro still felt moved to point out that the Soviet commitment to revolution in Latin America was less than convincing.

The Russians, meanwhile, could be reasonably satisfied with their balance sheet in Latin America as the 1960s drew to a close. Cuba had undergone a revolution and was a major propaganda and strategic thorn in the side of the United States. Moscow had successfully helped to prevent the United States from destroying the revolution. At the same time Cuba had been isolated from obstructing Moscow's broader strategies. It was not linked to China. Its effort at exporting revolution to the rest of the continent had failed. It was sufficiently dependent on Moscow for oil and grain not to be able to step very far out of line.

Cuba was also a potentially valuable strategic asset for Moscow, although the Kremlin was careful not to repeat the mistakes of Khrushchev during the missile crisis of 1962. With the gradual growth of an ocean-going global navy, Moscow saw Cuba as a useful site for providing refueling, storage, and support facilities for its military and merchant fleet, as well as for long-range aircraft. The first visit to Cuba by a Soviet naval force took place in July 1969. A few months later Soviet Defense Minister Marshal Grechko toured the island. In September 1970 the United States claimed to have evidence that the Russians were building a permanent naval base for nuclear-powered submarines at the port of Cienfuegos on Cuba's southern coast. But when the Nixon administration raised the issue with Moscow as a violation of the 1962 U.S.–Soviet understanding that no nuclear missiles would be established on the island, Moscow quietly halted its construction. Subsequent American administrations remained satisfied that the

Kremlin was honoring the distinction between nuclear and conventional facilities in Cuba.

With Cuba isolated from any serious risk of upsetting Moscow's general foreign policy, the Kremlin could proceed with its long-term policy of developing trade and diplomatic relations with the major Latin American states. These were useful for several reasons. They helped to enhance Soviet prestige and influence. They provided an opportunity for building on the growing anti-American nationalism of Latin America with the eventual aim of minimizing Washington's hegemony. They also gave Moscow a chance to import valuable raw materials and semimanufactured goods, such as coffee, cocoa, wool, cotton, nonferrous metals, vegetable oils, fruit, grain, and meat. Unlike Cuba, which was an economic drain on the Soviet Union because of the vast subsidies necessary to keep it going, the other Latin American states traded with Moscow on a genuine basis of mutual advantage. By the end of the decade, the number of countries trading with Moscow had gone up from three to nine.

The next major ripple in the apparently calm waters of Soviet–Latin American relations came in the autumn of 1970 with the election and inauguration of Salvador Allende as president of Chile. It was the most significant event in the hemisphere since Castro's revolution. For the first time a Marxist had come to power by free vote in Latin America at the head of a coalition, Popular Unity, based on his own Socialist party, the Communists, and dissident Christian Democrats. The precedent aroused great interest in Western Europe among Euro-Communists and other left-wing movements. From Moscow's point of view, Allende's triumph was potentially more beneficial than Castro's. It seemed to justify the Soviet advocacy of a peaceful transition to socialism. It opened the way to political power for Chile's Communists, who had traditionally been close to Moscow. It looked as though it could be a model for the other major Latin American states. And of course it was a blow to the United States, but one that Washington could not so openly oppose. There could be no Bay of Pigs in Chile.

Nevertheless, there were potential dangers for Moscow. First, Moscow might be asked to support the Chilean experiment more firmly than it would like. Overidentification with Chile could lead to a falling-out with other Latin American nations and the United States, if the Allende government turned out to be too radical. A second danger was that Chile might become another financial drain down which Moscow would find itself pouring endless rubles or even hard currency. The Kremlin reacted to Allende's inauguration with extremely guarded optimism, clearly mindful of the lessons of its ten years of experience with Castro. Speaking a few days later at the November 7 anniversary of the Russian Revolution, normally an occasion for boasting of Communist successes, Mikhail Suslov, the Kremlin's veteran ideologist, mentioned Chile only once and that in passing: "The national-liberation struggle of the peoples of Latin America is broadening and deepening. More than ten years ago the Cuban revolution broke the chain of imperialist oppression in the Latin American countries. Recently new weak links have been discovered—Peru, Chile, and Bolivia."[23]

Although the Russians signed an agreement on scientific and technical cooperation with Chile a month later, it was not until the following May that the first hint came of Soviet aid to Chile. On a visit to Moscow, Socialist Foreign Minister Clodomiro Almeyda was promised credits to buy a prefabricated housing factory and some industrial equipment. But the question of major Soviet aid in launching a chemical industry and constructing the fishing port that the Chileans asked for was only said to be "under study." At the Soviet party congress a conspicuous difference emerged in the tone of the Chilean and Soviet speeches. Luis Corvalan, the general secretary of the Chilean Communist party, made an implicit plea for help as he warned that "the struggle in our country is entering a more acute phase . . . nothing is excluded—neither attempted coups d'état nor armed clashes of all sorts."[24] Brezhnev ignored his request. Although he conceded that the Popular Unity victory had "incensed Yankee imperialism," he gave no promise of Soviet solidarity or help. The Russians were clearly hoping that Allende would be moderate and not alienate his neighbors and the United States. When Allende met the Argentinian president a few months later on the Chilean–Argentinian border, *Pravda* hailed the encounter with an editorial under the headline "Realism gains the upper hand."[25] "Experience shows that differences in social systems and forms of government by no means impede countries having mutually advantageous and good-neighborly relations."

Moscow continued this distant attitude to Chile throughout Allende's three years in power. The only high-level visit by a Soviet politician to Santiago was a party, not government, delegation led by Andrei Kirilenko, a Politburo member, on the occasion of the fiftieth birthday of the Chilean Communist party. President Allende paid only one visit to Moscow—in December 1972. The communiqué afterward was extremely vague. It pledged further economic aid to unspecified industries, power plants, and agriculture without giving a concrete figure. It said nothing about Chile's main problem, which was how to sell its copper in the face of an American-inspired boycott. In practice, the record of the credits actually used by Chile between 1970 and 1973 shows that the Allende government had more help from Western Europe and other Latin American countries, particularly Mexico and Argentina, than from the Soviet Union or Eastern Europe.

When the military junta under General Augusto Pinochet overthrew Allende in September 1973, the Soviet reaction was astonishingly restrained. This was the high point of détente with Washington. Brezhnev had just visited the United States and was expecting President Nixon to repay the visit the following year. Moscow was careful to keep its reaction to the Chilean coup within the bounds of controlled and mild indignation. A Central Committee statement blamed reactionary forces in Chile for promoting the coup in violation of the Chilean constitution. In only one passage did the statement say that they had "the support of foreign imperialist forces," but without specifying the United States. Two weeks later *Pravda* carried its first major analysis of the coup. By this time the American media had come out with stories of CIA and multinational corporate involvement in the destabilization of the Allende government. The *Pravda* article reported some of these stories as "allegations." It still did not mention Nixon or Kissinger by name as having had any hand in the affair.[26]

A long, theoretical analysis of the Chilean experience was published a few months later under the name of Boris Ponomarev, a candidate member of the Soviet Politburo and head of the international department of the Central Committee. Such analyses are meant for a wide readership throughout the Communist movement and can be expected to take a more militant line than the Soviet leadership's diplomatic pronouncements. But even he had few concrete practical recommendations for comrades worried about the lessons of the Chilean Revolution for their own struggles. The Chilean experiences had been the first example of a "peaceful" revolutionary development for a long time and had proved "most valuable to Marxist–Leninists" who wanted to perfect revolutionary strategy and tactics. Revolutionary forces must move more decisively than they had done in Chile to deprive the old regime of control of the army and mass media. Communists had to remain in the vanguard and adopt the "boldest" forms of struggle. The opposition was the first to use unconstitutional means, and the government should also have been ready to use unconstitutional as well as constitutional means. After its first political success, the government should realize that the economy becomes the main battlefield.[27] All of which is safe comment, but little use as a serious guide to future action in other revolutions. Nor was it accurate. The left wing of the Socialist Party Movimiento de Accion Popular Unitaria (MAPU) and Movimiento de Izquierda Revolucionaria (MIR) (the latter even threatening Allende with guerrilla action to enforce change) were far "bolder" than the Communists.

Moscow's low-key reaction to the Chilean counterrevolution fitted in with the general trend of Soviet attitudes to Latin America throughout the Brezhnev period. Although Moscow kept up a diplomatic boycott of the Pinochet regime and conducted a relatively vigorous press campaign against it, this stood in contrast to its growing links with the other right-wing regimes on the continent, from Bolivia and Brazil to Argentina and Uruguay. The Chilean disaster confirmed the Kremlin in its view that revolution in Latin America was not just around the corner. In the meantime its aims of fostering long-term Soviet influence and developing trade could equally be served by the middle class and the military, with the added bonus that these strata might turn out to be anti-American. Castro appeared to draw a similar lesson. As the 1970s proceeded, his own relations with the other states in the hemisphere began to improve. Cuba's diplomatic isolation and the OAS boycott of the island were slowly whittled away. Castro's attention switched to Africa.

Toward the end of the decade, however, the focus shifted back to Central America as the Sandinista movement in Nicaragua began to increase its armed challenge to the Somoza dictatorship. The Sandinistas were the spearhead of a broad anti-Somoza coalition that included right-wing businessmen and Christian Democrats. Cuba played a role in encouraging the different factions within the guerrilla movement to unify their strategy, and may have helped to coordinate some of their arms supplies. But the Sandinistas had wide support among Central American governments, including Costa Rica, Panama, and Venezuela, and their weapons came from several different sources, including those captured from Somoza's National Guard. As with the Cuban revolution twenty years earlier, the Soviet Union watched Nicaragua's autonomous armed uprising with only remote interest and no active involvement. Central America had long been the colonial backyard of the United States. For the Soviet Union it had little strategic significance. Cuba provided whatever benefits Moscow wanted in the Caribbean in terms of facilities for serving Soviet submarine operations in the western Atlantic. Even after Somoza's overthrow in July 1979 the Soviet Union was slow to exploit the new opportunity the Sandinistas might provide. Once again caution was the watchword. The Russians were reluctant to forge links with a regime that was not yet stable.

For their part the Nicaraguans did not want to give the United States any excuse to intervene. It took eight months before Soviet–Nicaraguan relations began to develop. In March 1980 a delegation went to Moscow to sign agreements under which Russian experts would help Nicaragua with agriculture, power engineering, transport, and communication. But it was only after the Reagan administration cut its own assistance and food aid and hinted at a blockade at the beginning of 1981 that Moscow stepped up its economic help and supplied some military hardware and a few military advisors. Soviet support was small, late, and reluctant. When the Soviet Communist party held its congress in February 1981, the dialogue between the Nicaraguan delegation and their Soviet hosts was an almost exact replay of what had transpired with the Chileans ten years earlier. Carlos Nuñez Tellez, the president of the governing council in Nicaragua, made an impassioned speech warning of American pressure and the threat of intervention. He pleaded for help and solidarity from the socialist countries, "even though they are thousands of kilometers away." His appeal appeared to fall on deaf ears. Brezhnev made no mention of Central America in his congress speech, and although he had publicly announced meetings with the leaders of Ethiopia and Angola, he awarded Carlos Nuñez Tellez no such honor. The Soviet line was graphically expressed to visiting journalists by one official: "If the Americans invaded Nicaragua, what would we do? What could we do? Nothing."[28]

By this time the United States was already expressing great anxiety about the guerrilla movement in El Salvador. U.S. military aid to the small Central American nation had been cut off in 1980 after the murder of three American nuns and an American lay worker by right-wing forces supported by the civilian-military junta. But a few days before leaving office, Carter restored the military supply line. Then, within a month of taking office, the Reagan administration issued a White Paper claiming to prove that the Soviet Union, Cuba, and their allies were delivering massive amounts of arms to the Salvadorean guerrillas. But even the White Paper did not claim that the guerrilla movement was not autonomous. Numerous independent observers have testified to the gradual polarization of Salvadorean society during the 1970s, which led to an armed struggle by the Left. In October 1979 the military government of General Humberto Romero, which had been faithfully supported by the United States, was overthrown by a five-man civilian-military junta. The junta only lasted three months before its three civilian members resigned, after protesting the army's unwillingness to curb the activities of paramilitary death squads. Many Christian Democrats and other liberal reformists joined the center-left Democratic Revolutionary Front, an umbrella grouping that also encouraged four different guerrilla movements.

To back up its White Paper, the Reagan administration produced a collection of allegedly captured documents that were said to show that two hundred tons of arms were delivered to the guerrillas by the Soviet Union and its allies before the uprising of January 1981. But critical analysis of the documents by the *Washington Post* and the *Los Angeles Times* indicated that only about ten tons ever actually crossed the border.[29] They also showed that Shafik Handal, the general secretary of the Salvadorean Communist party, who visited Moscow twice during 1980, was disappointed with the low level of his reception. He was seen by Mikhail Kudachkin, the deputy chief of the Latin American section of the Central Committee's international affairs department. In one of the captured documents, Handal complained of Soviet "indecisiveness" which, he feared, might limit the amount of arms available from the Communist countries. All that the Russians did was to give military training to thirty youths already studying in Moscow. In response to Washington's long history of supplying the right wing in El Salvador, the Soviet Union's support of the opposition was limited.

At the Soviet party congress in February 1981, it was noticeable how little emphasis was given to Central America. The Soviet Union made it clear that it did not want to turn the issue into an East–West clash, let alone a challenge to a new American administration. There were giveaway clues in the small signs, such as the difficulty shown by Leonid Zamyatin, the Central Committee's chief spokesman, in remembering at a press conference whether Nicaraguans spoke Spanish or Portuguese. Or the fact that no Salvadorean Communist party representative addressed the congress. But the main factor was Brezhnev's deliberate effort to be conciliatory to the new American president on all the central issues of East–West arms control. With his offer of a summit meeting with Mr. Reagan, Brezhnev emphasized that the Soviet Union had too many important things to discuss with the United States to allow itself to be side-tracked by the fate of two small and distant countries in Washington's back-yard.

The lack of Soviet interest in Central America was not matched by Castro. The Cuban vice-president, Carlos Rafael Rodrigues, told an invited group of Americans in March 1982 that Cuba had given some arms to the Salvadorean guerrillas before the January 1981 offensive.[30] But he maintained that this had subsequently stopped. A discrepancy between Moscow and Havana over El Salvador is easy to believe. In Angola in 1975 Castro had been bolder than the Russians, and it is quite probable that a similar divergence occurred over El Salvador, to which Castro feels geographically, culturally, and emotionally attached in a way that no Russian could be. The Russians have weaker links with the Left in Central America, and those whom they do know tend to be wary of the guerrilla strategy (such as the Moscow-backed Guatemalan Labor party which was slow to take up arms). "We are always careful in aiding foreign guerrilla movements. We take our time. We want to know who the people are, and what they are going to do with the help," as one Soviet official in Moscow put it in March 1981.[31] Castro was much better connected.

Nevertheless, the failure of the guerrilla offensive in El Salvador in January 1981 and the American decision to make a major issue of Central America had an effect on Castro. He stopped his arms supplies and told the Americans he wanted a political settlement to the crises in the region and his own dispute with the USA. Wayne Smith, the senior U.S. diplomat in Havana, treated the Cuban overtures as serious, but his advice was not accepted in Washington. For another year the secretary of state, Alexander Haig, continued to argue that it was not only Cuba but the Soviet Union who lay behind the trouble in El Salvador. "This situation is global in character," he told a Senate committee. "The problem is worldwide Soviet interventionism that poses an unprecedented challenge to the free world. Anyone attempting to debate the prospects for a successful outcome in El Salvador who fails to consider the Soviet menace is dealing with only the leg or the trunk of the elephant."[32]

The Reagan administration even hinted that it might invade Cuba itself. If one purpose of its policy was to win domestic support in the United States for a more active policy in Central America by claiming that Moscow was playing a major role, the effort failed. The American public remained skeptical of "another Vietnam" and seemed to accept that the rising instability in the region, in Guatemala as well as El Salvador, was due to local social and economic injustice. If the policy was designed to isolate Cuba, it also failed. Moscow supplied Castro with more military equipment in the first eight months of 1981 in order to defend himself against the threat of American intervention than in any previous year since 1962. Haig promptly cited these shipments as new proof of Cuban aggressiveness and claimed that the administration had solid evidence that some of these weapons were being transshipped to Central America. But as Wayne Smith later wrote: "The Administration never produced any such solid evidence. As for the size of the shipments, surely the United States could not expect the Cubans to disarm in the face of U.S. threats."[33]

While American tensions mounted with both Cuba and Nicaragua, Moscow was careful to draw a distinction between the two countries. When Nicaragua sent its defense and foreign ministers to Moscow in November and December 1981, in part to discuss Soviet arms supplies, there were no statements of unequivocal Soviet support such as the Russians had given Castro. Although the Americans subsequently claimed that Moscow had given Nicaragua twenty-five older model tanks, two helicopters, and some armored personnel carriers, this was considerably less than the amount Castro received during the crisis of 1981. Six months later when Daniel Ortega, one of the Sandinista leaders, headed a delegation to Moscow, Brezhnev urged him to improve his relations with Washington. Far from trying to exploit the differences between Managua and Washington, the Soviet president said, "We understand perfectly well the persevering efforts of the leadership of Nicaragua to remove through talks the difficulties and tension in relations with her neighbors and with the United States."[34]

The Falklands War found Moscow split several ways over the best way of handling a conflict in a region that is probably farther from the Soviet Union than any other inhabited part of the world. If there was any single line of principle in the Soviet reaction, it was hard to see. Moscow abstained in the UN Security Council on Resolution 502 which condemned the Argentinian use of force and called for an immediate withdrawal of Argentinian troops. If it had supported the resolution, it would have prejudiced relations with one of its largest trading partners in the Third World and one that had defied the American call to join the West's embargo in 1980 and continued to sell meat and grain to Moscow. If it had vetoed the resolution, it would have given the impression that the Soviet Union supported the use of force to settle sovereignty disputes—a precedent that Japan might in theory adopt in order to repossess the southern Kurile Islands from the Soviet Union.

Although Moscow had traditionally endorsed the Argentinian claim to the Falklands for many years, it played this down during the crisis until after Britain had recaptured them. When Athos Fava, general secretary of the Argentine Communist party, met Boris Ponomarev, the Central Committee secretary who deals with nonruling parties, in Moscow in May 1982, the communiqué said that the Argentinian stressed "the ardent desire of the Argentine people to restore their sovereignty over the Malvinas [Falklands]," but did not say whether Moscow agreed.[35] The Soviet media hardly mentioned Argentina's initial use of force, but denounced Britain for launching military action "from the very beginning of the conflict."[36] The main focus of Soviet coverage was aimed at widening the split between the United States and Latin America. Moscow also showed concern at the possibility that the Falklands might become the site of an eventual Anglo–American military base, or be linked to a future South Atlantic Treaty Organization.

In terms of concrete support for Argentina, Moscow gave the military junta of Lieutenant General Leopoldo Galtieri intelligence data on British ship movements obtained by satellite. Soviet technicians also helped to improve Argentina's radar system, but there was no evidence of any Soviet arms deal, or of any request by the junta for arms. Cuba, as usual, sounded more militant than the Russians. A government statement on May 1 said that the countries of Latin America had a duty to support Argentina with all means necessary, and at the end of the month Castro acted as host to a special meeting of the Non-Aligned Movement which supported Argentina. But Cuba also gave no military aid.

The final twist in the Soviet position came when Galtieri resigned after the Argentinian surrender. The Soviet media referred to the "military junta" for the first time in the crisis and talked of the chance of a successful "process of democratization" in which Moscow presumably hoped that its friends, the Argentine Communist party, would take part, now that the regime was coming under popular criticism for mishandling the crisis.[37] There had been little talk of democracy from Moscow in the months before the crisis, when it looked on Argentina as a valuable trading partner. There was little talk of it afterward, once it became clear that Galtieri's resignation would not produce a real opening in the political process. In Argentina, just as it had been in most of the hemisphere for the previous decade and a half, Moscow's policy was business as usual.

Conclusion

For Moscow Latin America has always been remote, geographically and psychologically. When Castro came to power, the Kremlin was slow to react. It was not until after Castro had repulsed the Bay of Pigs invasion and shown that he was in firm control of the island that Moscow began to move toward an alliance with him. Even then the Russians were more interested in Cuba's strategic potential, so close to the mainland of the United States, than in Castro's ideas for promoting revolution throughout Latin America. In the early years of the Brezhnev era, the Kremlin was continually at odds with Castro as it sought to restrain him from upsetting its trade and diplomatic relations with the major states of the western hemisphere.

Allende's advent to power in Chile in 1970 left Moscow relatively unmoved. It made no effort to forge an alliance with the democratically elected Marxist leader, and when his government began to succumb to U.S.-supported destabilization it remained aloof. The left-wing coup in Grenada and the military overthrow of the Somoza regime in Nicaragua took place without any substantial Soviet assistance. Even the mounting civil war in El Salvador and the turbulence in Guatemala in the early 1980s remained low on the list of Soviet priorities. Where there was evidence of outside arms supplies from Cuba, it appeared that they had been organized without the prompting of the Soviet Union.

Indeed, no continent demonstrates more clearly than Latin America Moscow's willingness to support the political status quo. While the Kremlin has frequently given military supplies to guerrilla movements in Asia and Africa, it has rarely done so in the western hemisphere. Partly this has been because of unwillingness to provoke the United States in its own backyard. Partly it is a judgment that the governments of South America (less so, of Central America) are stable and secure. Partly it is because the Kremlin believes that it has more to gain from trading with these nations than in seeking to promote the dubious prospect of revolutionary change.

12

AFRICA

*The Soviet Union never fails to take into account the
fact that African countries have much in common in
spite of their different socio-political orientations. All
of them are still part of the capitalist system.*

Yevgeni Tarabrin, deputy director
of the Africa Institute in Moscow[1]

Every Sunday evening as the sun begins to set over the Atlantic, hooting trucks
drive slowly along Luanda's beach front. Amid much shouting and gesticulation,
reluctant men detach themselves from the sand and race through the palm trees
to the impatient trucks. "It's the weekly Cuban roundup," sympathetic locals
explain. "Time to get back to base." On the outskirts of Angola's capital city
there is a growing ring of five- and six-story blocks of brightly painted new flats,
built by Cubans for the Angolan people. In many of the country's hospitals and
in the medical school in Luanda, Cuban doctors train and work with Angolans.
Cuba's military and civilian presence in Angola is easy to see. The Angolan
government feels no need to hide it. Here, probably more than in most places in
Africa, the presence of expatriate helpers is welcomed and accepted as legitimate.

More than five years after their initial arrival the reason for the Cubans'
appearance on the scene has not changed. They came in large numbers to defend
a new African state from a South African invasion. They remain in Angola for
exactly the same reason. After a lull following its withdrawal in the aftermath of
Angolan independence, South Africa stepped up its undeclared war on the vast

territory in 1977. Repeated bombing raids and the occupation by South African troops of a large part of southern Angola have reminded most observers that the Cubans are there in a vital defensive capacity. Although they no longer play so prominent a role as they did in the 1975–76 campaign, they remain as a last line of defense against any full-scale South African effort to seize the country.

It is important to stress the widely held African and international view that the Soviet-sponsored Cuban presence in Angola is legitimate. Although the United States likes to talk of Soviet and Cuban "adventurism" in Angola, this is a minority view. Three successive U.S. administrations, first under Gerald Ford, then Jimmy Carter, and now Ronald Reagan, have refused to recognize the Angolan government, but in doing so they are flying in the face of most of the rest of the world. In January 1976 the United States tried hard to persuade the Organization of African Unity (OAU) to deny recognition to the MPLA (Movimento Popular de Libertação de Angola) at the OAU's first summit meeting after the South African invasion, on the grounds that the new Angolan government depended on Soviet and Cuban help. But twenty-two African governments advocated immediate recognition and the rest of the organization soon followed suit. At no time has a single African government given recognition to the rival faction, UNITA (União Nacional para Independência Total de Angola), which South Africa and the United States preferred. When the Reagan administration sought to link a Cuban withdrawal from Angola to a South African withdrawal from Namibia, it was told repeatedly by African governments of all political complexions that Pretoria must pull out first.

The truth about Soviet involvement in Angola is not that it was a violation of international law, but that the Russians made their reentry into African politics suddenly and dramatically. For the first ten years of the Brezhnev era Africa had been virtually ignored in Moscow. The Middle East, Southeast Asia, and the western hemisphere were higher on the list of priorities than sub-Saharan Africa. Moscow had had dealings with Africa under Khrushchev. When Ghana became the first European colony to gain independence in 1957, Moscow's interest was aroused. But its brief flirtation with Nkrumah in Ghana and Sekou Touré in Guinea, as well as Khrushchev's effort to play a role in the Congo crisis, achieved less than the Kremlin hoped. Within a space of roughly eight years Soviet policy in Africa moved in a circle—from disinterest to eager optimism and then back to a disappointed realism, under which Africa was relegated to a minor position. Africa, the Kremlin decided, was a continent that mattered little on the world stage and where socialism would not be built soon.

This remains essentially the Kremlin's point of view today, after a second cycle of reawakened interest and renewed disappointment in the second half of the 1970s. The Kremlin's second period of activism, focused this time in Angola and the Horn of Africa, excited more alarm in Washington than the first interventions in the 1970s for two simple reasons. They involved a considerably larger display of Soviet military might, and they were successful, at least in the short term. But as time went on, the benefits that Moscow gained from acquiring new allies in Angola and Ethiopia began to erode, and by the early 1980s Moscow's enthusiasm for Africa had conspicuously waned. It realized, as the quotation at the head of this chapter makes clear, that Africa has a long way to go before reaching economic independence from the West, however "socialist" some of its countries' governments attempt to be. Less than 10 percent of all the Soviet and Eastern European civilian technicians in the Third World were working in sub-Saharan Africa. Soviet financial aid was minimal. While paying lip service to the struggle against colonialism and apartheid in southern Africa, the Soviet Union supplied mainly hand-held weaponry to the Southwest Africa People's Organization (SWAPO), which was waging a guerrilla war in Namibia, and to the African National Congress of South Africa. For help in the effort to divert their economies and transport links away from dependence on South Africa, the apartheid state's black neighbors turned overwhelmingly to the West. There is no likelihood that the Andropov era will see a change in Moscow's line.

Any understanding of the Soviet role in Africa requires a careful analysis of the chronology by which the two superpowers renewed their interest in an obviously crucial area of instability in the mid-1970s. In opposing the Soviet Union's activity in the Angolan civil war Kissinger described it as a "blatant power play."[2] The primary American principle was that "Angola is an African problem and should be left to Africans to solve."[3] In fact, the record shows that the United States was already intervening in the civil war and that it, rather than the Soviet Union, took the decisive step in seeking a one-sided military solution to the Angolan problem. As with so many other Third World trouble spots, Moscow did not come in because there was a "power vacuum" but because Washington was already there.

The collapse of the Portuguese dictatorship in April 1974 had taken both the Russians and the Americans unawares. Although Moscow had given military aid to the MPLA during the Portuguese colonial period, it had scaled this down in 1972 and brought it to an end by early 1974. The United States, by contrast, strongly supported the colonial status quo. A small amount of secret CIA assistance was given to Holden Roberto, the leader of the FNLA, as a fallback option in case of a Portuguese collapse, but this was almost entirely phased out in 1969. The unexpected Portuguese revolution thus found the superpowers on the sidelines.

Then suddenly the future of the white-ruled colonies was up in the air again. After safely watching the advent of independence in almost all of sub-Saharan Africa over a twenty-year period, the first bastions of white supremacy in southern Africa seemed seriously under threat.

The first contingent of foreign military advisors in Angola actually came from China, which sent 112 men, led by a major general, to train Roberto's FNLA army at the end of May 1974. They chose the FNLA because it was anti-Soviet and had good relations with Zaire. In July the CIA began to increase its funding to Roberto without the knowledge of the U.S. National Security Council's so-called 40 Committee which was supposed to oversee its activity.[4] Three months later the Soviet Union started to send military supplies to the MPLA through Congo-Brazzaville. With the prospect of a civil war mounting between the guerrilla movements as the Portuguese relaxed their hold, the OAU persuaded the three guerrilla leaders to promise to seek a trilateral accord. In January 1975, after negotiations which lasted for three weeks at Alvor in the Portuguese Algarve, they reached an agreement with the Portuguese on a transitional government. For a brief moment there was a fleeting chance for a peaceful approach to independence.

Washington, however, rejected the chance of using diplomacy to reinforce the compromise. Only days after the Alvor accord the 40 Committee authorized a grant of $300,000 to the FNLA, which already had the largest army and was more committed to a military strategy than either of the other two movements. With the United States choosing unilateral intervention to support a victory by anti-Communist forces, the Soviet Union "was left to draw its own conclusions"—in the words of Professor John Marcum, the leading U.S. expert on Angola.[5] Wayne Smith, who was director of the State Department's Office of Cuban Affairs from 1977 to 1979 and then the senior American diplomat in Havana until 1982, put it more bluntly: "The fact is that the United States had done more to provoke the fighting in Angola than the Cubans. Washington encouraged Holden Roberto and the FNLA to ignore the agreement to share power with the MPLA and UNITA."[6]

In other circumstances Moscow might have decided to do nothing. But fear of being outflanked by the United States and China, and irritation that its long-time protégé, the MPLA, might lose, probably prompted it to involve itself more deeply. It stepped up its supplies.

The Russians flew weapons to Congo-Brazzaville which were transferred to small craft for unloading along the Angolan coast. Luanda was still under the control of a strongly anti-MPLA Portuguese governor and direct transfer of equipment through the Angolan capital was impossible. When Zaire aided the FNLA in its attacks on the MPLA forces, the MPLA was able to enlist the help of Katangese rebels from Zaire who had no love for the MPLA but were even more hostile to the Zairean ruler, President Mobutu. With this extra manpower and the new supplies, the MPLA began to win the military ascendancy. American aid was dramatically increased in July after the 40 Committee decided to give arms not only to the FNLA but also to Jonas Savimbi's UNITA.

It was now almost inevitable that Angola's future would be decided on the battlefield after a bloody civil war. Outside aid was pouring in to both sides, the MPLA and FNLA/UNITA, which were hoping to seize as much territory as possible before the demoralized Portuguese abandoned the colony on the projected day of independence, November 11. Two key decisions in foreign capitals, Pretoria and Havana, eventually precipitated the final outcome. On one side South Africa chose to intervene directly in the hope of using the cover of the civil war to destroy the MPLA as well as SWAPO, which was fighting for the independence of Namibia. Pretoria felt it was a low-risk chance of contriving a moderate, pro-Western alternative in both territories. It may even have thought that it would be rewarded in the West for helping to defeat the side backed by Moscow. At what point the South Africans conceived these ambitions is not clear, but it is known that their forces had already moved across the Cunene River on the Angolan border in June. On August 9 they occupied the site of the South African-financed Cunene hydroelectric project which straddles both sides of the border. In early September troops backed by helicopters advanced thirty-five miles north of the Namibian border through the regions of Ongiva and Roçadas (later renamed Xangongo). If this was the beginning of a planned thrust much farther north, it was not yet recognized as such by the MPLA.

A senior Cuban officer, Commandante Raul Diaz Arguelles, had led a delegation in August to Luanda where he was asked to send military instructors to train new MPLA recruits. The supply operation proceeded at a leisurely pace. Three ships with 480 specialists left Cuba in mid-September for the roughly three-week transatlantic trip to Angola, where the first one arrived on October 4 at Porto Amboim. The crucial South African escalation took place on October 14 when South Africa launched Operation ZULU from Namibia. As Wayne Smith describes it, "In August and October South African troops invaded Angola with full U.S. knowledge. No Cuban troops were in Angola prior to this intervention."[7] Accompanied by mortars and protected by helicopter gunships, a column of armored cars stormed northward toward Luanda with UNITA units coming up behind. Within three weeks they had captured Benguela and were only 120 miles south of the capital. From the other direction, twelve miles to the north of Luanda, the FNLA was preparing for its final advance. It had American weapons brought in on CIA-organized C–130 transport planes from Zaire and South African artillery pieces. CIA and South African advisors were with them. At this point Cuba's intervention moved into a second stage. With the prospect that the South Africans might seize Luanda, the MPLA sent Henrique dos Santos (known by his nom de guerre as Onambwe) to Havana. A graduate of a Cuban university, Onambwe was an obvious choice for the mission. He told the Cubans that the MPLA desperately needed help and was thinking of declaring independence in advance of the official date, in the hope of boosting international support for its difficult position. The Central Committee of the Cuban Communist party met on November 5 and quickly agreed to the MPLA request. Some Cuban advisors had died in the battle for Benguela, and with his own men under direct threat Castro took the risk of a major new operation. Under the code name Carlota, after a slave who led an uprising in Cuba in 1843, combat troops were rushed to Angola in Cuban planes. Heavy Soviet equipment, including mobile Katyusha rocket launchers known as Stalin organs, was sent. With these the Cubans helped to rout the FNLA column marching on Luanda at a ridge called Quifandongo, where Cuban and Angolan flags now fly at a memorial site. South of Luanda, the South African column was halted and forced to turn back.

The South African intervention had proved to be a disaster for both Pretoria and Washington. At a stroke it removed any legitimacy the anti-MPLA side might have had. The Chinese withdrew their advisors in October. Several African states, led by Nigeria, moved to recognize the MPLA. The South African incursion also prompted and justified a far bigger Cuban intervention than Castro originally intended. In December with the MPLA tide turning, "Cuba sent the men and weapons necessary to win," as Castro put it. The Cuban contingent rose to fifteen thousand troops. Over the next few weeks they drove the FNLA and the South Africans out of the country.

The dramatic Soviet and Cuban backing for the MPLA was an operation without precedent. For the first time Moscow and its allies had been able to project their power decisively by air thousands of miles from their own shores and turn the tide of a revolutionary situation. Not only had they been successful, but they had done it in circumstances that most Africans considered legitimate. South Africa had been forced into retreat. Perhaps there were superficial similarities with Soviet aid for the North Vietnamese who had just swept their way into Saigon in triumph a few months earlier. But the differences were greater. Soviet aid to Hanoi had been extended over a long period and, though important, was subsidiary to the Vietnamese's own efforts in building up a well-trained, disciplined, and experienced army. In Angola the Soviet and Cuban intervention had been sudden, urgent, and highly visible, and had undoubtedly been the primary factor in the MPLA victory.

Where did this new Kremlin boldness come from? It has become fashionable in the West to talk of Moscow acting increasingly in the Third World through "surrogates" or "proxies." Kissinger told the Senate that in Angola the "culprits are the Soviet Union and its client state, Cuba."[8] It was a "blatant challenge" by Moscow. In fact there is no firm evidence that the most dramatic part of the Angolan operation, the dispatch of Cuban combat troops, was a Soviet initiative, and that Cuba was simply acting in response to Moscow's bidding. The short time between the MPLA request and Cuban action tends to support the Cuban claim that they had acted on their own. Certainly Cuba had shown more interest and concern than the Russians earlier in the crisis. In August the MPLA sent one of its senior commanders, "Iko" Carreira, to Moscow to ask for help. He was told to try the Cubans. In late August the Cuban foreign minister, Raul Roa, told a Conference of Non-Aligned Nations in Lima that the nonaligned states ought to act "in whatever manner" to speed the decolonization of Angola.[9] Direct Cuban involvement in the Third World was already long-standing. From the mid-1960s Cuba had sent antiaircraft and construction crews to Vietnam.

Military advisors were working in several African countries. Reporters who were in Angola after the arrival of the Cubans saw much greater intimacy between them and the Angolans than between the Russians and the Angolans.

Cuba's Angolan expedition may well have been the outcome of growing Cuban self-confidence. Several weeks before the civil war, Castro had told a meeting in November 1974 that Cuban armed forces would be "on the side of the peoples who face up to imperialism in all parts of the world." Ironically, at that time Cuba was just embarking on a series of secret talks with the Ford administration designed to relieve U.S. pressures on the island. In July 1975 the Organization of American States finally voted to lift the sanctions on Cuba that it had imposed more than a decade earlier. Castro could well feel buoyed and encouraged that international events were moving in his direction. The triumph of the Vietnamese must also have been cheerful news. Faced with the most important breakthrough in the liberation struggle in Africa since the Algerian revolution in 1962, and directly asked for help by the MPLA, it is not very surprising that Castro agreed.

Moscow's agreement was clearly essential, since the Russians would have to help to supply weapons and arrange transport. Whether the Russians were reluctant is hard to say. They were traditionally more concerned than Castro not to upset the United States and jeopardize détente. But they had recently been shut out of Chile and Egypt, and may have wanted to redress the balance. Besides, Angola's decolonization was a major event by any yardstick. After a decade of difficulties in the postcolonial states of East and West Africa, the focus was shifting again to the vital minority-ruled white South. For years the Russians had backed the liberation movements diplomatically and with modest supplies of arms, albeit intermittently. They could hardly turn their backs on Angola when the Americans and Chinese were clearly looking for a military victory for one side.

Moscow's willingness to take part in Castro's bold involvement in the Angolan civil war came in marked contrast to its restrained and almost dismissive attitude to Africa over the previous few years. Before the Angolan crisis Moscow's lack of enthusiasm about Africa was little different from what it had been two decades earlier when Africa's approach to political independence had found Soviet policymakers woefully unprepared. In the mid-1950s the number of Soviet African experts who had ever been to Africa could be numbered on the fingers of one hand, and there was no separate Africa Institute in the Academy of Sciences. Although Ghana's independence was the most momentous event in postwar Africa, it seemed to leave the Soviet Union unmoved. The foreign pages of *Pravda* and *Izvestia* frequently alluded to the demands of colonial and independent peoples in Latin America, Indonesia, Cyprus, and the Middle East. Africa was barely mentioned. When the journal *New Times* tried to wax lyrical over Ghana with the comment that decolonization had "spread to the very heart of the Dark Continent,"[10] its unfortunate phrase revealed more about

Soviet thinking than the writer intended. While the Soviet Union promptly congratulated the new country, it made no effort to set up quick trade or diplomatic relations.

To be fair, Soviet hesitation over Ghana was not just a result of ignorance. As students of Lenin, the Soviet leaders were convinced that victory over colonialism had to be followed by victory over neocolonialism, and that political independence was only significant if it led on to economic independence. Was Ghana's Prime Minister Nkrumah, with his appeals for foreign investment and his membership in the British Commonwealth, really a man to back? Should one trust a member of the "national bourgeoisie" or rather try to work through local Communists, given that they were very few in number? This question was quickly decided. The Russians felt that Ghana's handful of young Marxists was too small, dilettante, and undisciplined to warrant close support. Nor did the Kremlin wish to antagonize Nkrumah by pressing for the creation of a Communist party. By urging the Marxists to work within Ghana's existing institutions, the Russians proved they were realists. But the argument showed that the Russians wanted to wait and see what Nkrumah did before risking a close relationship. Had his foreign policy been helpful, they might have been more excited, but his rhetoric on international issues appeared to make little distinction between the East and the West, with its warnings about the "new" imperialism as well as the "old."

Strong Soviet interest in Africa was first kindled a year and a half later when Sekou Touré took Guinea to independence out of the French community. Here was a different situation from Ghana's. France angrily isolated Guinea, giving it economic as well as political independence. All French civil servants were recalled. Guinea's social structures seemed ripe for socialism. There was almost no local bourgeoisie, and its single political party called itself Socialist. By contrast to Nkrumah, who seemed inclined to opportunism, Touré was well versed in Marxism. A final factor was the growing challenge from China to the Soviet Union's credentials as a supporter of revolution. The Kremlin rushed to embrace Guinea, offering it economic and military aid, and inviting Touré to Moscow where he was lavishly received.

Attracted by the hope that African independence could produce other left-wing allies, Moscow soon found itself embroiled in the Congo crisis. The crisis aroused strong emotions up and down Africa and throughout the Third World, and gave the Soviet Union its first lessons in the complications of "direct action" in Africa. It arose within days of the Congo's independence, when the Congolese army mutinied, the copper-rich province of Katanga moved to secede, and Belgian forces reentered the country. President Kasavuba and the Prime Minister Patrice Lumumba ordered the Belgians to withdraw to their camps, and when the order was ignored, they appealed to the United Nations for help. Moscow was suspicious that the UN was under excessive Western control, but reluctantly voted for the resolution authorizing a UN peace force. Problems mounted when the UN showed itself slow to move against the Katanga seces-sion, giving credence to the Soviet charges. At this point the Congolese government sought to take action on its own. Lumumba and his chief of staff, Joseph Mobutu, mounted a military campaign against Katanga's neighboring state of South Kasai which had also seceded. The Soviet Union answered a request for help from Lumumba by sending fifteen transport planes and pilots. The unilateral Soviet move outside the framework of the United Nations alarmed the Belgian and U.S. governments and anti-Lumumba factions in the Congolese government. Lumumba was dismissed and imprisoned and the UN closed the airfields to all but UN planes. In fury, Moscow launched a fierce attack on UN Secretary-General Dag Hammarskjold, suggesting he be replaced by a "troika." A few days later Mobutu mounted a coup and ordered the Soviet Union and Czechoslovakia to withdraw their entire embassy staffs. The Soviet Union complied and withdrew its planes. A final appeal from Lumumba for arms and military aircraft shortly before he was deposed was rejected by an angry and disappointed Moscow.

Lumumba was murdered shortly afterward. For a time Moscow suggested it would aid the regime of Antoine Gizenga which had been set up by Lumumba supporters in Stanleyville, but it did not do so. Although there is some evidence that it arranged an indirect supply of arms via Ghana and Egypt, none ever reached the Congo. By the time the UN force finally ended the Katanga secession in January 1963, the Soviet Union was playing no role. Even when civil war flared up again in 1964, Soviet involvement was modest and belated, and only came after Belgian paratroopers had dropped from U.S. planes to occupy Stanleyville. Again Soviet supplies were indirect, in line with the argument, enunciated in *Pravda*, that the Congo problem was an African one to be solved by Africans. Egypt and Algeria were to pass on Soviet arms which Moscow agreed to replace.

The experience of "direct action" in 1960 had left Moscow with a number of lessons. First, it showed how attached nearly all Third World countries were to the United Nations. Khrushchev's notion of a three-man group to replace the secretary-general received almost no support, however upset many countries were by UN slowness in the early stages of the crisis. Second, it revealed that the Kremlin did not yet have the ability to use military power effectively outside Europe. This was not as humiliating as the similar lesson learned in the Cuban missile crisis soon afterward, but it probably helped to strengthen backing in the Kremlin for an upgrading of Soviet naval and airlift forces. It also ensured that in the second and third stages of the Congo troubles when Stanleyville was the focus, the Russians' involvement was indirect and small-scale. The third mes-sage of the Congo events was that even a superpower often has no choice but to comply with smaller nations' wishes. Asked to withdraw, the Russians did. This was to be repeated later in Egypt and Somalia. The notion that only countervail-ing Western power ever forces the Russians to retreat is a hawkish myth.

Russian reluctance to advance was well illustrated in the next African dilemma. With the Algerian war of independence reaching a climax, Soviet backing for national liberation movements was put to a test. All-out support for the FLN, the Algerian independence movement, would have won Moscow credit among African radicals. But this might have undercut Soviet hopes of reinforcing de Gaulle's disenchantment with NATO, as well as embarrassing the French Communist party which was afraid of the domestic effect of the Soviet backing for the FLN. In an attempt to square the circle Moscow expressed public sympathy for the rebels but refused them official recognition. It urged both sides to negotiate. Soviet caution over Algeria and its attempt to steer between contradictory interests fueled the scorn of the Chinese, who were beginning to attack Moscow more and more openly. They argued that the Soviet policy of peaceful coexistence with the West required oppressed peoples to accept colonial domination. Irritating though the Chinese efforts to woo African and Asian radicals were, Moscow did not let them modify its policy. In the last two years of his power, Khrushchev improved relations with even the more right-wing African states, such as Dahomey, Kenya, Nigeria, and Senegal. The Kremlin's switch to a line that largely ignored domestic trends in African countries and hoped merely to influence their foreign policies may have been prompted by disappointment over the volatility of the few left-wing countries which had emerged. In early 1961, President Brezhnev had toured Guinea to an enthusiastic reception. Shortly afterward the new American President John Kennedy, who had impressed Touré on a visit to the United States, offered Guinea aid. By the end of the year after antigovernment student demonstrations in which it was claimed that the Soviet embassy was involved, Touré had asked the Soviet ambassador to leave. Here was the Soviet Union's most reliable ally in sub-Saharan Africa suddenly blowing cold.

After Khrushchev's removal, the Kremlin's new leaders reverted to a kind of isolationism. They cut back on aid to Africa and tried to protect their investments by warning other African friends that, in order to mobilize people for the gradual building of a new social system, it was necessary to have a disciplined political party. In Cuba at this time the Kremlin was urging Castro to create a tightly organized party in the obvious hope of reducing the subjectivism and wavering of a charismatic but vulnerable individual leader. Moscow urged the same policies in Ghana and Mali, the two African states that seemed most promising.

The Ghana case was instructive of Moscow's new line. The Kremlin refused to pay Ghana the hard currency that its foreign minister, Kojo Botsio, desperately sought on a mission to Moscow in early 1965. It agreed to a debt moratorium and an increase in purchase prices of cocoa, but refused to grant cash. The Kremlin was impatient of Nkrumah's large and uneconomic development schemes. The Russians also urged Nkrumah to give more power to the party and move away from the personality cult which was becoming daily more grotesque. Their access to Nkrumah by this time was close. After two assassination attempts against him, Nkrumah had put them in charge of his personal protection. Even this degree of closeness was not enough for the Russians to persuade him to minimize the personality cult. With domestic opposition growing and his influence waning among other African leaders, Nkrumah had become a wasting asset. The Russians specifically refused to take part in the subversion camps where he was training men to overthrow the regimes of his neighbors.[11] If the Russians ever saw Nkrumah as another Castro, the notion looked increasingly thin—although the CIA still feared the analogy. The 40 Committee in Washington rejected a CIA proposal to oust Nkrumah, but local CIA men in Accra maintained contacts with army dissidents. When Nkrumah was overthrown while on a trip to Peking, the Accra station of the CIA was given full credit by headquarters.[12]

The Kremlin's effort to curb Nkrumah's excesses was part and parcel of the new leadership's differentiated approach to Africa. If there was a single theme, it could be called consolidation. Those countries that seemed to have some eventual prospects of building socialism must be advised to be methodical and patient and work through a properly administered political party. Those countries that were still under the sway of Western neocolonialism ought to have trade and diplomatic relations with the Soviet Union. Embassies were exchanged with the Ivory Coast and Upper Volta, the most reactionary African states. Official comments on Senegal became complimentary. Moves were made to restore relations with the Congo. All this was in contrast to China's attitude which was still closely linked to West and Central Africa's handful of militant revolutionaries. The Soviet Union preferred to judge African countries by their geopolitical and strategic importance. Key places were the Congo, Senegal, and Nigeria. As Andrei Gromyko put it in July 1969, "We do not consider ideological differences or differences in social systems. We are motivated by the wish to coexist. We regard the Congo as playing an important role in Africa." Senegal was useful because of its port facilities, which serviced a growing number of Soviet trawlers in the late 1960s. Its airport was an important leg on Soviet flights to Latin America.

The clearest example of Moscow's recognition of the strategic value of particular African states came with the Nigerian civil war. Moscow had not welcomed the July 1966 coup which was launched by northerners who, it was feared, would revive an anti-Soviet foreign policy. As tension mounted between the new government and the Ibo leaders of Nigeria's eastern region, the Kremlin maintained a neutral policy urging both sides to make concessions. Even after the eastern region's secession and the start of the civil war, it avoided bias toward either side. But when the British rejected a request from the federal leader, General Gowon, for aircraft, the Russians stepped in and sent MiG–17s. From then on until the end of the war they remained committed to the federal side. At the beginning the Russians probably calculated that the war would be over quickly. They knew that most African leaders had condemned Biafra's secession, and that the territorial integrity of African states was a cardinal value upheld by the OAU. But they also could not resist the opportunity of filling the gap left when the British initially refused to supply offensive weaponry. Nigeria was too important a country to ignore.

In general, over the whole first ten years of the post-Khrushchev period, Moscow's relations with sub-Saharan Africa declined in intensity. North Africa remained important, but even this was secondary by contrast with Soviet interest in the Middle East and Asia. Although southern Africa was clearly a region of significance, it was still under white minority rule. At least it provided Moscow with no awkward choices. Moscow could support the liberation movements rhetorically and to some extent militarily without giving itself any diplomatic difficulties. The chance of a breakthrough by any of the liberation movements seemed remote.

The collapse of the Portuguese empire changed everything. With the onset of the Angolan civil war and the efforts by the United States, Zaire (formerly the Congo) and South Africa to aid the anti-Communist side, Moscow became involved in the most successful intervention in Africa that it had ever made. Yet those observers who expected that the Russians would follow up their triumph in Angola by escalating their commitments in the Namibian and Zimbabwean liberation struggles were soon proved wrong. The Russians had been supplying small arms to SWAPO and to Joshua Nkomo's Zimbabwe Africa People's Union (ZAPU) for some years. There was no discernible increase in the arms supplies in the months following the Angolan civil war. At the Geneva Conference in October 1976, at which the Zimbabwean nationalist movements met Rhodesian Prime Minister Ian Smith under a British chairman to try to agree on independence, the Russians and Cubans played only a minor supporting role. Their locally accredited diplomats kept contact with the Zimbabweans, who found them confused over why guerrilla movements should be arguing about the details of a classic Westminster-style constitution. Confusion was, in fact, the hallmark of Moscow's whole approach to the decolonization of Rhodesia. They never understood the role that Britain still played more than ten years after apparently losing control at the time of Smith's unilateral declaration of independence, nor did they appreciate that the nationalists still preferred a negotiated solution. When Britain reached agreement with the nationalists to hold the Lancaster House talks, the Russians did not know how to react. Even while the conference was on, Moscow never expected it to succeed and made no plans in case it did. Worse than this mistake was the Russians' failure to appreciate the power and appeal of ZAPU's rival, the Zimbabwe African National Union (ZANU) which was eventually to lead the colony to independence. Moscow refused military aid to ZANU throughout the war. It was a mistake that cost the Russians dearly. The ZANU leader Robert Mugabe declined to invite them to the independence celebrations and made them wait a year before opening diplomatic relations. He wanted to show that he would not allow himself to be used.

The reasons for Moscow's neglect of ZANU are not entirely clear. One theory is that since China began training ZANU guerrillas in 1963 the Russians deliberately cold-shouldered ZANU. This may be so, but there are other cases where Moscow competed with Peking, as for example the Dhofari rebels in Oman, whom the Russians chose to train after learning that Peking was already training them. More plausible is the argument that Moscow accepted the predictions that Joshua Nkomo, the president of ZAPU, would end up as Zimbabwe's leader because he was the senior nationalist leader, "the father of Zimbabwean nationalism." ZAPU had close links with the African National Congress of South Africa, which in turn worked with the South African Communist party. When the ANC recommended ZAPU, Moscow took their advice. Three of ZAPU's military leaders, Jason Moyo, Debisa Dibengwa, and Alfred Mangena, were trained in Moscow and the Russians trusted them, whatever they thought of Nkomo personally. The Russians also appear to have accepted the line that tribalism had been eradicated in the two liberation movements, and that ZAPU would win any political competition between them. With their traditional emphasis on class-based politics and their underestimation of nationalism, it was easy for the Russians to fall into a line of wishful thinking which Western liberals also wanted to believe. They did press Nkomo to unite with ZANU, but when Mugabe won the 1980 preindependence election for ZANU, the Russians were amazed. Afterward they tried to hint that they had helped ZANU by channeling arms aid through Mozambique. While it is true that Mugabe's army had received help from the Mozambicans who had good relations with Moscow, the most that can be said of the Russian contribution is that Moscow turned a blind eye to the flow of weapons into Zimbabwe. Mugabe was not impressed.

In Angola itself, in the aftermath of independence, the Russians and Cubans showed no inclination to use their gains as a springboard for advances on the southern frontier with Namibia. Although Moscow made up for the losses sustained by the MPLA during the civil war and dispatched aircraft, tanks, and antiaircraft missiles, the number of Cuban troops in the country is admitted by Western sources to have gone down at the end of the war.[13] From a peak of 16,000 troops the numbers declined to 10,000 in 1976. It was only in the following year, when South African incursions into southern Angola picked up again and the South African-aided UNITA groups renewed their operations in the central highlands, that the Cubans were reinforced, reaching a total of 19,000 by the end of 1977. But the Cubans were no longer used as front-line combat troops. They helped to man the air-defense systems and their officers acted as military advisors in the field. The bulk of the troops remained in reserve.

Although the Soviet Union, Cuba, and several Eastern European countries also sent hundreds of civilian technicians who made up in part for the exodus of

Portuguese—as they had done for the same reason in Mozambique a year earlier—the Kremlin showed no eagerness to turn its new responsibilities into a confrontation with the West. It did not seek naval base facilities in either Mozambique or Angola, knowing that the appearance of Soviet submarines on patrol so close to the Cape route would only have fueled the alarmist fears of Western hawks about alleged Soviet expansionism. In March 1977 when several hundred armed Lunda tribesmen from Katanga in Zaire who were hostile to President Mobutu marched back from their camps in Angola and seized three towns, no serious analyst believed the Russians or Cubans were involved. The Carter administration said it had no evidence of any such involvement. A year later when a similar incursion took place, this time via Angola and Zambia, the American reaction was sharper. But this appeared to have more to do with Western anger over recent Soviet advances in Ethiopia and reflected the growing influence of Carter's hard-line national security advisor, Zbigniew Brzezinski, compared with the more dovish secretary of state, Cyrus Vance. The CIA director, Stansfield Turner, claimed to have at least circumstantial evidence of a Cuban role: "We have sufficient evidence to draw the conclusion that there must have been Cuban involvement in the training and equipping, although no intelligence conclusion is ever black or white."[14] Castro denied that Cuba had had contact with the Katanga rebels since the end of the civil war. Two months later, when French and Belgian troops had repelled the rebels, Angola and Zaire set up diplomatic relations and the Angolan President Agostinho Neto promised to disarm and move them 150 miles from the Zairean border. The Shaba crisis was not a sign of an increase in Soviet activity in Central Africa, but one more episode in the continuing instability in Zaire in which the West had itself repeatedly intervened.

Zimbabwe's independence and Reagan's victory in the 1980 presidential election in the United States prompted a new aggressiveness in South African policy toward the front-line African states. It stepped up its ground and air attacks into southern Angola up to two hundred miles north of the Namibian border. In Mozambique, besides arming and equipping an antigovernment guerrilla movement, which operated mainly in the northwest of the country, it sent commandoes on a mission against ANC representatives in Maputo and killed twelve people. The Soviet response was the minimum consistent with its treaties of friendship with both countries. Moscow answered Samora Machel's request for a demonstration visit by Soviet warships to Maputo in February 1981. In Angola the Soviet Union continued to supply antiaircraft missiles and radar, and military advisors to help man them. But politically Moscow maintained a low profile. When the South Africans killed two Soviet military advisors and two Soviet women and captured another technician in southern Angola in August 1981, it took Moscow three weeks even to admit the losses to its own public. Had American advisors been killed in a war in the Third World, one can imagine the immediate outcry and the pressures on the administration to take action. The Kremlin ensures that this does not apply in the Soviet Union. If it wants to escalate, it will do so regardless of public opinion. If it wants to remain cautious, it will also ignore the public. In the Angolan case it was clear that the Russians wanted no direct confrontation with South Africa.

Nor was Moscow's interest in South Africa itself very great. Since the October Revolution it had had links with the South African Communist party, in those days essentially a European party. Through it the Russians developed links with the ANC, to whom it continues to give military training and some small arms. But Moscow has no illusions that an ANC military victory or an internal revolution are likely in the next few years. South Africa is a useful international issue with which to keep the West on the defensive at the United Nations. It costs Moscow little and the returns are good. When the South African government claims to be facing a "total onslaught" from the Soviet Union, it is using an exaggerated argument designed only to win Western support. The Soviet onslaught is minimal to the point of nonexistence.

The one area of Africa where the Soviet Union followed its Angolan success with some vigor was not in the South but in the Horn. There again Moscow moved to ensure that its role would be seen as legitimate. This time the conflict was not a civil war but a border war between two sovereign states over disputed territory, the Ogaden. For some years Somalia had laid claim to this Ethiopian-controlled area, as well as to parts of Kenya. For the Russians, the issue was apparently of little interest, although they must have asked themselves why the Somalis wanted Soviet tanks, artillery, and MiG–21s. In spite of almost a decade of Soviet involvement in Somalia, there is no evidence that they ever encouraged the Somali president, Siad Barre, to pursue his irredentist ambitions against Ethiopia and Kenya.[15]

Somalia was valuable to Moscow because of its position on the Arabian Sea. They enjoyed facilities in the base at Berbera, which was aimed at supporting their patrols in the Indian Ocean against the threat of U.S. Polaris submarines. The Soviet contingent in Somalia had reached approximately 3,600, including 1,400 military advisors, by the time that President Podgorny visited Mogadishu to sign a Treaty of Friendship in 1974. This heavy Soviet presence caused divergent reactions in the United States. Kissinger saw it as a useful justification for an American buildup on the island of Diego Garcia in the Indian Ocean.[16] American officials in Saudi Arabia favored ways of having the Russians expelled. After King Faisal's assassination in 1975, the Saudis developed a more active policy of using "petro-dollar diplomacy" to buy out radical influence in the region. Major targets of the new Saudi line were the Soviet Union's two friends, Somalia and South Yemen.

The Russians were aware of these moves. Having been expelled from Egypt and the Sudan, they were not anxious to lose in Somalia too. They had reacted with caution to the change of regime in Somalia's neighbor Ethiopia in 1974. The political coloration of the young officers who overthrew Emperor Haile Selassie was unclear. When they approached the Russians for arms aid soon after the coup, Moscow refused for fear of alienating Siad Barre by arming his neighbors. For two years the Russians maintained this line. It was only in December 1976 that they finally agreed to supply arms, apparently satisfied by then that the Ethiopian revolution could be useful to them. The Russians were in an obvious dilemma. In Somalia and Ethiopia they saw two progressive-sounding, left-leaning regimes commanding a strategically important position. The trouble was the border dispute between them. Ideally, they would have liked to insulate the conflict from their own relations with each side, in the manner of the American approach to Greece and Turkey.

This was what they attempted. First, they told Siad Barre that they would not help him in his increasingly open efforts to intervene in the Ogaden. Second, they tried to mediate between Ethiopia and Somalia in the hope of creating a broad federation of Socialist states in the region, possibly including Eritrea, Djibouti, and South Yemen. In March 1977 Castro visited the Horn. He saw both Siad Barre and the Ethiopian leader, Mengistu Haile Mariam, and tried to arrange a meeting between them. The next month Podgorny also saw both men.

Although the mediation efforts failed, the Russians were still not keen to take sides in the conflict. When their arms supplies to Ethiopia arrived in May, they were initially transferred to the north to deal with resistance to the new regime rather than to the Ogaden.[17] At that point the future of the dispute over the Ogaden was not clear. The Russians must have calculated that at some point the conflict might explode, forcing them to take action. They may also have calculated that in that event Ethiopia, as the larger and more influential country, was the better side to be on. Its case in the Ogaden, though weak historically, was supported by the OAU. But to suggest that the Russians made a cynical switch from Somalia to Ethiopia is too simple. Nor is it accurate to accuse the Russians of "betraying" Somalia.

The break in relations between Somalia and Moscow was precipitated by Siad Barre after significant American overtures for better relations. In July 1977 the United States announced its willingness to send Somalia "defensive weapons." Although Washington denied that this was a commitment to aid Somalia in an attack on the Ogaden, it was described by Chester Crocker, who later became Reagan's assistant secretary of state for Africa, as "apparent American encouragement of the Somali invasion of the Ogaden."[18] Even after the invasion of the Ogaden in July, the Russians tried to preserve a stake in both countries. Siad Barre flew to Moscow in August to seek Soviet support and to protest about Soviet arms supplied to Ethiopia. Although he was given nothing, the Russians waited until October before announcing that all arms supplies to Somalia had ceased. Had Moscow simply wanted to switch to Ethiopia's side, the moment for this would have come with the invasion in July. It was Siad Barre who made the break. Angry and frustrated with Moscow, he expelled all Soviet and Cuban advisors from Somalia on November 13.

Now the Russians had nothing left to lose. Two weeks later they started a massive airlift of Soviet heavy equipment to Ethiopia in what turned out to be a bigger operation than the one in Angola two years earlier. In December thousands of Cuban troops arrived. The Russians were established in the eyes of the OAU and of most international observers as supporters of the victim of aggression. No one doubted that Somalia's invasion was unjustified. In order not to waste the prestige that their help for Ethiopia had won them, the Russians successfully urged Mengistu not to go across the border into Somalia once the Somalis had been pushed back out of the Ogaden.

The Eritrean independence movement posed a more difficult problem for Moscow. The official Soviet line had been to call for a negotiated solution within a unitary Ethiopian state. This put Moscow against Mengistu's aim of achieving a military victory against the Eritreans. The Cubans were in an even more awkward position. While Haile Selassie was in power, Castro had endorsed the Eritrean demand for independence and trained about 130 guerrillas.[19] Although he later stopped the aid because of a split within the Eritrean movement, Castro continued to describe it as "a national liberation movement," even after the change of regime in Ethiopia. Flushed by his victory in the Ogaden, Mengistu was eager to turn on his other enemy in the north. During his first offensive against Eritrea in May 1978, Moscow and Havana refused to take an active role. At the second attempt in July 1978, the Russians and Cubans supported Mengistu with up to 2,000 Cuban troops and hundreds of Soviet advisors. By the end of November the Ethiopians had regained every major town in Eritrea, leaving the Eritreans to fight a tenacious guerrilla war.

There is little doubt that if the Russians had not wanted to go along with the second offensive against Eritrea they need not have done so. They had refused to support Siad Barre in the Ogaden, and then, after joining the Ethiopian side, had held Mengistu back when the Cubans had given him the upper hand. Had the Russians refused to go forward against Eritrea, Mengistu would have had no alternative but to agree. The Russian argument was presumably strategic. Ethiopia's ports on the Red Sea are all in Eritrea, and the Russians are not willing to forgo the chance of acquiring access to them to help to make up for the loss of Berbera in Somalia. In practice their intervention on Mengistu's side did them little good. Although the second 1978 offensive was a severe blow to the Eritreans, it was not final. The Eritreans continued to harass the Ethiopians and in the spring of 1982 a thousand Soviet advisors were again reported to be with the Ethiopian army in Eritrea in yet another offensive.[20]

In spite of his total dependence on Moscow for arms, Mengistu proved to be as difficult a client as the Vietnamese and Cubans. He resisted repeated Soviet efforts to persuade him to form a political party so that his military regime could put down roots on the classic Soviet model of a central administration with subservient local organs. He permitted Moscow anchorage for its warships bound for the Indian Ocean on the barren Dahlak Islands off the port of

Massawa, but did not grant the Russians use of better onshore facilities.[21] He fell behind on his payments for Soviet arms. Meanwhile, in Somalia, the United States gained access to Berbera in place of the Russians.

In July 1982 there came the first signs of a slight shift in Soviet policy. After a number of alleged Somali incursions close to Soviet oil-drilling operations in Ethiopia, Ethiopian armored columns and mechanized infantry pushed into Somalia. The Ethiopians denied they were intervening and claimed the fighting was an uprising by the dissident Somali Salvation Democratic Front against the Siad Barre regime. Independent observers supported the evidence of Ethiopian involvement, but saw the action as an attempt to embarrass Siad Barre and provoke political disaffection within Somalia, particularly among the army, rather than as a classic invasion.[22] Cuban advisors were believed to have helped with the planning. The Soviet role and its motivation were not entirely clear, but it seemed to suggest that the Russians were still interested in recovering their position in Somalia under a new regime. To be allied with both Somalia and Ethiopia and to achieve a settlement between the two of them would be a major coup. But Moscow's investment in planning the new fighting was obscure and may have amounted to little more than giving it reluctant approval, provided it did not turn into a major international crisis. Given the Kremlin's preoccupation with Brezhnev's declining health in the summer of 1982, it is unlikely that Moscow would have wanted to take decisive new steps in an already difficult situation in the Horn of Africa.

In the event, the uprising in Somalia never occurred and the Ethiopian intervention petered out. Almost twenty years after their first arms supplies to Somalia, and five years after their new alignment with Ethiopia, the Russians were being reminded yet again that there is no direct link between giving military aid and reaping strategic or political rewards.

CONCLUSION

Africa has been in some ways the most disappointing continent for the Kremlin. Moscow has twice found itself stirred by the prospect of an upsurge in Soviet influence—only to be disillusioned later. In the late 1950s the Soviet Union hoped to develop a number of clients such as Ghana, Guinea, and Mali. In the Congo crisis of 1960 it sought to play a major role. But after a series of rebuffs it lost interest in the region. In the mid-1970s the collapse of the Portuguese empire in Africa renewed Moscow's attention in sub-Saharan Africa after a lapse of several years. Its successful involvement in the Angolan civil war appeared to open the prospect of significant influence in the whole of southern Africa. It was not to be. Miscalculations in Zimbabwe plus unwillingness to take on the military might of South Africa in Namibia in any major way led to the blocking of any further political advance by the Soviet Union. Only in the Horn of Africa—as a result of another revolution that Moscow had done nothing to foster—was the Kremlin able to win a useful position.

But even there Moscow found that its influence was limited to the military field. The West's ability and readiness to exert economic power left African countries, however radical they wished to be, essentially linked to the international Western-dominated economy. By the end of the Brezhnev era, Soviet strategists were conceding that even those African countries, such as Angola, Ethiopia, and Mozambique, which were defined as "socialist-oriented", continued to depend on the capitalist market. If Moscow's experience in Latin America showed that it was hard to shift a country's politics in a socialist direction, its experience in Africa was perhaps more depressing. Here the lesson was that countries could shift to a nominally socialist economy (with a centralized system of distribution, state farms, and the nationalization of the basic industries and banks) but still be tied to the international capitalist system. The outcome was likely to be that Moscow would increasingly scale down its investment in Africa throughout the 1980s. Only a political explosion in South Africa itself would arouse Moscow's interest for the third time.

PART THREE

Conclusion

13

PROSPECTS
FOR THE 1980s

We must put a stop to this destructive militarization of the public discussion of relations between East and West, an end to this constant talk about the horrible things the Russians could do to us and we to them in a supposedly imminent war. And we must also stop making the intentions and military preparations of a possible opponent appear to the public in a threatening and alarming light.

George Kennan, 1982[1]

The prophets of doom began to work overtime in the early 1980s in predicting the grimmest scenarios of likely Soviet actions in the rest of the decade. As interest switched to the Brezhnev succession, a change overcame those who had previously portrayed him as the leader of a brutal, expansionist power. Suddenly, by comparison with the successor generation, Brezhnev became a senile moderate, a rather bumbling, somewhat pathetic creature whose departure might even be regretted in the West. After him would come a new breed of younger, more wicked men. "It is my nightmare," Kissinger confessed, "that his successors, bred in more tranquil times and accustomed to modern technology and military strength, might be freer of self-doubt; with no such inferiority complex they may believe their own boasts and with a military establishment now covering the globe, may prove far more dangerous."[2] Brzezinski shared

Kissinger's vision of a stronger and more dangerous Soviet Union. "The most critical period will be roughly from 1983 to 1987 when the Soviet leadership will probably pass to younger men," he told reporters after a two-week visit to China in July 1982. "This successor generation may see these first years as the optimum period to use military power."[3]

Other spokesmen for the West's security establishment had a similar nightmare, though its origin was different. The horrific factor for them was the Soviet Union's weakness, not its strength. In 1981 John Nott, Britain's defense minister, asked: "Who can tell what problems will come for Brezhnev's successors, with popular discontent inevitable over living standards, with demographic problems—a steep increase in the birth rate of non-Slavic peoples, especially the fifty million Muslims in Central Asia—and all this held together by a repressive bureaucracy and supplied by a heavy, over-centralized and inefficient economic system? Can we disregard totally even the possibility in years to come of a disintegrating Soviet empire with, as an act of desperation, the dying giant lashing out across the central front?"[4]

Whether the Soviet Union was judged to be strong or weak, posing a threat over the next few years or, as Nott seemed to be saying, as far ahead as one could see, the message was the same as it had been for almost forty years. The West must keep up its guard and spend more on defense. The fact that their assessments of the Soviet threat were so vague and contradictory did not seem to worry the West's hawks. Even if one admitted that policy was being made on the basis of a "nightmare" rather than a cool analysis of probabilities, it did not matter. Planners, the public was told, have to deal with "worst-case scenarios" and prepare accordingly. Vigilance and an increase in military strength were the West's best response.

Such reflex reactions ought to be suspect. By 1982 the evidence was that the Western public had grown suspicious of them. A detailed transatlantic opinion poll, sponsored by the *International Herald Tribune* and the Atlantic Institute, found that the Soviet military buildup was not a major worry for almost two-thirds of the people polled, and that in the United States and every Western country except West Germany less than 10 percent felt that the West's defenses were inadequate.[5] The argument of this book reflects the survey's mood. After looking at Moscow's record in every region of the globe, whether on the Soviet Union's borders or in remoter areas of the Third World, it concludes that although the instruments of Soviet military power have grown, its influence has declined. For a Soviet strategic planner the prospect for the 1980s offers little encouragement.

The dispute with China is deeply entrenched. It is already twenty years since the last period of détente, and although there are signs of Chinese willingness to show more even-handedness between the superpowers, Moscow probably cannot look forward to anything better than peaceful coexistence with China. The chances of a Sino–Soviet alliance are virtually nil. In the Middle East Islam has proved to be as unpredictable a problem for the Soviet Union as for the West. Moscow has shown no sign of being able to handle resurgent Islamic nationalism. The consequences of this are more serious for the Soviet Union because of its geographical closeness to the Middle East and the fact that almost a fifth of its people have Muslim backgrounds. Moscow is bogged down in Afghanistan. Its relations with Iran are worse under Khomeini than they were under the Shah. Its influence in Libya is much less than suggested by alarmist reports in the Western media. Soviet–Libyan ties are a marriage of convenience and cannot be relied upon. Qadaffi might change his mind tomorrow and expel the Russians, as did Sadat in Egypt and Siad Barre in Somalia.

In Eastern Europe Moscow faces a deep crisis of loyalty. The upsurge of Solidarity showed that thirty-five years of Soviet-style socialism has failed to win the allegiance of large sections of the Polish working class, even among the young who have had no experience of any other system. The Kremlin has to presume that disaffection might equally break out publicly in Hungary, Czechoslovakia, and East Germany. If the upheavals of 1956 and 1968 might be written off by wishful thinkers in Moscow as the outcome of Stalin's repression and his successors' failure to develop enough consumer goods, this explanation could no longer work for the early 1980s.

At the heart of Soviet foreign policy, its relations with Western Europe and the United States, the view from the Kremlin is hardly more comforting. A new round in the nuclear arms race with the United States is underway, with damaging implications for the chance of developing the civilian economy. West Germany, France, and Britain, the three leading countries in Western Europe, are governed by determined anti-Communists. The brief period of détente has given way to a new Cold War, as the West has reverted to the strategy of economic pressure that marked the early postwar years.

Soviet ideological influence is at a low ebb. Although the Kremlin is still respected in parts of the Third World as a supplier of diplomatic support and military hardware, the Soviet Union has lost its image as the inspiration for revolution. The invasion of Afghanistan confirmed what a majority of Third World countries had long suspected, if they had not said it out loud before. The Soviet Union is a superpower that has no hesitation in defining its own security in a way that can threaten the security of its neighbors. In Afghanistan it was no longer a force in support of national liberation but against it. As for the Soviet model as an example for other developing countries to follow, this had already lost most of its impetus by the early 1970s. The concept of socialism, in a general and undefined way, might still be influential as a source of theoretical legitimacy for many authoritarian Third World nations, but the Soviet Union's particular experience is not studied with admiration or enthusiasm.

Nor are Soviet citizens respected abroad as ambassadors of an alternative life style. In the Third World they tend to be seen as just another group of arrogant Europeans, aloof, patronizing, and often racist. They usually do not have the

informality, self-confidence, and individual generosity of their American counterparts, or the sophistication of Western Europeans. Official Soviet atheism has
cut them off from close relations with deeply religious cultures in Asia, Latin
America, and the Middle East.

Declining foreign influence is only one of the Kremlin's worries. On the
domestic front Andropov has to face a daunting series of problems, in spite of
the underlying stability of the system. The basic Soviet problem is the economy.
Brezhnev admitted this at the Twenty-Sixth Party Congress in 1981, when he
launched what amounted to the rewriting of the future. Twenty years after
Khrushchev published a party program whose proud boast was that by 1980 the
Soviet Union would be the world's most prosperous state, with free rents, free
medicine, and free public transport, the party had decided to think again.
Brezhnev said that it was time to redraft the program, thus formally abandoning
the Khrushchev prediction that by 1970 the Soviet Union would have overtaken
the United States in industrial and agricultural output. In practice the Soviet
leadership had already downgraded the 1961 targets. Its targets for 1980 in the
1976–80 Five-Year Plan were only 65 percent of Khrushchev's 1980 figure for
national income and 50 percent for agriculture. Brezhnev's ceremonial discard-
ing of his predecessor's piece of science fiction marked the final de-
Khrushchevization of the Soviet Union. Cautious pragmatism, the hallmark of
Brezhnev's long rule in international relations and economic management, was
extended to the field of ideology as well. The advance to communism no longer
had a time limit, but would require—as Brezhnev put it—an "historically long"
and undefined period.

The gap between Soviet space achievements and the backwardness of large
parts of the country is still great. The USSR is a kind of Third World superpower, "the most developed of the developing countries and the least developed
of the developed countries."[6] Brezhnev's successors have no choice but to
accept the reality of the country's economic difficulties. The guidelines for the
1980–85 Five-Year Plan talked of an annual growth rate of 4 percent compared
with 6 or 7 percent a decade earlier. The old process of extensive development in
which growth comes from a surplus of labor and natural resources has come to an
end. The economy is running into a shortage of labor in general, and skilled
labor in particular. When it was a question of mobilizing unskilled labor to build
an industrial base, the centralized command economy was sufficient. But its
limited system of incentives was and still is too weak to stimulate innovation and
economize on labor. Future economic growth will have to rely increasingly on a
more subtle mixture of investment and production decisions than a command
economy can make, and on a more efficient application of new technology.

Andropov raised the problems in a gloomy rundown of economic issues in his
speech at the first Central Committee meeting after Brezhnev's death. "Labor
productivity is growing at a rate which cannot satisfy us. The problem of lack of
coordination between the development of raw-material and processing branches

still remains. . . . Plan targets continue to be met at the price of large outlays and production costs. . . . Inertia and conservatism are still at work. Some people just do not know how to set about doing the job. . . . Progress is slow. To introduce a new method or new technology, production has to be reorganized and this affects the fulfillment of plan targets. You may be taken to task for failing production plans but only scolded at the most for poor introduction of new technology."[7]

Future economic growth will have to rely increasingly on a more subtle mixture of investment and production decisions than a command economy can make, and on a more efficient application of new technology. Soviet agriculture is also facing severe problems. In spite of massive investment in farming, reaching about 27 percent of total investment in recent years, output has been declining. Production of virtually all major crops—grain, potatoes, sugar beet, oilseeds, fruit, and vegetables—peaked in the late 1970s and began to drop. Milk output peaked in 1977 and largely because of shortage of feed stuffs, milk production per cow has also been dropping. Meat output peaked in 1978 and in some parts of the Soviet Union rationing has had to be reintroduced. In announcing a new long-term food program in May 1982, Brezhnev blamed the crisis on shortages in mechanization, migration of peasants to the cities, short-ages of fertilizer and herbicides, an antiquated and irrational pricing policy, and transport and storage problems that led to immense waste through rot or loss.

Another problem is the incipient energy shortage. In spite of its huge reserves, the Soviet Union faces an increasingly difficult job in extracting them from Siberia. The high price of oil on the world market makes it costlier for Moscow to subsidize its Eastern European allies. Finally, there is a looming demographic problem brought about by a reduction in the number of children reaching the age of eighteen. For most of the Brezhnev period the labor force was being enlarged by the coming to age of those born during the postwar baby boom. In the 1980s the children of the relatively small number of wartime babies will be maturing, leading to an estimated drop of almost 25 percent in the new generation of young adults. This will affect both the labor force and the availability of manpower for the armed forces.

This formidable array of imminent problems is bound to be a serious factor in the Kremlin's future decision making. But before an observer leaps to embrace John Nott's image of a "dying giant," it is important to remember the strengths of the Soviet system. Its staying power is too often ignored in the West. A socioeconomic crisis does not become a political crisis until it is perceived as such. Soviet citizens may grumble and complain, but it does not follow that they are, or will soon be, on the verge of revolt. Communism is associated with the loss of national independence in Poland, but with the achievement of national goals in Russia, as one observer has pointed out.[8]

There are other important cushions in the system.[9] Although centrifugal forces of nationalism and ethnic identity have reemerged in non-Russian regions

such as the Baltic states and the Ukraine, the Caucasian republics and among
Soviet Jews, they have not produced serious symptoms of political disintegra-
tion. Second, there has been no political fallout from the generation gap
between young Soviet citizens and their parents. Rising popular expectations
are almost entirely confined to the material sphere and not to political or cultural
areas. Third, the Brezhnev period produced a considerable advance in living
standards which affected all groups and all fifteen Soviet republics. The minimum wage went up 50 percent. Pensions were increased. Peasants were included
in the social security system, and collective farms were insured by the state
against loss of earnings caused by bad harvests.

Soviet Living Standards, 1965 and 1980[10]

Indicator	1965	1980
Monthly wage	96.5 rubles	168.5 rubles
Number of doctors	554,000	993,000
Families with TV sets	24%	85%
Families with refrigerators	11%	84%
Living space per person in towns	10 sq. meters	13.2 sq. meters
Consumption of meat and meat products per person	41 kilos	57 kilos
Consumption of vegetables per person	72 kilos	93 kilos
Consumption of potatoes per person	142 kilos	120 kilos
Consumption of bread and grain per person	156 kilos	139 kilos

The table shows how Soviet living standards improved during the Brezhnev
period. In spite of chronic uncertainties in the delivery of food to the shops, and
the recent decline in farm output, the switch in traditional Russian eating habits
from a high reliance on bread and potatoes to meat and vegetables is a significant
historic change. It is important to remember that the Politburo decision to start
importing grain in the early 1970s was not prompted by a domestic disaster, but
by a conscious effort to improve Soviet diets. Much of the imported grain went to
feedstuff to rear cattle.

Fourth, the Kremlin has kept down price increases. Consumers have been so
cushioned against steep rises by a massive system of state subsidies that it would
be politically difficult for the leadership to alter the system abruptly. Nevertheless, price stability has helped to reduce the level of popular grumbling. Fifth,
the increase in living standards has partly been achieved by individual social
mobility. The system clearly has an effective safety valve against discontent, if a

peasant can migrate easily into an urban job, if an unskilled worker has a fair opportunity to improve his or her skills, and if the educational system is egalitarian enough to allow young people to advance financially and socially to a level that was not open to their parents.

Over and above these specific improvements during the Brezhnev era, there are two other stability-enhancing features of Soviet society that reduce the chances of political upheaval. One is the pervasive Russian respect for order and fear of chaos which is shared by the leadership and most of the population alike. Famine, war, and massive social dislocation have been too frequent in Russian history for people to relish the possibility of another social outburst. Russians long for a strong leader, and part of the nostalgia for Stalin, found even among people too young to remember his rule, can be attributed to the sense that social discipline slipped under Brezhnev. This suspicion of troublemakers was a powerful asset for the Kremlin in its successful campaign against the dissident movement of the 1970s. However large the movement was numerically, the leadership was able to isolate it from the mainstream of society. Pavel Litvinov, who demonstrated in Red Square against the invasion of Czechoslovakia and is the grandson of Maxim Litvinov, Stalin's foreign minister, has commented: "Under the Czars we had an authoritarian state and now we have a totalitarian state but it still comes from the roots of the Russian past. You should understand that the leaders and the ordinary people have the same authoritarian frame of mind. Brezhnev and the simple person both think that might is right. That's all. It is not a question of ideology. It's simply power. Solzhenitsyn acts as if he thinks this has all come down from the sky because of Communism. But he is not so different himself. He does not want democracy. He wants to go from a totalitarian state back to an authoritarian one."[11]

A second stabilizing factor is the broad support given by the population to the Kremlin's foreign policy. The sense that the country is encircled by enemies, which is one of the fundamental motivating forces in Soviet attitudes to international issues, is widely shared. Whether out of habit, a lifetime of indoctrination, patriotism, or genuine conviction, most people accept the Kremlin's self-characterization as "peace-loving" and its assertion that the Soviet Union has sponsored most of the relevant disarmament initiatives of recent years. The Soviet Union's achievement of strategic parity with the United States was a source of pride to Soviet citizens. Even people with the most reason to feel alienated from the regime often reveal a deep and simple patriotism. One Soviet dissident tells the story of a late-night taxi ride through Moscow in 1980. The driver, a man of about sixty, started to tell her about his life. His parents had had a medium-sized farm. During Stalin's collectivization campaign the party confiscated their land and sent the family to Siberia as kulaks. Came the war and the boy, now a young man, was called up and sent to the front. Captured by the Germans, he spent years as a prisoner of war. On release he was promptly reimprisoned by Stalin, like most ex-POWs. Eight years later he finally emerged from the camps at the age of thirty-five. "I had nothing," said the taxi driver. "I had done nothing. I had no training, no qualifications, nothing—and half my life was already gone." He managed to get a job as a driver, then he married and had children, but now, late in the Moscow night, as he sat at the wheel of his taxi, he complained that his life had been as empty as the streets they were passing through. As they reached the dissident's destination, he finished, "And now Carter is putting all this pressure on us, all these new missiles. And we have to suffer." When she said mildly that the Soviet Union had been building missiles too, the driver replied, "Yes, but we have to defend our native land." A native land, she thought to herself, as his taxi disappeared, that exiled him, sent him to war, and put him into labor camps . . . but he will still do whatever it asks him.

Even the Kremlin's failures have not broken the popular bond of trust in the leadership's efforts to defend Soviet national security. They may have strengthened it by heightening the feeling of encirclement and isolation. In the United States, the "loss" of China caused a period of public soul-searching and a hunt for scapegoats. In Russia, the break with China only seemed to magnify the feeling that no allies could be trusted. Likewise, the collapse of détente is not considered by most Russians as in any way the Kremlin's fault.

"We must recognize the tendency of the Soviets to escape their dilemmas by foreign adventures," Kissinger wrote in July 1981.[12] His remark is suspect on several counts. It assumes a similar degree of linkage between domestic and foreign affairs as exists in Western countries, with their volatile public opinion and regular elections. In the Soviet Union there is no such pressure on the leadership. Foreign affairs are not an issue for public debate. Moreover, Kissinger's remark is belied by the record. The Kremlin sought to escape its dilemmas of declining growth rates, spiraling defense costs, and relatively backward technology by the opposite of foreign adventures. It tried to foster cooperation with the West through détente, hoping thereby to control the arms race and forestall the pressure for internal economic reforms by importing ready-made solutions from abroad.

The whole concept of Soviet "adventurism" and "expansionism" needs to be reexamined. Do these words accurately describe reality or are they merely labels of abuse? One of the central conclusions of this book is that Soviet moves described as "adventurist" have often been low-risk policies, cautiously arrived at and in some cases internationally approved by a majority of the world community. As for expansionism, this may be nothing more sinister than the normal search for diplomatic and political influence that other states also follow.

The grave problems that confront Andropov as Brezhnev's successor involve awkward decisions between competing priorities and, in some cases, the possibility of a radical break with previous policies. The most fundamental one is how the Soviet Union ought to react to the sharpening mood of anti-Soviet confrontation in the United States. At a time when Soviet growth rates are certain to decline, the choice of whether to allocate scarce resources to investment, consumption, or defense spending has never been more difficult. With the White House apparently set on a new round in the arms race, should the Kremlin make a costly outlay of funds, which would clearly have to be renewed for several years, so as to prevent the United States from getting ahead, or should it make the kind of arms control concessions in the Strategic Arms Reduction Talks (START) in Geneva which Washington is demanding?

Three other questions are linked to the new Cold War. First, China. At the moment the Soviet Union is believed to be spending only some 10 percent of its defense budget on its deployments in the Far East, facing China. There must be a strong case for arguing that this relatively small amount of money is preventing Moscow from patching up its twenty-year-old dispute with China. If Moscow pulled back most of its troops, as China is demanding and as the Kremlin hinted in the days following Brezhnev's death, it could probably remove the danger of a Sino-American alliance, which has been one of the Kremlin's greatest concerns in recent years.[13] The counterargument holds that the financial gain of reducing the Soviet troop and missile presence in the Far East is not significant enough to trade in against the loss of security. "How can we be sure that the Chinese will not take advantage of our withdrawal and threaten Siberia?" the conservatives in the Kremlin must be asking.

Second, Western Europe. As long as Washington seems set on a collision course with the Soviet Union, the Kremlin will have to decide how far to press its efforts to persuade Western Europe to stick by détente. If it tries to insert itself too blatantly into the transatlantic debate by wooing Western European governments too urgently, it may encourage the hawks in the West to redouble their economic pressures or merely solidify the Western alliance. Linked to this is the third issue, the problem of trade dependence. Western doubts about dependence on the Soviet Union for energy supplies are matched by Soviet doubts over the West's commitment to long-term credits and technology transfers. Brezhnev opened the Soviet Union to an unprecedented degree of East–West commercial cooperation. His successors must work out how far they are prepared to rely on that in the future, and whether to revert in the next five-year and ten-year plans to a strategy of greater self-sufficiency.

In the Third World, the Soviet Union faces the prospect of at least as much turbulence and instability as occurred in the 1970s. The transition from a colonial world to a postcolonial one in which the United States has supplanted France, Britain and Europe's other former imperial powers as the major political and economic force has not diminished the strength of local nationalism. Internal political tensions, as well as conflicts between regional neighbors, are bound to continue in the 1980s. The Soviet Union will have a role to play. It is one of the chief arms suppliers to several Third World governments and has set itself up—and is looked to—as a global rival to the United States. Moscow would like to separate its role in Third World conflicts from the issue of East–West détente, but the experience of the 1970s suggests that Washington will not accept the argument. "Linkage" between Soviet "behavior" in the Third World and the state of East–West political relations will continue to be made in Washington, whether formally or not. The Kremlin must decide whether it is worth provoking the United States into a tougher overall confrontation for the sake of marginal gains in a particular Third World dispute.

The last two succession periods in the Kremlin, after Stalin's death and Khrushchev's overthrow, had some common features. In the first phase there was a publicly subdued but nevertheless real rivalry between two contenders—from 1953 to 1957 between Khrushchev and Malenkov, from 1964 to 1970 between Brezhnev and Kosygin. In the second phase one man emerged victorious and produced a compromise program, incorporating some of the policies of his defeated rival. In the case of the succession to Khrushchev, the tensions were not as sharp as in the earlier case, and the losing contender remained in a significant position. Nor had the dispute between them dealt with foreign policy.

The succession to Brezhnev followed neither of the earlier patterns. By arranging a political alliance with Ustinov, the minister of defense, Andropov was able to outflank his main rival Chernenko in the weeks before Brezhnev died. Within hours of Brezhnev's death Andropov emerged as the new general secretary of the party. Nevertheless, it would clearly take time for him to achieve the political preeminence of Brezhnev at its height. In the meantime the Politburo would reflect different nuances on the crucial issues of foreign and domestic policy, and Andropov cannot be sure of an automatic majority for his point of view. At sixty-eight years of age, he was older than the contenders in earlier succession periods. His regime is likely to be a cautious, transitional one in which major initiatives are postponed until the next succession.

There are other important differences between the current succession and the earlier ones. The Soviet Union is now incomparably stronger militarily than it was in 1953 or 1964. Its achievement of strategic nuclear parity with the United States is bound to give the generation that follows Brezhnev and Andropov a self-confidence that the latter rulers lacked. Whatever difficulties Moscow faces with China, Eastern Europe, or the West, it can now enjoy the fundamental security of a massive military arsenal. This does not mean that the old Soviet fear of encirclement will fade away, especially in the context of a nuclear world where there is no such thing as total security. But it should give the next generation a more solid basis on which to plan foreign policy.

Unfortunately, the second difference partly cancels out the first. Andropov took over after the collapse of détente. In the earlier periods the Kremlin still hoped that strategic parity would force the United States to treat the Soviet Union as an equal, and minimize the element of confrontation in the partly adversary, partly collaborative relationship between them. The downturn in détente under Carter and Reagan showed that parity could provide no guarantee of stability in U.S.–Soviet relations. This lesson came as a shock to Brezhnev and his colleagues. They had no quick or ready explanation for it. Once bitten, the Kremlin appears less eager to invest such hopes in détente again. From the moment of his succession, Andropov was less enthusiastic and more matter-of-fact about détente than Brezhnev. "We favor the search for a healthy basis, acceptable to the sides concerned, for the settlement of very complicated problems, especially, of course, the problems of curbing the arms race, involving both nuclear and conventional arms. But let no one expect unilateral disarmament from us. We are not naive people," he told the Central Committee within days of Brezhnev's death.[14] The extra confidence that Andropov's own successors are likely to have as a result of Moscow's increased might will be tempered by a sense of Washington's unreliability as a partner.

Under Andropov and whatever leadership may follow his in the mid- or late-1980s, certain fundamental positions will never be abandoned. The Kremlin will permit no weakening of monolithic party rule in the Soviet Union, no destabilization of Eastern Europe, no return by the United States to nuclear superiority, and no unilateral ideological disarmament, that is, the renunciation of Moscow's self-appointed role as the chief international standard-bearer in the competition with capitalism. If these are the minimum conditions on which any Soviet foreign policy will be built, there are a number of major restraints on Soviet power that provide the framework for and, in a real sense, impose a ceiling on its future growth. One of these, clearly, is American policy. The nature of American power—how and where it is used in the 1980s—will play a crucial role in determining Soviet actions. But it is important to remember that the two are not linked in direct proportion to each other. There is no simple mathematical formula by which a certain application of U.S. power will deter or repulse an equivalent amount of Soviet power. By injecting an element of superpower competition into a Third World conflict, the United States may attract rather than repel Soviet interest, as it did in the case of the Angolan civil war in 1975. Even if Moscow does not actively intervene, it will never concede that Washington has a right to intervene or that Moscow has no right to intervene. In spite of the distant clients that Moscow has acquired in the last twenty years, such as Cuba and Vietnam, the Soviet Union still maintains a broadly geographical and territorial notion of security. The United States, by contrast, has an outward-bound, forward-based concept of security related to the need for access to raw materials and markets. Moscow recognizes this essential asymmetry between itself and the United States, but it will not readily tolerate any American effort to give it a military dimension. The Carter administration's declaration of the Persian Gulf as a "vital interest" of the United States that had to be defended by U.S. military power excited a strong Soviet reaction.

Some Western observers mistakenly assume that Western power is the only restraint on Soviet actions. If the West does not have the military muscle or political will to resist Moscow, the Russians are bound to advance. Such a view tends to be encouraged by the duality involved in the notion of a world dominated by two antagonistic superpowers. To some extent each side fosters this view itself. But the centrality of the Soviet–American conflict in world politics over the last thirty years is an aberration.[15] Modern history offers no precedent for the degree of concentration which these two nations have devoted to each other, so much so that each assesses its relations with third countries almost entirely in the light of its effect on their mutual competition. Now the period of superpower dominance is coming to an end. Even within their own alliance systems each superpower is facing strains. The United States is having to adjust to the relative growth of Western European and Japanese economic power, and to demands both from elites in Western Europe for more consultation on alliance policy and from substantial sectors of the public for greater independence. Beyond their alliances, the superpowers face a world in which regional powers are gaining strength, where historical disputes that were often held in check by colonialism are breaking out again, and where the political boundaries drawn by the Western imperial nations are coming under challenge. At the same time there is a growth in local nationalism, and a new vigilance in many Third World countries about foreign access to their raw materials. The example of OPEC is only the most dramatic case of Third World determination to protect their primary products and ensure that they are no longer exploited on the advanced industrial countries' terms. All these factors suggest that while the Third World of the 1980s will be increasingly turbulent, the chances for either superpower to intervene successfully in local or regional conflicts are likely to diminish. The Iran–Iraq war, which left both superpowers impotent on the sidelines, may be the pattern for the decade.

In the second half of the 1970s Soviet attitudes to the prospects of economic and political development in the Third World underwent a significant shift. The old effort to detach Third World countries from the West was modified. Soviet analysts began to talk of a single interdependent world economy, in which the developing countries should participate by producing raw materials in exchange for technology and industrial goods from the advanced countries, of which the Soviet Union was one. This was not very different from the Western conception, although it went strongly against the Chinese view of local and regional self-reliance for Third World nations. The shift in Soviet thinking clearly militated against a policy aimed at encouraging developing countries to cut the West off from raw materials. Some Soviet economists even envisaged a kind of vast triangular arrangement of world trade whereby the advanced Western capitalist economies would invest in Soviet raw materials, the Socialist countries with their less advanced technology would deal with the developing countries, and the developing countries would produce natural resources for all industrial states, both East and West, in return for capital and know-how in building up their local processing industries. While this rather visionary internationalization of the Soviet economy may have lost some of its attraction in the Kremlin as a result of the West's deliberate cutback in trade with the Soviet Union, there is likely to be little change in its basic premise that the Third World's advance to industrialization and thence to socialism will be a long and gradual process.

The Kremlin's increasing recognition of the complexity of the Third World is not lost on Andropov. In his first policy speech, he hinted at a kind of isolationism when he argued that the Soviet Union's primary task was to develop its own economy—"We exercise our main influence on the world revolutionary process through our economic policy."[16] The next generation will have more experience of the Third World and is likely to have even fewer illusions about prospects of rapid change. This goes against those Western politicians who argue that because the emerging Soviet leadership will be younger, more vigorous, and more self-confident than Brezhnev, it is likely to be more aggressive. It is also sometimes said that the new men will be more willing to take military risks because, unlike Brezhnev and his contemporaries, they have had no experience of the Second World War. The theory is based on weak demographic ground. Although the new generation are not war veterans, many lost fathers and, in some cases, mothers among the twenty million Soviet citizens who died. It will be at least another fifteen or twenty years before the children of the postwar baby bulge, whose links with the war are really weaker, reach senior positions.

The notion of increased Soviet "adventurism" in the future rests on nothing but a hunch. It is just as likely that people who have lived through the relatively good years since the war and have enjoyed a gradual increase in prosperity will be more materialistic and less willing to risk everything than those who went through the 1930s and 1940s. The views of the growing pool of foreign policy advisors with direct experience of service abroad suggest a sense of realism and the limitations of Soviet power in a complicated world. They are well aware that instability in the Third World is no automatic signal of imminent revolutionary change. They also know that foreign revolutions may demand more of Moscow than Moscow wants to give or can hope to give. Revolutions also complicate Soviet relations with the capitalist world. Stability in the Third World may be better for Moscow, provided it is not founded on a Pax Americana in which the United States enjoys new military facilities from which to threaten the Soviet Union. What the new generation shares with Brezhnev and Andropov are old Russian attitudes—a desire for docile buffer states or friendly neighbors on their immediate borders, and a fear of encirclement. World revolution is something that they do not expect to see in their lifetime, or would unreservedly welcome, if it seemed to be approaching.

NOTES

PAGES ix–xii: INTRODUCTION

1. *International Herald Tribune*, January 31, 1981.

2. *Istoria Sovetskoy konstitutsii, 1917–1956* (History of the Soviet constitution, 1917–1956) (Moscow, 1957), p. 460.

3. Estimate made by John Stremlau, assistant director of international relations for the Rockefeller Foundation, quoted in the *International Herald Tribune*, October 8, 1982.

4. "Report on Russian and Russian Studies in British Universities," prepared under the chairmanship of Professor R. J. C. Atkinson for the University Grants Committee, December 1979.

PAGES 3–14: THE ANDROPOV INHERITANCE

1. *Pravda*, November 13, 1982.

2. *Pravda*, November 16, 1982.

3. Ibid.

4. Willy Brandt, *Begegnungen und Einsichten* (Hamburg: Hoffman und Campe, 1976), p. 481.

5. Richard Nixon, *Memoirs* (London: Sidgwick and Jackson, 1978), p. 884.

6. Henry Kissinger, *Years of Upheaval* (London: Weidenfeld and Nicolson, and Michael Joseph, 1982), p. 235.

7. Hearings before the U.S. Senate Foreign Relations Committee, U.S./Soviet Strategic Options, January, March 1977, p. 142.

8. Georgi Arbatov, *Der Sowjetische Standpunkt über die Westpolitik der USSR* (Munich: Rogner und Bernhard, 1981), p. 163.

9. Interview with the author, September 1981.

10. *Guardian*, January 30, 1982.

11. *International Herald Tribune*, October 26, 1982.

12. Proceedings of the Twentieth Party Congress of the CPSU, 1956 (Moscow: Gospolitizdat, 1956), vol. I, p. 323.

13. Jerry Hough, *Soviet Leadership in Transition* (Washington, D.C.: The Brookings Institution, 1980), p. 122.

14. Ibid., p. 128.

15. *Pravda*, November 23, 1982.

PAGES 15–25: THE SOVIET VIEW OF NATIONAL SECURITY

1. *Pravda*, November 8, 1982.

2. *Pravda*, September 15, 1957.

3. Nikita Khrushchev, *Khrushchev Remembers* (New York: Bantam Books, 1971), p. 643.

4. Interview with the author, September 1981.

5. Roy and Zhores Medvedev, "The USSR and the Arms Race," in *Exterminism and Cold War* (London: Verso Editions and New Left Books, 1982), p. 163.

6. *Khrushchev Remembers*, pp. 443 ff.

7. Richard Nixon, *Memoirs* (London: Sidgwick and Jackson, 1978), p. 882.

8. Interview with Robert Scheer, *Guardian*, September 8, 1982.

9. Ibid.

10. *New York Times*, March 21, 1982.

11. *Pravda*, November 4, 1967.

12. Georgi Arbatov, *Der Sowjetische Standpunkt über die Westpolitik der USSR* (Munich: Rogner und Bernhard, 1981), p. 67.

13. Ibid., p. 62.

14. Nixon, *Memoirs*, p. 619.

15. Henry Kissinger, *The White House Years* (London: Weidenfeld and Nicolson, and Michael Joseph, 1978), p. 1141.

16. Willy Brandt, *Begegnungen und Einsichten* (Hamburg: Hoffman und Campe, 1976), p. 447.

17. *New York Times*, January 30, 1981.

18. Arbatov, *Der Sowjetische . . .*, p. 114.

19. Address to Members of both Houses of Parliament, June 8, 1982. Official text, published by the U.S. Embassy, London.

20. Charles Bohlen, *Witness to History 1929–69* (New York: W. W. Norton, 1973), pp. 495–6.

21. *Istoria vneshnei politiki SSSR*, vol. 2 ed. Khvostov (Moscow, 1971), p. 480.

22. "Report of the Central Committee of the CPSU to the Twenty-Fourth Congress" (Moscow: Novosti Press Agency Publishing House, 1971), p. 34.

23. Georgi Arbatov, "U.S. Foreign Policy at the Onset of the 1980s," in *Peace and Disarmament* (Moscow: Progress Publishers, 1980), p. 76.

24. "Report of the Central Committee of the CPSU to the Twenty-Third Congress" (Moscow: Novosti Press Agency Publishing House, 1966).

25. Constitution of the USSR (Moscow: Novosti Press Agency Publishing House, 1978).

26. *Pravda*, July 23, 1981.

27. "The International and the National in the Revolutionary Process," *New Times*, no. 7, (1981).

28. I. D. Ovsyany, ed., *A Study of Soviet Foreign Policy* (Moscow: Progress Publishers, 1975), p. 30.

29. M. A. Suslov, *Pravda*, June 21, 1972.

30. Georgi Arbatov, "American Foreign Policy at the Threshold of the 1970s," *SSha*, no. 1, (January 1970), p. 25.

31. A. A. Grechko, "Vooruzhennyye sily Sovetskogo gosudarstva," (Moscow: *Voenizdat*, 1974), p. 401.

32. *Guardian*, March 20, 1981.

33. Arbatov, *Der Sowjetische . . .*, p. 51.

PAGES 26–46: THE GROWTH OF SOVIET POWER

1. June 5, 1980, quoted in *The Defense Monitor*, vol. 9, no. 5 (Washington, D.C.: The Center for Defense Information).

2. This paragraph is based on a report by George Lardner in the *Washington Post*, September 14, 1982.

3. Henry Kissinger, *Years of Upheaval* (London: Weidenfeld and Nicolson, and Michael Joseph, 1982), p. 88.

4. *Diplomacy of Power: Soviet Armed Forces as a Political Instrument* (Washington, D.C.: The Brookings Institution, 1981), pp. 689 ff.

5. Ibid., p. 53.

6. *Force without War: U.S. Armed Forces as a Political Instrument* (Washington, D.C.: The Brookings Institution, 1978), p. 16.

7. *Soviet Naval Influence: Domestic and Foreign Dimensions*, eds. Michael MccGwire and John McDonnell (New York: Praeger, 1977), p. 653.

8. "The Rationale for the Development of Soviet Seapower," in *Soviet Strategy*, eds. John Baylis and Gerald Segal (London: Croom Helm, 1981), p. 235.

9. Quoted in *The Defense Monitor*, vol. II, no. 1 (Washington, D.C.: The Center for Defense Information, 1982), p. 2.

10. Ibid. p. 9.

11. Press release of the North Atlantic Military Committee, Brussels, December 8, 1981.

12. Quoted in William Stivers, "Doves, Hawks, and Détente," in *Foreign Policy*, no. 45 (Winter, 1981–82), p. 129.

13. Michel Tatu, *Power in the Kremlin* (New York: Viking, 1969), p. 232.

14. Henry Kissinger, *The White House Years* (London: Weidenfeld and Nicolson, and Michael Joseph, 1978), p. 83.

15. Ibid., p. 84.

16. Quoted in Chalmers Roberts, *The Nuclear Years* (New York: Praeger, 1970), p. 97–98.

17. Quoted in George Kistiakowsky, "False Alarm: The Story Behind SALT Two," in *New York Review of Books*, March 22, 1979.

18. "Report of the Central Committee of the CPSU to the Twenty-Sixth Congress" (Moscow: Novosti Press Agency Publishing House, 1981).

19. *New York Times*, May 30, 1982.

20. *Arms Control Today*, Journal of the Arms Control Association, March 1982, p. 10.

21. *Guardian Weekly*, November 1, 1981.

22. Ibid.

23. *Pravda*, July 25, 1981.

24. Ibid.

25. Quoted in H. S. Dinerstein, *War and the Service Union* (New York: Praeger, 1962), p. 187.

26. V. D. Sokolovsky, *Voennaya Strategiya* (Moscow: Voenizdat, 1962), p. 237.

27. David Holloway, *The Soviet Union and the Arms Race* (New Haven and London: Yale University Press, 1983), p. 57.

28. *Sovetstkaya voennaya entsiklopediya*, vol. 7 (Moscow: Voenizdat), p. 564.

29. "The Soviet View of INF," in *Arms Control Today*, March 1982, p. 4.

30. *Diplomacy of Power . . ., p. 54.*

PAGES 47–69: THE UNITED STATES: THE RISE AND FALL OF DÉTENTE

1. "The United States in Soviet Perspective," in *Prospects of Soviet Power in the 1980s*, pt. 1 (London: The International Institute for Strategic Studies, 1979), p. 13.

2. Richard Nixon, *Memoirs* (London: Sidgwick and Jackson, 1978), p. 883.

3. Ibid., p. 880.

4. Ibid., p. 879.

5. Henry Kissinger, *Years of Upheaval* (London: Weidenfeld and Nicolson, and Michael Joseph, 1982), p. 1160.

6. *Pravda*, October 17, 1964.

7. George Breslauer, *Khrushchev and Brezhnev as Leaders* (London: George Allen and Unwin, 1982), p. 166.

8. Willy Brandt, *Begegnungen und Ein-sichten* (Hamburg: Hoffman und Campe, 1976), p. 444.

9. "Report of the Central Committee of the CPSU to the Twenty-Fourth Congress" (Moscow: Novosti Press Agency Publishing House, 1971).

10. Ibid.

11. Morton Schwartz, *Soviet Perceptions of the United States* (Berkeley: University of California Press, 1978), p. 149.

12. Vernon Aspaturian, "The Soviet Military-Industrial Complex—Does It Exist?", *Journal of International Affairs*, vol. 26, no. 1 (1972), p. 3.

13. Marshall Shulman, "Toward a Western Philosophy of Co-existence," *Foreign Affairs*, vol. 52 (October 1973).

14. *Pravda*, June 20, 1973.

15. "Report of the Central Committee of the CPSU to the Twenty-Fifth Congress" (Moscow: Novosti Press Agency Publishing House, 1976).

16. Interview with the author, September 1981.

17. "Report of the Central Committee of the CPSU to the Twenty-Sixth Party Congress" (Moscow: Novosti Press Agency Publishing House, 1981).

18. Georgi Arbatov, "O sovetsko-amerikanskikh ototnosheniakh," *Kommunist* (February 1973).

19. Nixon, *Memoirs*, p. 610.

20. Henry Kissinger, *The White House Years* (London: Weidenfeld and Nicolson, and Michael Joseph, 1978), p. 1208.

21. Ibid., p. 1132.

22. Press release, July 3, 1974. Office of the White House Press Secretary. Transcript of Henry Kissinger's press conference.

23. Kissinger, *The White House Years*, p. 1255.

24. Kissinger, *Years of Upheaval*, p. 468.

25. Ibid., p. 519.

26. Kissinger, *The White House Years*, p. 622.

27. Richard Barnet, *The Giants* (New York: Simon and Schuster, 1977), p. 76.

28. Arbatov, "O sovetsko . . .," p. 32.

29. Ibid., p. 41.

30. Kissinger, *The White House Years*, pp. 135–36.

31. Quoted in Robert Legvold, "The Concept of Power and Security in Soviet History," in *Prospects of Soviet Power in the 1980s*, pt. 1 (London: The International Institute of Strategic Studies, 1979), p. 6.

32. Nixon, *Memoirs*, p. 878.

33. *Pravda*, December 22, 1972.

34. Henry Trofimenko, "The Third World and the U.S.–Soviet Competition: a Soviet View," *Foreign Affairs*, vol. 59, no. 5 (1981).

35. *Pravda*, April 28, 1981.

36. "The Concept of Power and Security in Soviet History," in *Prospects of Soviet Power in the 1980s*, pt. 1 (London: The International Institute of Strategic Studies, 1979), p. 6.

37. Speech marking the centenary of Lenin's birth, in *Pravda*, April 22, 1970.

38. *New York Times*, January 30, 1981.

39. *Pravda*, June 17, 1979.

40. Kissinger, *The White House Years*, p. 898.

41. "The New Challenge to Russia," *US News and World Report*, May 30, 1977.

42. Trofimenko, "The Third World and the U.S.–Soviet Competition."

43. "Dateline Havana: Myopic Diplomacy," *Foreign Policy*, no. 48 (Fall 1982).

44. Interview with Zbigniew Brzezinski, *Observer*, January 18, 1981.

45. Trofimenko, "The Third World and the U.S.–Soviet Competition."

46. Leonid Brezhnev, *Rebirth* (Moscow: Novosti Press Agency Publishing House, 1978), p. 114.

47. Ibid., p. 115.

48. Tass, June 22, 1982.

49. October 28, 1982.

50. *Pravda*, November 23, 1982.

51. *Izvestia*, August 5, 1982.

52. *Foreign Trade*, no. 6 (Moscow, 1978).

PAGES 70–86: WESTERN EUROPE: IS THERE A SOVIET THREAT?

1. Quoted in Richard Barnet, *The Giants* (New York: Simon and Schuster, 1977), p. 35.

2. Willy Brandt, *Begegnungen und Einsichten* (Hamburg: Hoffman und Campe, 1976), p. 445.

3. "Report of the Central Committee of the CPSU to the Twenty-Third Congress" (Moscow: Novosti Press Agency Publishing House, 1966).

4. Brandt, *Begegnungen . . .*, p. 453.

5. Ibid., p. 447.

6. Ibid., p. 455.

7. Ibid., p. 447.

8. *Pravda*, December 17, 1981.

9. Henry Kissinger, *The White House Years* (London: Weidenfeld and Nicolson, and Michael Joseph, 1978), p. 200.

10. *The Military Balance, 1969–70* (London: The International Institute for Strategic Studies, 1969), p. 63.

11. "Nuclear Weapons and the Atlantic Alliance," *Foreign Affairs* (Spring 1982).

12. "Beyond First Use," *Foreign Policy*, no. 48 (Fall 1982), p. 43.

13. *International Herald Tribune*, October 6, 1982.

14. *The Military Balance 1981–82* (London: The International Institute for Strategic Studies, 1982), p. 131.

15. *International Herald Tribune*, September 15, 1982.

16. Ibid.

17. Interview with author, September 1981.

18. *Reuters*, January 12, 1982.

19. *Pravda*, January 14, 1982.

20. "Report of the Central Committee of the CPSU to the Twenty-Sixth Congress" (Moscow: Novosti Press Agency Publishing House, 1981).

21. Ibid.

22. *Pravda*, March 13, 1981.

23. Kissinger, *White House Years*, p. 410.

24. Ibid., p. 412.

25. Ibid.

26. Eugene Rostow, "The Unnecessary War," speech delivered at the English-Speaking Union, London, November 30, 1981.

27. Ibid.

PAGES 87–115: EASTERN EUROPE: UNUSUAL EMPIRE

1. Quoted in Seweryn Bialer, *Stalin's Successors* (Cambridge: Cambridge University Press, 1980), p. 266.

2. *Pravda*, September 24, 1981.

3. Zdenek Mlynar, *Night Frost in Prague* (London: C. Hurst, 1980), pp. 238 ff.

4. Quoted in *Freies Deutschland*, no. 12, 4 (November–December 1945), p. 3.

5. *International Herald Tribune*, March 20, 1981.

6. Paul Marer, "Has Eastern Europe Become an Economic Liability to the Soviet Union?", in *The International Politics of Eastern Europe*, ed. Charles Gati (New York, London: Praeger, 1976), p. 59.

7. C. H. McMillan, "Factor Proportions and the Structure of Soviet Foreign Trade," ACES Bulletin 15, no. 1 (Spring 1973).

8. Marer, "Has Eastern Europe . . .?", p. 143.

9. Philip Windsor, "Security Seen from the East," in *The Soviet Union and Eastern Europe*, ed. George Schopflin (London: Anthony Blond, 1970).

10. Mlynar, *Night Frost in Prague*, p. 70.

11. Ibid., p. 71.

12. *Pravda*, March 30, 1968.

13. Mlynar, *Night Frost in Prague*, p. 162.

14. Keesing's *Contemporary Archives* (Bristol: 1968), p. 22887.

15. Mlynar, *Night Frost in Prague*, p. 163.

16. Ibid., p. 168.

17. Pavel Tigrid, *Why Dubček Fell* (London: Macdonald, 1969), p. 86.

18. Prague Radio, August 28, 1968, quoted in Galia Golan, *Reform Rule in Czechoslovakia* (Cambridge: Cambridge University Press, 1976), p. 235.

19. Pavel Tigrid, *Why Dubček Fell*, p. 94.

20. Keesing's *Contemporary Archives* (Bristol: 1958), vol. 9, p. 16237.

21. *Pravda*, September 26, 1968.

22. Lyndon Johnson, *The Vantage Point* (New York: Holt, Rinehart & Winston, 1971), p. 490.

23. Keesing's *Contemporary Archives* (Bristol: 1976), p. 27795.

24. Keesing's *Contemporary Archives* (Bristol: 1969), p. 23858.

25. "Report of the Central Committee of the CPSU to the Twenty-Fifth Congress"

(Moscow: Novosti Press Agency Publishing House, 1976).

26. Interview printed in *L'Unità*, September 10, 1980.

27. Neal Ascherson, *The Polish August* (London: Allen Lane, 1981), p. 228.

28. *Izvestia*, November 24, 1980.

29. Ascherson, *Polish August*, p. 215.

30. *Pravda*, December 11, 1980.

31. *Pravda*, December 18, 1980.

32. "Report of the Central Committee of the CPSU to the Twenty-Sixth Congress" (Moscow: Novosti Press Agency Publishing House, 1981).

33. *Der Spiegel*, no. 53/81, December 28, 1981.

34. Radio Warsaw, October 23, 1981.

35. Bruce Porter, "The USSR and Poland on the Road to Martial Law," Radio Free Europe/Radio Liberty, RL 4/82.

36. *Financial Times*, December 14, 1981.

PAGES 116–130: AFGHANISTAN

1. Quoted in *Soviet News*, Press Department of the Soviet Embassy, London, April 22, 1980, p. 191.

2. Interview with the author, quoted in the *Guardian*, November 11, 1981.

3. *Pravda*, January 13, 1980.

4. *Soviet News*, April 22, 1980, p. 191.

5. "Report of the Carnegie Endowment for International Peace's Conference on Soviet Muslims and Their Political Destiny" (New York: 1981), p. II.8.

6. Quoted in David Newsom, "America Engulfed," *Foreign Policy*, no. 43 (Summer 1981), p. 18.

7. Nikita Khrushchev, *Khrushchev Remembers* (New York: Bantam, 1971), p. 561.

8. "The Shah, Not Kremlin, Touched Off Afghan Coup," *Washington Post*, May 13, 1979.

9. *Guardian*, September 8, 1979.

10. *Time*, November 22, 1982.

11. Interview with the author, October 1981.

12. See Selig Harrison, "A Breakthrough in Afghanistan?", *Foreign Policy*, no. 51 (1983), for a good discussion of Soviet military strategy and the chances of a settlement.

13. Interview with the author, *Guardian*, November 9, 1981.

14. *Krasnaya Zvezda*, January 23, 1982.

15. *Krasnaya Zvezda*, May 17, 1981.

16. Interview with the author, July 1980.

17. Carl Bernstein, "Arms for Afghanistan," *New Republic*, July 19, 1981.

PAGES 131–160: ASIAN ANXIETIES

1. Quoted by Richard Nixon, *Memoirs* (London: Sidgwick and Jackson, 1978), p. 621.

2. *Survey of the Sino–Soviet Dispute: A Commentary and Extracts from the Recent Polemics, 1963–1967* (Oxford: Oxford University Press, 1968), p. 21.

3. John Gittings, "China: Half a Superpower," in *Superpowers in Collision: The New Cold War*, by Noam Chomsky, Jonathan Steele, and John Gittings (London: Penguin Books, 1982), p. 69.

4. Ibid., p. 70.

5. Konrad Adenauer's memoirs, quoted in *Superpowers in Collision*, p. 106.

6. November 21–22, 1964; in *Peking Review*, November 27, 1964.

7. Johnson, *The Vantage Point* (New York: Holt, Rinehart & Winston, 1971), p. 121.

8. Ibid., p. 123.

9. Ibid.

10. Douglas Pike, "The Impact of the Sino–Soviet Dispute on South-East Asia," in *The Sino–Soviet Conflict*, ed. Herbert Ellison (Seattle: University of Washington Press, 1982), p. 190.

11. *People's Daily*, March 22, 1965; in *Peking Review*, March 26, 1965.

12. Unpublished letter of the Central

Committee of the Chinese Communist Party to the Central Committee of the CPSU, quoted in the *Observer*, November 14, 1965.

13. Ibid.

14. *Pravda*, October 1, 1965.

15. Quoted in Melvin Gurtov and Byong-Moo Hwang, *China under Threat* (Baltimore: Johns Hopkins Press, 1980).

16. Thomas Robinson, "The Sino–Soviet Border Dispute: Background, Development and the March 1969 Clashes," Rand RM-6171-PR (August 1970), Santa Monica, California, pp. 11 ff.

17. Allen S. Whiting, *Siberian Development and East Asia* (Palo Alto: Stanford University Press, 1981), p. 92.

18. Gurtov, *China under Threat*, p. 212.

19. Ibid.

20. *Pravda*, November 8, 1967.

21. Gurtov, *China under Threat*, p. 215.

22. Ibid., p. 217.

23. Michael Yehuda, *China's Role in World Affairs* (London: Croom Helm, 1978), p. 185.

24. *Peking Review*, no. 40 (1968), p. 15.

25. Kenneth Liberthal, "The Background in Chinese Politics," in *The Sino–Soviet Conflict*, p. 13.

26. Kissinger, *The White House Years* (London: Weidenfeld and Nicolson, and Michael Joseph, 1979), p. 172.

27. Whiting, *Siberian Development . . .*, p. 91.

28. Quoted in Kissinger, *White House Years*, p. 183.

29. Ibid., p. 184.

30. Ibid., p. 178.

31. Ibid., p. 524.

32. Ibid., p. 836.

33. Ibid.

34. *Pravda*, March 21, 1972.

35. *Pravda*, December 22, 1972.

36. *Far Eastern Affairs*, Moscow, no. 3 (1978) pp. 14–22.

37. *Guardian*, November 27, 1980.

38. "Report of the Central Committee of the CPSU to the Twenty-Sixth Congress (Moscow: Novosti Press Agency Publishing House, 1981), p. 18.

39. Ibid., p. 19.

40. *Guardian*, October 20, 1981.

41. *Pravda*, January 31, 1982.

42. *Pravda*, March 25, 1982.

43. *International Herald Tribune*, November 18, 1982.

44. Kissinger, *Years of Upheaval*, p. 233.

45. Quoted in Gerald Segal, *The Great Power Triangle* (London: Macmillan, 1982), p. 92.

46. *Los Angeles Times*, September 13, 1971.

47. Kissinger, *Years of Upheaval*, p. 1146.

48. Quoted in John Dornberg, *Brezhnev* (London: André Deutsch, 1974), p. 265.

49. Kissinger, *Years of Upheaval*, p. 1226.

50. Frank Snepp, *Decent Interval* (London: Penguin Books, 1980), p. 115.

51. Ibid., p. 110.

52. Gareth Porter, *Vietnam's Soviet Alliance in Indochina Issues*, The Center for International Policy, Washington (May 1980).

53. Jimmy Carter, *Keeping Faith* (London: Collins, 1982), p. 195.

54. Gareth Porter, *Vietnam's Soviet Alliance . . .*, p. 5.

55. *Observer*, February 25, 1979.

56. Radio Moscow, February 26, 1979.

57. Quoted in *Soviet News*, Press Department of the Soviet Embassy, London, September 1, 1981.

58. *Pravda*, February 21, 1976.

59. *The Times* (London), July 10, 1980.

60. Donald Hellman, "The Impact of the Sino–Soviet Dispute on Northeast Asia," in *The Sino–Soviet Conflict*, p. 181.

61. Ibid., p. 179.

62. "Report of the Central Committee to the Twenty-Sixth Congress of the CPSU."

63. Whiting, *Siberian Development . . .*, p. 95.

64. Ibid., p. 97.

PAGES 163–178: APPROACHES TO THE THIRD WORLD

1. "Report of the Central Committee of the CPSU to the Twenty-Sixth Congress (Moscow: Novosti Press Agency Publishing House, 1981).

2. Roy Medvedev, *Khrushchev* (Oxford: Basil Blackwell, 1982), p. 244.

3. Ibid., p. 244.

4. *Current Soviet Policies II. The Documentary Record of the 20th Communist Party Congress and Its Aftermath*, ed. Leo Gruliow (New York: Praeger, 1957), p. 37.

5. Bhabani Sen Gupta, "The Soviet Union and South Asia," in *The Soviet Union and the Developing Nations*, ed. Roger Kanet (Baltimore: Johns Hopkins University Press, 1974), p. 122.

6. V. Tyaguneko, "Tendencies in the Social Development of the Liberated Countries in the Contemporary Epoch," *Mirovaya ekonomika i mezhdunarodniye otnosheniya* (1962), p. 33.

7. A. Arzumanyan, "Results of World Development over the Last 100 Years and Current Problems of the International Revolutionary Movement," *Mirovaya ekonomika i mezhdunarodniye otnosheniya* (1964), no. 12, p. 95.

8. N. I. Gavrilov, quoted in *Mizan* (London) 7 (October 1965), p. 6.

9. Central Intelligence Agency, *Handbook of Economic Statistics* (Washington, D.C.: National Foreign Assessment Center, 1980), p. 107.

10. Ibid., pp. 105–6.

11. Henry Kissinger, *White House Years* (London: Weidenfeld and Nicolson, and Michael Joseph, 1978), p. 203.

12. *New York Magazine*, March 9, 1981.

13. "Report of the Central Committee of the CPSU to the Twenty-Sixth Congress," p. 20.

14. Ibid., p. 22.

15. Central Intelligence Agency, *Handbook of Economic Statistics*, p. 113.

16. Central Intelligence Agency, *Communist Aid Activities in Non-Communist Less Developed Countries, 1978*, ER 79–10412U (September 1979), p. 4.

17. *International Herald Tribune*, June 10, 1982.

18. Ibid.

19. V. I. Popov, I. D. Ovsyany, and V. P. Nikhamin, eds., *A Study of Soviet Foreign Policy* (Moscow: Progress Publishers, 1975), p. 90.

20. Yuri Krasin, "The International and the National in the Revolutionary Process,"*New Times*, no. 7, 1981.

21. Ibid.

22. Yevgeni Tarabrin, ed., *USSR and the Countries of Africa* (Moscow: Progress Publishers, 1980), p. 222.

23. Ibid., p. 124.

24. Yuri Krasin, "The International and the National . . ."

25. Elizabeth Kridl Valkenier, "The USSR, the Third World, and the Global Economy," in *Problems of Communism* (July–August 1979).

26. *Foreign Trade*, no. 7 (1976), p. 7.

27. "Report of the Central Committee of the CPSU to the Twenty-Fifth Congress," p. 98.

28. Ibid., p. 97.

29. Ibid., p. 98.

30. *Foreign Trade*, no. 6 (Moscow: 1979), p. 12.

31. Valkenier, "The USSR, the Third World . . ."

32. *Pravda*, April 12, 1974.

33. N. I. Lebedev, *A New Stage in International Relations* (London: Pergamon Press, 1978), p. 178.

PAGES 179–206: THE MIDDLE EAST

1. Mohammed Heikal, *Sphinx and Commissar: the Rise and Fall of Soviet Influence in the Arab World* (London: Collins, 1978), p. 278. Heikal was editor of the Cairo newspaper, *Al Ahram*, from 1957 to 1974, and a close confidant of Nasser.

2. Tass, July 9, 1982.

3. Heikal, *Sphinx and Commissar*, p. 155.

4. *New York Times*, March 2, 1949.

5. "The Conferences at Malta and Yalta"—*Foreign Relations of the United States*, Diplomatic Papers (Washington, D.C.: U.S. Government Printing Office, 1961).

6. *Foreign Relations of the United States*, U.S. Department of State, 1944–1/2, vol. 5 (Washington, D.C.: U.S. Government Printing Office, 1961), p. 470.

7. *Pravda*, February 24, 1981.

8. General Assembly, First Special Session, 77th Plenary Meeting, vol. 1, pp. 127–35.

9. Christopher Sykes. *Crossroads to Israel* (London: New English Library, 1967), p. 353.

10. Heikal, *Sphinx and Commissar*, p. 65.

11. Ibid., p. 63.

12. Ibid., p. 69.

13. Jon D. Glassman, *Arms for the Arabs* (Baltimore: Johns Hopkins University Press, 1975).

14. BBC: Summary of world broadcasts. May 25, 1967.

15. Mohammed Heikal, *The Cairo Documents* (London: New English Library, 1972), p. 242.

16. Anthony Nutting, *Nasser* (London: Constable, 1972), p. 419.

17. Lyndon Johnson, *The Vantage Point* (New York: Holt, Rinehart & Winston, 1971), p. 302.

18. Ibid.

19. Heikal, *Sphinx and Commissar*, p. 182.

20. Heikal in an article in *Al Ahram*, August 25, 1967.

21. Ibid.

22. Heikal, *Sphinx and Commissar*, pp. 185–88.

23. Heikal in an article in *Al Ahram*, August 25, 1967.

24. Henry Kissinger, *The White House Years* (London: Weidenfeld and Nicolson, and Michael Joseph, 1979), p. 346.

25. Ibid., p. 360.

26. Heikal, *Sphinx and Commissar*, p. 221.

27. Kissinger, *White House Years*, p. 1289.

28. Heikal, *Sphinx and Commissar*, p. 253.

29. Anwar Sadat, *In Search of Identity: An Autobiography* (New York: Harper and Row, 1977), p. 246.

30. Henry Kissinger, *Years of Upheaval* (London: Weidenfeld and Nicolson, and Michael Joseph, 1982), p. 580.

31. Kissinger told a London press conference on April 27, 1982, in reference to America's approaches to Israel, "We would like to think we pursued them independent of the Soviet threat but certainly the consciousness of the potential dangers was in our minds."

32. Kissinger, *Years of Upheaval*, p. 752.

33. Ibid., p. 753.

34. *Pravda*, February 24, 1981.

35. *Pravda*, September 16, 1982.

36. Michael MccGwire, "The Soviet Navy in the Seventies," in *Soviet Naval Influence*, ed. Michael MccGwire and John McDonnell (New York and London: Praeger, 1977), p. 656.

37. Ibid.

38. Ibid., p. 491.

39. State of the Union address, January 1980.

40. *Soviet News*, December 16, 1980 (London: Press Department of the Soviet Embassy).

41. *International Herald Tribune*, April 16, 1980.

42. *International Herald Tribune*, July 15, 1981.

43. *Financial Times*, September 4, 1981.

44. *Economist*, May 9, 1981.

45. Dina Spechler and Martin Spechler, "The Soviet Union and the Oil Weapon," in *The Limits of Power*, ed. Yaacov Roi (London: Croom Helm, 1979), p. 98.

46. Ibid., p. 116.

PAGES 207–225: LATIN AMERICA

1. *Pravda*, May 5, 1982.

2. "Mezhdunarodnaya zhizn," no. 11, 1958, quoted in *Soviet Relations with Latin America*, ed. Stephen Clissold. Issued under the auspices of the Royal Institute of International Affairs (Oxford: Oxford University Press, 1970), p. 43.

3. "Manuel Gomez," quoted in *Survey*, no. 53 (October 1964).

4. M. N. Roy, *Memoirs* (Bombay, 1964), p. 346.

5. William Ratliff, *Castroism and Communism in Latin America, 1959–1976* (Washington, D.C.: American Enterprise Institute for Public Policy Research, 1976), p. 8.

6. Nikita Khrushchev, *Khrushchev Remembers* (New York: Bantam Books, 1971), p. 546.

7. Michel Tatu, *Le Pouvoir en U.R.S.S.* (Paris: Editions Grasset, 1967), p. 84.

8. *Pravda*, October 17, 1964.

9. *Pravda*, July 10, 1960.

10. Jean Daniel, "Unofficial Envoy: An Historic Report from Two Capitals," *New Republic*, December 14, 1963.

11. Interview with Claude Julien, *Le Monde*, March 22, 1963.

12. *Khrushchev Remembers*, p. 555.

13. Ibid., p. 554.

14. *Peking Review*, March 15, 1964.

15. *Cuba Socialista*, no. 17, December 1962.

16. "First Afro–Asian–Latin American People's Solidarity Conference and Its Projections," O.A.S., Washington, vol. 2, pp. 66 and 71.

17. Ibid., p. 71.

18. *Cuba Socialista*, August 1966.

19. *Pravda*, March 19, 1968.

20. *Granma*, English edition, February 11, 1968.

21. *Bohemia*, March 15, 1968.

22. *Granma*, English edition, August 25, 1968.

23. *Pravda*, November 7, 1970.

24. *Pravda*, April 4, 1971.

25. *Pravda*, July 29, 1971.

26. *Pravda*, September 26, 1973.

27. Boris Ponomarev, *World Marxist Review*, vol. 17, no. 6 (June 1974).

28. Interview with the author, reported in The *Guardian*, March 5, 1981.

29. *Los Angeles Times*, March 17, 1981.

30. *International Herald Tribune*, March 7, 1982.

31. *Guardian*, March 5, 1981.

32. *Time*, March 22, 1982.

33. Wayne Smith, "Dateline Havana: Myopic Diplomacy," *Foreign Policy* (Fall 1982), p. 164.

34. *Soviet News*, Press Department of the Soviet Embassy, London, May 11, 1982.

35. *Soviet Weekly*, May 5, 1982 (London: Novosti Press Agency).

36. Ibid., May 29, 1982.

37. Radio Peace and Progress, July 3, 1982.

PAGES 226–244: AFRICA

1. Y. A. Tarabrin, ed., *The USSR and Countries of Africa* (Moscow: Progress Publishers, 1980), p. 314.

2. U.S. Senate, *Angola: Hearings before the Subcommittee on African Affairs of the Committee on Foreign Relations, 94th Congress, Second Session, 1976*, p. 19.

3. Ibid., p. 18.

4. John Stockwell, *In Search of Enemies* (New York: W. W. Norton, 1978), p. 67.

5. John Marcum, *The Angolan Revolution*, vol. II, 1962–1976 (Cambridge, Mass.: MIT Press, 1978), p. 257.

6. Wayne Smith, "Dateline Havana: Myopic Diplomacy," *Foreign Policy* (Fall 1982), p. 170.

7. Ibid.

8. U.S. Senate, *Angola, Hearings . . .*, pp. 8, 14.

9. Quoted in Edward Gonzales, *Problems of Communism*, November–December 1977.

10. *New Times*, no. 10 (1957), p. 19.

11. Robert Legvold, *Soviet Policy in West Africa* (Cambridge, Mass.: Harvard University Press, 1970), p. 252.

12. Stockwell, *In Search of Enemies*, p. 201.

13. Central Intelligence Agency, *Communist Aid to the Less Developed Countries of the Free World, 1976*, Central Intelligence Agency (August 1977), pp. 4–5.

14. Keesing's *Contemporary Archives* (Bristol: 1978), p. 29128.

15. James Mayall, "The Battle for the Horn," *The World Today*, September 1978.

16. Fred Halliday, *Soviet Policy in the Arc of Crisis* (Washington, D.C.: Institute for Policy Studies, 1981).

17. Fred Halliday and Maxine Molyneux, *The Ethiopian Revolution* (London: Verso Editions and New Left Books, 1982), p. 246.

18. *Foreign Policy*, no. 35 (Summer 1979).

19. Halliday, *Soviet Policy . . .*, p. 251.

20. *International Herald Tribune*, May 17, 1982.

21. *International Herald Tribune*, November 27, 1980.

22. *The Times* (London), July 22, 1982.

PAGES 247–259: PROSPECTS FOR THE 1980S

1. George Kennan, former American ambassador in Moscow and scholar of Soviet affairs, in a lecture in Frankfurt, reported in the *International Herald Tribune*, October 11, 1982.

2. Henry Kissinger, *The White House Years* (London: Weidenfeld and Nicolson, and Michael Joseph, 1978), p. 1141.

3. *Los Angeles Times*, July 20, 1982.

4. *Hansard*, July 7, 1981.

5. *International Herald Tribune*, October 25, 1982.

6. Seweryn Bialer, *Stalin's Successors* (Cambridge: Cambridge University Press, 1980), p. 162.

7. *Pravda*, November 23, 1982.

8. Jerry Hough, "Soviet Perspectives," in the *Brookings Bulletin*, vol. 17, no. 3 (1981), p. 3.

9. I am indebted for this list to Seweryn Bialer's *Stalin's Successors* (Cambridge University Press, 1980), pp. 142ff.

10. All figures except living space come from *The USSR in Figures for 1980*, the Central Statistical Board, Moscow (Moscow: Finansy i Statistika Publishers, 1981), pp. 41, 163, 182, and 184. Living space figures come from *Narodnoe Khoziaistvo SSSR v 1980 g.*, (Moscow: Statisticheskii ezhegodnik, 1981), pp. 7 and 392.

11. Hedrick Smith, *The Russians* (New York: Ballantine Books, 1976), p. 332.

12. *The Times*, July 30, 1981.

13. Viktor Afansayev, editor of *Pravda*, and a member of the Central Committee, told Japanese journalists that China and the USSR might agree to reduce their troops on the border, according to the *International Herald Tribune*, November 17, 1982.

14. *Pravda*, November 23, 1982

15. Bialer, *Stalin's Successors*

16. *Pravda*, November 23, 1982.

INDEX